Freshwater Fishes of the Northeastern United States

Freshwater Fishes

Northeastern United States

A FIELD GUIDE

Robert G. Werner

SYRACUSE UNIVERSITY PRESS

First Edition 2004
12   13   14   15   6   5   4   3

∞The paper used in this publication meets the minimum requirements
of American National Standard for Information Sciences—Perma-
nence of Paper for Printed Library Materials, ANSI Z39.48–1992.

Publication of this book is made possible by a grant from
Furthermore: a program of the J. M. Kaplan Fund.

The digitizing of color plates was made possible by a grant from the
New York State Department of Environmental Conservation.

For a listing of books published and distributed by Syracuse University
Press, visit our website at SyracuseUniversityPress.syr.edu.

ISBN: 978-0-8156-3020-3

Library of Congress Cataloging-in-Publication Data
Werner, Robert G.
Freshwater fishes of the northeastern United States : a field guide /
Robert G. Werner.— 1st ed.
p. cm.
Includes bibliographical references.
ISBN 0-8156-3020-4 (alk. paper)
1. Fishes—Northeastern States—Identification. I. Title.
QL628.N92W47   2004
597.176'0974—dc22
2004000345

Printed in Canada

To my wife, Jo

Robert G. Werner's interest in fishes and aquatic ecosystems began when he was a child growing up on Lake Maxinkuckee in northern Indiana. He studied zoology at Purdue University and undertook graduate work in zoology at the University of California, Los Angeles, and at Indiana University, ultimately obtaining a Ph.D. under the direction of Dr. Shelby Gerking. After service in the Marine Corps and upon completion of his studies, he joined the faculty of the State University of New York College of Environmental Science and Forestry (ESF) at Syracuse, New York, where he taught ichthyology, limnology, fishery biology, ecology of Adirondack fishes, and tropical ecology. While at ESF, he was director of the Thousand Islands Biological Station, Clayton, New York, and codirector of the Great Lakes Research Consortium. He received a Fulbright fellowship to work in Argentina and was a visiting scientist at the Scottish Marine Biological Station in Oban, Scotland, as well as at the National Marine Fisheries Service, Southeastern Fisheries Research Laboratory, Beaufort, North Carolina. His research has focused on the early life-history stages of fishes, fish movements, and the ecology of pike and muskellunge in the St. Lawrence River. He has published two books: *Freshwater Fishes of New York State: A Field Guide* (Syracuse University Press) and *Fishery Science: The Unique Contribution of Early Life Stages* (with Lee Fuiman).

Contents

Tables

Preface

The northeastern United States, although well known for its beautiful lakes and streams and its superb fishing, has no recent comprehensive field guide to the fishes found in its waters. A number of excellent works dealing with the fishes of the individual states of this region have been published, such as C. L. Smith's *The Inland Fishes of New York State* (1985), W. R. Whitworth's *Freshwater Fishes of Connecticut* (1996), J. F. Scarola's *Freshwater Fishes of New Hampshire* (1973), and W. H. Everhart's *Fishes of Maine* (1976), but most of these books are out of print, and none of them encompasses the fish fauna of the entire Northeast. This book was written to serve as a field guide to the fishes of the Northeast for anglers, students, naturalists, ecologists, environmentalists, and anyone interested in fishes and the natural world around them.

The book is designed to facilitate field identification by focusing, to the extent possible, on characteristics and techniques that can be effective in identifying fishes in the field. In most cases, for a proper identification it is necessary to have the fish "in hand," but one can sometimes make an identification of a fish in its natural habitat. Observing fishes in their natural setting, or "fish watching," can be as enjoyable as bird-watching. Fishes are as colorful as birds, particularly during the breeding season. They often gather in large numbers at certain times of the year in preparation for either migrating or spawning. Moreover, under certain circumstances, they are in shallow enough water to be observed from land. C. L. Smith developed this idea in his book *Fish Watching* (1994). The major obstacle to identifying fish in the field is that they occupy a habitat that is often turbid and alien to humans. In addition, some of the most interesting fishes are quite small, with distinguishing characters that are not easy to see in the field without the aid of a magnifying lens. You should not despair, however. To be successful, you must use a set of clues similar to that used by field ornithologists: shape, size, color pattern, behavior, habitat, location, and time of year observed. These clues are useful in narrowing the choices and ultimately making an identification.

Unlike the bird-watcher, however, the dedicated student of fishes very often has the advantage of being able to capture the fish for closer inspection either through angling or collecting it using a small seine or dip net. In addition, the use of a hand lens and a photo tank can aid in viewing characters helpful in identifying small fishes.

Accurate portraits of fishes are also very important aids to identification. In the preparation of this book, I have been very fortunate to have access to the superb paintings of Ellen Edmonson and Hugh Chrisp from the New York State Biological Survey for the bulk of the fishes in the region. The paintings of the greater redhorse prepared by Elizabeth Burckmyer and the rainbow trout by Wilifred Bronson are the only paintings in the original collection not painted by Chrisp or Edmondson. These paintings were prepared as a part of an extensive survey of all of the watersheds in New York and are unusually accurate depictions of both the morphology and color of the fishes. A few important species were not present during the survey and thus were not painted, such as the introduced Pacific salmon. Peter Thompson recently painted these species for New York Sea Grant, and I was fortunate to gain access to them as well. All of the paintings are very useful because they bring the natural colors of the fish to life and carefully outline the morphological characters that are so important in identification.

After some experience, you should be able to identify roughly one-third of the species of fishes in the region just as you might identify birds—that is, while they are in their natural habitat. This assumes that you can get a good sustained view and are able to see key characteristics. Most of the fishes in this group are large animals with distinguishing characters or readily visible colors. Many are sport fishes; others are large and conspicuous, such as carp, American eels, or longnose gars. Another one-third of the species require that you have the fish in hand so that you can get a more sustained and detailed look. These fishes include many average-size fishes from several different families, such as cutlips minnows, several of the suckers, and some of the smaller sunfishes. The final one-third of the fishes in the region require some magnification to allow you to see relatively small characters. These fishes include many of the minnows and the darters. Although the practice of identifying fishes in the field is not as well developed as bird-watching, it is probably easier than you might think. In the Northeast, approximately two-thirds of the fish species can be identified in the field without magnification, and essentially all can be identified with the aid of a good hand lens.

Once an identification is made, you can use this book to learn a great deal more about the life history and distribution of the fishes by reading the species accounts. If you wish to pursue the topic further, consulting the references listed at the end of the book offer a rich source of detailed information.

All of this will lead to a better understanding of the community of fishes with which we share the region and of the significance of their well-being to our own. I hope that this book will encourage respect for fishes and promote conservation not only of the fishes, but also of their habitat.

The book focuses on freshwater and anadromous fishes in the states composing the Northeast, specifically New York and the six New England states—Connecticut, Massachusetts, Rhode Island, Vermont, New Hampshire, and Maine.

Acknowledgments

Biological surveys of the fishes of several of the states in the northeastern region of the United States provided the groundwork for this book. *The Fishes of the Watershed,* prepared by John Greeley and colleagues and published in the New York Biological Surveys in fourteen volumes from 1927 to 1940, were especially useful.

Guides to the fishes of the individual states have been very helpful as well. Everhart's *Fishes of Maine* (1976); Scarola's *Freshwater Fishes of New Hampshire* (1973); Smith's *The Inland Fishes of New York State* (1985); Werner's *Freshwater Fishes of New York State* (1980); and Whitworth, Berrien, and Keller's *Freshwater Fishes of Connecticut* (1968), as well as the more recent version, Whitworth's *Freshwater Fishes of Connecticut* (1996), have served as valuable resources. I took additional information on fish distribution from several recent publications (Carlson, Daniels, and Eaton 1999; Halliwell, Whittier, and Ringler 2001; Whittier, Halliwell, and Paulsen 1997; Whittier, Halliwell, and Daniels 1999, 2000). For the descriptions and life histories of each species, I relied on several general texts, including: Becker 1983; Carlander 1969, 1977; Jenkins and Burkhead 1994; Scott and Crossman 1973; Smith 1985; Trautman 1981; and Werner 1980. The comprehensive studies by Kuehne and Barbour (1983) and by Page (1983) greatly aided preparation of descriptions and life histories of fishes in the family Percidae. I gratefully acknowledge the work of all these authors.

Three individuals read portions of the book while it was being prepared. Douglas Carlson, New York State Department of Environmental Conservation, and Stephen Coghlan, State University of New York College of Environmental Science and Forestry (SUNY ESF) read the species accounts. Dr. Henry Mullins, Syracuse University, read the section on the geological history of the region.

Several people contributed to the line drawings. Dawn Gorham, SUNY ESF, prepared the base map for the drainages of the region. Approximately one-fourth of the line drawings came originally from *Freshwater Fishes of New York State: A Field Guide* (Werner 1980) and were prepared by Henry Schmidt. Margaret Goloski prepared figures 1, 8, and 32, as well as the line drawing for the family Gobiidae. As part of an earlier uncompleted project, Dr. Edward C. Raney supervised the preparation of numerous line drawings of the freshwater fishes of the region. They provide the bulk of the line drawings utilized in this guide. It was Dr. Raney's wish that material from his libraries continue to be used for educational purposes. John Homa Jr. purchased Dr. Raney's corporate and personal libraries in 1986 and gave his permission for their use in this field guide. It is our hope that the use of these illustrations continues to fulfill Ed's wish.

Dr. Robert Daniels was very helpful in locating and scanning the color plates of New York fishes. The New York State Department of Environmental Conservation provided funds for digitizing the plates from the New York Biological Surveys. These plates provided the majority of the paintings and were prepared by Ellen Edmonson and Hugh Chrisp as a part of the New York Biological Survey conducted from 1927 to 1940. These paintings are held in trust for the people of New York State by the New York State Museum, New York State Archives, and the New York State Department of Environmental Conservation.

The paintings of Pacific salmon and rainbow trout were commissioned by the New York Sea Grant and prepared by Peter Thompson. Duplication or copying of these paintings without the permission of New York Sea Grant is not permitted. David MacNeil and David White were instrumental in obtaining permission to use these illustrations. I gratefully acknowledge all of those who have helped illustrate this book.

Freshwater Fishes of the Northeastern United States

Introduction

Imagine that you are standing on the edge of a mountain stream. Overhanging branches of hemlock and pine shelter the stream from the sun. Dark, clear, cold water from farther up the mountain rushes by your feet. Large rocks partially buried in the gravel bottom divert the flow of the brook, creating small pockets of still water downstream, perfect shelter for small fishes. Not far from where you are standing a small waterfall cascades into the stream, creating a pool from the force of the bubbling, well-oxygenated water. Just downstream is a larger pool, and you notice a small trout rising to feed on a tiny insect that has inadvertently dropped onto the water. As you walk downstream a short way, you begin to notice a pattern of deep pools and runs separated by shallow riffles. This is the natural habitat of many cold-water stream fishes in the Northeast. Brook trout, slimy sculpins, and blacknose dace swim in these waters now just as they did as the glaciers were receding some 10,000–14,000 years ago.

Or imagine you are on the shore of a pond at sunset. The wind is still, and the pond has a mirrorlike quality to it. To your right is a small bay covered with yellow water lilies just beginning to bloom. Closer to shore, rushes protrude into the air. Under the water lilies, pumpkinseed sunfish defend their nests while smallmouth bass cruise the shoreline looking for prey. In the center of the pond, the water is much deeper and cooler. Here, black crappies and yellow perch spend the hot summer days.

These generalized pond and stream habitats are two of the most common natural aquatic habitats in the northeastern United States. But there are others. The Northeast has large and magnificent rivers—the Hudson, the St. Lawrence, and the Connecticut, to name a few. It has large lakes such as Lake Erie, Lake Ontario, Lake Champlain, and Moosehead Lake. Intermingled with these waters are small marshes, bog lakes, and springs—all habitats for fishes.

The states in the northeastern corner of the United States (Maine, New Hampshire, Vermont, Massachusetts, Rhode Island, Connecticut, and New York) form a discrete geographic region: bounded on the north and west by Lakes Erie and Ontario, the St. Lawrence River, and the Canadian border; on the east by the Atlantic Ocean; and on the south by the southern border of New York, Connecticut, Rhode Island, and Massachusetts. It is a region of more than 100,000 square miles blessed with abundant water and a myriad of lakes and streams. Many streams have their origins in the mountains of Maine, New Hampshire, Vermont, and New York. Others are linked to the vast Great Lakes-St. Lawrence drainage. A small but significant portion of the region drains to the west as a part of the Mississippi River drainage. Because the precipitation in the region is relatively high, averaging 43 inches per year, sufficient water is produced to keep the streams and rivers flowing and the lakes full. As a consequence, this region provides habitat for an interesting array of fishes that are explored in this field guide.

What is a fish? This seems like an obvious question with an equally obvious answer, but in reality it is not always clear. Almost everyone recognizes a trout or a perch as a fish, but there are some 24,600 other fish species in the world, nearly as many as all of the other vertebrates combined. Fishes occupy essentially the entire aquatic world and have developed corresponding adaptations that allow them to live successfully in some very extreme environments. The living forms that we currently recognize by the term *fishes* are divided into five classes: class Myxini, the hagfishes; class Cephalaspidomorphi, the lampreys; class Chondrichthyes, the sharks, skates, and rays; class Sarcopterygii, the coelacanth and lungfishes; and class Actinopterygii, the ray-finned fishes. In the freshwater fish communities of the Northeast, we find only lampreys and the ray-finned fishes. The other classes are marine, or if they are freshwater fishes, such as the lungfishes, they are not found in North America.

With such a diverse group, it is difficult to produce a precise definition of a fish that encompasses all species. The various classes of fish have as many differences between them as between any of the other classes of vertebrates. The difference between a frog and a bird is no greater than the difference between a lamprey and a perch. But for our purposes in the Northeast, a fish can be defined as a cold-blooded vertebrate that respires using gills and swims using fins, spending all of its life cycle in water.

The fishes included in this field guide are those that either spend their entire life cycle in freshwater or are required to spend a critical portion of their life cycle in freshwater. For example, Atlantic salmon or American shad spend much of their adult life in the ocean but migrate into freshwater to spawn. The young grow and develop in freshwater before migrating back to the ocean. This type of life cycle is called anadromous. Alternatively, the American eel spends the adult portion of its life in freshwater but migrates to sea to spawn, a life cycle referred to as catadromous. This book includes not only the fishes that spend their entire life cycle in freshwater, but also the anadromous and catadromous species as well.

It is true that a number of nearshore marine fishes and estuarine fishes may occasionally be found in freshwater and at times may even be abundant there. When they are added to the freshwater fauna, the grouping is often referred to as the inland fishes of a region.

Several species known to be in the Northeast in the past but not seen for decades and considered extirpated have been included here. The reason for including them is that, in some cases, such as the paddlefish, efforts are being made to reintroduce them to regional waters. In other cases, it is not known definitely that these species are completely gone from the area.

Based on these criteria, at least 162 species of fish are known to live or spawn in the freshwaters of the Northeast, representing twenty-eight families and sixteen orders. This diversity results mainly from the variety of freshwater habitats. Fish habitats include some of the largest lakes in the world; large and complex river systems; deep, clear lakes such as Lake George and the Finger Lakes; many soft-water lakes in Maine and the Adirondack Mountains of New York; and a myriad of small lakes, bogs, marshes, and streams.

Information on the 162 species has been gathered from research done mostly in the Northeast, but also elsewhere. Important information has been derived from state biological surveys undertaken during the first half of the twentieth century. Detailed accounts of the fishes of the northeastern states have also been very useful in the preparation of this field guide, in particular C. L. Smith's *The Inland Fishes of New York State* (1985); W. R. Whitworth's *Freshwater Fishes of Connecticut* (1996); and J. F. Scarola's *Freshwater Fishes of New Hampshire* (1973). I also gathered much information over the past three decades during collecting trips with students of ichthyology at the State University of New York College of Environmental Science and Forestry at Syracuse, New York. Literature sources can be found in the reference section of the book, a rich mine of information for pursuing a species or family in much greater detail than is possible in a field guide. The scientific name of fishes follows the International Code of Zoological Nomenclature.

Background

Geological History

A good place to start a discussion of a region's fishes is to outline the formation of the landforms that determine the drainage patterns and ultimately the fish habitat in the area. Our current understanding of the processes involved in the geological development of the Northeast is based to a large extent on the theory of plate tectonics. The center of the Earth is extremely hot, composed of massive amounts of molten rock, which is moving in large convection cells similar to what one might imagine if water were to boil in very slow motion.

The movement of molten rock at the center of the Earth tends to displace a portion of the Earth's outermost layer, or lithosphere, causing it to spread apart in some areas and to sink back toward the center of the Earth in others. These pieces of the Earth's lithosphere are the large plates referred to in the term *plate tectonics*. The net effect is to move large continental landmasses slowly around the surface of the Earth. The rate of movement is very sluggish, as you might expect, measured in centimeters per year.

We can begin the story approximately 1 billion years ago when it is thought that a large land mass collided with Laurentia, the precursor to the North American continent. The force of that collision drove the Laurentian landscape upward, forming a chain of high mountains stretching from what is now southeastern Canada to Mexico. This period of mountain building is called the Grenville Orogeny. Over time, these mountains eroded, and in most places they have essentially disappeared, covered by sediment. The Grenville Orogeny is important to us in the Northeast, however, because a remnant of that mountain-building period can still be found. The Adirondack Mountains of New York are one of the largest exposed portions of the Grenville Orogeny in the United States. Although the Adirondacks have been worn down over time, they have also been pushed up to a significant degree so that their "roots" have been exposed. This is what we now see when we travel through the Adirondacks. The Grenville Orogeny produced mountains composed of a mixture of sedimentary, metamorphic, and igneous rock. Most of the softer sedimentary rock has long since been eroded away, leaving only the harder and more resistant material behind. Because this type of rock is not easily eroded or chemically weathered, streams and lakes in this area contain very soft water, with little buffering capacity, making them vulnerable to the effects of acid precipitation.

The erosion of the mountains created during the Grenville Orogeny extended over many hundreds of millions of years, producing massive amounts of sediment that accumulated on the ocean floor near the margin of the continent. Additional calcareous material produced in the overlying sea contributed calcium carbonate to the mix, eventually leading to the formation of a thick layer of limestone.

Around 500 million years ago, a large land mass called Baltica, which would later form much of northern Europe, began drifting toward Laurentia. As it did, an arc of volcanic islands developed between Baltica and Laurentia and moved toward Laurentia. These islands joined with the layers of sedimentary rock formed at the bottom of the intervening sea to form the Taconic Highlands. This process of uplift lasted for approximately 60 million years, creating a mountain range extending for nearly 1,000 miles. It was an impressive array of mountains with peaks 15,000–20,000 feet high. Over the next 25 million years, this majestic mountain range was eroded down to near sea level. Eroded material deposited to the west formed the Queenston Delta, a mix of rock, sand, and mud extending along what is now the Mohawk River in New York and south from the shores of Lake Ontario. Remnants of the Taconic Orogeny exist on either side of the border between New York and three New England states—Vermont, Massachusetts, and Connecticut. The Berkshire Hills, Taconic and Green Mountains, and the area between the Hudson River-Lake Champlain valley and the Connecticut River valley are, at least in part, the result of the Taconic Orogeny.

As Baltica continued to move toward Laurentia, small landmasses collided with the Laurentian coastline, forming structures called exotic terranes. Terranes are distinctive strips of volcanic arcs or crust that are found attached to the continent and that have unique features separating them from the typical continental material. They seem to be geologically out of place. The first of these terranes was the Dunnage Terrane, which runs from around Montpelier in northern Vermont across northern New Hampshire through Maine north of Moosehead Lake. A larger terrane, called the Gander Terrane, runs north through central Connecticut and Massachusetts, eastern Vermont, and most of New Hampshire before turning northeast, forming most of central Maine. The last terrane, called Avalonia, is much smaller and is found in eastern Connecticut, Massachusetts, Maine, and Rhode Island.

Baltica collided with Laurentia, striking first what is now the Canadian coast and eventually making contact in the New England area around 380 million years ago. The collision led to the Acadian Orogeny and the formation of another major mountain chain. It also crushed and modified the existing terranes, attaching them firmly to Laurentia. As time went on, these new mountains, too, were eroded, leaving only a few remnants. The erosional debris covered many of the earlier sediments and stretched in the Northeast from the Catskill Mountains across southern New York to Lake Erie.

Finally, the last major mountain-building event in this region, called the Alleghenian Orogeny, occurred when the supercontinent Gondwana collided with Laurasia, or what would become the present North American continent, around 290 million years ago. Gondwana was composed of the contemporary landmasses of Africa, South America, Antarctica, India, and Australia. The joining of Gondwana with the North American and European continents created an enormous land mass called Pangaea. The portion of Gondwana that collided with the current New England was what is now the northwestern portion of Africa. The collision caused the crumpling of the edge of the continents, forming the Appalachian Mountains.

So there were four mountain-building periods:

1. The Grenville Orogeny (approximately 1 billion years ago), which created the Adirondack Mountains.

2. The Taconic Orogeny (approximately 500 to 440 million years ago), which formed the Taconics, Green Mountains, and Berkshire Hills.

3. The Acadian Orogeny (approximately 380 million years ago), which cemented the various terranes to the continent; and

4. The Alleghenian Orogeny (approximately 290 million years ago), which created the Appalachian Mountains.

After the Alleghenian Orogeny, Pangaea began to break apart, allowing the oceans to enter between North America and Africa and between the other landmasses. Separation took place along a rift line off the eastern coast of North America. Additional rifts occurred during this time; in particular, a rift valley developed along what are now the lower Connecticut and Hudson River Valleys.

Over approximately the next 200 million years, a tremendous amount of erosion took place, wearing down the mountains, creating enormous quantities of sediment, and leveling the landscape in the Northeast. A few resistant structures remained standing in relatively flat areas, such as Mount Monadnock in southern New Hampshire.

Rivers draining this land began to cut into the sediment, gradually forming valleys. An appreciation of the flatness of the original landscape can be had today by viewing the region from the top of one of the hills. It is quite striking to look out across the landscape and observe the uniform height of most of the ridges and hills. This uniformity can be explained if we assume that the region began as a relatively flat plain, and the erosion of rivers over millions of years cut valleys into the plain, creating a ridge-and-valley terrain.

All of these geological occurrences were prelude to a much more recent geological event that transformed the topography of the entire region, the Pleistocene glaciation.

The dominant geological force structuring the present landscape in the Northeast over the past 3 million years has been continental glaciation. Glaciers have expanded and contracted numerous times with great regularity in that period. The movement of glaciers in and out of the region appears to be cyclical, with a period of about every 40,000 to 100,000 years. The most recent glacier reached its maximum southward extension around 21,000 years ago, completely covering the Northeast with a layer of ice. As the climate warmed some 16,000 years ago, the glacier began to retreat and by 10,000 years ago had largely disappeared from the region.

Glaciers are extremely important in structuring the landscape. They are massive, erosive forces that flow over the land, covering everything but the highest mountains. They tend to follow preexisting valleys, widening and deepening them and forming major river and lake basins when they recede. They are also very dirty, redistributing large quantities of rock, sand, and mud. When a glacier recedes, it simply melts in place, producing enormous volumes of glacial melt water that sorts, transports, and deposits the material it has carried. This process results in numerous distinctive geological structures such as moraines, drumlins, eskers, and kettle lakes.

Moraines are often formed at the terminus of the glacier, where material that the glacier had been carrying southward is deposited as the glacier recedes. When this process occurs, moraines often become dams that hold water behind them, thus creating a lake. Some of the more remarkable lakes of this type are found in the Northeast and include the Finger Lakes in upstate New York. Moraines can also create substantial peninsulas and islands, such as Cape Cod and Long Island.

Eskers are formed under the glacier as melt water sorts and shapes elongate narrow ridges in subglacial tunnels. Drumlins are also formed under the glacier and develop into rounded, elongate hills similar in shape to a giant loaf of bread as the glacier surges forward and molds unconsolidated material. Both of these geological formations are locally quite common in the Northeast.

As a glacier recedes, large blocks of ice often become buried in glacial material. These blocks of ice melt over time, creating a depression that, when filled with water, becomes a kettle lake. Kettle lakes are among the most common types of small lakes in the region; the best known is probably Walden Pond.

The great weight of a glacier depresses the land under it, and after the glacier retreats, a long period of glacial rebound ensues when the land returns to its original state. This process is still going on right now, with rebound occurring along the shores of large lakes such as Erie, Ontario, and Champlain. Glacial rebound can change the direction of flow of water out of a lake or separate a lake from the sea, as in the case of the rebound at the northern end of what is now Lake Champlain.

Major Drainages in the Northeastern United States

The geological activity discussed so far not only has created extensive freshwater fish habitat, but has shaped and formed the basins holding the water. It has determined the location of rivers and how they flow to the sea. The net effect is an area blessed with a multitude of diverse lakes and streams, many small ponds, wetlands, and various other kinds of places where fishes can live. The north-south orientation of many of the major river systems such as the

Hudson, Housatonic, Connecticut, and Merrimack are likely owing to the orientation of the major mountain-building events that occurred in the past. All of the lakes essentially were formed as a result of glacial activity.

The lakes and streams in an area are often organized into drainage basins. A drainage basin is a network of interconnecting lakes, streams, and rivers that empty into the ocean at the same point. For example, the water draining from the Connecticut Lakes in northern New Hampshire and the water from Knightville Reservoir in Massachusetts sooner or later join the Connecticut River and enter the sea at its mouth. All of the streams and lakes that drain to the ocean via the Connecticut River are collectively called the Connecticut River drainage basin. If there is no obstacle to swimming, such as a dam or waterfall, a fish might theoretically move unimpeded throughout this watershed.

Unfortunately, this is not the case in most of the drainage basins in the Northeast. Many early industries, which required water to generate power and run mills, were established in the region to take advantage of the abundant flowing water. Dams were built to ensure a constant and reliable source of power. The dams prevented the movement of fishes upstream to their ancestral spawning grounds. Times have changed; many of the industries are no longer operational, and most of the dams consequently no longer provide power. They do regrettably continue to block the passage of fishes moving up and down the streams and rivers, however.

Because freshwater fishes are confined to the network of streams and lakes that flow from the mountains to the sea, their distribution is heavily dependent on the geography of drainage systems. Freshwater fishes cannot travel between drainage basins because they cannot travel across dry land or traverse the salty waters of the ocean. Consequently, the network of interconnecting streams and lakes that form the drainage system where these fishes are found determines the potential area they might occupy. This potential area is further restricted by their habitat requirements.

During the time when the glaciers were receding, a tremendous amount of water drained to the sea. In this period, connections existed between drainage basins that are now separated. For example, glacial Lake Iroquois, which became Lake Ontario, drained to the east down the Mohawk-Hudson River system to the ocean. It was not until the ice had moved north that the current drainage down the St. Lawrence River was established. Fish were able to use these watery interconnections to enter drainage systems from refugia.

Humans have assisted much more recently in the exchange of fishes between drainage basins. They often help fishes overcome barriers to movement by stocking fishes or by digging canals that connect drainage basins. Because of the important role drainage systems play in fish distribution, ichthyologists tend to think in terms of drainage basins rather than political boundaries.

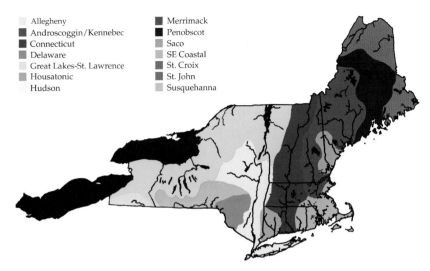

Fig. 1. Major drainage systems in the Northeast.

The major drainage systems in the region (figure 1), moving from west to east, are:

1. Allegheny
2. Laurentian Great Lakes and St. Lawrence
3. Susquehanna
4. Delaware
5. Hudson
6. Housatonic
7. Connecticut
8. Southeastern Coastal

9. Merrimack
10. Saco
11. Androscoggin
12. Kennebec
13. Penobscot
14. St. Croix
15. St. John

1. Allegheny: Drains a small corner of southwestern New York, eventually passing down the Ohio and Mississippi River to the Gulf of Mexico, and supports populations of species found nowhere else in the region.

2. Laurentian Great Lakes and St. Lawrence: One of the major drainages of the North American continent. Lake Erie, the Niagara River, Lake Ontario, Lake Champlain, and the St. Lawrence River are major components of this system in the Northeast. Vermont and much of northern and western New York drain to the Atlantic through this drainage system.

3. Susquehanna: Drains south-central New York, including the Chemung, Tioughnioga, and Chenango Rivers.

4. Delaware: Drains a portion of southeastern New York, including the southern Catskills, several New York City reservoirs, and many well-known Catskill trout streams.

5. Hudson: A major drainage for eastern New York and Vermont. Begins in the Adirondacks and drains south through the Capital District of New York, eventually to enter the ocean near New York City. It is under tidal influence from Albany to New York.

6. Housatonic: Primarily drains western Massachusetts and Connecticut, entering Long Island Sound in southwestern Connecticut.

7. Connecticut: A major drainage running from northern New Hampshire and Vermont south through Massachusetts and Connecticut, emptying into Long Island Sound.

8. Southeastern Coastal: A group of independent coastal streams extending from the Thames Rives in the South to Massachusetts Bay in the North.

9. Merrimack: Drains south-central New Hampshire, including Lake Winnipesauke and northeastern Massachusetts, where it enters the Atlantic Ocean.

10. Saco: Drains eastern New Hampshire and southwestern Maine.

11. Androscoggin: Drains northern New Hampshire and southwestern Maine, including the Rangeley Lakes.

12. Kennebec: Drains central Maine, including Moosehead Lake.

13. Penobscot: Drains central Maine, including Sebec and Chesuncook Lakes.

14. St. Croix: Drains northeastern Maine.

15. St. John: One of the most remote and least developed rivers in the region; drains northern Maine, including Baker Lake.

Zoogeography of Freshwater Fishes of the Northeast

Table 1 summarizes the distribution of fish species in the Northeast.

TABLE 1

Species List of Freshwater Fishes of the Northeast by State

Common Name	Species Name	N.Y.	Conn.	Mass.	R.I.	Vt.	N.H.	Me.	Total States
PETROMYZONTIDAE									
Ohio lamprey	*Ichthyomyzon bdellium*	x							1
northern brook lamprey	*Ichthyomyzon fossor*	x				x			2
mountain brook lamprey	*Ichthyomyzon greeleyi*	x							1
silver lamprey	*Ichthyomyzon unicuspis*	x				x			2
American brook lamprey	*Lampetra appendix*	x	x	x	x	x	x		6
sea lamprey	*Petromyzon marinus*	x	x	x	x	x	x	x	7

Common Name	Species Name	N.Y.	Conn.	Mass.	R.I.	Vt.	N.H.	Me.	Total States
	ACIPENSERIDAE								
shortnose sturgeon	*Acipenser brevirostrum*	x	x	x	x		x	x	6
lake sturgeon	*Acipenser fulvescens*	x				x			2
Atlantic sturgeon	*Acipenser oxyrhynchus*	x	x	x	x		x	x	6
	POLYODONTIDAE								
paddlefish	*Polyodon spathula*	x							1
	LEPISOSTEIDAE								
longnose gar	*Lepisosteus osseus*	x				x			2
	AMIIDAE								
bowfin	*Amia calva*	x	x	x		x	x		5
	HIODONTIDAE								
mooneye	*Hiodon tergisus*	x				x			2
	ANGUILLIDAE								
American eel	*Anguilla rostrata*	x	x	x	x	x	x	x	7
	CLUPEIDAE								
blueback herring	*Alosa aestivalis*	x	x	x	x	x	x	x	7
alewife	*Alosa pseudoharengus*	x	x	x	x	x	x	x	7
American shad	*Alosa sapidissima*	x	x	x	x	x	x	x	7
gizzard shad	*Dorosoma cepedianum*	x	x	x		x			4
	CYPRINIDAE								
central stoneroller	*Campostoma anomalum*	x	x						2
goldfish	*Carassius auratus*	x	x	x	x	x	x	x	7
redside dace	*Clinostomus elongatus*	x							1
lake chub	*Couesius plumbeus*	x		x		x	x	x	5
satinfin shiner	*Cyprinella analostana*	x							1
spotfin shiner	*Cyprinella spiloptera*	x				x			2
common carp	*Cyprinus carpio*	x	x	x	x	x	x	x	7
streamline chub	*Erimystax dissimilis*	x							1
gravel chub	*Erimystax x-punctata*	x							1
tongue-tied minnow	*Exoglossum laurae*	x							1
cutlips minnow	*Exoglossum maxillingua*	x	x	x		x			4

Common Name	Species Name	N.Y.	Conn.	Mass.	R.I.	Vt.	N.H.	Me.	Total States
brassy minnow	Hybognathus hankinsoni	x				x			2
eastern silvery minnow	Hybognathus regius	x		x		x	x	x	5
ide	Leuciscus idus	x	x					x	3
striped shiner	Luxilus chrysocephalus	x							1
common shiner	Luxilus cornutus	x	x	x	x	x	x	x	7
redfin shiner	Lythrurus umbratilis	x							1
silver chub	Macrhybopsis storeriana	x							1
pearl dace	Margariscus margarita	x	x			x		x	4
hornyhead chub	Nocomis biguttatus	x							1
river chub	Nocomis micropogon	x							1
golden shiner	Notemigonus crysoleucas	x	x	x	x	x	x	x	7
bigeye chub	Notropis amblops	x							1
comely shiner	Notropis amoenus	x							1
pugnose shiner	Notropis anogenus	x							1
emerald shiner	Notropis atherinoides	x		x		x		x	4
bridle shiner	Notropis bifrenatus	x	x	x	x	x	x	x	7
silverjaw minnow	Notropis buccatus	x							1
ironcolor shiner	Notropis chalybaeus	x							1
bigmouth shiner	Notropis dorsalis	x							1
blackchin shiner	Notropis heterodon	x				x			2
blacknose shiner	Notropis heterolepis	x				x	x	x	4
spottail shiner	Notropis hudsonius	x	x	x	x	x	x	x	7
silver shiner	Notropis photogenis	x							1
swallowtail shiner	Notropis procne	x							1
rosyface shiner	Notropis rubellus	x	x			x			3
sand shiner	Notropis stramineus	x				x			2
mimic shiner	Notropis volucellus	x	x	x		x			4
northern redbelly dace	Phoxinus eos	x		x		x	x	x	5
finescale dace	Phoxinus neogaeus	x				x	x	x	4

Common Name	Species Name	N.Y.	Conn.	Mass.	R.I.	Vt.	N.H.	Me.	Total States
bluntnose minnow	Pimephales notatus	x	x	x	x	x	x		6
fathead minnow	Pimephales promelas	x	x	x	x	x	x	x	7
blacknose dace	Rhinichthys atratulus	x	x	x	x	x	x	x	7
longnose dace	Rhinichthys cataractae	x	x	x	x	x	x	x	7
bitterling	Rhodeus sericeus	x							1
rudd	Scardinius erythrophthalmus	x	x	x		x		x	5
creek chub	Semotilus atromaculatus	x	x	x		x	x	x	6
fallfish	Semotilus corporalis	x	x	x	x	x	x	x	7
tench	Tinca tinca	x	x	x					
CATOSTOMIDAE									
quillback	Carpiodes cyprinus	x				x			2
longnose sucker	Catostomus catostomus	x	x	x		x	x	x	6
white sucker	Catostomus commersoni	x	x	x	x	x	x	x	7
creek chubsucker	Erimyzon oblongus	x	x	x	x		x	x	6
lake chubsucker	Erimyzon sucetta	x							1
northern hog sucker	Hypentelium nigricans	x							1
silver redhorse	Moxostoma anisurum	x				x			2
river redhorse	Moxostoma carinatum	x							1
black redhorse	Moxostoma duquesnei	x							1
golden redhorse	Moxostoma erythrurum	x							1
shorthead redhorse	Moxostoma macrolepidotum	x				x			2
greater redhorse	Moxostoma valenciennesi	x				x			2
ICTALURIDAE									
white catfish	Ameiurus catus	x	x	x	x	x	x	x	7
black bullhead	Ameiurus melas	x	x						2
yellow bullhead	Ameiurus natalis	x	x	x		x	x		5
brown bullhead	Ameiurus nebulosus	x	x	x	x	x	x	x	7

Common Name	Species Name	N.Y.	Conn.	Mass.	R.I.	Vt.	N.H.	Me.	Total States
channel catfish	Ictalurus punctatus	x	x	x		x	x		5
stonecat	Noturus flavus	x				x			2
tadpole madtom	Noturus gyrinus	x		x			x		3
margined madtom	Noturus insignis	x		x			x		3
brindled madtom	Noturus miurus	x							1
ESOCIDAE									
grass/redfin pickerel	Esox americanus	x	x	x	x	x	x	x	7
northern pike	Esox lucius	x	x	x	x	x	x	x	7
muskellunge	Esox masquinongy	x	x			x		x	4
chain pickerel	Esox niger	x	x	x	x	x	x	x	7
UMBRIDAE									
central mudminnow	Umbra limi	x	x	x		x			4
eastern mudminnow	Umbra pygmaea	x							1
OSMERIDAE									
rainbow smelt	Osmerus mordax	x	x	x	x	x	x	x	7
SALMONIDAE									
cisco or lake herring	Coregonus artedii	x				x			2
lake whitefish	Coregonus clupeaformis	x				x	x	x	4
pink salmon	Oncorhynchus gorbuscha	x						x	2
coho salmon	Oncorhynchus kisutch	x		x			x		3
rainbow trout	Oncorhynchus mykiss	x	x	x	x	x	x	x	7
sockeye/kokanee salmon	Oncorhynchus nerka	x	x	x		x		x	5
Chinook salmon	Oncorhynchus tshawytscha	x	x	x		x	x	x	6
round whitefish	Prosopium cylindraceum	x	x			x	x	x	5
Atlantic salmon	Salmo salar	x	x	x	x	x	x	x	7
brown trout	Salmo trutta	x	x	x	x	x	x	x	7
Arctic char	Salvelinus alpinus					x	x	x	3

Common Name	Species Name	N.Y.	Conn.	Mass.	R.I.	Vt.	N.H.	Me.	Total States
brook trout	Salvelinus fontinalis	x	x	x	x	x	x	x	7
lake trout	Salvelinus namaycush	x	x	x		x	x	x	6
	PERCOPSIDAE								
trout-perch	Percopsis omiscomaycus	x	x			x			3
	APHREDODERIDAE								
pirate perch	Aphredoderus sayanus	x							1
	LOTIDAE								
burbot	Lota lota	x	x	x		x	x	x	6
	ATHERINIDAE								
brook silverside	Labidesthes sicculus	x							1
	FUNDULIDAE								
banded killifish	Fundulus diaphanus	x	x	x	x	x	x	x	7
	POECILLIDAE								
western mosquitofish	Gambusia affinis	x	x						2
	GASTEROSTEIDAE								
fourspine stickleback	Apeltes quadracus	x	x	x	x		x	x	6
brook stickleback	Culaea inconstans	x	x			x		x	4
threespine stickleback	Gasterosteus aculeatus	x	x	x			x	x	6
ninespine stickleback	Pungitius pungitius	x	x	x	x		x	x	6
	MORONIDAE								
white perch	Morone americana	x	x	x	x	x	x	x	7
white bass	Morone chrysops	x							1
striped bass	Morone saxatilis	x	x	x	x	x	x	x	7
	CENTRARCHIDAE								
mud sunfish	Acantharchus pomotis	x							1
rock bass	Ambloplites rupestris	x	x	x	x	x	x		6
bluespotted sunfish	Enneacanthus gloriosus	x							1
banded sunfish	Enneacanthus obesus	x	x	x	x		x		5
redbreast sunfish	Lepomis auritus	x	x	x	x	x	x	x	7

Common Name	Species Name	N.Y.	Conn.	Mass.	R.I.	Vt.	N.H.	Me.	Total States
green sunfish	Lepomis cyanellus	x	x	x					3
pumpkinseed	Lepomis gibbosus	x	x	x	x	x	x	x	7
warmouth	Lepomis gulosus	x							1
bluegill	Lepomis macrochirus	x	x	x	x	x	x		6
longear sunfish	Lepomis megalotis	x							1
redear sunfish	Lepomis microlophus					x			1
smallmouth bass	Micropterus dolomieu	x	x	x	x	x	x	x	7
largemouth bass	Micropterus salmoides	x	x	x	x	x	x	x	7
white crappie	Pomoxis annularis	x	x	x		x			4
black crappie	Pomoxis nigromaculatus	x	x	x	x	x	x	x	7

PERCIDAE

Common Name	Species Name	N.Y.	Conn.	Mass.	R.I.	Vt.	N.H.	Me.	Total States
eastern sand darter	Ammocrypta pellucida	x				x			2
greenside darter	Etheostoma blennioides	x							1
rainbow darter	Etheostoma caeruleum	x							1
bluebreast darter	Etheostoma camurum	x							1
Iowa darter	Etheostoma exile	x				x			2
fantail darter	Etheostoma flabellare	x				x			2
swamp darter	Etheostoma fusiforme	x	x	x	x		x	x	6
spotted darter	Etheostoma maculatum	x							1
johnny darter	Etheostoma nigrum	x							1
tessellated darter	Etheostoma olmstedi	x	x	x	x	x	x		6
variegate darter	Etheostoma variatum	x							1
banded darter	Etheostoma zonale	x							1
yellow perch	Perca flavescens	x	x	x	x	x	x	x	7
logperch	Percina caprodes	x				x			2
channel darter	Percina copelandi	x				x			2
gilt darter	Percina evides	x							1
longhead darter	Percina macrocephala	x							1
blackside darter	Percina maculata	x							1
shield darter	Percina peltata	x							1
sauger	Sander canadense	x							1

Common Name	Species Name	N.Y.	Conn.	Mass.	R.I.	Vt.	N.H.	Me.	Total States
walleye	Sander vitreum	x	x	x		x	x		5
	SCIAENIDAE								
freshwater drum	Aplodinotus grunniens	x				x			2
	GOBIIDAE								
round goby	Neogobius melanostomus	x							1
tubenose goby	Proterorhinus marmoratus	x							1
	COTTIDAE								
mottled sculpin	Cottus bairdi	x				x			2
slimy sculpin	Cottus cognatus	x	x	x		x	x	x	6
Total species in state[a]		160	77	74	48	94	69	64	

[a] Total species in all states: 162.

New York, which makes up approximately 43 percent of the area of the Northeast, has the most diverse fish fauna in the region, with 160 of 162 species. The only species missing from New York's faunal list are the arctic char and the redear sunfish. Such high diversity is owing not only to the large size of New York, but also to its diverse array of major drainage systems, including the Laurentian Great Lakes, the Susquehanna, Delaware, Hudson, and—probably most important from the point of view of diversity—the Allegheny. The Allegheny is a very small system in the Northeast, draining only a small corner of southwestern New York, but it links through the Ohio River to the Mississippi River drainages and thus to an array of fishes not found in other portions of the Northeast. There are 60 species of fish in the Allegheny drainage system in New York, 14 of which are found nowhere else in the region. Maine, which is nearly the size of New York, has a total of only 64 species. Vermont, with 94 species, has the second greatest diversity of fish fauna, owing in large part to Lake Champlain. Rhode Island, because of its small size and limited coastal drainages, has the fewest species (only 48). The other states fall somewhere between these extremes. Some regions of the United States with comparable area, such as the Southeast, have many more species than the Northeast. The lower diversity in the Northeast is owed in part to the relatively short time that it has been open and available to fishes. The glaciers left the area some 10,000–16,000 years ago, providing little time for development of a diverse fish community.

Habitat

Freshwater fishes occupy a surprising range of habitats. They can be found in very small streams, large rivers, small ponds, marshes, and large lakes. One prominent ichthyologist, Carl Hubbs, has written, "Where there is water there are fishes, and where there are fishes they can be caught." In other words, if there is a permanent source of water, the odds are very good that at least one species of fish will be occupying it no matter how small and inconspicuous the source of water might appear.

Fishes have adapted to particular kinds of habitat so that some are better in open water; others prefer the bottom; many function more effectively in streams; and some can tolerate low-oxygen conditions. The adaptations often involve irreversible morphological changes. For example, darters, which are often found in swift-flowing riffle areas in streams, have lost their swim bladder in many cases. The swim bladder functions in most fishes as a hydrostatic organ conferring neutral buoyancy on the fish. A species that spends its time resting on the bottom does not need the buoyancy of a swim bladder. In fact, such a bladder may be disadvantageous in that it would subject the darter to the danger of being swept downstream.

Adaptations to different modes of feeding are also quite apparent in fishes. Compare, for example, the sea lamprey, northern pike, and sturgeon. In one case, the sea lamprey, we have a species that is very well adapted for attaching to the side of a fish, rasping the skin away, and feeding on the body fluids of its prey. In the case of the northern pike, we have a classic predator with a large mouth full of teeth that is well adapted to capturing smaller fish as prey. The third example, the sturgeon, has a long, protrusible mouth extending ventrally from the under side of the head, which facilitates feeding off of the bottom. Each is very well adapted for the type of feeding mode it uses. Observation of a fish's mouth can provide insight into the types of prey on which the species feeds and the habitat in which it feeds.

The majority of species in the region are found in moderate-size streams, where they can occupy a series of critical habitats over the course of a year. They often require deep water for protection from wading predators or for surviving the icy winter. On other occasions, they may search out overhanging banks or logs to provide protection from above. During the spawning period, swift-flowing water over gravel provides an ideal habitat for laying eggs. Most species move through these habitats as needed according to the demands of their life history or to pressures from predators or weather.

Human Impacts on Fish Distribution

At the peak of the Ice Age, the region was completely covered by glaciers. To the best of our knowledge, no fish lived in the Northeast during this period, although some researchers have suggested that life might have existed in "nunataks"—areas of high ground surrounded by glacial ice—near the Gulf of St. Lawrence. But, for the most part, the history of fishes in the region begins with an essentially blank slate some 16,000 years ago. As the glaciers receded and open-water habitat became available, fishes began to work their way into the region from what are called refugia. During the Ice Age, fishes survived outside of the glaciated regions in areas that had open water and allowed for aquatic life to persist through the period. At least three refugia served as sources for the Northeast: the Atlantic Coastal Plain Refugium, the Atlantic Coastal Uplands Refugium, and the Mississippi Valley Refugium (Schmidt 1986). The Atlantic Coastal Plain Refugium probably occupied much of what is now the continental shelf region from southern Virginia and North Carolina. Sea levels were lower during the Ice Age, and thus the coastline was approximately 60 miles farther out than it is now. This refugium would have been a low-lying, slow-moving aquatic habitat. The Atlantic Coastal Uplands Refugium was farther inland and occupied higher-elevation streams and lakes with more rapid flows. As you might expect, the types of fishes found in the flat lowland refugia would be quite different from those found in the rapidly moving streams of the uplands refugia. The third major refugium supplying the Northeast was the Mississippi Valley Refugium, a large area encompassing the lower Mississippi River valley and later the Great Lakes. The initial makeup of the community of fishes of the Northeast was determined by the location of the refugia, its species composition, and the pattern and nature of the glacial retreat. Changes in drainage pattern and stream capture later provided additional opportunities for adding species to the fish fauna. The fishes that established themselves in the region at that time are what we refer to as native species.

In more recent times, humans have brought in new species, either intentionally or inadvertently, and thus have substantially modified the original species composition. They accomplished these additions in a number of ways. Because transportation systems were dependent to a large extent on water during the colonial and postrevolutionary history of the region, humans constructed many canals linking one watershed to another. One of the best-known examples is the Erie Canal, which allowed vessels (and fish) to move from the Mohawk-Hudson drainage into the Great Lakes and vice versa. Hundreds of other canal systems developed throughout the Northeast. Canals provided routes for fish passage from one watershed to another, which was not possible before the construction of the canal.

Humans also have intentionally or inadvertently released exotic species of fish into a water body. Some of these introductions have been quite successful, such as rainbow and brown trout stocked in lakes and streams. Others, such as introductions of carp or round goby, are more problematic. Introductions of this type have come either by planned efforts of fish management agencies or by inadvertent releases of bait fish by anglers, of pets by aquarists, or of ballast water from ocean-going vessels. Such introductions continue to occur.

The net effect of human activities—including the introduction of exotic species, habitat destruction, and overfishing—has been to reduce or eliminate many species of native fishes. States and the federal government have developed lists of species that they feel are threatened by extinction to one degree or another. In the Northeast, thirty-seven species have been placed on those lists (table 2).

TABLE 2

Freshwater Fishes of the Northeast on State or Federal Lists
of Endangered Species, Threatened Species, or Species of Special Concern

Species	U.S.	N.Y.	Conn.	Mass.	R.I.	Vt.	N.H.	Me.
Northern Brook Lamprey						E		
Mountain Brook Lamprey		SC						
American Brook Lamprey			E	T		T		
Shortnose Sturgeon	E	E	E	E	E		E	
Lake Sturgeon		T				E		
Atlantic Sturgeon			T	E				
Mooneye		T						
Lake Chub				E				
Silver Chub		E						
Streamline Chub		SC						
Gravel Chub		T						
Eastern Silvery Minnow				SC				
Pugnose Shiner		E						
Bridle Shiner				SC				
Redfin Shiner		SC						
Ironcolor Shiner		SC						
Northern Redbelly Dace				E				
Longnose Sucker			SC	SC				
Lake Chubsucker		T						
Black Redhorse		SC						
Stonecat						E		
Round Whitefish		E						

TABLE 2 (*continued*)

Species	U.S.	N.Y.	Conn.	Mass.	R.I.	Vt.	N.H.	Me.
Arctic Char (Sunapee Trout)							E	
Burbot			E	SC				
Threespine Stickleback				T				
Mud Sunfish		T						
Banded Sunfish		T	T					
Longear Sunfish		T						
Eastern Sand Darter		T				T		
Bluebreast Darter		E						
Swamp Darter		T						T
Spotted Darter		T						
Longhead Darter		T						
Channel Darter						E		
Gilt Darter		E						
Spoonhead Sculpin		E						
Deepwater Sculpin		E						

Key: **E**: Endangered, any species in danger of extinction throughout all or a significant portion of its range; **T**: Threatened, any species likely to become an endangered species within the foreseeable future throughout all or a significant portion of its range; **SC**: Special Concern, any species for which a welfare concern or risk of endangerment has been documented. Federally endangered species, such as the shortnose sturgeon, are considered endangered in all states in the region whether or not they are specifically listed by the individual states.

Observing, Collecting, and Studying Fishes

Observing

Although fishes are more difficult to observe than birds, it is possible to see and often identify them in their natural habitat, particularly if the water is clear and shallow. Quietly observing from a stream bank, from a country bridge, or along a lakeshore often provides the opportunity to see fishes and to view their behavior. It helps to wear polarized sunglasses to cut the glare, allowing you to see into the water much more clearly, and to have a pair of binoculars handy to magnify the fishes for easier identification. Dr. C. L. Smith's book *Fish Watching* (1994) outlines the techniques to finding and identifying fishes in their natural habitat. One key is to know the fish species that you are likely to find within a state or region. This field guide provides that information. A second key is to narrow the range of species expected by understanding what species might occupy the habitat under view. For example, if you are observing a riffle area in a small mountain stream, you should be looking for small darters or minnows and not expect to see lake sturgeon. A third key is the behavior of the fish. Some tend to be bottom dwellers who rarely approach the surface, such as sculpins and darters; others commonly feed near the surface, such as trout or killifishes. A final important key is timing. Many fish spawn during relatively short time intervals, and when they do, they gather in large numbers and are often quite conspicuous. The males typically are brightly colored and thus easy to identify at this time. Their behavior is often very distinctive. So, with all of these key factors in mind, it is possible to make interesting observations not only of what fish are present, but also of what behaviors they are exhibiting at the time.

Another approach to observing fishes is to get directly into the water with the fish using a mask and snorkel. Surprisingly, fish are relatively unafraid when a swimmer is in the water with them. They are much more likely to disperse when a person suddenly appears on the bank of a stream than they are if a swimmer works his or her way down into a pool from upstream. In the water, you can often get a very good close-up view of the fish to make firm identifications and observe their behavior.

Collecting

Ichthyologists and fishery biologists use a variety of techniques to collect fishes for study, most of which are not readily available to the average person. But fishes can be taken using relatively simple techniques available to all. One obvious way is angling. Large sport fish taken this way provide anglers with a close-up look of the fish and allow them to make a positive identification. Small fishes can be taken using smaller lures and lighter tackle. Small flies work for many minnows as well as for trout. Seines or dip nets can also be used. Seines are small nets, typically 6 to 8 feet wide and 3 to 4 feet deep, with a lead line on the bottom and floats on top. You pull the seine through the water and then drag it up on shore or, alternatively, drive the fishes into a stationary net. Either method provides an excellent opportunity to collect many species of small fish. Permits are often required, however, if you plan to use a seine. Check with your state natural-resource agency before beginning.

Once a fish is in hand, it is possible to make close-up observations of the key characteristics needed to identify it. A hand lens or other types of magnification help, but a photo tank can also be very useful. A photo tank is a small aquarium, usually less than 5 or 6 inches long, 4 to 5 inches high, and 1 or 2 inches deep, with a moveable glass plate inside that can be used to restrict the fish to the front of the tank for easy viewing. The tank is an excellent way to make close-up observations of small, hard-to-identify fishes, such as minnows or darters, in a more natural condition. Barbels, fin rays, and other anatomical structures are often easier to see when the fish is submerged in water than when it is being held in dry air. In addition, this method puts less stress on the fish and makes it more likely that it can be returned successfully to the water without serious damage. Once a small fish is in such a tank, it can be examined closely, and many of the characters that are difficult to see when the fish is in hand become apparent. In the absence of a photo tank, which you normally would have to build yourself, a small clear plastic container can serve as a substitute.

Studying

One of the more rewarding ways of interacting with native fishes is to attempt to rear them in an aquarium. To be successful, you need to know their basic requirements with regard to water quality, temperature, and food. If they do well in the tank, you may want to attempt to take the experiment one step further and try to get them to breed. Success at breeding often requires a trial-and-error approach before a solid understanding of their requirements can be achieved. Because many of the fishes in the region have not been thoroughly studied, rearing them may lead to additions to our knowledge of their habitat and breeding requirements. Members of the North American Native Fishes Association have reared many native fishes and have provided tips to their proper husbandry. Their Web page is: http://www.nanfa.org/index.html.

If you plan to collect fishes, you will most likely require a permit from your state natural-resource agency. The addresses for state agencies in the region are:

Connecticut
Department of Environmental Protection
79 Elm Street
Hartford, CT 06106–5127

Maine
Maine Department of Inland Fisheries and Wildlife
284 State Street
41 State House Station
Augusta, ME 04333–0041

Massachusetts
Massachusetts Wildlife
Division of Fisheries and Wildlife
251 Causeway Street, Suite 400
Boston, MA 02114–2152

New Hampshire
New Hampshire Fish and Game Department
2 Hazen Drive
Concord, New Hampshire 03301

New York
New York State Department of Environmental Conservation
625 Broadway
Albany, NY 12233

Rhode Island
Department of Environmental Management
Bureau of Natural Resources
235 Promenade Street
Providence, RI 02908–5767

Vermont
Vermont Agency of Natural Resources
103 South Maine Street
Waterbury, VT 05671

How to Use This Book

Naming Fishes

One of the first things we typically want to know when we encounter a fish is its name. If the name given to a fish is to be of value, then everyone needs to agree on a consistent name. For a long time, no organized plan existed for naming fish (or any other plant or animal for that matter). People from one region had one name for a fish, but people from another region had a different name for the same fish. This led to considerable confusion. In 1735, Carolus Linnaeus developed a system that gave each creature two names: the first its generic, or genus, name to indicate its relationship to other closely related species, and the second a specific name to distinguish it from all other species of that genus. He used Latin for these names because it was widely used by scholars at the time. Scientists throughout the world have used Linnaeus's system ever since.

For example, the scientific name of the smallmouth bass is *Micropterus dolomieu*. *Micropterus* is the name of the genus that includes the largemouth bass, redeye bass, Suwannee bass, spotted bass, and Guadalupe bass, all reasonably close relatives of the smallmouth bass. The species name is *dolomieu*, which distinguishes the smallmouth from the other bass in the genus *Micropterus*. The smallmouth bass is the only animal in the world with this Latin name. By consulting the appropriate references, any zoologist in the world can find a complete description of *Micropterus dolomieu* and from that will know exactly what fish he or she has. The zoologist, however, might have some difficulty if he or she relies only on common names because this fish is also called bronzeback, black bass, brown bass, or white trout.

The American Fisheries Society has developed a list of accepted common names, along with the scientific names, for all of the fishes in the United States and Canada. This list makes it possible to use common names for fishes in the Northeast without confusion. In this field guide, I initially list both the common and scientific names, but in subsequent references I use only the common names recommended in the fifth edition of *Common and Scientific Names of Fishes from the United States and Canada* (Robins et al. 1991).

Fish Morphology

In order to identify a fish, you must know some basic facts about fish anatomy. Spend a few minutes here before going on to the keys. Figures 2 and 3 and the accompanying discussion should help.

Most fishes have three unpaired median fins and two sets of paired fins. The median unpaired fins are the dorsal, caudal, and anal fins. Some species also have an adipose fin, and in others the dorsal fin comprises two or more parts.

The dorsal fin is located in the middle of the back, running fore and aft. It is

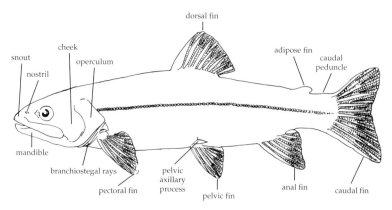

Fig. 2. External anatomy of a typical soft-rayed fish.

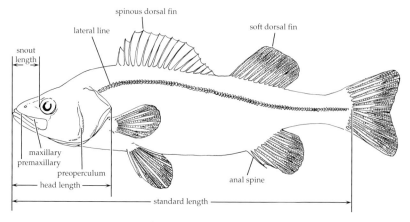

Fig. 3. External anatomy of a typical spiny-rayed fish.

simply a membrane supported by skeletal elements, which, depending on the species, may be spines, rays, or spinous rays. The type of element that supports the fin is quite important in identifying fishes. You will frequently have to distinguish spines from rays. Note in figure 4a the unsegmented character of spines, how they do not branch at the ends, and how they are of one solid piece when viewed from the front or back. A soft ray, in contrast, is segmented, quite often flares out at the end (is branched), and appears to be split lengthwise when viewed from the front or back (figure 4b). A spinous ray is intermediate in that it is unbranched and quite massive, but it is divided lengthwise into two halves, and the segmentation is still present in the form of toothlike projections along its posterior (rear) edge (figure 4c). Spinous rays are found only in the carp, goldfish, and catfishes.

When counting rays in the minnow and sucker families, start the count from the forward edge of the fin with the first principal unbranched ray as shown in figure 5. This is the first full-length ray, just in front of the first branched ray. Ignore the short rudimentary rays that lie in front of the first principal ray, for they may vary in number. Then count every ray until you reach the last two. If two rays are joined at the base or are angled in such a way that it appears they will join shortly after they enter the body, count them as one ray. If, however, they appear to be separate

a. spines

b. soft rays

c. spinous ray

Fig. 4. Three types of skeletal support in the fins of freshwater fishes: *(a)* spines; *(b)* soft rays; and *(c)* spinous ray.

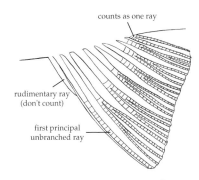

counts as one ray

rudimentary ray (don't count)

first principal unbranched ray

Fig. 5. Method of counting rays of minnows and suckers. Begin count with the first principal unbranched ray, then count each ray to the end. If the last two rays are joined, count them as one. The fish illustrated has 8 rays.

and distinct, count them as two rays. When counting rays in the catfish, trout, or pike families, count all rudimentary rays.

Between the dorsal fin and the caudal fin in trout, smelt, trout-perches, and catfishes, there is a small flap of tissue unsupported by spines or rays. This is the adipose fin.

Soft rays support the tail—or, more properly, the caudal fin—of fishes. Three types of caudal fins are found: heterocercal, abbreviate heterocercal, and homocercal. In the heterocercal caudal fin, the vertebral column extends well into the upper lobe of the fin. The sturgeon is a fish with a well-developed heterocercal caudal fin, as shown in the top drawing in figure 6. The homocercal caudal fin (bottom drawing in figure 6) is distinguished in that the vertebral column does not enter the caudal fin at all, but terminates at the base of the fin. Most fishes in the Northeast possess this type of fin. The abbreviate heterocercal condition is intermediate and is found only in the bowfin and gar (center drawing in figure 6).

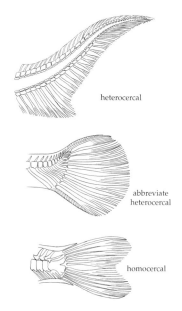

Fig. 6. Heterocercal, abbreviate heterocercal, and homocercal caudal fins. The vertebral column extends into the upper lobe of the heterocercal fin, but it stops at the base of the homocercal fin. It is intermediate in the abbreviate heterocercal fin.

The anal fin is located on the ventral midline just behind the vent. All of our freshwater species have only one anal fin, except the brackish-water tomcod, which has two. The anal fin may have one or more spines at its leading edge, but soft rays support the remainder of the fin.

The pelvic fins are paired and lie on either side of the midline. They are posterior and more ventral than the pectoral fins. In more evolutionarily advanced fishes, such as the sunfishes or perches, they tend to be found in a more anterior position, sometimes directly under the pectoral fins. In more primitive teleosts, such as minnows or pikes, they tend to be well posterior of the pectoral fins.

The pectoral fins are also paired but are found farther up the side and more toward the head than are the pelvic fins.

The head of a fish extends from the tip of the snout to the posterior edge of the gill cover. The lower jaw is called the mandible. It is formed by the fusion of several bones, the major one being the dentary bone. On occasion, the lower jaw possesses holes on its ventral side, called mandibular pores. Two bones form each half of the upper jaw, an anterior tooth-bearing bone called the premaxilla and a posterior bone called the maxilla. In some fishes, the premaxilla is said to be protractile, which simply means that a distinct groove crosses all the way over the midline of the snout separating the premaxilla from the snout. If the premaxilla is nonprotractile, this groove is bridged at the midline by a strip of flesh called a frenum.

The nostrils lie a short way back on the snout—normally two pair, one pair on either side of the midline. Each nostril generally has two openings separated by a fleshy flap. The eyes are set in a bony cavity called the orbit. The gills are protected by a flexible bony structure called the operculum. Anterior to the operculum is a narrow, crescent-shaped bone called the preoperculum. Anterior to the preoperculum is the cheek region. Ventral to the operculum is a membranous region supported by branchiostegal rays. By lifting the operculum, you can see the gills. Most species have four gills on either side of the head. The red feathery portion is composed of gill filaments, which are attached to a white bony gill arch. Protruding forward from the gill arch are small projections called gill rakers.

The teeth of fishes may be found in several places. In the upper jaw, teeth are found on the premaxilla. Moving toward the center of the oral cavity, the next set of teeth are the palatine teeth. Then on the midline near the front are the vomerine teeth. In the lower jaw, teeth are found on the mandible, but they may also be found on the tongue, and in some species pharyngeal tooth pads are present as well.

Scales cover the body of most fishes. In the primitive fishes, sturgeon and gar, the scales are large, heavy, and bony; in most fish, however, they are thin, transparent, bony ridge scales. Two types of bony ridge scales occur in fishes: cycloid scales, which are circular and relatively smooth; and ctenoid scales, which possess small toothlike projections (ctenii) on the exposed portion of the scale.

Scales sometimes become specialized for certain purposes. Three such cases are important in identifying fishes. In some species, just above the point where the pelvic fin joins the body, an enlarged pointed scale has grown. This is called the pelvic axillary process. A second special case occurs along the sides of most fishes, where a faint line runs the length of the body from the head to the tail. At closer inspection, you may note that the line is simply a series of holes in a row of scales. These scales are called lateral line scales. Of course, some fishes without scales have lateral lines, and some fishes with scales do not have lateral lines, but they are the exceptions. The third type of specialized scale is called a scute. It is a raised series of scales located on the ventral midline of herrings, giving them a sawtooth appearance.

A thin membrane called a peritoneum lines the body cavity of fishes internally.

Arrangement of Species Accounts

Ichthyologists traditionally have organized the families of fishes in order of their suspected evolutionary relationships. Families thought to be more primitive and thus to have had a longer evolutionary history are placed first, and those more advanced fishes with a shorter evolutionary history are placed last. I follow that approach here, arranging the families from the primitive lampreys through the more advanced sculpins. The common name is listed first, then the family or species name.

Key to Families

Using the Key

The purpose of this book is to provide an opportunity to learn more about the fascinating world of fishes found in the streams and lakes of the Northeast. The first and most crucial step in this process is to learn the names of the fishes. Once the name is known, it is possible to gather a great deal of additional information from the scientific literature. This guide begins that process by providing a summary of the species' life history and distribution. More information can be found in the references listed at the end of the book. The essential initial element, however, is to determine the name of the fish.

A fish can be identified in at least two ways. One is simply to compare it to the pictures in the field guide. The pictures have arrows that point to the important distinguishing characters on the fish. Does it resemble any of the fishes pictured? If so, a little further reading on its distribution to determine if it is likely to be in the area where you found it will help confirm the identification. A second approach is to use a dichotomous key. Ichthyologists and fishery biologists widely use keys because they are specifically designed to assist in identifying a fish. A key requires that you make a choice between two alternatives regarding the morphology of the unknown specimen. Because choosing between alternatives often requires careful observation of characteristics, it is best to have the specimen in hand. It can be examined fresh or, if necessary, preserved in 10 percent formalin.

At the end of the alternative you choose, you will see a line pointing either to a name or to a number that tells you where to go next. Follow the numbers, making the appropriate choice at each dichotomy until you find a name. In the "Key to Families," this name is the family name of your specimen; if a family has more than one species, an additional key to the species is given in the section where the family is discussed. In most cases, you can verify the identification by comparing your specimen with the illustration and with its distribution in relation to the area where it was taken.

For example, suppose you have an American eel in hand but cannot identify it. First go to dichotomy 1 in the "Key to Families." Read *both* alternatives 1a and 1b to see which best describes your unknown specimen. Dichotomy 1 asks if the fish's mouth is a round sucking disk or if the fish has jaws; if the fish has pectoral or pelvic fins or both, or it is lacking such fins; and if it has several gill openings on each side or just one. Other contrasts are presented. Your fish has jaws, pectoral fins, one gill opening on each side, and a pair of nostrils, so you would choose 1b and be instructed to go to dichotomy 2. There you will decide whether the vertebral column extends into the upper lobe of the caudal fin or not. Because it does not, you then go to dichotomy 4. Here you are asked to decide whether the snout is greatly elongate. It is not, so you move to dichotomy 5, where you are asked if a flat bony plate protects the ventral surface of your fish's lower jaw. There is no flat bony plate on your fish, so you go to dichotomy 6, where you must decide whether pelvic fins are present or absent. They are absent, and you also note that the body of the fish in question is eel shaped. This identification leads to the conclusion that your specimen is in the eel family Anguillidae. Verify this conclusion by comparing the fish with the drawing. If by chance the drawing and the specimen do not agree, go back and run through the key again, rechecking your choices.

Once you have determined the family, you should look it up in the main body of the guide. In the species accounts for that family, run through the "Species Keys" just as you went through the "Key to Families" and determine the exact identification of your fish. In this example, there is only one species of eel in the region, *Anguilla rostrata*, the American eel. It is widely distributed in all states in the Northeast.

Key to Families

1a. Mouth a round sucking disc, no jaws; no pelvic or pectoral fins; 7 porelike gill openings on either side of head; single median nostril → **Lampreys, Family Petromyzontidae**

1b. Mouth with true jaws; normally with both pectoral and pelvic fins present (pelvic fins missing in eels); one large slitlike gill opening on either side of head; pair of nostrils on snout → **2**

2a. Vertebral column extends nearly to tip of dorsal lobe of caudal fin (visible as ridge extending into tail); caudal fin forked; dorsal lobe much larger than ventral lobe in sturgeon, lobes of approximately the same size in spoonbill→ **3**

2b. Vertebral column does not extend to tip of dorsal lobe of caudal fin; caudal fin rounded or forked; if caudal fin forked, both lobes are of approximately the same size→ **4**

3a. Snout extends considerably beyond mouth, forming an unusually long, paddlelike structure, which is approximately 20 to 33 percent of the total body length; scales absent from body (some scales are present on tail)→ **Paddlefishes, Family Polyodontidae**

3b. Snout extends beyond mouth, forming a relatively short pointed snout that is less than 20 percent of the total body length; barbels extend downward from snout in front of mouth; body protected by several rows of bony plates→ **Sturgeons, Family Acipenseridae**

4a. Snout greatly elongate, at least 20 percent of total length; body covered with heavy, diamond-shaped ganoid scales→ **Gars, Family Lepisosteidae**

4b. Snout of normal length; body with normal scales or scaleless→ **5**

5a. Ventral surface of lower jaw protected by a flat bony plate; long dorsal fin with more than 45 soft rays extending over half the length of the body→ **Bowfins, Family Amiidae**

5b. Ventral surface of lower jaw fleshy, protected only by mandibular bones; dorsal fin either long or short→ **6**

6a. Pelvic fins absent; body eel shaped→ **Freshwater Eels, Family Anguillidae**

6b. Both pelvic and pectoral fins present→ **7**

7a. A small fleshy adipose fin located on back in front of caudal fin→ **8**

7b No small fleshy adipose fin present → **11**

8a. Four to eight barbels surrounding mouth; no scales; adipose fin may merge with caudal fin in some small species→ **Bullhead Catfishes, Family Ictaluridae**

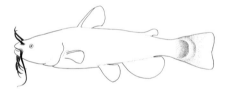

8b. No barbels around mouth; scales present→ **9**

9a. Small flap of tissue (pelvic axillary process) present at base of pelvic fin→ **Trout, Salmon, and Whitefishes, Family Salmonidae**

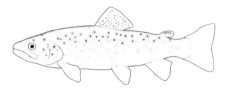

9b. No pelvic axillary process→ **10**

10a. Body covered with ctenoid scales that feel rough when rubbed from the rear forward; pectoral fin extends well backward beyond base of pelvic fin→ **Trout-Perches, Family Percopsidae**

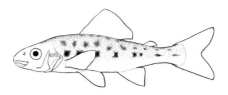

10b. Body covered with cycloid scales that feel smooth when rubbed; tip of pectoral fin does not reach back to base of pelvic fin→ **Smelts, Family Osmeridae**

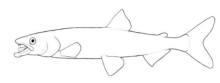

11a. A single barbel located at the tip of the lower jaw→ **Cuskfishes, Family Lotidae**

11b. No barbel at tip of lower jaw→ **12**

12a. Body without scales→ **13**

12b. Body with scales→ **14**

13a. Dorsal fin with 2–10 stout spines; membrane connects spines to back, not to adjacent spine→ **Sticklebacks, Family Gasterosteidae**

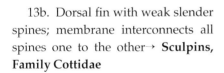

13b. Dorsal fin with weak slender spines; membrane interconnects all spines one to the other→ **Sculpins, Family Cottidae**

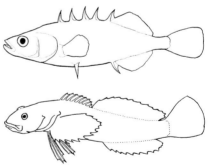

14a. Small flap of tissue (pelvic axillary process) present at base of pelvic fin→ **15**

14b. Pelvic axillary process absent→ **16**

15a. Base of dorsal fin located over pelvic fin base, not over anal fin base; no lateral line; belly with row of strong spiny scales (scutes) down midline, forming a sawtooth edge→ **Herrings, Family Clupeidae**

15b. Base of dorsal fin located, in part, directly over base of anal fin; straight lateral line present; belly without scutes down midline→ **Mooneyes, Family Hiodontidae**

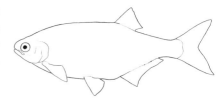

16a. Either a single dorsal fin composed entirely of segmented soft rays or a dorsal fin with only a single stout serrated spine at anterior edge followed by soft, segmented rays→ **17**

16b. Two distinctly separated dorsal fins, or, if dorsal fins are continuous, the anterior portion contains 2 or more unsegmented spines→ **23**

17a. A large, stout spine with double serrations on its posterior edge, located at front of dorsal fin (may be preceded by small unserrated partial spines) → **Carp and Goldfish, Family Cyprinidae** (in part)

17b. A single dorsal fin composed entirely of segmented soft rays→ **18**

18a. Head completely scaleless→ **19**

18b. Head with some scales; the cheeks always with scales→ **20**

19a. Usually 8 dorsal rays; anal fin set more anterior; distance from base of first anal ray to base of caudal fin contained less than 2.5 times in distance from base of first anal ray to tip of snout (see figure 7)→ **Minnows, Family Cyprinidae** (in part)

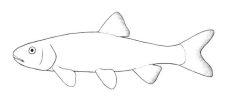

19b. Dorsal rays, 10 or more; anal fin set far posterior; distance from base of first anal ray to base of caudal fin contained at least 2.5 times in distance from base of first anal ray to tip of snout→ **Suckers, Family Catostomidae**

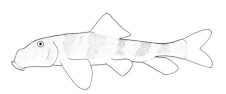

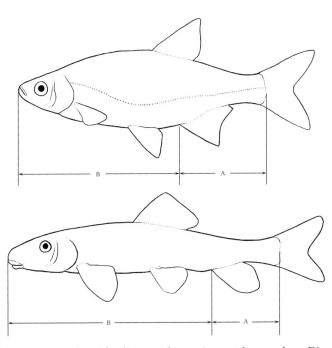

Fig. 7. Relative position of anal fin distinguishing minnows from suckers. Distance A from the base of first anal ray to the base of caudal fin fits less than two and one-half times into distance B from base of first anal ray to the tip of the snout for minnows *(top)*, but more than two and one-half times for suckers *(bottom)*.

20a. Caudal fin rounded; no lateral line→ **21**

20b. Caudal fin forked; lateral line present; jaws forming a ducklike snout→ **Pikes, Family Esocidae**

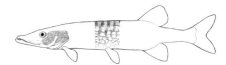

21a. Mouth terminal (pointing forward); groove separating upper lip from snout not continuous across snout; majority of length of pelvic fin lies posterior to an imaginary line drawn vertically down from the base of first ray in dorsal fin→ **Mudminnows, Family Umbridae**

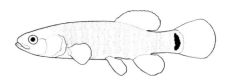

21b. Mouth superior (pointing upward); groove separating upper lip from snout continuous across snout, separating upper lip from snout; majority of length of pelvic fin lies anterior to an imaginary line drawn vertically down from the base of first ray in dorsal fin→ **22**

22a. Base of first ray of dorsal fin located anterior to base of first ray of anal fin; anal fin rounded in male→ **Topminnows (Killifishes), Family Fundulidae**

22b. Base of first ray of dorsal fin located posterior to base of first ray of anal fin; anal fin of male modified into an intromittent organ adapted for internal fertilization→ **Livebearers, Family Poecillidae**

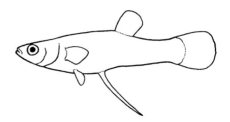

23a. Anus located on throat, anterior to pectoral fins in adults, more posterior in juveniles→ **Pirate Perches, Family Aphredoderidae**

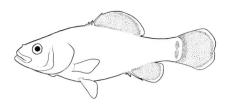

23b. Anus located directly in front of anal fin→ **24**

24a. Pelvic fins clearly posterior to pectoral fins; a small anterior dorsal fin well separated from posterior dorsal fin; anal fin base much longer than dorsal fin bases→ **Silversides, Family Atherinidae**

24b. Pelvic fins located under pectoral fins; anterior spiny dorsal fin joined to or slightly separated from posterior soft-rayed dorsal fin; anal fin base shorter than dorsal fin bases→ **25**

25a. Anal spines 1 or 2→ **26**

25b. Anal spines 3 or more→ **28**

26a. Pelvic fins joined into a single sucker-shaped fin→ **Gobies, Family Gobiidae**

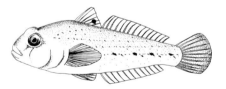

26b. Pelvic fins not joined, separated into a left and right fin→ **27**

27a. Dorsal fin separated into an anterior spiny dorsal and a posterior soft-rayed dorsal; lateral line (if present) ends at base of caudal fin→ **Perches, Family Percidae**

27b. Anterior and posterior dorsal fin joined into a continuous fin; lateral line extends onto caudal fin→ **Drums, Family Sciaenidae**

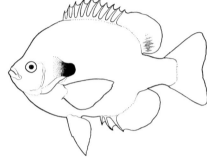

28a. Dorsal fin completely joined, may be notched, as in largemouth bass, but never completely separated; longest soft rays tend to be near center of soft dorsal fin→ **Sunfishes, Family Centrarchidae**

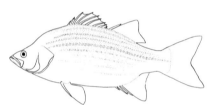

28b. Dorsal fin separated or only slightly connected; longest soft rays tend to be near front of soft dorsal fin→ **Temperate Basses, Family Moronidae**

Species Descriptions and Illustrations

Lampreys
Family Petromyzontidae

Lampreys are very primitive fishes. They have a cartilaginous skeleton, a round sucking disk in place of jaws, and a single nasal opening in the center of the snout; they lack pectoral and pelvic fins. All of the other fishes in the Northeast have a bony skeleton, true moveable jaws, a pair of nasal openings on either side of the snout, and either pectoral or pelvic fins or both. Lampreys resemble eels in overall body shape, but eels have well-developed jaws and a pair of pectoral fins. The lamprey life cycle typically involves several years as a filter-feeding larva called an ammocoete followed by 1–18 months as a free-swimming adult. Many lampreys do not feed as adults; a few are parasitic on other fishes.

Thirty-one species of lamprey are known in the world, six of which live in the Northeast. One of the more common and certainly the most significant economically is the sea lamprey, *Petromyzon marinus.* In the Northeast, the Ohio lamprey (*Ichthyomyzon bdellium*) and the mountain brook lamprey (*Ichthyomyzon greeleyi*) are found only in the upper reaches of the Allegheny drainage in the western portion of New York State. The American brook lamprey (*Lampetra appendix)* is uncommon but widely distributed throughout the region. The remaining two species, the silver lamprey (*Ichthyomyzon unicuspis*) and northern brook lamprey (*Ichthyomyzon fossor)* are uncommon and found only in New York and the Lake Champlain drainage of Vermont.

Species Key to Adults

1a. Dorsal fin divided into 2 separate distinguishable fins→ **2**

1b. Dorsal fin not divided, one continuous fin, although it may have a notch approximately halfway back→ **3**

2a. Large, pointed teeth, the 2 above oral opening close together; 7 or more bicuspid circumoral teeth (inner teeth in the buccal funnel, forming a circle around esophageal opening; see figure 8); sea-run spawning adults up to 47 inches long, landlocked forms between 13 and 30 inches long; oral disc, when expanded, wider than head; parasitic→ **Sea Lamprey,** *Petromyzon marinus*

2b. Small, blunt, relatively inconspicuous teeth, the 2 above oral opening widely separated; 6 bicuspid circumoral teeth; oral disc narrower than head; spawning adults 5–8 inches long; nonparasitic→ **American Brook Lamprey,** *Lampetra appendix*

3a. All circumoral teeth unicuspid (possess a single point); myomeres (muscle segments) fewer than 56 from last gill opening to anus→ **4**

3b. Some circumoral teeth are bicuspid; myomeres 55 or more from last gill opening to anus→ **5**

4a. Large, sharply pointed teeth; spawning adults 10–14 inches long; oral disc as wide or wider than head; parasitic→ **Silver Lamprey,** *Ichthyomyzon unicuspis*

4b. Small, blunt, partially hidden teeth; spawning adults 5–7 inches long; oral disc narrower than head; nonparasitic→ **Northern Brook Lamprey,** *Ichthyomyzon fossor*

5a. Teeth well developed; spawning adults 10–14 inches; oral disc as wide or wider than head; parasitic→ **Ohio Lamprey,** *Ichthyomyzon bdellium*

5b. Teeth poorly developed; spawning adults 5–8 inches long; oral disc narrower than head; nonparasitic→ **Mountain Brook Lamprey,** *Ichthyomyzon greeleyi*

Ohio Lamprey

Ichthyomyzon bdellium (Jordan, 1885)

Identification. The genus *Ichthyomyzon* is distinguished from all other lamprey genera in the Northeast by the presence of a single, continuous dorsal fin. There may be a dip or notch in the fin, but the fin is not completely separated. Of the four members of this genus, the mountain brook lamprey (*I. greeleyi*) and the Ohio lamprey (*I. bdellium*) have some bicuspid teeth, whereas the teeth of the silver lamprey (*I. unicuspis*) and northern brook lamprey (*I. fossor*) are unicuspid. Bicuspid teeth are teeth that end in two points, whereas unicuspid teeth terminate in a single point (see figure 8). Both the silver lamprey and the Ohio lamprey are parasitic on fishes and thus have sharply pointed teeth and a larger oral disc (length of disc front to back is as great or greater than the greatest width of head behind disc). The northern brook lamprey and mountain brook lamprey, in contrast, are nonparasitic and have blunt teeth and a smaller oral disc. In the Northeast, the Ohio and mountain brook lampreys are found only in the Allegheny drainage in southwestern New York.

The Ohio lamprey can be identified by a lack of jaws, no paired fins, a single continuous dorsal fin, a few well-developed bicuspid teeth near the mouth, and an oral disc longer than the head is wide. It has a parasitic adult stage, with adults 10–14 inches in length. Its color is blue to gray dorsally, grading to white ventrally.

Life History. The spawning behavior of the Ohio lamprey is not well known but is presumed to be similar to that of other members of the group. It is a relatively small parasitic lamprey and is found in small brooks to large streams or even rivers. In Ohio, it tends to be the first lamprey to spawn in the spring, normally moving into smaller tributaries. Adults feed on the blood and body fluids of other fishes, such as carp, suckers, or catfishes; ammocoetes feed on detritus and on a variety of algae and microscopic animals. Ohio lampreys range in size from 7 to 12 inches and live for approximately 6 years before spawning and dying.

Distribution. Ohio lampreys are found widely in the Ohio River basin as far east as the Allegheny River system in western New York, in particular French Creek, and they prefer streams and rivers. They are not known from any other drainage in the region.

Northern Brook Lamprey

Ichthyomyzon fossor Reighard and Cummins, 1916

Identification. The northern brook lamprey is a small fish (5–7 inches long) characterized by a lack of jaws; no paired fins; a single continuous dorsal fin; small, blunt, inconspicuous unicuspid teeth; a small oral disc; and a nonparasitic feeding habit. It is brown on the back, grading rather quickly from brown on the sides to white on the belly.

Life History. The life history of the northern brook lamprey is similar to that of other lampreys. It spawns at somewhat warmer temperatures (55–60°F) in moderate-size streams with sand, sand and silt, or gravel bottoms. Females carry 1,000 to 1,300 eggs. As with most lampreys, the female chooses a suitable nesting site. She attaches by her sucker disc to a rock at the upstream edge of the prospective nest and with the help of an accompanying male initiates nest building. Using lateral undulations of their bodies, the pair excavate a shallow nest in the gravel. At spawning, the male attaches to the back of the female's head using his sucker disc, and they simultaneously release gametes into the nest. Adults die after spawning. The larvae hatch in approximately 12 days and begin drifting downstream shortly afterward. They settle in areas with mud bottoms and develop burrows. They remain as ammocoetes for 3–6 years, at the end of which they enter a rest period for approximately a year. They feed very little during this time. At the end of the rest period, they transform into adults beginning in the fall and spawn the next spring. They are nonparasitic and do not feed as adults. The ammocoetes feed on detritus and a variety of algae and microscopic animals.

Distribution. Northern brook lampreys are most common in the upper Great Lakes and St. Lawrence basins, with some ranging south to Missouri and Kentucky. They are found in just a few localities in medium-size streams in northern and western New York and in tributaries to Lake Champlain in Vermont.

Mountain Brook Lamprey

Ichthyomyzon greeleyi Hubbs and Trautman, 1937

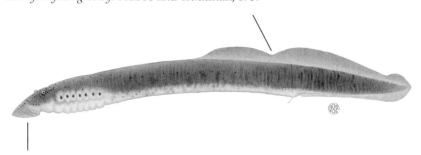

Identification. Mountain brook lampreys *lack jaws* and paired fins; possess *a single continuous dorsal fin; poorly developed bicuspid teeth;* and an oral disc shorter than the head. In the nonparasitic adult stage, they are 4–6 inches long. They are light brown dorsally, grading to a light tan ventrally.

Life History. The life history of the mountain brook lamprey parallels that of other nonparasitic lampreys in the region. They have been reported to spawn in small creeks or streams in the spring when the water temperature approaches 65°F. They build nests in gravel-bottom riffle areas and deposit the eggs in the nest. After hatching, the young drift downstream and begin the filter-feeding ammocoete lifestyle. Adults are nonparasitic, feeding little if at all; ammocoetes feed on detritus and a variety of algae and microscopic animals. Mountain brook lampreys may live for 5 to 6 years.

Distribution. Mountain brook lampreys are found in small creeks tributary to the Ohio River, including tributaries of the Allegheny River in western New York. The Allegheny drainage (French Creek) is the only place in the region that they are known to occur. They are a species of special concern in New York.

Silver Lamprey

Ichthyomyzon unicuspis Hubbs and Trautman, 1937

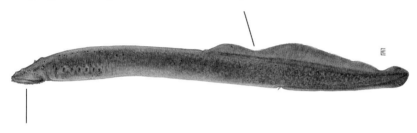

Identification. Silver lampreys are distinguishable by a *lack of jaws* and of paired fins; a *single, continuous dorsal fin;* sharp, unicuspid teeth; and a *large oral disc.* Adult silver lampreys average 4–13 inches in length. They are brown in color, appearing somewhat lighter on the lower sides and belly.

Life History. Spawning adult silver lampreys move upstream in the spring as water temperatures warm to approximately 50°F. Males build nests in moderate-size streams over sand or gravel bottoms. Females attach to a rock at the head of the nest; the male attaches to her head and winds his body around hers, and they spawn simultaneously. The eggs settle, fastening to the gravel at the bottom of the nest, and the adults die after spawning. Females have been known to produce 10,000–27,000 eggs. The young hatch in 5–7 days, depending on water temperature, and the young ammocoetes drift downstream, settling to the bottom. They spend 4–7 years in burrows in mud or silt in quiet water. They typically transform into adults in the fall and move downstream the next spring to feed and grow. This parasitic phase of their life lasts for 1–2 years, after which they move upstream to spawn and repeat the cycle. Adults feed on the blood and body fluids of other fishes; ammocoetes feed on detritus and a variety of algae and microscopic animals.

Distribution. Silver lampreys are found from the upper Great Lakes south through the Mississippi drainage to the Ohio River and then east to West Virginia and north to the St. Lawrence River. Isolated instances have been reported from as far north as Hudson Bay and as far south as Mississippi. In the Northeast, they are found only in New York and Vermont, specifically in tributaries to Lakes Erie, Ontario, and Champlain. They are also found in the St. Lawrence and Hudson Rivers in New York, and in Lake Champlain.

American Brook Lamprey

Lampetra appendix (DeKay, 1842)

Identification. The American brook lamprey lacks jaws as well as pectoral and pelvic fins, as do all other lampreys. It is distinguished from other lampreys by its relatively small size (5–8 inches as an adult), 2 separate dorsal fins, an oral disc narrower than its head, and small blunt teeth arranged in clusters. It is nonparasitic, explaining the relatively narrow oral disc. Spawning adults are typically brown to black dorsally, grading sharply to lighter shades ventrally.

Life History. American brook lampreys spawn at the head of riffles in streams in the spring when water temperatures reach 50–54°F, usually in late March or April. They prefer gravel-bottom areas for spawning, with the gravel averaging approximately ½ inch in diameter. Males fasten their oral disc to these small rocks and move them to the side, creating a depression approximately 6–7 inches long. When ready to spawn, the female attaches to a larger stone at the upstream edge of the nest, and the male, using his disc, secures himself to her head. He wraps his body around hers, and they release eggs and sperm simultaneously. As a result of the movement of the male's and female's bodies, the eggs and sperm become thoroughly mixed, and the fertilized eggs become bound to the sand and gravel in the nest. A female may produce up to 3,000 eggs. The male and female die after spawning. The eggs hatch in 10–14 days, depending on water temperature. After hatching and then absorbing the yolk sac, the young drift downstream and locate a quiet section with a sand and silt bottom. Each creates a U-shaped tube, where they remain for up to 5 years, feeding on detritus and other material carried to them by the current. In late summer or early fall of the last year before spawning, they transform into adults. In the spring, they make the upstream migration, spawn, and die, thus completing the cycle. Because the adults are nonparasitic, they do not feed at all and never feed on other fishes, as the sea lamprey does. All of this species' feeding is done by the ammocoetes larvae, on detritus and a variety of algae and microscopic animals.

Distribution. The American brook lamprey ranges from the upper Great Lakes to the St. Lawrence River and New Hampshire, then south through the Mississippi and Atlantic Slope drainages to Arkansas, northern Alabama, and the Roanoke drainage in Virginia. It prefers small to medium-size creeks and rivers with clear water and gravel bottoms; it occasionally is found over mud or rubble bottoms. In the Northeast, it is reported from New York and all of the New England states except Maine. It is considered threatened in Vermont and Massachusetts and is of special concern in Connecticut, where it is found in only one small tributary of the Connecticut River near Windsor Locks.

Sea Lamprey

Petromyzon marinus Linnaeus, 1758

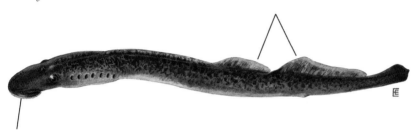

Identification. The sea lamprey is the largest adult lamprey in the Northeast, with marine forms approaching 4 feet in length. Landlocked forms rarely reach half that length. The sea lamprey has *2 separate and distinct dorsal fins* and an impressive *array of teeth in its sucking disc, which radiate out in all directions from the mouth opening* (figure 8). The only other lamprey in the region with 2 dorsal fins is the American brook lamprey (*Lampetra appendix*), which is a smaller fish (5–8 inches long) and can be distinguished from the sea lamprey by smaller teeth clustered in groups instead of radiating out from the mouth as in the sea lamprey.

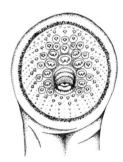

Fig. 8. Teeth in mouth of sea lamprey.

All of the other lampreys are in the genus *Ichthyomyzon* and have a single dorsal fin. Sea lampreys have a dark mottling over a brown background on the back and sides. The belly is a lighter brown.

Life History. Adult sea lampreys move into streams in the spring, usually in May, to spawn. The male normally arrives first, chooses a location in a shallow, swiftly flowing stretch and creates a small depression in the gravel bottom by attaching his sucker mouth to stones and displacing them. When the female arrives and the nest is finished, the male attaches to the back of her head, and they release eggs and sperm simultaneously into the gravel-bottomed nest. A single sea-run female can produce as many as 235,000 eggs. For freshwater forms, the number is much less, averaging 65,000–70,000 eggs per female. After spawning, the adults die. The young hatch in 10–12 days and leave the nest a week or so later as small larvae, drifting downstream until they find quiet water, where they settle into the soft mud on the bottom. They burrow into the mud and feed on organic material that washes to them. During this time, they are called ammocoetes and are quite harmless. In some areas, the ammocoete is occasionally used for bait. Ammocoetes feed and grow for approximately 5 years before transforming into adults. Upon transformation, the sea lamprey migrates downstream to the ocean (or to a lake if landlocked) and begins a parasitic existence. It feeds by attaching itself to another fish, using the teeth on its tongue to rasp a hole in the fish's side and consume its blood and body tissues. To facilitate feeding, the lamprey secretes an anticoagulant. After 1–1½ years in the parasitic phase, the adults achieve sexual maturity and migrate upstream to spawn, after which they die.

The sea lamprey has earned a bad reputation as a predator on desirable sport fishes. Fish taken from waters with large sea lamprey populations often have nasty-looking circular scars on their bodies. Sea lampreys have had a significant impact on fish populations in lakes where the species has become established. In the early 1970s, sea lamprey-control programs were implemented in the Great Lakes, including Lake Ontario and Lake Erie. The approach is to eliminate the ammoecetes in the tributary streams, thus reducing the adult parasitic population. A selective poison, usually TFM (3-trifluoromethyl-4-nitrophenol), is placed in streams known to contain lampreys. TFM is very effective on lampreys and is thought to have little effect on other organisms in the stream. Although not eliminating lampreys entirely, this program has resulted in a substantial decline in lamprey abundance, allowing for recovery of lake trout and other game fish populations.

Distribution. Sea lampreys are fundamentally marine fish that spawn in freshwater. They are found on both sides of the Atlantic from Greenland and Norway south to Florida and Africa. They have been collected in all of the states in the Northeast, commonly in coastal streams and rivers. In some places, they have become landlocked, spending their entire life cycle in freshwater, where they are often called lake lampreys. This has occurred in the upper St. Lawrence River and in Lakes Ontario, Erie, Seneca, Cayuga, Oneida, and Champlain in New York and Vermont. After the construction of the Welland Canal in 1829, the sea lamprey was able to move into the upper Great Lakes, where it multiplied rapidly and had severe effects on the native fish populations.

Sturgeons
Family Acipenseridae

Sturgeons are very large, long-lived fishes found in lakes and large rivers. They have long snouts with a ventral mouth preceded by 4 barbels; spiracles (a small respiratory opening behind each eye); and no teeth. The body is protected by 5 rows of large bony plates: 1 dorsal, 2 lateral, and 2 ventral. The tail is heterocercal; that is, the vertebral column extends into the upper lobe of the caudal fin, creating a large upper lobe and a relatively smaller lower lobe, similar to that of sharks. Some individuals become quite large, reaching up to 8 feet in length. Worldwide, twenty-three species are known, with three found in the Northeast. Of these three species, only the lake sturgeon remains in freshwater throughout its life cycle. The other two enter freshwater to spawn but spend the rest of their lives in brackish or marine environments. Essentially all members of this family are threatened by habitat loss, dams (which prevent migration), pollution, and exploitation.

Species Key

1a. Narrow mouth, with the width of mouth inside the lips less than 55 percent of the distance between eye sockets; 17–27 gill rakers; paired postdorsal and preanal shields; viscera light colored; primarily marine, may enter freshwater stretches of the Hudson River, Connecticut River, and other large rivers in the region to spawn.→ **Atlantic Sturgeon,** *Acipenser oxyrhynchus*

1b. Wide mouth, with the width of mouth inside the lips greater than 62 percent of the distance between eye sockets; 22–40 gill rakers; postdorsal and preanal shields in a single row; black viscera; freshwater or brackish-water species→ **2**

2a. Gill rakers 22–29; 8–13 dorsal shields; 25–32 lateral shields; 19–29 rays in anal fin; dorsal and lateral shields lighter in color than background; fish generally less than 40 inches long; an endangered species→ **Shortnose Sturgeon,** *Acipenser brevirostrum*

2b. Gill rakers 25–40; 9–17 dorsal shields; 29–42 lateral shields; 25–35 rays in anal fin; dorsal and lateral shields same color as background; fish commonly more than 40 inches long; found in large freshwater lakes or rivers→ **Lake Sturgeon,** *Acipenser fulvescens*

Shortnose Sturgeon

Acipenser brevirostrum LeSueur, 1818

Identification. The sturgeons are readily distinguished from other fishes in that their *vertebral column extends well into the upper lobe of their forked caudal fin* and by the 5 rows of large, platelike scales on their bodies. Shortnose sturgeons are small for sturgeon, less than 3½ feet long, and rare. They have *relatively wide mouths* (greater than 62 percent of distance between eye sockets). They have 22–29 gill rakers; 8–13 dorsal shields and 25–32 *lateral shields, which are lighter in color than the background color of the body;* and 19–29 rays in the anal fin. They are brown dorsally, grading to a light tan ventrally. Shortnose sturgeons have been placed on the federal endangered species list.

Life History. Adult shortnose sturgeons have been reported to spawn in the spring in the Connecticut River when water temperatures reach 54–59°F. They choose a rubble bottom with good current as a spawning site. First spawning occurs at 7–10 years of age, and then there is a considerable wait of 2–5 years until the individual spawns again. Males have a shorter waiting period than females. Females can lay large numbers of eggs, anywhere from 40,000 to 200,000 at a time. Eggs hatch in 1–2 weeks, depending on temperature. The larvae are approximately ¼ inch long at hatching. Juveniles can be found in relatively deep, swift-flowing water just above the salt wedge in estuarine regions.

Distribution. The shortnose sturgeon ranges along the coast from the St. John River in New Brunswick to northern Florida. It is currently quite rare and is endangered throughout its range. The only records since 1949 in the Northeast are in the Sheepscot and Kennebec Rivers in Maine, the Connecticut River in Massachusetts and Connecticut, and the Hudson River in New York. Two populations are known in the Connecticut River, one landlocked between the Holyoke Dam and the Turners Falls Dam and one in the lower Connecticut River south from the Holyoke Dam to the mouth of the river. The Hudson is thought to have the largest population, with somewhere between 13,000 and 50,000 individuals. In the Hudson River, they are found from the mouth of the river up to the Troy Dam near Albany. They prefer deep channels with good current.

Lake Sturgeon

Acipenser fulvescens Rafinesque, 1817

Identification. The lake sturgeon is the most common sturgeon in freshwater in the region, but the shortnose and Atlantic sturgeons may be locally abundant in large rivers near the ocean during their spawning season. The lake sturgeon has a *relatively wide mouth (greater than 62 percent of the distance between eye sockets),* whereas the Atlantic sturgeon has a narrower mouth (less than 55 percent of distance between eye sockets). The shortnose sturgeon has dorsal and lateral shields that are much lighter than the background color; it is also small (less than 40 inches) and rare, and it is found most commonly in brackish water. In contrast, the lake sturgeon has *dorsal and lateral shields that are approximately the same color as its background color;* it is larger (greater than 40 inches) and found exclusively in freshwater. The lake sturgeon is dark brown dorsally, grading to light tan or white ventrally. Fins are dark brown.

Life History. Lake sturgeons spawn in May or June, usually in large rivers, after the temperature has reached 50–60°F. They prefer stone or sand bottoms for the deposition of eggs, often in quite shallow water. Males wait for a ripe female to appear, at which time several of them join her. At spawning, the males vibrate their bodies in parallel with the female, and they release eggs and sperm. Females, depending on size, carry from 180,000 to 680,000 eggs and spawn once every 4 or 5 years after reaching maturity at anywhere from 14–26 years of age. Males normally spawn every other year after reaching maturity at 9–13 years of age.

Lake sturgeons are long-lived fish; one individual in Wisconsin was estimated to be 82 years old. Another individual taken in Lake of the Woods, Canada, was determined to be 154 years old. It weighed 208 pounds. The largest individual reported was taken in Lake Superior, Canada, weighing in at 310 pounds. Sturgeons grow throughout their life, even though the growth rate slows down after sexual maturity. In the St. Lawrence River, fish weighing more than 80 pounds and measuring more than $5\frac{1}{2}$ feet in length have been reported.

Lake sturgeons prefer large bodies of water and generally stay close to the bottom. Surprisingly, sturgeon on occasion will leap out of the water. They shoot straight up and fall back into the water with a big splash. No one knows why they do this, but one theory suggests that it is a means of communication. The loud splash can be heard up to $\frac{1}{2}$ mile away and may help keep a group of sturgeon together. They overwinter in deep, well-oxygenated water. They feed on a variety of bottom organisms, including insects, worms, mollusks (including zebra mussels), and crustaceans. The barbels around their mouths help them locate food, which they pick up rapidly with their protrusible mouth. Mud and dirt accompanying the food are expelled through the gill openings.

For many years, lake sturgeons supported a small commercial fishery in Lake Ontario and the St. Lawrence River. Unfortunately, populations have declined over the years owing to overfishing and habitat degradation, leading to the placement of the lake sturgeon on the endangered or threatened species list. It is considered endangered in Vermont and threatened in New York.

Distribution. The lake sturgeon is found from the Hudson Bay region of Canada southward down the Mississippi Valley to Alabama. It is found in the Great Lakes-St. Lawrence drainage. It occupies large rivers or lakes in New York and Vermont, including Lakes Erie and Ontario, the St. Lawrence River, Cayuga Lake, and Lake Champlain. Efforts by the New York State Department of Environmental Conservation are currently under way to restore the lake sturgeon to some of its original habitat in New York.

Atlantic Sturgeon

Acipenser oxyrhynchus Mitchill, 1814

Identification. The Atlantic sturgeon has a *heterocercal tail; 5 rows of bony plates on the body; a relatively long and pointed snout; and a narrow mouth.* The width of the mouth inside the lips is less than 55 percent of the distance between eye sockets. It is primarily a marine fish that migrates into coastal rivers and estuaries to spawn. Adults in freshwater or brackish water are generally more than $3^{1}/_{2}$ feet long, whereas adult shortnose sturgeons, which also occupy freshwater or brackish water, rarely exceed $3^{1}/_{2}$ feet in length. The Atlantic sturgeon's back is dark brown to black, grading to white on the ventral side.

Life History. Adult Atlantic sturgeons are long-lived and reach sexual maturity relatively late. Males are 12 years old or older and females are just under 20 years old when they first spawn. Males enter rivers earlier than do females, arriving in April in the Hudson River; females normally appear about a month later. Spawning occurs near the salt front. Larvae and early juveniles remain in the river until late summer or fall, when they drop downstream into deeper water to overwinter. Juveniles leave the river sometime between their second and sixth year. Although adults feed little during spawning, juveniles feed on benthic organisms such as crustaceans, mollusks, worms, insects, and some plant material.

Distribution. Atlantic sturgeons range southward along the coast from Labrador to northern Florida. Their populations have been greatly reduced over the years, and they are now relatively uncommon except in a few local areas. They have been recorded from large rivers near the coast in all of the states in the Northeast except Vermont. They may no longer be present in many of these rivers. They currently are considered endangered in Massachusetts and threatened in Connecticut. In the Hudson River, in contrast, the Atlantic sturgeon population has been estimated at around 150,000 individuals.

Paddlefishes

Family Polyodontidae

The paddlefish family is composed of just two species: one found in China, the other in North America. They have a cartilaginous skeleton and a heterocercal tail and are related to sturgeons. As the name implies, the unique characteristic that distinguishes all paddlefishes is the presence of a large, paddle-shaped snout. They cannot be confused with any other fishes in the region.

Paddlefish

Polyodon spathula (Walbaum, 1792)

Identification. The paddlefish is a large fish with a very unusual, long, paddle-shaped snout, which comprises 20 to 33 percent of the total body length. It has a heterocercal tail similar to the sturgeon, with the vertebral column extending into the upper lobe of the caudal fin, but in the paddlefish both the upper and lower lobes of the caudal fin are of approximately the same size. The paddlefish lacks the bony plates found on the sturgeon. It is distinct from any other freshwater fish in the region. It is gray to black on the back and sides, grading to white on the belly.

Life History. The paddlefish is primarily a fish of large, free-flowing rivers that are rich in zooplankton. It may also be found in large reservoirs formed from damming such rivers. It feeds by swimming slowly with its mouth open, filtering zooplankton out of the water by using its gill rakers as strainers. Electrosensory organs scattered across the surface of the large bill help the paddlefish locate plankton. The bill also serves to stabilize the fish in a horizontal plane, thus making swimming easier. Paddlefish spawn over gravel bars in rivers in the spring when the water is rising and the temperature is higher than 50°F. Eggs are scattered across the bottom, and because they are adhesive, they fasten to objects on the bottom. The young hatch in a week or so depending on temperature. When the young absorb their yolk sac, they begin to feed on plankton. Until they are approximately 10 inches long, they select individual prey items; after that they begin to adopt the adult filter-feeding habit. They are known to live to be 30 years old and eventually reach 4 feet and 28 pounds or more in size.

Distribution. Only two *Polyodon* species are known worldwide, and only one of these, *Polyodon spathula,* the paddlefish, is found in North America. In the Northeast, it has been reported only from Chautauqua Lake and the Allegheny River of western New York. Ichthyologists now assume that it has been extirpated in these waters. It is included in this guide, however, because efforts are being made to reestablish it in New York. From 1998 to 2001, the New York State Department of Environmental Conservation released young paddlefish into the Allegheny Reservoir. The paddlefish is not known from elsewhere in the Northeast.

Gars

Family Lepisosteidae

Gars are slender, cylindrical fishes well protected with heavy, diamond-shaped ganoid scales. They have a relatively long snout with nasal sacs at the tip (figure 9) and a jaw full of teeth, making them very effective predators. The vertebral column extends into the upper lobe of the caudal fin. In the young gar, this character is quite conspicuous. In older fish, the vertebral column is hidden, and the caudal fin appears symmetrical. The gas bladder is connected to the gut and is used as an accessory breathing organ, which allows the fish to survive in water with low oxygen levels. Only eight species are known world-wide, of which one, the longnose gar, is found in the Northeast.

Longnose Gar

Lepisosteus osseus (Linnaeus, 1758)

Identification. The longnose gar is easily identified by the *long, narrow, bony snout* and the *heavy, diamond-shaped ganoid scales* covering the body. The width of the snout measured at the nostrils is less than the diameter of the eye (figure 9).

As juveniles, longnose gars might be confused with pikes or muskellunge, but the abbreviate heterocercal tail of the gar allows for easy separation from young pikes and muskellunge. Longnose gars are dark green to olive on their back, grading to white on the belly. They have large dark spots on the vertical fins—dorsal, anal, and caudal. Young longnose gars have large dark spots on

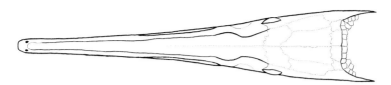

Fig. 9. Width of the snout in relation to the diameter of the eye in the longnose gar.

the body and a dark brown band running the length of the body directly above a distinctive white band.

Life History. Longnose gars gather in shallow water in late May or early June. Spawning occurs in groups composed of one female and several males. The adhesive eggs are broadcast across the bottom, hatching in 3–9 days. The $\frac{1}{2}$-inch-long larvae remain attached to objects in their environment by means of an adhesive organ on the ventral side of their snout until they absorb their yolk sac. Young gars feed on small crustaceans and insect larvae until they are 2 inches long, then switch to small fish as their primary source of food. It takes 3–6 years for gars to reach sexual maturity, and females may live for as long as 22 years. Males have a shorter life of around 11 years. A 2-foot female carries approximately 12,000 eggs, which are green and poisonous. Gars will grow up to 4 feet long, but most individuals are approximately 2 feet long and weigh around 2 pounds. Longnose gars are commonly found close to shore in weedy lakes or rivers. They swim or float rather sluggishly near the surface, usually in groups of three to twelve individuals, and can be mistaken for floating logs by the casual observer. When feeding, however, they can move rapidly to capture small fish. They slowly approach their prey from the side and with a rapid sideways swipe of the head capture and consume it. The movement is so rapid that it is almost undetectable. They feed only on living prey but seem to have little impact on native fish populations.

Distribution. Longnose gars range from the Dakotas to Quebec and south to Florida and northern Mexico. In the Northeast, they are commonly found in New York in the Great Lakes and St. Lawrence River, Lake Champlain, and Chautauqua Lake, as well as in the Oswego, Seneca, and Niagara Rivers. They are also found in Vermont in Lake Champlain but are not reported east of the Lake Champlain drainage.

Bowfins
Family Amiidae

Bowfins are stocky fish, shaped somewhat like the black bass. The presence of a flat bone on the underside of their lower jaw, called the gular plate, distinguishes them from all other species in the region. The vertebral column extends partway into the upper lobe of the caudal fin, a condition referred to as abbreviate heterocercal (figure 6). The gas bladder is connected to the gastrointestinal tract and thus gives the bowfin a limited air-breathing capability.

The family is composed of only one species, which is found exclusively in the freshwaters of eastern North America.

Bowfin

Amia calva Linnaeus, 1776

Identification. The bowfin has a *very long and uniform dorsal fin*, containing more than 45 soft rays and extending over most of the length of the back. The *heavy, bony gular plate stretching across the under side of the lower jaw* is also distinctive. The bowfin is dark olive green to brown on its back and head, grading to a pale yellow on its underside. A *dark spot is present on the dorsal side of the base of the caudal fin*, which is very conspicuous in males, less so in females.

Life History. In May or June, the male bowfin enters shallow, weedy areas and begins to construct a nest. He clears out any vegetation by using his mouth and head to uproot it, eventually creating a circular depression 4–8 inches deep and $1\frac{1}{2}$–$2\frac{1}{2}$ feet in diameter. In a day or two, usually after dark, a female visits. She rests on the bottom of the depression while the male circles her for 10–15 minutes. He eventually joins her; they lie side by side, mate, and leave several thousand fertilized eggs. The female may repeat this process with other males, and more than one female may visit the male. Eventually 2,000–5,000 eggs are deposited. The eggs hatch in 8–10 days, and the young larvae attach themselves to roots and pebbles at the bottom of the nest using an adhesive organ on their snout. They remain there for 7–9 days before they begin swimming freely and leave the nest in a tightly packed school. The male actively guards the young during the time they are in the nest. He normally remains nearby, often with his head resting at the edge of the circular depression. If an intruder appears, he attacks it viciously. Bowfins are the only species of primitive freshwater fishes (primitive fishes include lampreys, sturgeons, gars, and bowfins) in the Northeast that exhibit parental care of their young. This trait is typically found in more advanced fishes.

Bowfins are long-lived fish, some having been kept in captivity for up to 30 years. The average adult bowfin weighs $2\frac{1}{2}$–$3\frac{1}{2}$ pounds and measures $1\frac{1}{2}$–2 feet in length, although some individuals that were 34 inches long and weighed nearly 12 pounds have been reported. They live in weedy, clear lakes and sluggish rivers, usually in shallow water. In addition to using their gills for respiration, they can also use their swim bladder to breathe air when oxygen levels in the water are low. They feed very heavily on fish and crayfish and for this reason are thought to be undesirable. They may, however, play a beneficial role by controlling populations of panfish. Overabundant panfish lead to stunted populations where individual growth is greatly restricted. Little intentional effort is made to capture bowfin for commercial or sporting purposes. A few anglers have discovered their fighting qualities. They can be taken on live bait or plugs and put up a strong fight.

Distribution. Bowfins are found in the United States from the Mississippi River east. They range from southern Canada to Florida. In New York, they are fairly common, being found in the Great Lakes and St. Lawrence River, Lake Champlain, the Finger Lakes, and Oneida Lake, as well as in the lower Raquette and Seneca Rivers. They are somewhat less common elsewhere in the region but are found in all states except Maine and Rhode Island.

Mooneyes
Family Hiodontidae

Mooneyes resemble herrings in shape and color, and both have an adipose eyelid, cycloid scales, and a pelvic axillary process. Mooneyes differ from herrings in that they lack scutes (sharp scales on the ventral midline), possess a lateral line, and have large teeth on the tongue. The middle of the dorsal fin rests directly above the first ray of the anal fin in mooneyes, whereas essentially all of the dorsal fin is forward of the anal fin in herrings. Two species make up this family, the mooneye and the goldeye. Both are found exclusively in freshwater habitats of North America. In the Northeast, the only representative is the mooneye (*Hiodon tergisus*).

Mooneye

Hiodon tergisus LeSueur, 1818

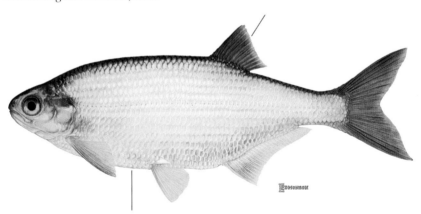

Identification. The mooneye is often confused with freshwater representatives of the herring family such as the shad and alewife. It is easily distinguished from them in the field by the *lack of scutes or a sawtooth edge on the midline of its*

62

belly; in addition, *the mooneye's dorsal fin rests, at least in part, directly over the anal fin.* Freshwater herrings have a dorsal fin that is anterior to the anal fin, possess scutes, and lack well-developed teeth and a lateral line. Mooneyes have well-developed teeth on their jaws and tongue, which leads to the name "toothed herrings" for the family. The mooneye is light gray on its back, which grades quickly to a silvery white on its sides and belly. The lower fins are silvery white as well. The upper part of the head is delicately shaded with yellow and green.

Life History. Mooneyes are not commonly seen because they normally live in the open waters of large, clear lakes and rivers. Although little is known of their breeding habits, what is known suggests that they spawn in tributary streams and rivers in the spring beginning as early as March and continuing into May. Females lay 10,000–20,000 eggs during the spawning period. The eggs have a gelatinous coating, similar to frogs' eggs. The young hatch at around $^1/_3$ inch in length. Eight-year-old mooneyes have been collected from Lake Erie. In Canada, they are reported to live up to 11 years of age. They may grow up to 17 inches in length and exceed 2 pounds in weight. They feed on insect larvae, plankton, and an occasional small fish.

Their populations are declining throughout their range, possibly owing to siltation of spawning habitat. They can be taken on a fly. Anglers often incorrectly use their common name, mooneye, for other species such as the alewife and shad.

Distribution. The mooneye's range extends from south central Canada through the southern Great Lakes to the St. Lawrence-Champlain drainage and then southward west of the Appalachians to Alabama and Arkansas. They have been reported from only two states in the Northeast, New York and Vermont. In New York, they are found in Lakes Erie, Ontario, and Champlain, in Black Lake and Butterfield Lake, as well as in the St. Lawrence and Oswegatchie Rivers. Older records indicate their presence in the Allegheny River. In Vermont, they are fairly common in Lake Champlain. They still occupy all of these areas, except the Allegheny River, where they are considered extirpated. They are on the threatened list in New York.

Freshwater Eels
Family Anguillidae

Eels have an elongate body, pectoral fins but no pelvic fins, a pneumatic duct leading to the gas bladder, soft-rayed fins, and an elongate skull with jaws. The only other species with elongate, eel-like bodies are the lampreys, but they lack jaws and paired fins. Approximately fifteen species of eels are known worldwide. Only one, the American eel (*Anguilla rostrata*), is found in the Northeast.

American Eel

Anguilla rostrata (LeSueur, 1817)

Identification. *Jaws and an elongate body* distinguish the eel from all other species. The only fish with an elongate body bearing any resemblance to the eel is the lamprey. Because the lamprey has no jaws, 7 pairs of porelike gill openings, and no pectoral fins, whereas the eel has jaws, pectoral fins, and a single pair of gill slits, the two species are easily distinguished. The color of the eel changes with its stages of development. For most of its life in freshwater, it is yellow brown to olive brown in color, with the back darker and the belly lighter. As the eel reaches sexual maturity and prepares for its migration to the sea, its back becomes almost black, and its belly changes to a silvery color.

Life History. The eel has an extremely interesting life history. It is the only fish in the region that undertakes a catadromous migration, that is, a migration from freshwater to the sea to spawn, followed by a return to freshwater by the young eel or elver. Early in the spring, the mature fish, which have been living in freshwater, begin to migrate downstream at night toward the ocean. Upon reaching the ocean, they migrate to the vicinity of the Sargasso Sea, where they spawn and presumably die. The eggs drift back northward with the current, eventually hatching into transparent, ribbonlike larvae called leptocephali. Approximately a year later the leptocephali transform into small eel-like fish called elvers and migrate up coastal rivers and streams. The young eels then feed and grow for 5 to 20 years until they reach sexual maturity and return to the Sargasso Sea. Females are generally larger than males, sometimes reaching a length of $3\frac{1}{2}$ feet. Eels are very effective carnivores, feeding heavily at night on a variety of prey organisms, including fish. Eels are considered an excellent food fish.

Distribution. The eel is found in streams and lakes along the eastern coast of North America from Labrador south to the West Indies and including the coast of the Gulf of Mexico. It is found in all of the states and major drainage basins of the Northeast. Unfortunately, its numbers have been declining in many areas over the past two decades.

Herrings
Family Clupeidae

Herrings are slender, silvery, laterally compressed fishes with scutes (specialized, sharply pointed scales) along the ventral midline and with the gas bladder connected to the gut (physostomous). They have no lateral line or adipose fin. Their eyes are furnished with an adipose eyelid, and there is an extension of the swim bladder into the inner ear called the bulla. Most of the 180 species of herrings are marine. Four species in two genera are found in freshwater in the Northeast. They are the gizzard shad (*Dorosoma cepedianum*) and three species of river shad: American shad (*Alosa sapidissima*), alewife (*Alosa pseudoharengus*), and blueback herring (*Alosa aestivalis*). On occasion, river shad may intermingle with bay anchovies. Although bay anchovies are primarily marine fish, they are known to enter freshwater for short periods. The anchovy is easily distinguished from any of the river shads in that it lacks the scutes of the herrings and has an unusually large mouth, which extends posteriorly to the edge of the preoperculum.

Species Key

1a. Posterior ray in dorsal fin much longer than any of the preceding rays; snout short and blunt, protruding over mouth; origin of dorsal fin posterior to base of pelvic fins (figure 10)→ **Gizzard Shad,** *Dorosoma cepedianum*

1b. Posterior ray in dorsal fin not elongated; snout more pointed, lower jaw more or less protruding; dorsal fin directly above or in front of base of pelvic fin (river shads, *Alosa*) (figure 11)→ **2**

2a. Lower jaw wide, dorsal surface rising abruptly to form a raised crest halfway back (must open mouth to see) (figure 12); posterior end of maxilla (upper jaw bone) extends no farther than middle of eye; a single dark spot on

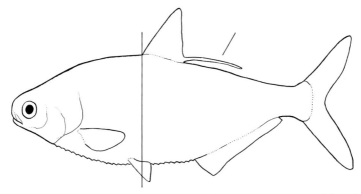

Fig. 10. Shape of snout, position of dorsal fin, and elongate posterior ray of dorsal fin in the gizzard shad.

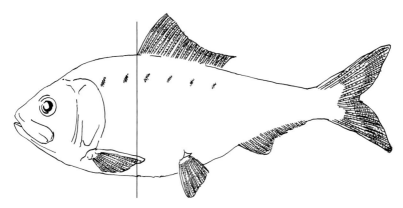

Fig. 11. Shape of snout, position of dorsal fin, and posterior ray of dorsal fin (not extended) in river shads.

side of body just behind upper end of gill opening→ **3**

2b. Lower jaw slender, dorsal surface rising less abruptly and failing to form a raised crest halfway back; posterior end of maxilla extends to directly below posterior edge of eye; often a row of 3 or more dark spots running posteriorly along side of body from upper end of gill opening→ **American Shad,** *Alosa sapidissima*

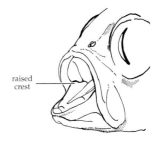

Fig. 12. Raised crest on alewife's lower jaw.

3a. In adults, eye diameter less than or equal to snout length (figure 13); in fresh specimens, the back is bluish black to bluish green, and the peritoneum is black; 45–50 gill rakers on lower limb of gill arch→ **Blueback Herring,** *Alosa aestivalis*

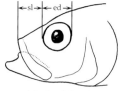

blueback herring

Fig. 13. Size of eye (ed, eye diameter) in relation to snout length (sl) in the blueback herring *(top)* and alewife *(bottom).*

3b. In adults, eye diameter greater than snout length (see figure 13); in fresh specimens, the back is gray to grayish green, and the peritoneum is pale; 38–43 gill rakers on lower limb of gill arch→ **Alewife,** *Alosa pseudoharengus*

Blueback Herring

Alosa aestivalis (Mitchill, 1814)

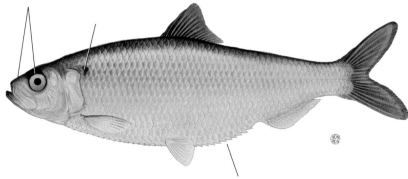

Identification. All of the members of the herring family (Clupeidae) are characterized by a series of *specialized scales called scutes, which form a sawtooth edge down the midline of the belly.* You can readily appreciate this edge by running your finger forward from the front of the anal fin toward the throat. It feels very much like the teeth on a saw blade. Members of the genus *Alosa*, or river herrings, lack the extended last dorsal ray characteristic of the gizzard shad (*Dorosoma).* Blueback herrings most closely resemble alewives except that *their eyes are relatively small (eye diameter less than snout length);* they typically have more rays in their dorsal fin (16–18 versus 12–16 for alewives); and they have a dark peritoneum. They are bluish black to blue green on their backs, grading through tan or silver on the sides to white on the belly in fresh specimens. They often have a *dark spot just behind the upper corner of the gill cover.*

Life History. Blueback herrings spawn in coastal rivers, often migrating long distances upstream. They have an extended spawning season beginning in April and extending to July. Waves of spawners will swim up rivers and streams, interspersed with quiet periods when no fishes are moving. Blueback herrings prefer faster and deeper water than alewives for spawning and usually wait until the water temperature is a little warmer (57°F). They also prefer a hard substrate as opposed to sand or gravel. Each female may carry from 50,000 to 350,000 eggs. They feed on plankton and larval fishes, as do the other members of the river herring group.

Distribution. Blueback herrings range along the coast from Prince Edward Island to northern Florida. They are found in every state in the region. They are primarily a coastal species, but they are expanding their range up the Mohawk River and into the Great Lakes and Lake Champlain. It is anticipated that land-locked populations will develop in these large bodies of water.

Alewife

Alosa pseudoharengus (Wilson, 1811)

Identification. Alewives resemble both blueback herring and shad and are often confused with them. Their *eye diameter is equal to or greater than the snout length;* their peritoneum is gray to white; and they are deeper bodied than the blueback herring. They are distinguished from the American shad by the presence of a raised crest on the lower jaw (figure 12); a *somewhat shorter upper jaw that reaches only back to the middle of the eye;* a cheek patch that is wider than it is deep; and a *single dark spot behind the gill opening on their sides.* Shad have a row of 3 or more spots in this area. Alewives are dark gray to green on their backs, abruptly shading to silver and white on their sides and belly.

Life History. Alewives are anadromous like the shad and leave the ocean to spawn in freshwater in the spring after the water has warmed to 51°F. They usually spawn in very shallow water in quiet areas in rivers or bays over sand and gravel or vegetated substrate. Each female produces between 60,000 and 100,000 eggs. After the young hatch, they migrate to the sea and return when they are approximately 3 years old to spawn and complete the cycle.

The region has a number of landlocked populations; the best known are those in the Great Lakes. These fish are smaller than their oceanic counterparts, reaching only 4–5 inches as opposed to 11–12 inches for the sea-run fishes. The landlocked alewife spawns from late March to late June, with each female producing 10,000 to 20,000 eggs. Spawning often occurs at night in water 6–12 inches deep over sand or gravel bottoms. The eggs hatch in 2–6 days, and the larvae are pelagic. Adult fish, too, live in open water, usually well below the surface. They feed primarily on plankton throughout their lives. Alewives can strongly influence the character of the zooplankton population in lakes where they are abundant by reducing the numbers of large species of zooplankton in favor of the smaller forms. They also feed on the larvae of other fishes, such as yellow perch, walleye, and lake trout. Landlocked alewives can live to 8 years of age. Alewife populations in the Great Lakes increased rapidly in the mid-1900s to the detriment of certain native species. Many cisco and whitefish populations have been depressed or, in some cases, possibly driven to extinction by alewives. In addition, when alewife populations are high, they are subject to massive die-offs. They wash up on beaches, causing an unpleasant smell and generally creating a nuisance. The introduction of Pacific salmon in the Great Lakes has lowered the alewife population and greatly reduced these problems. Interestingly, research has recently identified a significant unpredicted feedback in this predator-prey relationship: Early Mortality Syndrome (EMS). Both alewives and smelts, two exotic species in the Great Lakes, have unusually high levels of an enzyme called thiaminase. The levels are approximately one hundred times that of native coregonids and may be attributable to bacterial flora associated with the viscera of alewives and smelts. Because salmonids feed heavily on both alewives and smelt, they consume large quantities of thiaminase in the process. It is thought that thiaminase lowers the thiamine level in the developing embryos and larvae of salmonids, which leads to EMS. The symptoms of EMS are loss of equilibrium, disoriented swimming behavior, hyperexitability, lethargy, and hemorrhage, ending ultimately in death.

Alewives, although not taken on hook and line, contribute significantly to the sport fishery by providing forage for game fish. The Pacific salmon, coho, and Chinook introduced into Lake Ontario, as well as lake trout, are heavily dependent on alewives as forage. In many of the Finger Lakes of New York, lake trout also feed heavily on alewives.

Distribution. The marine form of the alewife is found along the Atlantic Coast from Newfoundland to North Carolina. It has been introduced into many lakes throughout the United States and Canada. In the Northeast, it is found in every state in the region.

American Shad

Alosa sapidissima (Wilson, 1811)

Identification. The American shad can be distinguished by the presence of scutes, a normal dorsal fin without an extended posterior dorsal ray, a slender lower jaw without the raised crest, a cheek patch that is deeper than it is wide, and a *maxilla that extends to the posterior edge of the eye*. It is blue gray on the back, grading through silvery on the sides and belly. *A series of 3 or more dark spots commonly runs posteriorly from the upper corner of the gill opening.*

Life History. American shad normally spend most of their adult life in salt water and enter freshwater only to spawn in the period from April to June. They migrate into large coastal rivers when the water reaches 50–55°F, and they travel far inland. Spawning occurs at sunset, usually in shallow water near the mouth of tributary creeks. Males and females pair up, swim toward shore, and deposit eggs and sperm as they go. Each female carries an average of 25,000 eggs. The eggs sink to the bottom and are left to fare for themselves. Young shad remain in the stream through the summer, migrating to sea during their first autumn. After 2–5 years in the ocean, where they feed on plankton and grow as large as 12 pounds and 30 inches (the average is much less, more like 2–3 pounds and 19–21 inches), they return to spawn. American shad do not die after spawning and in some cases are known to return in later years to spawn again; 11-year-old shad have been found in the Hudson River. They also develop landlocked populations that fail to return to the sea after hatching and simply grow and reach maturity entirely in freshwater.

American shad provide an excellent sport-fishing experience and can be taken readily during their spawning run. Many anglers use a "shad fly" at dusk, and others use spinning gear and a lead jig. Once a shad is hooked, it puts up a strong fight.

Major problems to the management of the American shad fishery are dams in the spawning rivers, overfishing, and high egg and larval mortality. If the adults are unable to reach the spawning grounds, or if the young suffer very high mortality during their seaward migration, the fishery suffers.

Distribution. American shad are found all along the Atlantic coast from Newfoundland to Florida. They have been introduced into the Pacific Ocean and now range from California to Alaska. They are found in all of the states in the Northeast, primarily in large coastal streams and rivers during spawning season. The Connecticut, Hudson, and Delaware Rivers are well known for their shad fisheries.

Gizzard Shad

Dorosoma cepedianum (LeSueur, 1818)

Identification. The gizzard shad is easily distinguished in the field from all other fishes in the region by the scutes on its ventral midline and by the greatly elongated posterior ray in its dorsal fin. It is blue on the back and silver to white on the sides and belly.

Life History. Gizzard shad spawn between April and June, after the water reaches 50–70°F. The female produces 200,000–400,000 adhesive demersal (heavy and sticky) eggs that hatch in 2–4 days. Sexual maturity is reached at 2 years of age. Some individuals taken from Lake Erie were 19 inches long and weighed just a shade less than 3 pounds. Most fish, however, are little more than half that size. They typically live for approximately 6 or 7 years. Gizzard shad sometimes suffer extensive die-offs after spawning. Large numbers of dead fish have been reported washed up on shore in the spring. As larvae and juveniles, gizzard shad begin feeding on zooplankton but quickly shift to feeding on algae and organic matter filtered out of the water and bottom mud. They are equipped with a large number of long, thin gill rakers for this purpose. This straining mechanism can be seen by lifting the operculum (gill cover) and observing the white gill rakers on the inside edge of the gills. The gizzard shad is one of the few herbivorous fish species in the Northeast and possesses a unique muscular stomach, called the gizzard, that is used to grind and break up plant tissue.

Young gizzard shad serve as forage for many game fishes. Unfortunately, if not kept under control, gizzard shad populations can increase to the point where they become a nuisance. They are not considered a food or game fish.

Distribution. The gizzard shad ranges from the Great Lakes-St. Lawrence drainage west through the Mississippi drainage to South Dakota and south to northeastern Mexico and Florida. It appears to be expanding its range farther into the Northeast, where it has been reported from lakes and large rivers in New York, Vermont, Connecticut, and Massachusetts. It prefers warm lakes and large, slow-moving rivers with large phytoplankton populations. It can enter brackish water.

Carp and Minnows
Family Cyprinidae

Most minnows are small fish with cycloid scales, soft rays supporting their fins, and toothless jaws. Some possess barbels on their upper jaw, and many species develop nuptial tubercles during the breeding season. They are generally omnivorous. This is one of the largest families of fish in the world, with nearly two thousand described species. Forty-seven are found in the Northeast, six of which were introduced.

Minnows are arguably the most difficult group of freshwater fishes to identify, in part because they are often small and thus the characters distinguishing them are correspondingly small. Fortunately, once you have scaled your perspective down to their size, it is possible to simplify the identification of minnows in the Northeast by the process of elimination. Each of eleven species has a unique trait that helps to separate it from any other minnow in the region. These traits are outlined in detail in the key and species descriptions for this family. The minnows in this group include six introduced species (carp, goldfish, rudd, ide, tench, and bitterling), plus the stoneroller, cutlips minnow, tongue-tied minnow, silverjaw minnow, and golden shiner. The remaining minnows can be broken up into smaller groups to facilitate identification. For example, chubs and related groups and the introduced tench have a barbel located at the end, or just up from the end, of the maxilla. The three species of dace—redside, finescale, and northern redbelly—have very small scales. A blunt anterior half ray in the dorsal fin distinguishes the fathead and bluntnose minnows. Breaking the minnows into small categories makes it possible to address this admittedly difficult group of fishes.

The shiners are probably the most difficult of the minnows to identify. Nearly twenty species of small fish are called shiners in the genera *Cyprinella, Luxilus, Lythrurus,* and *Notropis,* and they look pretty much alike upon initial inspection. It is possible to learn to distinguish among them, however, by dividing them into smaller subgroupings (see table 3). For example, the shiners

TABLE 3

Method for Subdividing the Shiners Found in the Northeast *(see text for details).*

	Number of Anal Rays			
	7	8	9	10 or more
Deep-bodied fish		spotfin shiner	satinfin, striped, and common shiner	redfin shiner*
Black stripe extending onto head	bridle and swallowtail shiners	blackchin, blacknose, pugnose,* and ironcolor* shiners		
Pallid species	sand shiner	mimic, bigmouth, and spottail shiners		emerald, comely, rosyface, silver* shiners

*Species not commonly found or one with a very localized distribution. See species description for specific location.

can be divided into four groups based on the number of anal rays they possess: 7, 8, 9, and 10 or more (see figure 5 for the method of counting anal rays). They also can be divided based on certain external characteristics, such as deep or slender bodies, possession of a black stripe, or pale color. Once such a matrix has been established, then no subgroup will have more than four species, and supplemental characters such as the presence of spots on the fins, the size and shape of the mouth, or the shape and number of scales can help in making the final identification. As with any identification, it is important to note also the distribution of each species. Many species have very limited distributions and are not likely to be found outside of these waters, thus providing one more clue to help you with the identification. Although the minnows are clearly a challenge, the effort to be able to distinguish these beautiful and interesting fishes is well worth it.

Species Key

1a. Dorsal fin elongate, containing 14 or more rays (carp and goldfish) → **2**

1b. Dorsal fin shorter, containing fewer than 12 rays (minnows) → **3**

2a. Upper jaw with 2 fleshy barbels on each side; introduced → **Carp, *Cyprinus carpio***

2b. Upper jaw with no barbels; introduced → **Goldfish, *Carassius auratus***

3a. Cartilaginous ridge in front of lip on lower jaw, separated by a definite groove from the lip (figure 14); basic coloration light brown; no distinct lateral band or caudal spot; peritoneum black; intestine wound around swim bladder→ **Stoneroller,** *Campostoma anomalum*

3b. No cartilaginous ridge on lower jaw, ridge is separated by a groove from lip; coloration variable; peritoneum silvery in most, black in *Pimephales;* intestine not wound around swim bladder→ **4**

4a. Small (less than 3 inches long), deep-bodied fish; lateral line incomplete (5–6 pores); introduced (uncommon, known from only two streams in southeastern New York)→ **Bitterling,** *Rhodeus sericeus*

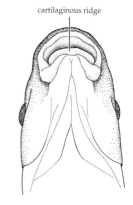

Fig. 14. Cartilaginous ridge on stoneroller's lower jaw.

4b. Fishes of varying size and depth; lateral line contains 10 or more pores→ **5**

5a. Barbels present at or near posterior tip of maxilla (sometimes hidden in groove; see figure 15)→ **6**

5b. Barbels absent→ **18**

6a. Barbel large and conspicuous at corner of mouth; scales small, 95–105 in lateral line; square tail; deep caudal peduncle; first ray of dorsal fin spinelike; introduced (figure 16)→ **Tench,** *Tinca tinca*

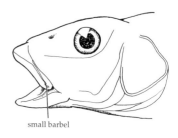

Fig. 15. Barbel present near tip of maxilla.

6b. Barbel small and often hidden (see figure 15); scales larger, less than 95 in lateral line; tail forked; caudal peduncle narrower; rays of dorsal fin approximately same length→ **7**

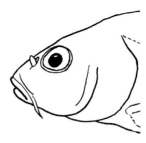

Fig. 16. Tench *(Tinca tinca)* showing barbel.

7a. Premaxillae nonprotractile (upper lip connected to skin of snout by a bridge of fleshy tissue, a frenum, that interrupts the premaxillary groove) (figure 17, *top*); barbel at tip of maxilla (figure 18, *top*)→ **8**

7b. Premaxillae protractile (snout and upper lip separated by a groove) (figure 17, *bottom*); barbel either at tip of maxilla (figure 18, *top*) or in advance of tip of maxilla (figure 18, *bottom*), sometimes concealed in groove→ **9**

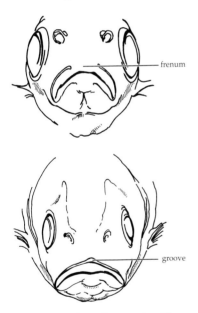

frenum

groove

Fig. 17. Protractile and nonprotractile premaxillae *(top)*. In the nonprotractile condition, a bridge of flesh called a frenum bridges the groove between the snout and upper lip *(bottom)*. In the protractile condition, the upper lip is separated from the snout by a groove.

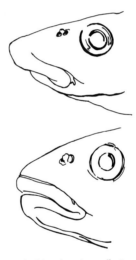

Fig. 18. Barbel *(top)* at tip or *(bottom)* in advance of tip of maxilla.

8a. Snout projects less than 1 millimeter beyond the oblique mouth (figure 19, *left*); distinct dark lateral band that passes through center of eye; dorsal fin not in a forward position (criterion: base of first ray of dorsal fin approximately at midpoint of line extending from caudal base to anterior edge of eye)→ **Blacknose Dace,** *Rhinichthys atratulus*

8b. Snout projects more than 1 millimeter beyond the horizontal mouth (figure 19, *right*); dark lateral band indistinct, fusing with basic coloration of side and passing through lower half of eye; dorsal fin positioned forward (criterion: base of first ray of dorsal fin in advance of midpoint of line extending from caudal base to anterior edge of eye)→ **Longnose Dace,** *Rhinichthys cataractae*

9a. Barbel in groove above maxilla and located forward of tip of maxilla (sometimes difficult to see in small specimens; you may need to pull lower jaw down to help expose barbel in groove above upper jaw; see figure 20)→ **10**

9b. Barbel at tip of maxilla→ **12**

10a. Mouth large, posterior end of upper jaw reaches at least to the forward edge of eye, often farther (figure 20); scales large, usually less than 61 in lateral line→ **11**

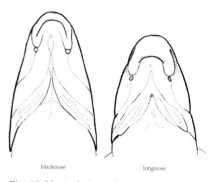

blacknose   longnose

Fig. 19. Ventral view of snout of the two *Rhinichthys* species: blacknose dace *(left)* and longnose dace *(right)*.

Fig. 20. Creek chub's mouth.

10b. Mouth small, posterior end of upper jaw does not reach forward edge of eye (figure 21); scales small, usually 65–75 in lateral line; no conspicuous black spot on base of dorsal fin→ **Pearl Dace,** *Margariscus margarita*

Fig. 21. Pearl dace's mouth.

11a. A dark spot at base of first rays in dorsal fin; 52–61 scales in lateral line→ **Creek Chub,** *Semotilus atromaculatus*

11b. No dark spot at base of first rays in dorsal fin; less than 50 scales in lateral line→ **Fallfish,** *Semotilus corporalis*

12a. Scales small, more than 55 scales in lateral line→ **Lake Chub,** *Couesius plumbeus*

12b. Scales larger, less than 50 scales in lateral line→ **13**

13a. Eye small, its diameter less than length of upper jaw; snout extends only slightly beyond upper lip (figure 22)→ **14**

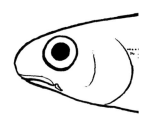

Fig. 22. Size of hornyhead chub's eye.

13b. Eye large, its diameter equal to or greater than length of upper jaw; snout extends a noticeable distance beyond upper lip (figure 23)→ **15**

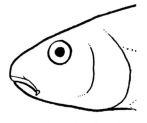

Fig. 23. Size of bigeye chub's eye.

14a. Large distinct caudal spot; snout shorter, length fits more than nine times into standard length; conspicuous red spot behind eye of spawning males; dark line down middle of back→ **Hornyhead Chub,** *Nocomis biguttatus*

14b. No distinct caudal spot; snout longer, length fits nine or fewer times into standard length; no red spot behind eye of spawning males; no dark line down middle of back→ **River Chub,** *Nocomis micropogon*

15a. Body decorated with spots or other dark markings along side (figure 24)→ **16**

15b. Body without spots or dark markings arrayed along side; may have a confluent lateral stripe→ **17**

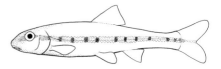

Fig. 24. Body markings on streamline chub.

16a. Relatively large, rounded dark spots aligned in a row along lateral line (see figure 24)→ **Streamline Chub,** *Erimystax dissimilis*

16b. Body lacking a row of dark spots along lateral line; X-, W-, V-, or Y-shaped markings scattered on sides and back→ **Gravel Chub,** *Erimystax x-punctata*

17a. Origin of dorsal fin over or behind origin of pelvic fin; dark lateral band extends along sides and onto snout→ **Bigeye Chub,** *Notropis amblops*

17b. Origin of dorsal fin anterior to origin of pelvic fin; silver color; no dark lateral band→ **Silver Chub,** *Macrhybopsis storeriana*

18a. Lower jaw composed of 3 lobes, a large medial lobe and 2 smaller lateral lobes (figure 25)→ **19**

18b. Lower jaw without lobes→ **20**

19a. Medial lobe prominent, protruding like a tongue, and bony; lateral lobes fleshy (see figure 25); no barbel→ **Cutlips Minnow**, *Exoglossum maxillingua*

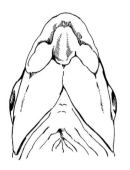

Fig. 25. Lower jaw of cutlips minnow showing 3 lobes.

19b. Medial lobe thin, not protruding like a tongue; lateral lobes less well developed; may have a barbel in groove between upper lip and snout just ahead of tip of maxilla→ **Tongue-tied Minnow**, *Exoglossum laurae*

20a. Body compressed, deep bodied; midline of abdomen posterior to pelvic fins may have a keel (figure 26); lateral line somewhat decurved, or bent downward; body color variable, but often yellowish to orange, with reddish fins on lower body→ **47**

20b. Body more rounded; midline of abdomen posterior to pelvic fins rounded and scaled; lateral line straighter; body color silvery, often with dark lateral band→ **21**

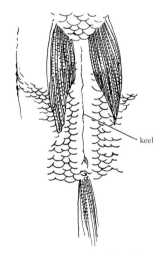

keel

21a. Sensory canals in head create cavernous spaces visible on ventral side of head and lower cheeks; head appears honeycombed in these areas (figure 27)→ **Silverjaw Minnow**, *Notropis buccatus*

Fig. 26. Ventral side of golden shiner showing fleshy, unscaled keel running anteriorly from anus.

21b. No obvious sensory canals in head→ **22**

22a. Scales small, more than 60 scales in lateral line→ **23**

22b. Scales larger, fewer than 55 scales in lateral line→ **25**

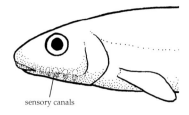

sensory canals

Fig. 27. Sensory canals in silverjaw minnow.

23a. Mouth large, upper jaw length fits no more than two and four-fifths times into head length; lower jaw protrudes beyond upper; complete lateral line (figure 28)→ **Redside Dace, *Clinostomus elongatus***

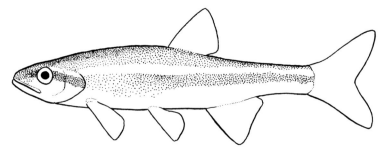

Fig. 28. *Clinostomus* mouth.

23b. Mouth small, upper jaw length fits more than three and one-fifth times into head length; jaws equal; incomplete lateral line (figure 29)→ **24**

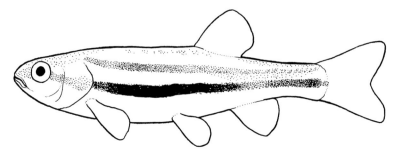

Fig. 29. *Phoxinus* mouth.

24a. Two distinct, dark, longitudinal stripes on sides (see figure 29); approximately 80 scales in lateral line→ **Northern Redbelly Dace,** *Phoxinus eos*

24b. A single dark, longitudinal stripe on sides, above which lies a pale, longitudinal stripe; approximately 90 scales in lateral line→ **Finescale Dace,** *Phoxinus neogaeus*

25a. First obvious dorsal ray somewhat thickened and separated from next posterior ray by a membrane (figure 30a); scales small and crowded on the flattened predorsal region→ **26**

25b. First obvious dorsal ray a thin splint closely attached to next posterior ray (figure 30b); predorsal scales more or less evenly spaced→ **27**

26a. Mouth does not extend as far forward as tip of snout (figure 31a); conspicuous spot at base of caudal fin; complete lateral line→ **Bluntnose Minnow,** *Pimephales notatus*

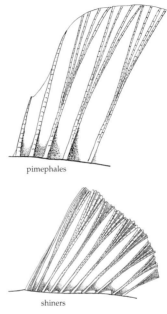

pimephales

shiners

Fig. 30. *(a)* First ray of dorsal fin as a blunt anterior half ray separated from the next ray posterior, as in *Pimephales*. *(b)* First ray as a thin, splintlike ray tightly adjoined to the next ray posterior, as in shiners and other minnows.

26b. Mouth extends as far forward as tip of snout (figure 31b); spot at base of caudal fin faint; incomplete lateral line⇢ **Fathead Minnow,** *Pimephales promelas*

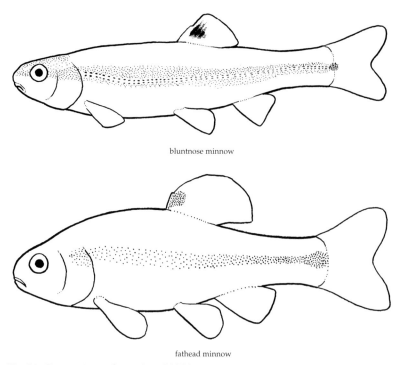

bluntnose minnow

fathead minnow

Fig. 31. Comparison of mouths of *(a)* bluntnose minnow and *(b)* fathead minnow.

27a. Lower jaw shaped like a C when viewed from below—that is, a shallow curved outline (figure 32a); intestine long, more than twice the length of the head and body; peritoneum black (shows through skin)⇢ **28**

27b. Lower jaw shaped like a U when viewed from below that is, a deeply curved outline (figure 32b); intestine short, less than twice the length of the head and body; peritoneum silvery, rarely brown or black ⇢ **29**

28a. Yellowish color in fresh specimens; 14–20 radii on scales⇢ **Brassy Minnow,** *Hybognathus hankinsoni*

28b. Silvery color in fresh specimens; 10–12 radii on scales⇢ **Eastern Silvery Minnow,** *Hybognathus regius*

29a. Anal rays 7⇢ **30**

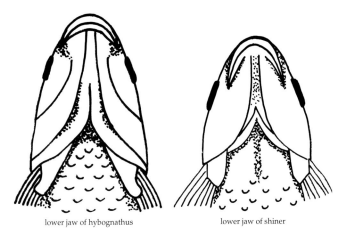

lower jaw of hybognathus   lower jaw of shiner

Fig. 32. *(a)* C-shaped lower jaw of *Hybognathus* in contrast to *(b)* U-shaped lower jaw of shiners.

29b. Anal rays 8 or more→ **32**

30a. Lateral line incomplete; dark lateral band extends along flanks and across snout→ **Bridle Shiner, *Notropis bifrenatus***

30b. Lateral line complete; no lateral band or, if present, does not extend onto snout→ **31**

31a. Dark lateral band present on sides and extending beyond midpoint of body, interrupted on head just behind eye, leaving a dark blotch anterior to eye→ **Swallowtail Shiner, *Notropis procne***

31b. Dark lateral band poorly developed; if present, band is darkest posteriorly and fades as it passes midpoint of body→ **Sand Shiner, *Notropis stramineus***

32a. Anal rays 8→ **33**

32b. Anal rays 9 or more→ **40**

33a. Dark spots on the membranes between the posterior rays of the dorsal fin; diameter of eye goes into head length four or more times→ **Spotfin Shiner, *Cyprinella spiloptera***

33b. No dark spots on membranes of dorsal fin; diameter of eye goes into head length less than four times→ **34**

34a. Dark spot at base of caudal fin, occasionally masked by silvery pigment in large individuals; blunt snout overhanging mouth→ **Spottail Shiner,** *Notropis hudsonius*

34b. No dark spot at base of caudal fin or, if present, broadly confluent with dark lateral band→ **35**

35a. Black lateral band extends around head and onto snout; lateral line incomplete (except for in pugnose shiner)→ **36**

35b. Lateral band, if present, is dusky and does not extend across head and onto snout; lateral line complete→ **39**

36a. Mouth small and nearly vertical, upper jaw extends only as far back as nostril (figure 33)→ **Pugnose Shiner,** *Notropis anogenus*

36b. Mouth larger and generally horizontal, upper jaw extends beyond nostril→ **37**

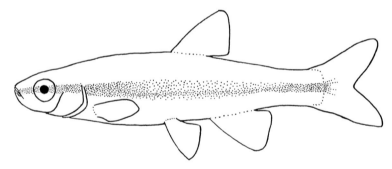

Fig. 33. Small and nearly vertical mouth of the pugnose shiner.

37a. Dark lateral band on snout does not include tip of chin; chin is not black (figure 34a)→ **Blacknose Shiner,** *Notropis heterolepis*

37b. Dark lateral band on snout includes tip of chin, creating black mark on chin (figure 34b)→ **38**

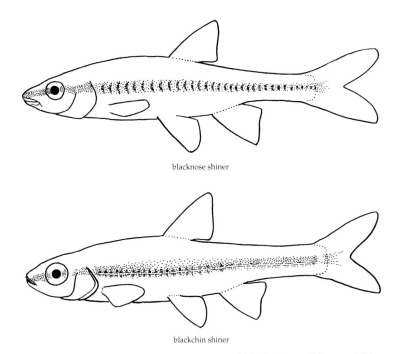

blacknose shiner

blackchin shiner

Fig. 34. Placement of dark lateral band on snout of *(a)* blacknose shiner and *(b)* blackchin shiner.

38a. Anterior half of lateral band has zigzag shape (figure 34b) → **Blackchin Shiner,** *Notropis heterodon*

38b. Anterior half of lateral band uniform, without zigzags → **Ironcolor Shiner,** *Notropis chalybaeus*

39a. Mouth small, upper jaw approximately as long as diameter of eye; scales in lateral line, in particular those anterior to pelvic fins, are much taller than wide; fewer than 16 predorsal scales → **Mimic Shiner,** *Notropis volucellus*

39b. Mouth large, upper jaw longer than diameter of eye; scales in lateral line similar to adjacent scales in shape; more than 16 predorsal scales → **Big-mouth Shiner,** *Notropis dorsalis*

40a. Anal rays 9 → **41**

40b. Anal rays 10–13 → **43**

41a. Dark pigmentation on posterior dorsal fin between the fifth and seventh dorsal rays; 35–37 lateral line scales→ **Satinfin Shiner,** *Cyprinella analostana*

41b. No pigmentation on dorsal fin; more than 36 scales in lateral line→ **42**

42a. Back with thin, dusky lines converging in posterior region to form a V; predorsal scales large, 22–25 on midline→ **Striped Shiner,** *Luxilus chrysocephalus*

42b. Back with thin, dusky lines running parallel to each other, not converging to form a V; predorsal scales small, 25 or more on midline→ **Common Shiner,** *Luxilus cornutus*

43a. A dusky spot at base of first 2 or 3 dorsal rays→ **Redfin Shiner,** *Lythrurus umbratilis*

43b. No dusky spot at base of dorsal fin→ **44**

44a. Base of first dorsal ray located directly over the forward edge of the pelvic fin base; two crescent-shaped marks between nostrils→ **Silver Shiner,** *Notropis photogenis*

44b. Forward edge of dorsal fin base located posterior to middle of pelvic fin base→ **45**

45a. Snout long, distance from forward edge of eye to tip of snout greater than eye diameter (figure 35a)→ **Rosyface Shiner,** *Notropis rubellus*

45b. Snout short, distance from forward edge of eye to tip of snout equal to or less than eye diameter (figure 35b)→ **46**

46a. Slender but relatively deep-bodied fish with pale silvery coloration→ **Emerald Shiner,** *Notropis atherinoides*

46b. Heavier-bodied fish with pale green coloration→ **Comely Shiner,** *Notropis amoenus*

47a. Fleshy keel, not covered with scales, extends along ventral midline from anus to pelvic fins (figure 26); 13 or more anal rays; lateral line strongly decurved; common, native of region→ **Golden Shiner,** *Notemigonus crysoleucas*

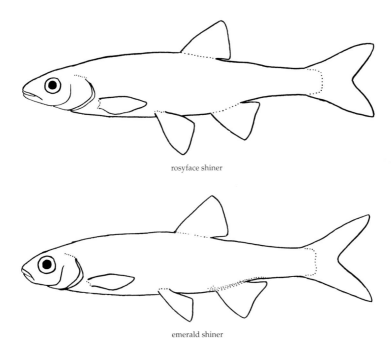

rosyface shiner

emerald shiner

Fig. 35. Length of snout of *(a)* rosyface shiner and *(b)* emerald shiner.

47b. Keel, if present, covered by scales; anal rays 12 or less; an uncommon species, but may be spreading by introduction→ **48**

48a. Scaled keel runs along ventral midline from anus to pelvic fins; body deeply compressed; 9–11 dorsal rays; introduced→ **Rudd,** *Scardinius erythrophthalmus*

48b. No ventral keel; body only slightly compressed, with a hump appearing behind head in adults; 8 dorsal rays; introduced→ **Ide,** *Leuciscus idus*

Central Stoneroller

Campostoma anomalum (Rafinesque, 1820)

Identification. The central stoneroller can be recognized by the *cartilaginous ridge on the lower jaw.* This ridge essentially replaces the lower lip, although vestiges of the lip can still be seen. You may need to depress the lower jaw to see the ridge clearly. Another interesting diagnostic characteristic is the fact that its intestine is coiled around its gas bladder, a trait not shared by other minnows in the region. The back is olive green to brown, grading through lighter shades to white on the belly. The fins are yellow green; *the dorsal fin has a dark horizontal band.* During breeding season, the dorsal and anal fins develop an orange color. the body is extensively covered with nuptial tubercles, and the eye is often red.

Life History. Stonerollers spawn from mid-April to June, beginning when the water temperature reaches 55–61°F. Males move upstream to small tributaries with strong current and a gravel or sand bottom. If you pick one up during the breeding season, the tubercles cause the fish to feel almost like coarse sandpaper. As soon as the male finds a suitable site, he begins to build a nest by pushing and rolling stones to create a small depression in the gravel. It is this rolling of stones that may have given rise to the common name, stoneroller. A female soon joins the male. They spawn over the nest, and the heavy eggs sink to the bottom, where they hatch in approximately 3 days. After spawning, the adults drop back downstream to deeper water.

Stonerollers scrape material off the rocks on the stream bottom, consuming diatoms, algae, microscopic animals of various sorts, and insects in the process. They live up to 5 years and reach 5–6 inches in total length.

In some areas, stonerollers are used as bait minnows. They are quite hardy. They are also interesting to watch in small streams in the spring as they go through their nest-building and spawning behavior.

Distribution. The central stoneroller is primarily a midcontinent species. It ranges from New York west to Minnesota and south to Texas and Georgia. In the Northeast, it is found in small- to medium-size gravel-bottom streams with strong current and clear water. It is found in New York in the Mohawk, Delaware, Susquehanna, and Finger Lakes and in drainages to the west. It had been reported from Connecticut in the Byram River drainage in the 1960s but has not been collected there since.

Goldfish

Carassius auratus (Linnaeus, 1758)

Identification. Goldfish, along with carp, have a *long dorsal fin with more than 14 rays*. No other minnows in the region have this trait. Goldfish are distinguished from carp in that they have *no barbels on their upper jaw*, whereas carp have two pairs of barbels. Goldfish are often orange, red, or black when bred in captivity but revert over time to an olive green coloration when returned to the wild.

Life History. Goldfish spawn in shallow vegetated areas, waiting until the water temperature reaches 77°F or warmer. Eggs are fertilized and broadcast over vegetation, where they develop for 3–6 days before hatching. Goldfish feed on algae, aquatic macrophytes, insects, crustaceans, mollusks, worms, and a wide range of other bottom-dwelling organisms. They are very tolerant of low oxygen and other environmental conditions that might affect more sensitive species.

Distribution. Goldfish are native to China and much of eastern Asia. They have had a long history of domestication by humans beginning in the Middle Ages in China. They are found in relatively quiet, heavily vegetated, often low-oxygen waters in all states in the Northeast. Not every locality in which they are found represents a self-sustaining population that reproduces each year, however. In many cases, the presence of goldfish simply indicates the recent release of aquarium fish.

Redside Dace

Clinostomus elongatus (Kirtland, 1838)

Identification. Redside dace have relatively small scales (more than 48 in lateral line) and an *unusually large, oblique mouth.* Throughout the year, adults have *a pinkish cast to their body just behind the head,* but during breeding season this pink becomes an intense reddish color, from which their name is derived. Their back is dark brown, grading abruptly to white on the belly. A lighter band extends along the side from the head to the tail.

Life History. Spawning of redside dace takes place in late May over gravel, often at the head of riffles. They sometimes use the large gravel nests built by creek chubs. They normally spawn at 3 years of age and may live until 4. Females carry 400–1,500 eggs each. Adults may reach 2½ inches in length. They feed heavily on terrestrial insects. They have been observed taking flying insects by jumping out of the water and capturing them in the air. The large mouth undoubtedly facilitates this behavior.

Distribution. Redside dace are found from Minnesota and Wisconsin south to Kentucky and West Virginia. Their range extends eastward to New York, where they are found in the upper Susquehanna, eastern Great Lakes, Allegheny, and upper Mohawk drainages. In the Northeast, they are found only in New York. They prefer pools in small streams with overhanging vegetation.

Lake Chub

Couesius plumbeus (Agassiz, 1850)

Identification. With a *barbel at the tip of the maxilla* and with *small scales* (more than 55 in lateral line), the lake chub is relatively easy to identify. The barbel in creek chubs, in contrast, is located up from the tip of the maxilla and partially hidden. Lake chubs are dark gray to brown on the back, grading through olive green to silver and white on the lower half of the body and belly. A dark band extends along the side from the head to the tail.

Life History. Lake chubs spawn in the spring from late April through May. They spawn in shallow water over a variety of habitats and in small tributary streams. The eggs are deposited on the bottom and abandoned. Growth is rapid, and young fish are 2–3 inches long by the middle of September. Young fish feed on zooplankton but switch to aquatic insects as they get older. Most fish do not live beyond age 5. Males are able to spawn at age 3; females typically wait another year and spawn at age 4.

Distribution. Lake chubs can be found across Canada and the northern United States from Washington and British Columbia to Maine and the Maritime Provinces. They extend southward to the upper reaches of the Delaware River. In the Northeast, they are found in a wide variety of habitats, both lakes and streams, in all states within the region except Connecticut and Rhode Island.

Satinfin Shiner

Cyprinella analostana Girard, 1859

Identification. The satinfin shiner is one of three deep-bodied shiners that have *9 anal rays.* It is distinguished from the others in this group by *dark pigmentation between the last 3 rays of the dorsal fin.* It also has 35–37 lateral line scales. The only other shiner to have dark spots on its posterior dorsal fin is the spotfin shiner, which has 8 anal rays. Satinfin shiners are gray to olive on the back, grading gradually to silver or white on the belly. The young have a dark midlateral stripe.

Life History. Satinfin shiners spawn throughout the summer. They are what is referred to as fractional crevice spawners because they often use crevices in rocks or logs as spawning sites. The female deposits only a portion of her eggs at each spawning event, coming back a few days to a month later to deposit more eggs. Males are known to make sounds during courtship. They feed primarily on small insects, in particular Diptera and Ephemeroptera. They may live for up to 4 years and achieve a size of 3 or so inches.

Distribution. The satinfin shiner is typically found in freshwater reaches of tidal creeks along the lowlands of the Atlantic Coast from the Mohawk and Hudson Rivers in New York south to North Carolina. In the Northeast, it is known only from the Mohawk-Hudson, Susquehanna, Black, and Delaware River systems in New York.

Spotfin Shiner

Cyprinella spiloptera (Cope)

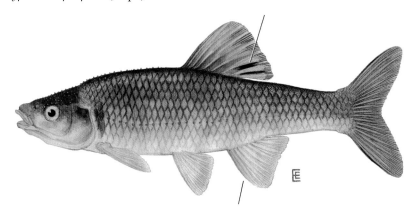

Identification. The spotfin shiner is the only shiner to have *8 anal rays* and a relatively deep body. It is also distinguished by *dark pigmentation on the membranes between the last 3 rays of the dorsal fin.* You may need to spread the fin to see this character clearly. The spotfin shiner is generally dark gray to brown on the back, grading to white on the belly.

Life History. Spotfin shiners may spawn throughout the summer from June to August. They are fractional crevice spawners-that is, they deposit their eggs in crevices in rocks or even logs. Females deposit only a fraction of the eggs they are carrying at a time, which allows them to repeat the egg-laying process, normally at approximately 5-day intervals throughout the spawning period. Spotfin shiners feed primarily on insects. They live for up to 4 years and achieve sizes of 3–4 inches at that age. Males tend to be a little larger than females.

Distribution. Spotfin shiners are found from the middle of the St. Lawrence River west through almost all of the Great Lakes (except Lake Superior) and in the upper Mississippi River south to Oklahoma and northern Alabama. In the Northeast, they have been reported only from lakes and creeks in New York and Vermont. They can tolerate relatively silty and turbid water.

Carp

Cyprinus carpio Linnaeus, 1758

Identification. The carp is one of the easiest members of the minnow family to recognize. Its large size, *long dorsal fin* supported by more than 14 rays, and *two pairs of barbels around its mouth* prevent you from confusing it with any other fish in the region. It is olive green or brown on its back, grading to white on its belly.

Life History. Carp spawn in late May or early June after the water has warmed to 62 or 63°F. Adults move into water so shallow that their backs and fins sometimes protrude into the air, creating a great deal of splashing and commotion as they go about their spawning activities. They are easily noticed at a distance during this time but are very wary and difficult to approach. Carp do not build nests or care for their eggs in any way; they simply broadcast their eggs over the bottom. Consequently, the eggs suffer a high mortality. To compensate, each female may carry up to 2 million eggs. The eggs hatch in 2–8 days, depending on water temperature, and the young quickly disperse. Carp fry feed initially on zooplankton but soon switch to feeding off the bottom. When bottom feeding, they draw material up into the mouth, spit it out, and then pick out any food items that suit them. Carp are omnivorous in their feeding habits, consuming both plant and animal material.

Carp are quite long-lived. There is a report of one individual that lived for 47 years in captivity. In nature, it is unlikely that many individuals exceed a life of 10 years or a size in excess of 10 pounds, although an angler in New York took a 50-pound fish.

As young fish, carp are quite susceptible to predation. After they reach adult size, however, they are relatively free of predators. They are too large to be killed and eaten by most other fishes, and their thick, heavy scales provide protection from lamprey attack. The only significant predators are humans.

The carp is one species underexploited by anglers in the United States. It is a sturdy fish that reaches large sizes and puts up a strong, if not spectacular, fight when hooked. Many anglers in Europe consider it an excellent sport fish. Interest in carp fishing is increasing in the United States.

Distribution. Carp were originally found in Asia and Europe. They were introduced into the northeastern United States on more than one occasion, one of the earliest was in a private pond near Newburgh, New York, where they subsequently escaped into the Hudson River around 1831 or 1832. Stocking policies in the late nineteenth century facilitated their spread so that now they are found throughout the United States and Canada. In the Northeast, carp are found in all states.

Streamline Chub

Erimystax dissimilis (Kirtland, 1840)

Identification. The streamline chub has a relatively large eye, its diameter greater than the length of the upper jaw, and a snout that extends beyond the upper lip. It has a line of rounded dark spots along the lateral line, in contrast to the gravel chub, which does not have the rounded spots, but instead has dark X-, W-, V-, or Y-shaped markings on its sides and back. Streamline chubs are olive green dorsally, grading through silver on its sides to white on its belly.

Life History. Very little is known of the life history of this species, but it is probably similar to that of other chubs discussed elsewhere. Streamline chubs feed on a variety of bottom-dwelling organisms, including insects and snails. Breeding adults are between $2\frac{1}{2}$ and 4 inches long.

Distribution. Streamline chubs are a primarily midwestern species found in the Ohio River drainage from Alabama and Tennessee northward to western New York. A western subspecies is also found in Arkansas and Missouri. They prefer gravel bars or riffle areas in moderately large clear streams. In the Northeast, they are found only in the Allegheny drainage of western New York.

Gravel Chub

Erimystax x-punctata (Hubbs and Crowe, 1956)

Identification. The gravel chub has a relatively large eye, its diameter greater than the length of the upper jaw, and a snout that extends beyond the upper lip. It can be separated from its closest relative, the streamline chub, by dark

X-, W-, V-, or Y-shaped markings on sides and back. The streamline chub, in contrast, has a line of rounded dark spots along the lateral line. The scientific name for the gravel chub, *x-punctata,* means spots that are shaped like an X. It is mostly silver in coloration, darker dorsally and grading to white ventrally.

Life History. This species is not common in the Northeast, and very little is known of its life history, but it is probably similar to that of chubs discussed elsewhere. Gravel chubs feed on a variety of bottom-dwelling organisms and have many taste buds on their barbels to facilitate prey location. Breeding adults range in size from 2½ to 3½ inches in length.

Distribution. The gravel chub ranges from southern Minnesota south to Arkansas and east to western New York in riffle areas of large creeks and rivers with fine gravel substrate. It seems to prefer somewhat deeper, slower water than the streamline chub. In the Northeast, it is found only in the Allegheny drainage of western New York. It is listed as threatened in New York.

Tongue-tied Minnow

Exoglossum laurae (Hubbs, 1931)

Identification. The *lower jaw of the tongue-tied minnow is composed of three lobes, a triangular medial lobe flanked by two smaller lateral lobes.* Its lobes are not as prominent as those in the cutlips minnow. Tongue-tied minnows are rather stocky fish with a small *dark spot at the base of their caudal fin* and a faint, dark lateral band. They have a brownish green to olive back, shading to a lighter olive belly.

Life History. Tongue-tied minnows spawn in early June, when the water has warmed to approximately 70°F. They build a nest similar to that of the cutlips minnow composed of a pile of small gravel located upstream of an obstruction such as a log or rock (see cutlips minnow for details). Males defend the nest. Little is known of their diet.

Distribution. Tongue-tied minnows are found in three separate locations in the United States: the New River drainage in North Carolina, Virginia, and West Virginia; the Great and Little Miami drainage in southwest Ohio; and the upper Allegheny and Genesee drainages in New York and Pennsylvania. In the Northeast, they are found only in New York in the Allegheny and upper Genesee River systems. They tend to be found in gravel-bottomed streams and rivers.

Cutlips Minnow

Exoglossum maxillingua (LeSueur, 1818)

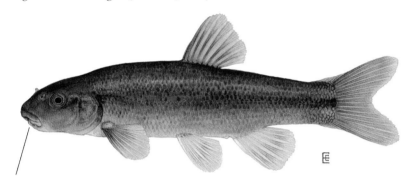

Identification. The cutlips minnow is easily identified. By simply looking at the *lower jaw, you will see that it is composed of 3 distinct lobes* (figure 25). Only the tongue-tied minnow (*Exoglossum laurae*) has a lower jaw that resembles the cutlips. The lobes in the cutlips minnow's jaw are very distinct, whereas the lobes on the tongue-tied minnow's jaw are relatively indistinct. Because the ranges for these two species do not overlap except in western New York, it is unlikely that they can be confused. The cutlips is dusky olive green dorsally, grading to a very light gray, green, or cream ventrally.

Life History. Cutlips minnows spawn from mid-May to mid-June, with most activity occurring in June. Males construct a nest by carrying carefully selected stones to the nest site and arranging them into a mound 1–1½ feet in diameter and 3–6 inches high. The nest is flat on top. The site chosen for the nest is usually in current and under some form of overhanging shelter. Spawning occurs on the upstream slope of the nest, and the eggs are lodged in the gravel nest by the current. The young hatch and leave the nest in approximately 6 days. Cutlips minnows feed on material taken from the bottom of the clear, gravelly streams they inhabit. Insects and mollusks dominate their diet. Cutlips minnows are also known to remove the eyes of other fishes when they are confined to a small space such as a bait bucket or aquarium, a habit that has led to the common name "eye-picker."

Distribution. Cutlips minnows range from the St. Lawrence River and eastern Lake Ontario drainages east to Vermont and south to North Carolina and Virginia. In the Northeast, they are found in small- to moderate-size creeks with gravel bottoms in New York, Connecticut, Massachusetts, and Vermont. In New York, they are found in all of the major drainages except the Allegheny, Lake Erie, and Long Island drainages. In Connecticut, they are found in western Connecticut in tributaries to the Hudson and Housatonic Rivers.

Brassy Minnow

Hybognathus hankinsoni Hubbs, 1929

Identification. Both the brassy minnow and the silvery minnow resemble shiners. If you pick them up, however, and look at their lower jaw from the underside, you will see that the *lower jaw of the brassy and silvery minnows is crescent or C shaped,* whereas in the shiners the lower jaw is U shaped (see figure 32). In living specimens, the brassy minnow can be distinguished from the silvery minnow based on color. The *brassy minnow has a distinct coppery tone,* whereas the silvery minnow has a somewhat more silvery sheen. Another useful character is the number of radii on the scales. Radii are lines that radiate out from the center of a scale. Brassy minnows have 14–20 radii per scale, whereas silvery minnows have only 10–12. Brassy minnows are dark olive green with a coppery tone on the back, changing rather abruptly halfway down the sides to a lighter olive gold and eventually to silver on the lower sides and belly. A dark stripe runs down each side.

Life History. Brassy minnows spawn in late spring or early summer in shallow water and in flooded marshes. They gather in large schools, with smaller groups breaking off to spawn. Eggs are scattered on the bottom and are left to fare for themselves. The young feed primarily on algae with a small amount of detritus and crustaceans. They mature and are ready to reproduce at the end of the first year or in some cases the second year. Adults may reach 4 inches in length.

Distribution. Brassy minnows are found from the upper St. Lawrence River and Lake Champlain west throughout the Great Lakes to the upper Mississippi and Missouri drainages. In the Northeast, they are reported only from New York and Vermont, and they are a species of special concern in Vermont. They prefer small, slow-flowing streams or bogs with abundant vegetation.

Eastern Silvery Minnow

Hybognathus regius Girard, 1857

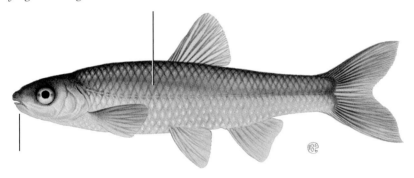

Identification. The silvery minnow looks a great deal like a shiner, except its *lower jaw is crescent or C shaped*, whereas the shiner's lower jaw is U shaped. In living specimens, the silvery minnow can be distinguished from the brassy minnow based on color. The brassy minnow is golden or copper colored, whereas the silvery minnow is *silver colored*. Another useful character is the number of radii on the scales. Silvery minnows have 10–12 radii per scale, whereas brassy minnows have 14–20. Silvery minnows are olive on the back, grading quickly to silver on the sides and belly. A diffuse dark stripe runs forward from the tail, fading as it approaches the head.

Life History. Silvery minnows spawn in shallow water, often over recently flooded grass, in late April to the middle of May. Eggs are scattered on the bottom, and the young are left to fare for themselves. Adults feed on algae and detritus. They become sexually mature at age 1 and may live for 2 or more years. Adult size is 3–3½ inches.

Distribution. The eastern silvery minnow ranges from the St. Lawrence River southward along the Atlantic Slope to Georgia. In the Northeast, it has been reported from all states except Connecticut and Rhode Island. It recently established a population in the Kennebec River in Maine. It prefers quiet water in lakes and medium to large streams and rivers.

Ide

Leuciscus idus (Linnaeus, 1758)

Identification. The ide is a relatively large minnow, often reaching 10–12 inches in length, and adults have a hump behind the head. It lacks a ventral keel and has 8 dorsal rays. It is golden brown on the back, grading through a lighter golden color on the sides to light yellow on the belly. The pelvic and anal fins are often red in adults.

Life History. The ide is found in clear water in lakes and ponds and sometimes in medium to large rivers. It spawns in the spring, scattering eggs over vegetation and then abandoning them. It feeds on invertebrates; larger individuals may consume small fish.

Distribution. The ide is a minnow of northern Europe that was brought to the United States in 1877 by the U.S. Fish Commission. It is found in various disjunct localities throughout the country, including Texas, Nebraska, Tennessee, Virginia, and Pennsylvania. In the Northeast, it is reported from New York in the Susquehanna River drainage, on Long Island, and in ponds in Connecticut and Maine.

Striped Shiner

Luxilus chrysocephalus Rafinesque, 1820

Identification. The striped shiner is a relatively large, deep-bodied shiner with *9 anal rays.* It lacks the dark spot on the posterior dorsal fin and has 37–41 lateral line scales, characters that separate it from the satinfin shiner. It is distinguished from the common shiner by a *set of thin, dusky lines that converge on the dorsal midline behind the dorsal fin to form V-shaped markings.* The scales above the lateral line and in front of the dorsal fin are relatively large and outlined in dark pigment. Counting from directly below the base of the first dorsal ray along the third to sixth scale row above the lateral line forward to the head gives an anterior dorsolateral scale count of 14–16 scales. In the common shiner, this same count is 18–24. Striped shiners are silvery gray dorsally and lighter ventrally.

Life History. Little is known of the striped shiner's life history. It is likely to have spawning habits similar to those of the common shiner (described next). It feeds primarily on aquatic insects. It is one of the largest shiners in the region, with some individuals reaching 8 inches in length.

Distribution. There are two subspecies of striped shiner, *L. chrysocephalus chrysocephalus* and *L. chrysocephalus isolepis. L. c. isolepis* is found in the lower Mississippi drainage, whereas *L. c. chrysocephalus* has a more northern range, extending northward from the Arkansas and Tennessee Rivers to the lower Great Lakes. In the Northeast, *L. c. chrysocephalus* is found only in the Allegheny River, Lakes Erie and Ontario, and the Finger Lakes of New York, preferring small- to moderate-size streams with gravel bottoms and little vegetation.

Common Shiner

Luxilus cornutus (Mitchill, 1817)

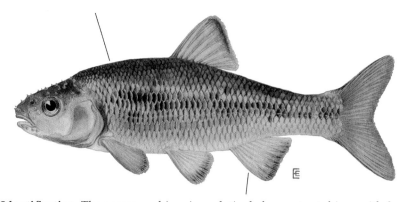

Identification. The common shiner is a relatively large, stout shiner with *9 anal rays*. It lacks the dark spot on the posterior portion of the dorsal fin and has 39–44 lateral line scales, characters that distinguish it from the satinfin shiner. It is distinguished from the striped shiner in that it does not have the set of thin, dusky lines that converge on the dorsal midline behind the dorsal fin to form the V-shaped markings so apparent in the striped shiner. *The scales above the lateral line and in front of the dorsal fin in the common shiner are relatively small and are not outlined in dark pigment* as they are in the striped shiner. Counting from directly below the base of the first dorsal ray along the third to sixth scale row above the lateral line forward to the head gives an anterior dorsolateral scale count of 18–24 scales. In the striped shiner, this same count is 14–16.

During the breeding season, the common shiner's fins are tinged with pink to red, giving rise to the name redfin. The remainder of the body is silvery, with an olive green back. Irregular dark blotches along the side are common.

Life History. Spawning occurs after the water has reached 60–65°F, which is usually in May or June. Males create a rather primitive depression in the gravel bottom of streams near the head of a riffle. They defend the nest area while the females wait downstream. A female eventually enters the nest and lays approximately 50 eggs, which the male then fertilizes. The eggs drift to the gravel bottom and, being adhesive, attach to the stones. Because females carry approximately 1,000 eggs, they probably repeat the spawning act more than once. Favored food organisms include insects, algae, and aquatic plants. The common shiner is one of the largest shiners in the region, reaching 7 or 8 inches in length, and lives for up to 5 years. It is a common fish, ranking fourth most common in streams and nineteenth most common in lakes in the region.

The common shiner serves as forage for many game fish. Anglers also use it as bait.

Distribution. The common shiner is found from Nova Scotia west to Saskatchewan and south to Kansas and Virginia. It occurs very frequently in small- to moderate-size streams and is found in all states and most drainage basins in the region.

Redfin Shiner

Lythrurus umbratilis (Girard, 1856)

Identification. The redfin shiner is the only shiner with *10–12 anal rays* and a relatively deep body. *A dusky spot located at the base of the first 2 or 3 dorsal rays* also distinguishes it. The creek chub has a dark spot at the anterior base of the dorsal fin, but it has a barbel just above the tip of its maxilla. The redfin lacks a barbel. Redfins are olive on the back, grading through silver on the sides to white on the belly. The fins of breeding males become quite red.

Life History. Redfin shiners are known to spawn in early June in Illinois. Males are territorial, choosing to defend locations over sand or gravel bottom. In some waters, they are reported to use sunfish nests as spawning sites. Females join the males, and the eggs are released, fertilized, and settle to the bottom. Little is known of the redfin shiner's diet. Adults are 2–3 inches in length.

Distribution. The redfin is common throughout the Mississippi and Ohio River drainages. It extends eastward into tributaries of Lakes Erie and Ontario in New York, typically in low-gradient streams. It is not abundant, however, and has been placed on that state's special concern list. It is not found elsewhere in the region.

Silver Chub

Macrhybopsis storeriana (Kirtland, 1847)

Identification. The silver chub has a barbel on the tip of its maxilla, a large eye with a diameter equal to or greater than the length of the upper jaw, and a snout extending a noticeable distance beyond its upper lip. The silver chub is most like the bigeye chub except that it has no lateral band, and the base of the first dorsal ray is anterior to the origin of the pelvic fin. It tends to be very light in color—hence the name silver chub.

Life History. Very little is known of the life history of silver chubs. In Ohio, they spawn in late May or early June, possibly in open water, after the water temperature reaches 70°F. As young fish, they are thought to feed on plankton and small insect larvae and to switch to mayflies when they get older. They live for at least 4 years, achieving a length of 6–7 inches.

Distribution. Silver chubs range from the mouth of the Mississippi River north to Minnesota and east to Lake Erie. In the Northeast, this species was last taken in 1928 in western New York, where it currently is on the endangered list. Silver chubs are found in large bodies of water such as Lake Erie and in the mouths of streams with fine gravel or sand bottoms.

Pearl Dace

Margariscus margarita Cope, 1868

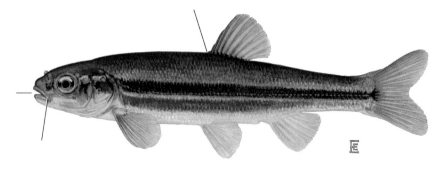

Identification. Pearl dace have a *small barbel in the groove between the maxilla and the snout* (it is occasionally absent), *lack the dark spot at the base of the dorsal fin* characteristic of creek chubs, and have a *relatively small mouth* when compared to other similar species, such as the creek chub and fallfish. In the pearl dace, the upper jaw does not extend far enough posterior to reach the forward edge of the eye, whereas in the creek chub and fallfish it extends at least to the front of the eye and often closer to the middle of the eye. Pearl dace have relatively small scales, 49–78 in the lateral line. They are gray to olive on the back, grading to white on the belly. Breeding males may have a red band running along the ventral side of the body.

Life History. Pearl dace spawn in the spring or early summer when the water temperature reaches 60°F or warmer. Unlike the creek chub and fallfish, pearl dace do not build nests. Instead, territorial males defend a small area of the stream bottom over gravel or sand. Females are attracted to the territory, deposit eggs, which are immediately fertilized by the male, and then depart for another territory. Pearl dace prefer insects as prey but will feed on a variety of other prey such as mollusks, plant material, and water mites. They normally live for 3 years and reach 3–4 inches in length.

Distribution. Pearl dace are found throughout Canada and the northern United States from Montana to Virginia. They are known from most states in the Northeast, except New Hampshire, Massachusetts, and Rhode Island. They inhabit spring-fed creeks, small lakes, and cool bog ponds.

Hornyhead Chub

Nocomis biguttatus (Kirtland, 1840)

Identification. Hornyhead chubs derive their name from the 60–100 sharply pointed nuptial tubercles on the upper part of breeding males' heads. The premaxillae are protractile, and a barbel is present at the tip of the maxilla, as with all of the chubs. Unlike the lake chub, the hornyhead chub has relatively large scales (less than 50 in lateral line), *a small eye with a diameter less than the length of the upper jaw, and a large distinct caudal spot. Breeding males have a distinct red spot behind the eye.* The hornyhead chub differs from the similar river chub in that the snout is relatively short, with the snout length fitting into the standard length more than nine times, whereas in the river chub it fits eight times or less.

Hornyhead chubs also have a dark line down the middle of the back, which is lacking in the river chub. They are a dark brown to olive on the back, grading rather abruptly to a yellowish white on the belly.

Life History. Male hornyhead chubs build elaborate nests in streams by carrying small stones in their mouths or rolling larger stones to the nest site using their heads. The nest is a circular pile of stones that the male defends vigorously using the sharply pointed nuptial tubercles on its head. Construction continues during spawning so that the nest increases in size, some reaching 3 feet in diameter and 6 inches deep. As many as ten females may deposit eggs in one nest during the breeding season, and other species of fishes—such as the blacknose dace, stoneroller, common shiner, rosyface shiner, redbelly dace, and the blackside darter—may also spawn in the nest. Hornyhead chubs feed on a variety of different prey items, including crustaceans, insects, worms, and, very important, snails. They may live for 4 or more years, achieving a length of 4 or 5 inches.

Distribution. Hornyhead chubs are found primarily in small- to medium-size gravel-bottom streams with low to moderate gradients. They are most abundant in the Great Lakes area and in the Ozarks but extend east into the Mohawk, Black, and Susquehanna drainages of New York. They are not known from any other state in the region.

River Chub

Nocomis micropogon (Cope, 1865)

Identification. River chubs have protractile premaxillae—that is, no frenum—and *a barbel at the tip of the maxilla.* They have relatively large scales (less than 50 in lateral line) and *a small eye with a diameter less than the length of the upper jaw,* but they lack the caudal spot and the red spot behind the eye found in the hornyhead chub. They are olive green on the back, grading to silvery white on the belly, with a dark lateral band.

Life History. As with many of the other chubs, river chubs construct large nests from the stones and gravel on the stream bottom. A considerable amount of effort is put into constructing the nests; one nest was estimated to have 70 quarts of pebbles and weigh 235 pounds. Some of the stones were brought from up to 20 feet away. Spawning occurs in late May or early June in New York. Other species sometimes use the nest as well, including the stoneroller, common shiner, and rosyface shiner. Young river chubs feed on plankton and algae; older fish switch to aquatic insects. They live for at least 4 years and achieve lengths up to 6 inches.

Distribution. River chubs range from the Susquehanna drainage in New York south to the James River in Virginia; southwest into North Carolina, Georgia, and Alabama; and north into Michigan. They are found in medium-size streams with relatively high gradient and gravel bottoms in the Susquehanna, Allegheny, Lake Erie, and Ontario drainages of New York. They are not found elsewhere in the region.

Golden Shiner

Notemigonus crysoleucas (Mitchill, 1814)

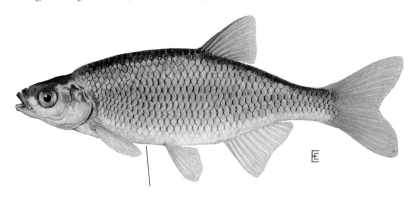

Identification. The golden shiner lacks barbels; has a *scaleless, fleshy keel running along the midline of the abdomen to the pelvic fins* and a long anal fin with 10–15 rays. As an adult, it possesses a distinctive golden color. It is a rather deep-bodied fish. The young are silvery and have a distinct dark lateral band running along their sides, which makes them easily confused with other shiners, except that they possess a fleshy keel even as juveniles.

Life History. Spawning occurs from May to August in ponds and lakes. No nest is built; the eggs are simply broadcast over aquatic vegetation and abandoned. The eggs are adhesive and remain attached to the vegetation until the young hatch and disperse. Golden shiners feed on zooplankton, phytoplankton, and small insects. If growth is rapid, they may be ready to spawn in their second summer; otherwise, they spawn in their third summer. Golden shiners may reach 10 inches in length and live for 8 or 9 years.

A substantial baitfish industry has grown up around this species. It is one of the most important bait fish in the region. It is cultured in ponds and sold to anglers. In addition, it is a valuable forage species for lake-dwelling game fish.

Distribution. The golden shiner is found throughout eastern North America from the Maritime Provinces of Canada to Florida and west to North Dakota and Texas. It has also been introduced in various parts of western North America. It is very common in all states in the region and is ranked the third most common fish in lakes and ponds. Golden shiners prefer relatively clear and quiet water with a great deal of aquatic vegetation in lakes and ponds, or large, slow-flowing streams and rivers. They generally swim in large schools, feeding at the surface on insects or in midwater on plankton.

Bigeye Chub

Notropis amblops (Rafinesque, 1820)

Identification. As you would expect from its name, the bigeye chub has a *large eye, its diameter equal to or greater than the length of the upper jaw,* and a *snout that extends a noticeable distance beyond the upper lip. It has a small barbel on the tip of its maxilla.* Unlike the members of the genus *Erimystax,* the bigeye does not have dark spots along its side, although it does have a dark stripe that extends along the side and onto its snout. It is a light-colored minnow except for the dark midlateral stripe. The back is light olive, and the belly is light gray to white.

Life History. Very little is known of the life history of this species, but it is likely to be similar to that of other chubs. Bigeye chubs can be expected to feed on crustaceans and insects. They are a relatively small chub, averaging less than 3 inches in length.

Distribution. The bigeye chub is found from the Tennessee River north through Illinois and Indiana and east to New York. It prefers small- to moderate-size streams with gravel bottoms. In the Northeast, it is found in New York in the Allegheny drainage and in streams tributary to Lake Erie. In 1987, one specimen was reported from Mopus Brook, Connecticut, but none have been reported there since.

Comely Shiner

Notropis amoenus (Abbott, 1874)

Identification. The comely shiner typically has *11 (10–12) anal rays,* a short snout (less than the eye diameter), and a *very distinct, well-defined band of anchor-shaped pigment on the under side of the chin. The forward edge of its dorsal fin is located behind the pelvic fin base.* It is a pale shiner, with an olive green back grading to a white belly. A pale silver band extends along the sides.

Life History. Very little is known of the life history of this species. It is thought to spawn in late spring or early summer based on the presence of males with breeding tubercles at that time. Comely shiners are generally 3 inches or less in length.

Distribution. The comely shiner is an eastern minnow ranging along the Atlantic Coastal Plain from New York to the Cape Fear drainage in North Carolina. In the Northeast, it is found only in the Hudson, Delaware, and Susquehanna River systems in New York. It occupies moderate to large streams, avoiding swift water.

Pugnose Shiner

Notropis anogenus Forbes, 1885

Identification. The pugnose shiner is one of four shiners that have *8 anal rays and a distinct dark lateral band.* It is distinguished, however, from all other shiners in the region by its unusually small mouth. The *mouth is nearly vertical and is so small that the maxilla does not extend back beyond the posterior nostril.* It is very rare in the region and is unlikely to be seen. It is a silvery-colored minnow with a thin midlateral band that runs from the tip of the snout to the base of the tail.

Life History. The life history of the pugnose shiner has not been well studied. It is thought to have very narrow tolerances for environmental conditions and thus is a good indicator of the quality of the environment. This low tolerance may be part of the reason for the decline in its numbers. Pugnose shiners are small fish, usually less than 2 inches in length.

Distribution. The range of the pugnose shiner extends westward from Lake Ontario through the Great Lakes into the upper Mississippi River in North Dakota. In the Northeast, it is reported only from New York in slow-flowing, vegetated bays of central and eastern Lake Ontario and the St. Lawrence River. It is very uncommon and has been placed on the endangered species list for New York.

Emerald Shiner

Notropis atherinoides Rafinesque, 1818

Identification. The emerald shiner has *10–13 anal rays;* the *base of its dorsal fin begins posterior to the base of the pelvic fin;* and it has *a relatively short snout (snout length is less than eye diameter).* It also lacks the distinctive pigment between the nostrils and on the under side of the chin characteristic of the silver, comely, and rosyface shiners. It has an olive green to silver back, grading to a white belly. An emerald band frequently extends from the upper corner of the gill cover along the side to the tail.

Life History. Little is known of the spawning behavior of emerald shiners. They may begin spawning as early as May, and some individuals may spawn as late as August. They are thought to spawn at night over a gravel or sand bottom. They grow rapidly, reaching 2 inches by late fall. Adults may reach 3–4 inches at the end of 3 years, their normal life span. They live in schools in the open water of large lakes and rivers, feeding on zooplankton and insects. They tend to move toward the surface at night and down into deeper water during the day, a movement pattern that parallels that of their prey.

The emerald shiner is widely used as bait. It also plays an important role as forage for many game fish.

Distribution. The emerald shiner ranges from the Lake Champlain drainage northwestward to northeastern British Columbia and south through the Mississippi drainage to the Gulf of Mexico. It is found in Maine, Vermont, Massachusetts, and New York. In New York, it is found in the Great Lakes-St. Lawrence and Mohawk-Hudson drainages. It tends to favor large bodies of water, where it commonly forms schools.

Bridle Shiner

Notropis bifrenatus (Cope, 1869)

Identification. The bridle shiner is the only shiner in the region that has 7 *anal rays; a continuous dark lateral band running along the sides, across the head, and onto the snout; and an incomplete lateral line.* It has a yellow silvery coloration dorsally that runs down to a dark midlateral stripe. It is silver white ventrally.

Life History. The bridle shiner spawns from early to midsummer at water temperatures ranging from 58 to 80°F in still water with vegetation. After the eggs are released, they either attach to the vegetation or sink to the bottom. The young remain sheltered in the vegetation until late summer, when they form schools. They feed primarily during the day on insects and crustaceans. They are small fish, usually no more than 2 inches long.

Distribution. Bridle shiners range from the St. Lawrence River in southern Quebec south to the Neuse River in North Carolina. They are found in warm-water lakes, in quiet-water streams, and in rivers with silt bottoms and high densities of vegetation in all states in the region. Unfortunately, populations in the Northeast seem to be declining at an alarming rate for reasons not understood. They are a species of special concern in Vermont.

Silverjaw Minnow

Notropis buccatus (Cope, 1865)

Identification. The silverjaw minnow is most easily recognized by the unusual sensory canals on its head and cheeks. In living specimens, the canals appear to be rectangular silver patches below the eye and on the lower jaw. This appearance changes to a honeycombed look in specimens that have been preserved. It is a pale fish, with silver sides and no dark lateral band.

Life History. Little is known of the life history of silverjaw minnows. They spawn from May to July. Their diet is predominantly insects. They range in size from 2 to 3 inches.

Distribution. Silverjaw minnows are found in two distinct populations: one southern population ranges from the Apalachicola drainage in Florida and Georgia west to Louisiana and Mississippi; and one northern population that ranges from Missouri east to Pennsylvania and West Virginia. In the Northeast, it is found only in the Allegheny drainage of western New York, where its numbers seem to be growing. It prefers small- to medium-size streams, tolerating some turbidity.

Ironcolor Shiner

Notropis chalybaeus (Cope)

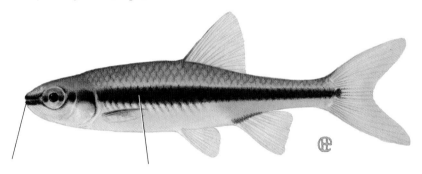

Identification. The ironcolor shiner has a *distinct, smooth, dark lateral band that does not demonstrate a zigzag pattern* and an incomplete lateral line. An important character for recognizing the ironcolor shiner is the *dark pigmentation inside its mouth.* This pigmentation and a lack of scales on its breast help separate it from the blackchin and blacknose shiners. Ironcolor shiners are dark-colored fish with a dark olive back, a broad and dark midlateral stripe, and a white belly.

Life History. Little is known of the life history of this species in the Northeast. In Florida, it spawns from April to September. No nests are constructed, and the eggs are apparently broadcast onto the vegetation or across the bottom. Ironcolor shiners school and feed on small insects. They are small shiners, rarely reaching beyond 2 inches.

Distribution. This species' range extends along the coastal lowlands in weedy, slow-moving waters from the lower Hudson drainage in New York to Florida and west to Texas, then north through the Mississippi drainage to Wisconsin. In the Northeast, it is reported only for southeastern New York and has been placed on the special concern list for that state.

Bigmouth Shiner

Notropis dorsalis (Agassiz, 1854)

Identification. The bigmouth shiner is a pallid shiner with *8 anal rays,* similar to the mimic and spottail shiners. It lacks the spot at the base of the tail that characterizes the spottail shiner, though, and *its mouth, as its name implies, is relatively large when compared to the mimic shiner (upper jaw length is greater than eye diameter).* The bigmouth shiner is a straw-colored fish with a slender midlateral stripe running from near the head to the tail, most prominently from just posterior to the dorsal fin to the base of the tail.

Life History. Very little is known of the life history of the bigmouth shiner. It is thought to have a relatively extended spawning season, ranging from May to August in Wisconsin. It feeds on aquatic insects, in particular mayflies and midges. It ranges from 2 to 3 inches in length.

Distribution. This species is most commonly found in Wisconsin, Iowa, Illinois, and Missouri. It is found in a few localities east of that area, including some populations in Michigan, Ohio, western Pennsylvania, and New York. In the Northeast, it is known only from the Allegheny, Genesee, Lake Erie, and Susquehanna drainages in New York.

Blackchin Shiner

Notropis heterodon (Cope, 1865)

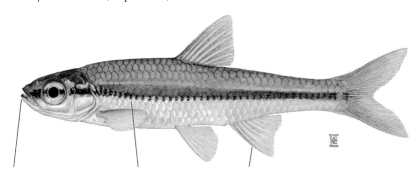

Identification. The blackchin shiner has *8 anal rays* and a very distinct dark lateral band similar to that of the blacknose shiner, except that in the blackchin shiner the *band passes across the head and snout in such a way as to produce a dark mark on the tip of the lower jaw.* The blackchin shiner is distinguished from the ironcolor shiner in that the *anterior half of the lateral band is not a smooth dark band, but appears to zigzag;* it lacks pigment inside the mouth; and its breast is covered with scales. The lateral line may be complete, but is often incomplete. Blackchin shiners are light olive dorsally, grading to white ventrally.

Life History. Little is known of the life history of blackchin shiners. Evidence suggests that they take a substantial portion of their diet from midwater as opposed to feeding off the bottom. Cladocerans and midges have been found in their guts. Adults range in size from 2 to 3 inches.

Distribution. The blackchin shiner is found throughout the Great Lakes basin and the upper Mississippi River. In the Northeast, it is found in shallow-water bays along the eastern shore of Lake Ontario and in the Thousand Islands section of the St. Lawrence River in New York. It has also been reported from inland lakes in New York, but populations there are thought to be declining. It is known from Vermont but has been placed in the special concern category in that state. It prefers clear but weedy standing water.

Blacknose Shiner

Notropis heterolepis Eigenmann and Eigenmann, 1893

Identification. The blacknose shiner is one of four shiners with *8 anal rays* and a very distinct dark lateral band. The *lateral band extends across the head and onto the snout* but does not cross any of the lower jaw. This characteristic separates it from the blackchin shiner (see earlier description of the blackchin) and the ironcolor shiner; its *larger and more horizontal mouth* separates it from the pugnose shiner. It also has an incomplete lateral line. It has an olive back, grading to a white belly. A distinct midlateral band extends from the snout to the base of the caudal fin.

Life History. Very little is known concerning the life history of the blacknose shiner. In the Niagara River, adult females ready to spawn have been collected in July. Based on its diet, it seems to prefer to feed off the bottom as opposed to open water. It is reported to reach $3\frac{1}{2}$ inches in length.

Distribution. The blacknose shiner ranges from Maine west to North Dakota and south to Missouri and Tennessee. In the Northeast, it is found in cool, weedy streams and lakes in Maine, New Hampshire, Vermont, and New York.

Spottail Shiner

Notropis hudsonius (Clinton, 1824)

Identification. The *dark spot at the base of its caudal fin,* its generally plain color, and its *8 anal rays* readily distinguish the spottail shiner. Be careful not to confuse it with the bluntnose minnow, which also has a black spot at the base of the caudal fin. In adult bluntnose minnows, the blunt anterior half ray in the dorsal fin is separated from the ray posterior to it (see figure 30a). In shiners, the first ray is a thin, splintlike ray that lies close to the rays behind it (see figure 30b). Most of the spottail's body is silvery, with the back a greenish gray and the belly white.

Life History. Spawning takes place in June or early July, when the fish gather in aggregations over a sandy bottom. There is no evidence of nest building. Each spottail female carries 1,300–2,600 eggs. The young begin life by feeding on microscopic algae and rotifers. They later transfer to small crustaceans, insects, mollusks, and even small fish. They live for 3–4 years and reach a length of 4 inches or more. The spottail is often used as bait and is an important forage species for game fishes.

Distribution. The spottail shiner is found in an area from the Lake Champlain drainage northwestward to the Northwest Territories and south to Missouri and Georgia. In the Northeast, it is found in all states in the region. It prefers clear water with little turbidity and is generally found in large rivers or lakes 3–60 feet deep with sand or gravel bottoms.

Silver Shiner

Notropis photogenis (Cope, 1865)

Identification. The silver shiner is one of four species of slender, graceful shiners with *10 or more anal rays.* The others are the comely, emerald, and rosyface shiners. The silver shiner can be distinguished from the other three by the presence of *2 crescent-shaped markings between the nostrils* and a *distinct middorsal stripe.* The other three shiners lack these markings. As its name implies, the silver shiner is a silver-colored shiner, darker on the dorsal side, grading to silver ventrally.

Life History. As with many shiners, very little is known concerning the silver shiner's spawning or life history. It feeds on aquatic insects and reaches a length of 4 inches.

Distribution. The silver shiner is found primarily in the Ohio River drainage. It extends into the Northeast only in the Allegheny drainage of western New York. It prefers riffle areas or pools below riffles in swift-flowing, clear, gravel-bottomed streams.

Swallowtail Shiner

Notropis procne (Cope, 1865)

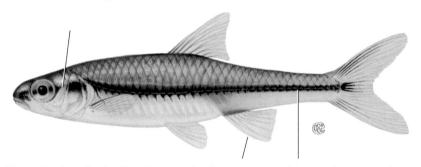

Identification. In the Northeast, only three species of shiners have *7 anal rays:* the sand, bridle, and swallowtail shiners. The swallowtail shiner is a small fish, less than 3 inches long, with a *dark stripe passing along the sides down the length of the body. The lateral band is briefly interrupted directly posterior to the eye.* It is the only shiner in the region with a dark lateral band, 7 anal rays, and a complete lateral line. The interruption of the lateral band behind the eye is a useful field character. The underlying color is olive dorsally, grading to light yellow or white ventrally.

Life History. Swallowtail shiners spawn in late spring to early summer, when water temperatures approach 78°F in riffle areas of streams. Males are territorial and defend a spawning area over sand or gravel bottom. Swallowtails feed on insects and algae and seldom live beyond 3 years. They typically are 2–3 inches long.

Distribution. The swallowtail shiner ranges along the Atlantic Slope northward from South Carolina to the Susquehanna and Delaware Rivers in New York. In the Northeast, it is found only in upland streams and small rivers in the Delaware and Susquehanna drainages of New York.

Rosyface Shiner

Notropis rubellus (Agassiz, 1850)

Identification. The rosyface shiner is a slender shiner with *10–11 anal rays* and a *bright brick-red head in breeding males.* It lacks the crescent-shaped markings between the nostrils and the middorsal stripe of the silver shiner. Its *snout is longer than the emerald shiner (distance from forward edge of eye to tip of snout is greater than eye diameter),* and it has a diffuse band of dark pigment that runs down the midline of the underside of the chin. The comely shiner has a similar band, but its band is much better defined. The rosyface shiner's basic color is light olive dorsally, grading to white ventrally.

Life History. Rosyface shiners spawn in late June in New York. They gather at the tail end of a riffle, just above a pool in shallow water. They tend to spawn in groups, using depressions in the gravel bottom as nests into which they deposit the eggs. They feed primarily on aquatic and terrestrial insects and achieve a length of 2–3 inches.

Distribution. The rosyface shiner ranges from Minnesota to the St. Lawrence River and south to Alabama and Arkansas. It is found only in New York, Vermont, and Connecticut in the Northeast. It prefers clear, nonturbid streams or small rivers with rock or gravel bottoms. Such habitats are becoming progressively less common, and thus the habitat available to rosyface shiners is declining.

Sand Shiner

Notropis stramineus (Cope, 1865)

Identification. The sand shiner is a pale-colored species with *7 anal rays* and a *complete lateral line.* No other shiners in the region combine these characteristics. Although the sand shiner normally does not have a dark lateral band, a poorly developed dark stripe does appear near the tail in some cases, but it fades quickly and does not extend past the midpoint of the body. Freshly caught specimens tend to be sandy to olive in color dorsally, grading to a silvery white belly.

Life History. Based on reports that sand shiners spawn at temperatures from 70 to 98°F, they apparently have an extended spawning season throughout the summer. They simply scatter their eggs across a sand or gravel bottom, providing no parental care. They feed on both aquatic and terrestrial insects, bottom ooze, and diatoms. They reach 2–3 inches in length.

Distribution. The sand shiner is widespread throughout the Midwest, ranging from Texas north to the Dakotas and Canada and east to the St. Lawrence River and Lake Champlain and then south to Tennessee. In the Northeast, it is found only in New York and Vermont, normally in moderately large streams with sandy bottoms or in lakes with silt-free bottoms.

Mimic Shiner

Notropis volucellus (Cope, 1865)

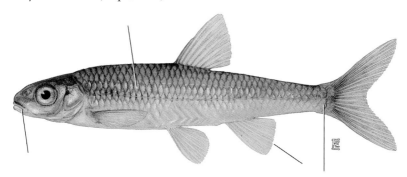

Identification. The mimic shiner is a relatively plain-colored shiner with *8 anal rays.* Only three shiners fit into this category: the mimic, bigmouth, and spottail shiners. The spottail is easily distinguished by the dark spot at the base of its tail. The mimic shiner *lacks such a spot.* The bigmouth shiner has a larger mouth (upper jaw length is greater than eye diameter) and normal lateral line scales, whereas the mimic shiner has a *small mouth (upper jaw length equals eye diameter) and elevated scales.* The mimic shiner is basically a silvery minnow, darker gray dorsally, grading to white ventrally.

Life History. Mimic shiners are thought to spawn over vegetation in relatively deep water during the middle of the summer. They feed on crustaceans, midge larvae, algae, and detritus. They are known to live for at least 3 years and approach 3 inches in length.

Distribution. Mimic shiners are found in the main channels of large rivers and in vegetated portions of lakes throughout a large region of the central United States. They range from along the Gulf Coast (Texas to Alabama) north to the upper Great Lakes and St. Lawrence River. In the Northeast, they are reported from New York, Vermont, Connecticut, and Massachusetts.

Northern Redbelly Dace

Phoxinus eos (Cope, 1862)

Identification. As with most dace, the northern redbelly dace has very small scales (more than 60 in its lateral line), which distinguishes it from most other minnows. The pearl dace, blacknose dace, and longnose dace have small scales, but they also have barbels on the upper jaw. The redside dace has a large oblique mouth, whereas the *redbelly dace's mouth is quite small.* The finescale dace is most similar to the redbelly dace, except that it has a single dark band extending along the side from the gill cover to the tail. The redbelly dace has *two dark lateral bands.* Additional characters to distinguish these two species are internal. The viscera in the finescale are pale in color, whereas the viscera in the redbelly are dark. The finescale has one primary loop in its gut, whereas the redbelly has two loops in addition to the primary loop. The northern redbelly dace is a darkly colored minnow with an olive brown back, grading to a white belly, with 2 dark stripes on its sides. Breeding males also develop a red band below the dark stripes.

Life History. Adults spawn any time from May to August in masses of filamentous algae. They feed on zooplankton, insects, larval fishes, and some plant matter. Adults are 2–2$\frac{1}{2}$ inches in length.

Distribution. Northern redbelly dace range from the Maritime Provinces of Canada and New England westward through the Great Lakes, upper Mississippi, and Missouri drainages. In the Northeast, they are found in boggy lakes, creeks, and ponds in all states except Connecticut and Rhode Island.

Finescale Dace

Phoxinus neogaeus Cope, 1868

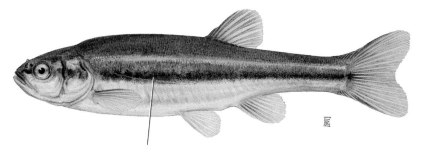

Identification. The finescale dace is very similar to the redbelly dace except that it has approximately *90 scales in the lateral line and a single dark stripe down its side instead of 2 dark stripes.* The viscera in the finescale are pale in color, whereas the viscera in the redbelly dace are dark. The finescale has one primary loop in its gut, whereas the redbelly has two loops in addition to the primary loop. Finescale dace are very dark brown to black dorsally, grading to white on the underside of the body.

Life History. Finescale dace spawn in the spring when the water temperature reaches approximately 63°F. They scatter their eggs on the bottom, often in sheltered areas. They feed on plankton and small insects. Finescale dace are larger than northern redbelly dace, averaging 3–3½ inches in length.

Distribution. The range of the finescale dace is similar to that of the northern redbelly dace, from the Maritime Provinces of Canada and Atlantic drainages of many New England states westward through the St. Lawrence and Great Lakes drainages to the Great Plains. In the Northeast, it is found in small boggy lakes, beaver ponds, and slow streams in all states except Connecticut, Massachusetts, and Rhode Island.

Bluntnose Minnow

Pimephales notatus (Rafinesque, 1820)

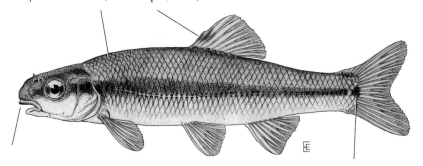

Identification. The bluntnose minnow has no barbels, no fleshy keel along the midline of its abdomen, a normal lower jaw, and a dark spot near the base of the first dorsal ray. The creek chub also has the dark spot at the base of the first dorsal ray, but it has a pair of barbels. The *first dorsal ray of the male bluntnose minnow is thickened and separated from the second dorsal ray by a membrane* (see figure 30a). Female and young bluntnose minnows resemble shiners in having a thin, splintlike first dorsal ray closely pressed against the second dorsal ray (see figure 30b). They can be separated from shiners, however, by the fact that the *scales on the back in front of the dorsal fin are crowded and irregularly arranged.* The bluntnose minnow can be distinguished from the fathead minnow by a *horizontal mouth overhung by the snout.* In addition, the bluntnose minnow has *a conspicuous spot at the base of the caudal fin* and a complete lateral line. Its body is olive green to brown on the back, grading to silvery white on the belly. A dark lateral band extends from the snout to the caudal spot.

Life History. The bluntnose minnow begins to spawn in May or June, waiting until the water temperature reaches 68°F. Intermittent spawning may occur throughout the summer. It spawns in still water, excavating a depression under a flat rock or board. The male builds the nest and defends it. The unusual feature of the bluntnose minnow's spawning behavior is that when the female lays her eggs in the nest, she does not deposit them on the bottom, but rather on the underside of a board or flat stone that forms the roof of the nest. The eggs are adhesive and stick to the board or rock. They are laid one or two layers thick and in a patch 4 or 5 inches in diameter composed of 200–500 eggs. The male guards the nest and tends the eggs, frequently rubbing them with a thick fatty pad that grows on the back of his head apparently for that purpose. If he is removed, the eggs die in less than a day. The eggs normally hatch in 1 or 2 weeks. The adults may spawn more than once during the year. The bluntnose minnow usually chooses to spawn in shallow water near shore and is thus easily observed. In fact, you can provide spawning sites for this interesting fish by laying empty flowerpots on their sides in an area where you suspect bluntnose minnows occur. Many hours of enjoyable watching can result from this simple expedient. Bluntnose minnows consume plankton and bottom organisms, including benthic diatoms. They may reach 3 years of age and 3 or more inches in length.

The bluntnose minnow is an important forage species and is widely used as a bait minnow. It is easily cultured, adapting to submerged flat boards as breeding sites.

Distribution. The bluntnose minnow is widespread throughout central North America from the Lake Champlain drainage west through the Great Lakes and south in the Mississippi River drainage to the Gulf States and east to Virginia. In the Northeast, it is found in clear lakes and ponds and occasionally in slow-flowing streams in all states except Maine.

Fathead Minnow

Pimephales promelas Rafinesque, 1820

Identification. The fathead minnow shares most of the characteristics of the bluntnose minnow, such as the presence of a *blunt, anterior half ray in the dorsal fin*. It differs in that its *mouth is somewhat oblique* and is not overhung by the snout. In addition, it has only a *very faint spot at the base of the caudal fin* and an incomplete lateral line. The fathead minnow's coloration is olive green on the back, grading to white on the belly. In the spring, males develop a nuptial coloration that is quite striking. The head becomes dark; a yellowish band encircles the body between the gill cover and the pectoral fin, behind which is another dark band. Under the dorsal fin, a second light band rings the body, but the remainder of the body remains dark.

Life History. Spawning takes place in late May or June when the water temperature reaches 60–64°F. Some individuals spawn throughout the summer. Spawning location and behavior are similar to those of the bluntnose minnow. Fathead minnows are omnivorous, feeding on insects, crustaceans, algae, and detritus. They are short-lived, normally dying after spawning at 2 years of age. If spawning does not occur, however, they may live longer. Individuals have been kept for 4 years in aquaria at the SUNY College of Environmental Science and Forestry at Syracuse. Adult size is 2 or 3 inches and is often reached at the end of the first growing season.

The fathead minnow is a valuable forage species, and it is cultured for sale as bait.

Distribution. The fathead is found throughout much of North America, ranging from New Brunswick to Alberta and south to Mexico. In the Northeast, it is found in all states in the region. It occupies a relatively wide range of habitats, being tolerant of turbidity and pollution. It prefers slow-moving streams and ponds.

Blacknose Dace

Rhinichthys atratulus (Hermann, 1804)

Identification. A *pointed snout, one barbel at the posterior tip of each maxilla, and nonprotractile premaxillae* distinguish the blacknose and longnose dace (genus *Rhinichthys*) from the other minnows. The snout of the blacknose dace does not protrude much beyond the mouth, whereas the snout of the longnose dace protrudes considerably (see figure 19). The blacknose dace is dark olive green to brown, grading to white on its underside. *A dark lateral band runs from the tail, along its side, and onto its head, passing through the center of the eye.* During breeding season, the males develop a rusty tinge to their fins.

Life History. Spawning occurs in late May or early June. The adults simply drop the fertilized eggs over a gravel stream bottom without preparing any nest. Females carry approximately 750 eggs. Blacknose dace probably do not live for more than 2–3 years, and small adults are usually only 2–3 inches long. They are stream dwellers, preferring small streams with a steep gradient. They are more common in the quieter parts of these streams than their close relative the longnose dace. The blacknose dace feeds on insect larvae, small crustaceans, small worms, and plant material. It is one of the few species found with brook trout in small headwater streams.

Distribution. The blacknose dace ranges from Nova Scotia to Georgia and west to Mississippi and the Dakotas. It is found most commonly in pools in small- to moderate-size streams with clear water and gravel bottoms in all states in the Northeast. It occurs more commonly in small streams than any other species in the region. It may also be found in small lakes.

Longnose Dace

Rhinichthys cataractae (Valenciennes, 1842)

Identification. The longnose dace has all of the characteristics outlined for the blacknose (see earlier description) except that its snout projects well beyond the mouth (see figure 19), and the lateral stripe, if present, is diffuse. It is olive green to dark brown on its back, grading to white on the undersides. The sides are somewhat mottled.

Life History. Little is known of the spawning behavior of this species. It is presumed to spawn in late spring or early summer in the gravelly riffle areas where it makes its home. The young are thought to be pelagic, living in still water, near shore. This habit lasts for approximately 4 months, quite unlike the behavior of the adults, who are bottom dwellers, hugging the bottom in riffle areas of the stream. The species is also found near shore in the rocky areas of large lakes. Longnose dace live up to 5 years and reach 4–5 inches in length. They appear to live a little longer and achieve larger size than the blacknose dace. They feed primarily on aquatic insect larvae and are considered particularly useful in reducing blackfly populations.

Distribution. The longnose dace is found from coast to coast in central North America, ranging south to Virginia and Mexico and north to Hudson Bay and the Northwest Territories. It is found in swift-flowing, small streams in all states in the Northeast. It is one of the more common species in small streams.

Bitterling

Rhodeus sericeus (Pallas, 1776)

Identification. The bitterling is a very small fish, typically less than 2 inches long. It has less than 12 rays in the dorsal fin and lacks the cartilaginous ridge of the stoneroller. Its unique characteristic is a very short lateral line. Only 4–7 scales in the lateral series have pores. Bitterlings are gray dorsally, grading to white ventrally.

Life History. Bitterlings have a very unusual type of reproductive behavior. As the time for spawning approaches, the female develops an ovipositor from her genital papillae. This elongate structure allows her to deposit her eggs carefully within the mantle cavity of certain freshwater clams. The eggs are then fertilized and are incubated within the mantle cavity, which provides protection and a steady current of water generated by the clam's activity. After the eggs hatch, the young leave the clam and fare for themselves.

Distribution. Bitterlings are originally from northern Europe and Asia. They are reported from only two streams in the region, the Bronx and Sawmill Rivers near New York City.

Rudd

Scardinius erythrophthalmus (Linnaeus, 1758)

Identification. The rudd is a large, slab-sided minnow with a sharp ridge running along the ventral midline. It has a lateral line that dips ventrally as it progresses along the side. It is most similar to the golden shiner except that it has 12 anal rays instead of 13 and a sharp ridge as opposed to the scaleless fleshy keel of the golden shiner. Adults are often orange in color, and males have bright red fins.

Life History. Little is known of the life history of this species in North America, but in Europe rudd spawn in the spring when the water warms to approximately 65°F. Females are very fecund, producing 80,000–100,000 eggs, which they broadcast over vegetation. These fish feed on crustaceans, aquatic insects, and some plant material.

Distribution. The rudd is an introduced species. It was originally from Europe but has been introduced in many areas of North America, possibly as the result of bait-bucket introductions. It appears to be spreading. At the present time in the region, it is known from Maine, Vermont, Massachusetts, and New York. It prefers quiet water.

Creek Chub

Semotilus atromaculatus (Mitchill, 1818)

Identification. The creek chub, pearl dace, and fallfish are easily recognized by the distinctive placement of the barbel on the maxilla. The *barbel is located up from the tip of the maxilla in the groove between the maxilla and the snout* and is thus sometimes hidden. If you open the mouth by pulling down on the lower jaw, you should easily see the barbel. The creek chub, with a *dark spot at the base of the dorsal fin* and with the *dorsal fin originating behind the origin of the pelvic fin,* is readily distinguished from all other minnows. Its mouth is large, reaching at least to the forward margin of the eye. Its back is olive green, its sides silvery white, and its belly white.

Life History. Creek chubs spawn in small streams in the spring. They build nests from gravel found on the bottom at the nesting site. The male picks up small stones and pebbles with his mouth and moves them a short distance upstream. He thereby excavates a pit downstream from a mound of gravel. He continues working downstream until he has created a long mound of gravel approximately a foot wide and several feet long, which parallels the current. At the downstream end of this mound is a pit, which the creek chubs use for spawning. The male defends this nest from other males in the region. Before long, a female enters the pit, and the male joins her. The male then performs one of the more interesting spawning acts found among our fishes. While resting next to her, head to head, and tail to tail, he slips his pectoral fin under her body, and with the combined effort of his head and pectoral fin he flips her up into a vertical position as if she were standing on her tail. He then wraps himself around her, and the two emit eggs and sperm. The female then drifts downstream, belly up, as if dead. All this takes less than a second or two to accomplish. The female quickly recovers and returns to this nest or another nest to continue spawning until her complement of 3,000–4,000 eggs is exhausted. The male covers the eggs with gravel and then abandons the nest. Creek chubs 7 years old have been collected in New York. They can reach 10 inches or more in length but are more commonly 4–6 inches long. They are opportunistic omnivores, feeding on a wide variety of foods, including insects, small fish, and a substantial amount of plant material. Creek chubs, as their name implies, are primarily inhabitants of streams. They are found in small lakes as well.

Distribution. The creek chub is found from the Maritime Provinces of Canada west to Montana and south to Texas and Georgia. It has been reported from small streams and lakes in all of the states in the Northeast except Rhode Island. It is a common resident of small- to moderate-size streams.

Fallfish

Semotilus corporalis (Mitchill, 1817)

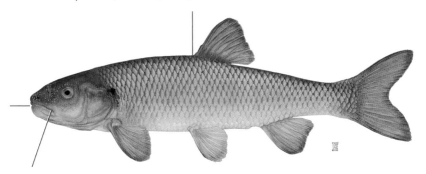

Identification. The fallfish is recognized as a member of the genus *Semotilus* by the *barbel located in the groove between the maxilla and the snout, just up from the tip of the maxilla.* It *lacks a dark spot at the base of the dorsal fin* but has *a large mouth (the maxilla extends to the forward edge of the eye)* and large scales (less than 50 in the lateral line). The fallfish has an olive brown back, olive to silvery sides, and a white ventral surface.

Life History. Fallfish are spring spawners, usually choosing May as the time for their nuptial activities. They prefer quiet water in streams or around the shores of lakes, where there is a clean gravel bottom. The male constructs one of the more spectacular nests among the fishes of the region. He picks up small stones and pebbles with his mouth and carries them to the nest site, piling them into a substantial elongate mound. The nest may reach 6 feet in length and 3 feet in height. A single male spawns over the nest with one or more females, each of which carries approximately 2,000 eggs. The eggs apparently fall into the interstices between the pebbles in the nest. Little is known of the early development of the fallfish. Young fallfish prefer the swifter, shallower water of a stream in contrast to the adults, who remain in deeper, quieter water. The young fish feed on plankton, switching to aquatic insects, crustaceans, and small fishes as they get larger. The fallfish is the largest native freshwater minnow in the region, exceeded in size only by the introduced tench, carp, and goldfish. Fallfish nearly 19 inches long and over 3 pounds in weight have been taken. The typical large fish is closer to 8–12 inches long, however. They have been known to live up to 6 years.

Because fallfish readily take a fly and are relatively large, they have provided a diversion for many anglers looking for trout.

Distribution. The fallfish is found in medium to large, clear, rubble- to gravel-bottom streams in the Atlantic Slope drainages from New Brunswick south to Virginia. It is found in every state in the Northeast.

Tench

Tinca tinca (Linnaeus, 1758)

Identification. Tench are very large minnows, often reaching 12–20 inches in length. They have a large and conspicuous barbel at the corner of their mouth. Their scales are small, 95–105 in the lateral line. They have a nearly square tail with a deep caudal peduncle. The first ray of their dorsal fin is heavy and spinelike in appearance. They are dark olive to light green dorsally, grading to white ventrally.

Life History. Tench occupy quiet vegetated water in lakes or ponds, sometimes in slow-moving stretches of rivers, usually with a mud bottom. They spawn in the spring to early summer in vegetated areas. They feed on a variety of invertebrate prey, including insects and crustaceans.

Distribution. The tench is a European minnow found throughout Europe and western Asia. The U.S. Fish Commission imported it into the United States in 1877. In the Northeast, it has been reported from New York, Connecticut, and Massachusetts. Some populations in these states may no longer be viable.

Suckers

Family Catostomidae

Suckers are soft-rayed fishes without an adipose fin, barbels, jaw teeth, or a pelvic axillary process. They have scales on the body, but none on the head. The lips are usually large and protruding, and the gas bladder is of the physostomous type.

Suckers are occasionally confused with minnows. An easy way to distinguish a sucker from a minnow in the field is to look at the placement of the anal fin on the body. If it is far enough posterior so that the distance from the base of the first anal ray to the base of the caudal fin fits more than two and one-half times into the distance from the front of the anal fin to the tip of the snout, it is a sucker; if less, it is a minnow (see figure 7). Carp and goldfish would be classified as suckers using this rule, but they have a large, hard spinous ray at the front of the dorsal fin; suckers do not.

Worldwide there are approximately fifty-eight known species of suckers. In the Northeast, twelve species have been recorded. These twelve include the quillbacks (*Carpiodes*), distinguishable by the long dorsal fin containing more than 20 principal soft rays; the chubsuckers (*Erimyzon*), whose distinctive characteristic is a complete lack of a lateral line; the hog sucker (*Hypentelium*), identifiable by the concave dorsal surface of the head; the catostomids (*Catostomus*), which have small scales (more than 55 in lateral line); and the redhorses (*Moxostoma*), which have 55 or fewer scales in their lateral line.

Species Key

1a. Dorsal fin long, containing more than 20 principal rays (figure 36)→ **Quillback,** *Carpiodes cyprinus*

1b. Dorsal fin short, containing fewer than 19 principal rays (figure 37)→ **2**

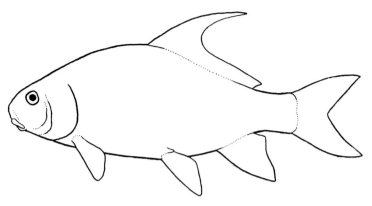

Fig. 36. Quillback sucker.

2a. Lateral line complete and well developed→ **3**

2b. Lateral line missing→ **11**

3a. More than 55 scales in lateral line→ **4**

3b. Fewer than 55 scales in lateral line→ **5**

4a. Bulbous snout projects well beyond tip of upper lip (figure 37a); posterior end of mouth extends back beyond nostrils; reddish lateral band on males in spring; dorsal rays 10; more than 80 scales in lateral line; scales oval in outline, with radii evenly dispersed→ **Longnose Sucker,** *Catostomus catostomus*

4b. Rounded snout projects only slightly, if at all, beyond tip of upper lip (figure 37b); posterior end of mouth extends back only to nostrils; no reddish lateral band on males in spring; dorsal rays 11–12; fewer than 80 scales in lateral line; scales approximately square, without radii in lateral fields→ **White Sucker,** *Catostomus commersoni*

5a. Head depressed between eyes, orbital rims raised (figure 38a); eye posterior to midpoint of head→ **Northern Hog Sucker,** *Hypentelium nigricans*

5b. Head rounded normally between eyes, orbital rims not raised (figure 38b); eye near middle of head (redhorse, *Moxostoma*)→ **6**

6a. Distinct dark spot at forward edge (base) of body; scales above the lateral line; in living specimens, caudal fin is pink to reddish→ **7**

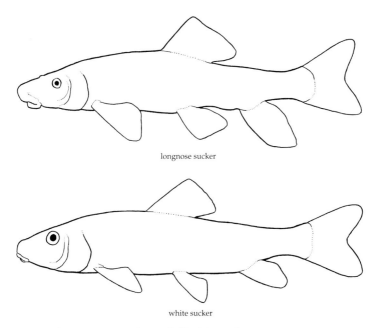

longnose sucker

white sucker

Fig. 37. Snout of (*a*) longnose sucker and (*b*) white sucker.

6b. No distinct dark spot on body scales; caudal fin gray in color→ **9**

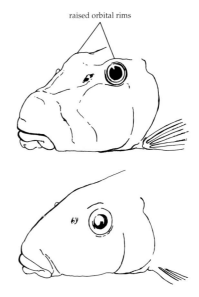

raised orbital rims

7a. Fifteen or sixteen horizontal scale rows cross an imaginary line describing the circumference of the caudal peduncle at its narrowest point, typically 7 above the lateral line, 7 below the lateral line, plus the 2 lateral line scales→ **Greater Redhorse, *Moxostoma valenciennesi***

7b. Twelve or thirteen scale rows cross the circumference of the caudal peduncle at its narrowest point→ **8**

8a. Head relatively small, head length fits into standard length between four and one-third and five and two-fifths times in yearlings

Fig. 38. Heads of (*a*) northern hog sucker and (*b*) redhorse sucker, illustrating concave shape of hog sucker's head.

and adults; mouth small; posterior edge of lower lip nearly a straight line (figure 39, *left*); folds on lower lip divided by transverse grooves, forming papillae; dorsal fin somewhat concave→ **Shorthead Redhorse,** *Moxostoma macrolepidotum*

8b. Head relatively large, head length fits into standard length less than four and one-half times; mouth large; posterior edge of lower lip approximates a 90-degree angle (figure 39, *right*); folds on lower lip not divided by transverse grooves, forming ridges not papillae; dorsal fin almost straight→ **River Redhorse,** *Moxostoma carinatum*

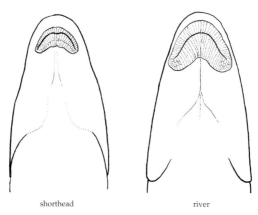

shorthead   river

Fig. 39. Ventral side of head of shorthead redhorse *(left)* and of river redhorse *(right)*.

9a. Dorsal fin has 15 rays; distance from base of first dorsal ray to base of last dorsal ray approximately equal to distance from base of first dorsal ray to back of head; folds on lower lip divided by transverse grooves; joining of right and left half of lower lip forms an angle of approximately 90 degrees (figure 40, *right*)→ **Silver Redhorse,** *Moxostoma anisurum*

9b. Dorsal fin has 12–14 rays; distance from base of first dorsal ray to base of last dorsal ray two-thirds to three-quarters of the distance from base of first dorsal ray to back of head; folds on lower lip not divided by transverse grooves; joining of right and left half of lower lip forms an angle greater than 90 degrees (figure 40, *left*)→ **10**

10a. Lateral line scales 44–47; pelvic rays 10; snout significantly overhangs mouth→ **Black Redhorse,** *Moxostoma duquesnei*

10b. Lateral line scales 40–45; pelvic rays 9; snout barely overhangs mouth, if at all→ **Golden Redhorse,** *Moxostoma erythrurum*

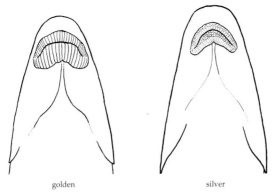

golden   silver

Fig. 40. Lips of golden redhorse *(left)* and silver redhorse *(right)*.

11a. Lateral scale rows 39–41; dorsal rays 9–10; dark markings on sides fused into a dark band in young, but forming distinct vertical bars in adults (figure 41a)→ **Creek Chubsucker,** *Erimyzon oblongus*

11b. Lateral scale rows 35–37; dorsal rays 10–12; dark markings on sides blend into a broad lateral stripe in adults (figure 41b)→ **Lake Chubsucker,** *Erimyzon sucetta*

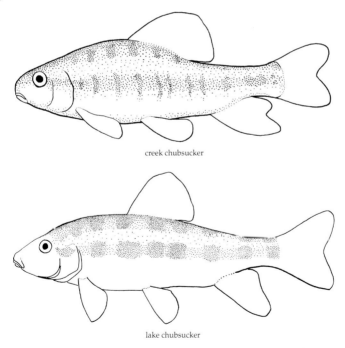

creek chubsucker

lake chubsucker

Fig. 41. Lateral markings on *(a)* creek chubsucker and *(b)* lake chubsucker.

Quillback

Carpiodes cyprinus (LeSueur, 1817)

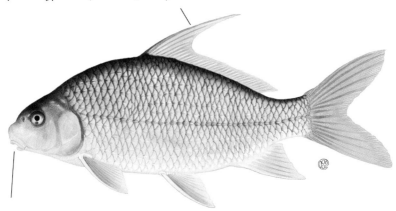

Identification. The quillback is relatively easy to identify with an inferior mouth; no barbels; and a *long dorsal fin containing 25–30 dorsal rays, the anterior rays being two to three times the length of more posterior rays, giving the fin a falcate shape.* It is a large, bulky fish, typically a foot or so long, and is not easily confused with any other sucker. It might be confused with the carp, another large and bulky fish, but the carp has barbels on its mouth and a stout, serrated spine at the front of its dorsal fin. The quillback has neither of these characteristics. It is a light cream to silvery fish, darker on the back and grading to white on the belly.

Life History. The quillback is thought to spawn in the spring or early summer at temperatures between 50 and 68°F. Populations living in lakes spawn in shallow water or enter the lower stretches of tributary rivers. Populations living in rivers move upstream and spawn in small creeks. Quillbacks are broadcast spawners, simply scattering their eggs over the bottom. They are not particular about the type of bottom. Eggs have been found over a range of bottom types, including gravel, mud, and vegetation. Quillbacks feed on a variety of invertebrates taken from the bottom.

Distribution. The quillback inhabits relatively large lakes and rivers throughout the Mississippi drainage east through the lower Great Lakes and St. Lawrence River and along the Atlantic Slope drainages from Delaware to Georgia. In the Northeast, it is found in New York in Lakes Erie, Ontario, and Champlain and in the Allegheny and Susquehanna drainages. It is also found in Vermont but is uncommon there. It is on Vermont's special concern list. It is found nowhere else in the region.

Longnose Sucker

Catostomus catostomus (Forster, 1773)

Identification. The longnose sucker deserves its name because the *snout projects well beyond the tip of its upper lip.* This feature and more than 80 scales in its lateral line distinguish it from all other suckers. The back is dark olive to black, grading to creamy white on the belly. A coppery tone underlies this basic color pattern. During spawning season, a broad rose- or wine-colored lateral band develops.

Life History. Longnose suckers live in cool, clear, deep lakes. They spawn in May or June in swift-flowing tributary streams with gravel bottoms. The male's rose-colored lateral band develops more noticeably at this time than does the female's. Unlike white suckers, longnose suckers appear to spawn in the day. The female releases 10,000–60,000 adhesive eggs over the bottom. The eggs are fertilized upon release and eventually hatch. The young leave the stream and move down into the lake before they are a half inch long, usually at the time that they have absorbed the yolk sac. Upon reaching the lake, they stay in shallow weedy areas until they are 2–6 inches long. They eventually move into deeper water, where the adults are normally found.

   The young initially feed on plankton, switching after several weeks to plant material, midge larvae, and amphipods. Adults feed heavily on midge larvae. The oldest fish reported was 19 years old, but the majority are less than 10 years old. Most fish are less than 24 inches long and less than 4 pounds in weight.

Distribution. The longnose sucker ranges from Siberia through Alaska and Canada and extends down into the northern part of the United States. In the Northeast, it has been reported from all states except Rhode Island.

White Sucker

Catostomus commersoni (Lacépède, 1803)

Identification. The white sucker is distinguishable from all other suckers in the region by having *only 10–13 soft rays in its dorsal fin* and 55–75 scales in its complete lateral line; in addition, *its snout projects very little beyond its upper lip, if at all.* The white sucker is gray to brown on its back, grading to creamy white on its underside.

Life History. White suckers spawn in April or May, moving at night into fast-flowing streams to mate. They seem to prefer gravel bottoms with good current, but some have been reported to spawn in pools or even in lakes. The males develop nuptial tubercles on their anal and caudal fins during the spawning season. Females also occasionally develop small nuptial tubercles. A single large female may carry up to 140,000 eggs, but the average is much lower. After spawning, the adults drop downstream, returning to the lake or deeper parts of the stream. The eggs are adhesive and remain attached to the gravel until hatching, which occurs in 5–10 days. The fry move downstream to deeper water shortly after absorbing their yolk sac. White suckers initially feed on microcrustaceans, rotifers, and algae; as they grow, they feed more commonly on insects, larger crustaceans, snails, and clams. Some anglers have assumed that they feed heavily on trout and salmon eggs, but there is little evidence of this behavior. Young suckers serve as forage for game fish. Suckers appear to be selective in what they eat and do not simply vacuum food off the bottom. White suckers rarely reach 10 years of age, although some dwarf varieties have been aged at 18 years. Adults may reach 18–20 inches and 3–4 pounds.

There are few places in the region where one cannot find white suckers. They are very tolerant of poor environmental conditions, but they can also be found in pristine lakes and streams. In the Northeast, they are one of the most common species in streams and only slightly less common in lakes.

Distribution. The white sucker's range extends from Labrador to the Northwest Territories and south to Oklahoma and Georgia. In the Northeast, it is found throughout the region.

Creek Chubsucker

Erimyzon oblongus (Mitchill, 1814)

Identification. The chubsuckers (*Erimyzon*) are the only suckers in the region *without a lateral line*. The creek chubsucker typically has approximately 40 (37–43) scales in the lateral row of scales (the row of scales where the lateral line would be if the chubsucker had a lateral line) and 8–11 dorsal rays, whereas the lake chubsucker has fewer scales (33–40) in the lateral row and more rays in the dorsal fin (10–13). The creek chubsucker also has a *dark, wide lateral band,* which is most prominent among younger individuals. In adults, it breaks up into a *series of connected dark blotches.* The back is dark brown, grading to a yellow green on the sides and cream on the belly.

Life History. Creek chubsuckers are thought to spawn in April and May, when water temperatures range between 59 and 72°F. Males develop nuptial tubercles and are very aggressive in defending spawning territories. These fish are reported to create a small depression in the bottom in which to lay their eggs. An analysis of stomach contents indicates that they feed on plant material and small crustaceans.

Distribution. Creek chubsuckers are found in small- to moderate-size rivers along the Atlantic Slope from Maine to Georgia and along the Gulf Coast from Florida to Texas. They are also commonly found in the Mississippi drainage from Louisiana north to Illinois and Indiana and then east in southern tributaries of Lakes Michigan, Erie, and Ontario. In the Northeast, they are reported from all states of the region except Vermont.

Lake Chubsucker

Erimyzon sucetta (Lacépède, 1803)

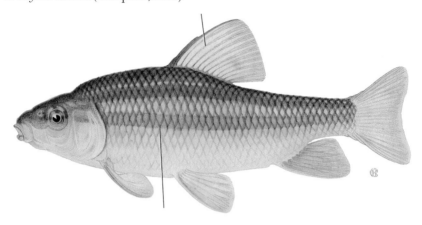

Identification. The lake chubsucker lacks a lateral line and has 35–37 scales in the lateral row and *10–13 dorsal rays.* It has a *distinct dark lateral band that runs from the gill cover back to the base of the tail.* This dark band is often paralleled with a lighter band above it. The back is dark olive green, grading across the sides to a light yellowish green on the ventral surface of body.

Life History. Lake chubsuckers spawn from March to July in bays and the mouths of tributary streams, broadcasting their eggs across the bottom over submerged vegetation. After hatching, young lake chubsuckers tend to stay in shallow, vegetated regions of the lake. Adults feed on small crustaceans and insect larvae.

Distribution. The lake chubsucker is found in quieter water than the creek chubsucker, preferring ponds, marshes, and impoundments. It ranges along the Atlantic Slope from Virginia to Florida and along the Gulf Coast to Texas. It is also found in the Mississippi drainage from Louisiana to Illinois and Indiana and in tributaries to Lakes Michigan, Huron, Erie, and Ontario. In the Northeast, it is found only in New York in tributaries to Lakes Erie and Ontario, where it is considered threatened. There are no records of this species being taken in New York since the 1930s.

Northern Hog Sucker

Hypentelium nigricans (LeSueur, 1817)

Identification. If you lay a straightedge across the top of the head to connect the eyes of a hog sucker, you will see that the head is depressed under the straightedge. This *concavity in the head* is a good field character to distinguish the hog sucker from the rest of the suckers in the Northeast, all of whom have a rounded dorsal surface to the head. The back is olive brown, grading through light brown or yellow on the sides to white on the belly. The back and sides are marked with *4–5 irregular dark saddles,* another good field character.

Life History. The hog sucker spawns in the spring, in April and May, in swift-flowing streams over sand or gravel, as do many other suckers. After the eggs hatch, however, the hog sucker remains in the stream. It is characteristically a stream fish, preferring clear and swift-moving water. It drops downstream into deeper areas to spend the winter. When the water temperature rises to approximately 60°F in the spring, it begins to move upstream, searching out rocky riffles for spawning sites. The hog sucker's food consists of a variety of bottom insects and crustaceans found in streams. It can reach 10–14 inches in length and 1–1½ pounds in weight. Nine-year-old individuals have been found, but the majority live less than 5 years.

Distribution. The hog sucker ranges from New York south to Alabama and west to Oklahoma and Minnesota. In the Northeast, it is found only in New York in the Great Lakes-St. Lawrence, Allegheny, Susquehanna, and Hudson drainages.

Silver Redhorse

Moxostoma anisurum (Rafinesque, 1820)

Identification. Suckers in the genus *Moxostoma* are relatively large, brassy-colored fish with a complete lateral line, rounded head, short dorsal fin, and fewer than 50 scales in their lateral line. The silver redhorse has *12 or 13 scale rows that cross an imaginary line describing the circumference of the caudal peduncle at its narrowest point. It also lacks dark spots at the base of the scales along its side. Its lips have folds that are subdivided by small cross grooves* (see figure 40, *right*). The dorsal fin has 13–17 rays. The back is brown to olive, grading to silver on the sides and belly.

Life History. The silver redhorse is thought to spawn earlier than most suckers, beginning when water temperatures approach 56°F, over gravel on riffles of rivers and streams. After hatching, the young drift downstream to quieter water. The silver redhorse feeds on aquatic insects, crayfish, mollusks, and some plant material. It may reach 2 feet in length and approach 7 pounds.

Distribution. The silver redhorse is found in streams and rivers along the Atlantic Slope from Virginia to Georgia and in the Ohio River, upper Mississippi, and Great Lakes drainages. In the Northeast, it is reported only from New York and Vermont, and it is a species of special concern in Vermont.

River Redhorse

Moxostoma carinatum (Cope, 1870)

Identification. The river redhorse has 12 or 13 scale rows that intersect the circumference of the caudal peduncle at its narrowest point, as in the silver redhorse. Its lips have folds that are not well divided by small cross grooves (see figure 39, *right*). It has a relatively large head and mouth, and the posterior edge of its mouth is slightly scalloped. The back is olive to bronze, grading to a manila color on the belly. It has dark spots on the base of the scales on the upper side of its body.

Life History. The river redhorse spawns later than most redhorses, typically over gravel shoals in rivers. In Quebec, evidence suggests that it may spawn from mid-June to early July. In Wisconsin, ripe adults were taken at temperatures ranging from 68–74°F. Males construct a nest, often 4–8 feet in diameter, which is unusual for suckers. They swim back and forth over the nest and eventually are joined by a female. Eggs are fertilized, deposited on the nest, and eventually covered with gravel. River redhorses feed primarily on mollusks and some aquatic insect larvae. They approach 30 inches in length and 11 pounds in weight.

Distribution. The river redhorse is found most commonly in the middle Mississippi River drainage. A disjunct population does exist in the Ottawa and St. Lawrence River drainages. In the Northeast, it is reported only from the Allegheny River drainage of New York. As its name implies, it is most commonly found in large rivers. Many river redhorse populations may be declining because of increased silt and turbidity in large rivers. In addition, declining clam and snail populations in rivers affect mollusk-feeding fishes such as the river redhorse.

Black Redhorse

Moxostoma duquesnei (LeSueur, 1817)

Identification. The black redhorse has 12–13 rays in its dorsal fin; no dark spots at the base of scales on its sides; 44–47 lateral line scales; 10 pelvic rays; and a snout that significantly overhangs the mouth. The back is dark brown, grading to silver on the belly.

Life History. Studies in Missouri show that black redhorses spawn in gravel shoals of rivers when water temperatures are between 56 and 72°F. After hatching, the young move into quieter water. Black redhorses feed on aquatic insects, crustaceans, and other invertebrates and may reach 10–16 inches and approximately 1 pound in weight.

Distribution. The black redhorse is found from the upper Mississippi River drainage east to New York and south to Alabama and the Ozark Mountains. In the Northeast, it is found only in New York in the Lake Erie and Ontario drainages and in the Allegheny River and its tributaries. It is uncommon, however, and is on New York State's special concern list. It prefers relatively clear, medium to large streams and rivers with moderate current.

Golden Redhorse

Moxostoma erythrurum (Rafinesque, 1818)

Identification. The golden redhorse has *12–13 rays in its dorsal fin;* no dark spots at the base of the scales on its sides; 40–45 lateral line scales; 9 pelvic rays; and a *snout that barely overhangs the mouth, if at all.* The back of the golden redhorse is gray to brown, grading to olive or golden on the sides and white on the belly.

Life History. Golden redhorses spawn over gravel shoals in rivers in the late spring when water temperatures approach 70°F. After hatching, the young drift into quiet water along the edges of the river. These fish feed on aquatic insects, mollusks, and some crustaceans. They may reach 1½–2 feet in length and 2–5 pounds in weight.

Distribution. Golden redhorses are found from the southern Great Lakes drainage east to New York and south to Alabama and Missouri. In the Northeast, they are found only in New York in the Allegheny, Genesee, Lake Erie, and Ontario drainages. They prefer moderate to large streams.

Shorthead Redhorse

Moxostoma macrolepidotum (LeSueur, 1817)

Identification. The shorthead redhorse's *head is small, fitting between four and one-third and five and one-half times into the standard length in yearlings and adults.* It has *12 or 13 scale rows across the circumference of the caudal peduncle* and a distinct *dark spot near the point of attachment of the scales above the lateral line.* In living specimens, the tail tends to be reddish in color, which contrasts with an olive- to brassy-colored body. The posterior edge of the lower lip is nearly straight. The folds on the lower lip are divided by transverse grooves (see figure 39, *left*).

Life History. Spawning of shorthead redhorses is similar to that of other redhorses. They migrate out of lakes into tributary streams, choosing shallow areas with sand to gravel bottoms and rapidly flowing, deeper water nearby. In Wisconsin, they spawn in April and May at water temperatures of 47–61°F. They are broadcast spawners, scattering eggs in small groups across the bottom. After hatching, young are found in areas with little current. Shorthead redhorses feed on bottom insects. They may approach 2 feet in length and 8–10 pounds in weight.

Distribution. The shorthead redhorse is widespread in the Mississippi, Missouri, Great Lakes-St. Lawrence, and Atlantic Slope drainages. In the Northeast, it is found only in New York and Vermont in moderate to large streams with rapidly flowing water.

Greater Redhorse

Moxostoma valenciennesi (Jordan, 1885)

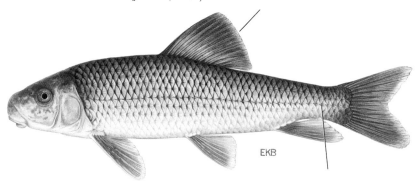

EKB

Identification. The greater redhorse is the only redhorse to have *15–16 horizontal scale rows that cross an imaginary line describing the circumference of the caudal peduncle at its narrowest point. The dorsal fin is convex in adults.* The back of the greater redhorse is dark brown to copper, grading to yellowish on the sides and eventually to white on the belly. The fins are often a bright orange color.

Life History. In the Thousand Islands section of the St. Lawrence River, greater redhorses spawn from June 28 to July 8 when water temperatures are 62–66°F. They choose spawning sites over large rubble and boulders in water around 10 feet deep, somewhat deeper than other suckers. They feed on crustaceans, mollusks, and aquatic insects. The greater redhorse is the largest of the redhorses and may approach 13 pounds in weight.

Distribution. The greater redhorse is found from the St. Lawrence River west through the Great Lakes to Wisconsin and south to southern Indiana and Ohio. In the Northeast, it is found only in New York and Vermont. In New York, it has been reported from Lakes Erie, Ontario, Oneida, and Champlain as well as from the St. Lawrence and Niagara Rivers. In Vermont, it is a species of special concern.

Bullhead Catfishes

Family Ictaluridae

The catfishes are scaleless fishes with flattened heads and a wide mouth surrounded by 8 barbels equipped with taste buds. The dorsal and pectoral fins are armed with a stout spinous ray, which in some species, notably the madtoms, is poisonous.

Approximately forty-eight bullhead catfish species are known, all from North America. There are nine species in the Northeast.

Species Key

1a. Adipose fin flaplike, free at posterior margin, not fused with back and caudal fin (figure 42, *top*); moderate to large fish→ **2**

1b. Adipose fin attached to back and fused with caudal fin, no free end (figure 42, *bottom*); small fish, usually less than 6 inches→ **6**

2a. Caudal fin slightly rounded, not deeply forked (figure 43a)→ **3**

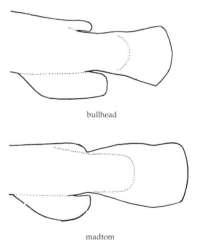

bullhead

madtom

Fig. 42. Attachment of adipose fin distinguishing bullheads *(top)* from madtoms *(bottom)*.

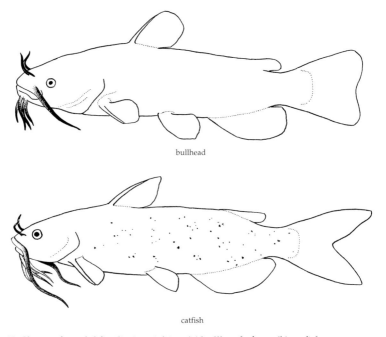

bullhead

catfish

Fig. 43. Shape of caudal fin distinguishing *(a)* bullheads from *(b)* catfishes.

2b. Caudal fin distinctly forked (figure 43b)→ **5**

3a. Four predominantly white barbels under jaw; anal rays 24–27, including rudimentary rays→ **Yellow Bullhead,** *Ameiurus natalis*

3b. Barbels under jaw are gray or black, not white; anal rays 15–24, including rudimentary rays→ **4**

4a. Posterior edge of pectoral spine has stout barbs (grasp pectoral spine between thumb and forefinger, with thumb at posterior edge of spine, and pull outward; thumb should be held by barbs; see figure 44); 21–24 anal rays, including rudimentary rays at front of fin; 13–16 gill rakers; mottled coloration without a white bar at base of caudal fin→ **Brown Bullhead,** *Ameiurus nebulosus*

4b. Posterior edge of pectoral spine without stout barbs; 15–21 anal rays, including rudimentary rays; 17–20 gill rakers; body not mottled, but with a white bar at base of caudal fin→ **Black Bullhead,** *Ameiurus melas*

5a. Body with black spots (more prominent in young individuals, spots fade on fish larger than 12 inches); anal rays 24–30; tail deeply forked, the shortest rays in caudal fin are less than half the length of the longest rays; lobes of tail pointed→ **Channel Catfish,** *Ictalurus punctatus*

5b. No black spots on body; anal rays 19–23; tail shallowly forked, the shortest rays in caudal fin are more than half the length of the longest rays; lobes of tail bluntly pointed→ **White Catfish,** *Ameiurus catus*

6a. Posterior edge of pectoral spine without barbs or teeth (feels smooth when you rub it with a finger; you must take care, however, not to allow poisonous spine to puncture skin)→ **7**

6b. Posterior edge of pectoral spine with strong barbs or teeth (figure 44)→ **8**

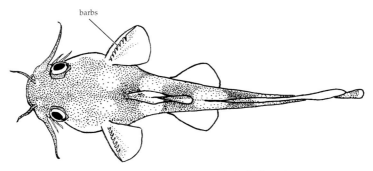

Fig. 44. Barbs on posterior edge of pectoral spine of brindled madtom.

7a. Premaxillary tooth patch without backward extensions (figure 45, *top*); jaws of about equal length; stocky body with oval caudal fin→ **Tadpole Madtom,** *Noturus gyrinus*

premaxillary tooth patch without backward extension

7b. Premaxillary tooth patch in upper jaw with curved extensions projecting backward (figure 45, *bottom*); upper jaw extends beyond lower jaw; slender bodied with elongate, rectangular caudal fin→ **Stonecat,** *Noturus flavus*

backward extension of premaxillary tooth patch

Fig. 45. Shape of premaxillary tooth patch with *(bottom)* and without *(top)* backward lateral extensions.

8a. Pectoral spine with moderate-length barbs (barbs do not exceed half the diameter of the pectoral spine); body without dark blotches; elongate body; dark margins on dorsal, caudal, and anal fins→ **Margined Madtom,** *Noturus insignis*

8b. Pectoral spine with large barbs (barbs exceed half the diameter of the pectoral spine; see figure 44); stocky body distinctly blotched→ **Brindled Madtom,** *Noturus miurus*

White Catfish

Ameiurus catus (Linnaeus, 1758)

Identification. The white catfish and the channel catfish are the only two members of this family in the region that have a *deeply forked tail* and an *adipose fin whose posterior end is free of the back.* Bullheads have a square to rounded tail, and the madtoms and stonecats' adipose fin is joined to the tail. The white catfish is distinguishable from the channel catfish in that it lacks black spots on its body and has *19–23 anal rays* instead of the 24–30 found in the channel catfish. It tends to be lighter in color than the channel catfish, with a gray to brown back, grading to a whitish belly. The barbels on the chin are white.

Life History. White catfish spawn in the summer when the water has warmed to approximately 70°F. They choose a site with a gravel or sand bottom, and both male and female clear out a depression to deposit the eggs. The nest can be up to 3 feet in diameter and a foot or so deep. They guard the eggs in the nest until they hatch. Adults are quite omnivorous, feeding on a variety of foods, including crustaceans, aquatic insects, and fish. As they get larger, they seem to prefer fish when available.

Distribution. White catfish are found in Atlantic coastal states from Maine to Florida and are reported from all of the states in the Northeast. They can tolerate some salinity and thus are often found in or near estuarine waters. They are also found in freshwater streams and small rivers.

Black Bullhead

Ameiurus melas (Rafinesque, 1820)

Identification. The black bullhead is distinguished by an adipose fin that is free of the back and tail; a caudal fin that is square to rounded; gray to black barbels under its chin; no barbs on the pectoral spine; 17–20 gill rakers; and 15–21 anal rays. The color of the black bullhead is dark brown to black on its back and upper sides, grading rapidly to light cream or white on its belly, and with a distinctive light bar at the base of its caudal fin.

Life History. Black bullheads may spawn over an extended period of time from April to July at temperatures ranging from 53 to 77°F. They build saucer-shaped nests in heavily vegetated areas and deposit eggs in gelatinous masses on the nest. The adults move the egg mass and fan it with their fins to provide oxygen to the developing eggs. Adults guard the nests and protect the young until they reach approximately an inch in length. These large aggregations of darkly pigmented young, with an accompanying adult, are often seen along the shores of lakes, ponds, and marshes where the vegetation is abundant. Black bullheads are omnivorous, feeding on aquatic insect larvae, crustaceans, mollusks, and plant material. As with other members of this family, they have taste buds on their barbels, which facilitates locating prey, particularly at night.

Distribution. The black bullhead ranges from Montana east to the Great Lakes and St. Lawrence River south to Alabama and Texas. In the Northeast, it is reported only from New York and from the Connecticut and Housatonic drainages in Connecticut. It prefers quiet, heavily vegetated water, either in low-gradient streams or in ponds or small lakes.

Yellow Bullhead

Ameiurus natalis (LeSueur, 1819)

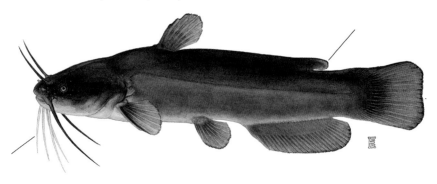

Identification. The yellow bullhead is the only bullhead to have *white barbels under its jaw.* It also has an *adipose fin free of the back and tail,* a *square to rounded caudal fin,* and 24–27 anal rays. Its color varies but is generally dark brown to olive brown on the back, grading to light tan or yellow on the belly.

Life History. Yellow bullheads may spawn a little earlier in the spring than other bullheads, usually over a short period in May or June. They construct nests in quiet water along the shores of rivers and ponds, often near a log or overhanging bank. Adults guard the nests and protect the young until they are ready to leave. Yellow bullheads feed on a variety of food items, including aquatic insects, mollusks, crustaceans, and, on occasion, fish.

Distribution. Yellow bullheads range from North Dakota and Texas to the Atlantic coastal states. In the Northeast, they are reported from all of the states except Maine and Rhode Island. They are more commonly found in relatively clear streams and ponds than are other bullheads.

Brown Bullhead

Ameiurus nebulosus (LeSueur, 1819)

Identification. The brown bullhead is readily distinguished by its *square to rounded caudal fin, free adipose fin, dark barbels under its jaw,* 13–16 gill rakers, and the large barbs on the inside edge of the pectoral spine. The black bullhead has much smaller barbs on its spines, and the yellow bullhead has white barbels under its chin. Coloration of the brown bullhead is mottled and quite variable but is basically dark brown to black on the back, grading through gray, green, and yellow on the sides to a yellowish cream on the belly.

Life History. Brown bullheads spawn in late spring or early summer, usually in shallow water at water temperatures between 62 and 72°F. The male constructs an irregular nest, preferring a site with some shelter, such as a log or rock. By lying close to the bottom and actively vibrating his body, the male is able to clear a space for the nest. Spawning takes place with the female lying side by side with the male. She releases 2,000–14,000 eggs as a result of several spawning acts. Both parents remain nearby: one, usually the male, guarding the nest; the other, presumably the female, incubating the eggs. Incubation consists of a rather violent agitation of the eggs by movement of the female's fins and body. If the eggs are removed from the nest and incubated under conditions of flow and oxygen concentration suitable for rearing trout eggs, they die. The only way the eggs can be induced to hatch is to place them in a container in which the flow is strong enough to cause them to be violently agitated. It is thought that the thick gelatinous sheath covering the eggs protects them from mechanical shock but inhibits oxygen movement to the egg, thus the need for a great deal of agitation. Incubation lasts 5–20 days. The young remain on the nest for a time after hatching, developing the characteristic coal black coloration. They eventually leave, swimming about in a tight aggregation of very black, small bullheads called a pod. The parents swim near the young, acting somewhat like sheep dogs, keeping the pod under control. This is a very characteristic trait of bullheads that can easily be observed in ponds or lakes during the summer because the young fish often swim quite near the surface.

Brown bullheads up to 6 years old have been caught. It is likely that they may live longer. They commonly grow to 14–16 inches in length and 1–2 pounds in weight. They are omnivorous, feeding at night with the aid of their barbels. The barbels contain very sensitive chemical receptors that enable the bullhead to locate its prey. Brown bullheads are found in lakes and ponds throughout the region. They prefer standing water to flowing streams. During the winter, they are known to bury themselves with their mouths protruding from the bottom mud, where they remain until the water warms up in the spring.

The bullhead is an excellent food fish. Its flesh is light and tasty, and it is easy to catch. Bullhead fishing is best done at night, using live bait such as worms or bits of fish.

Distribution. Brown bullheads range across southern Canada to the Great Lakes and south to Arkansas and Florida. They are found in all states in the Northeast. The brown bullhead is one of the most common species in lakes and relatively common in rivers in the Northeast.

Channel Catfish

Ictalurus punctatus (Rafinesque, 1818)

Identification. The channel catfish is characterized by a *deeply forked caudal fin;* a free adipose fin; *dark spots scattered along its side,* particularly in juveniles and females; and 24–30 anal rays. The only other catfish with a deeply forked caudal fin is the white catfish (*Ameiurus catus*), which has 19–23 anal rays and no spots. The color of the channel catfish is black to bluish gray on its back, grading to creamy white on its belly.

Life History. The spawning behavior of the channel catfish is similar to that of the brown bullhead except that channel catfish frequently spawn in streams or rivers over a broad range of temperatures from 65 to 85°F. Channel catfish also live longer and get much larger, some reaching 24 years of age and 13 pounds. The average, however, is considerably less. They live in large streams, rivers, or lakes with rocky or sandy bottoms. They are not normally associated with heavily vegetated habitat, as are the bullheads. They feed at night on all types of aquatic organisms.

The channel catfish is an excellent food fish as well as an excellent sport fish, providing fine angling when taken from swift water. They currently are being commercially reared in ponds in the southern United States.

Distribution. This fish was originally found throughout the central part of the United States from Florida north along the western slopes of the Appalachians to Canada, west to Montana, and south to northern Mexico. It has since been introduced east of the Appalachians and westward to California. Channel catfish are found in all states of the Northeast except Maine and Rhode Island.

Stonecat

Noturus flavus Rafinesque, 1818

Identification. The stonecats and madtoms (genus *Noturus*) are easily distinguished from other catfishes in that they are small fish whose *adipose fin is joined tightly to the back and caudal fin*. There is no free end to the adipose fin as there is in the bullheads and catfishes. Three other species of madtoms are known for the region: the margined madtom (*Noturus insignis),* tadpole madtom (*Noturus gyrinus),* and brindled madtom (*Noturus miurus).* The stonecat is a *slender, elongate fish* with a patch of teeth in the upper jaw associated with the premaxillary bones and extending backward from the lateral corner of the upper part of the mouth (figure 45, *bottom*). This character is not found in any of the other madtoms. The tadpole madtom has no barbs on the posterior margin of its pectoral spine, whereas the margined and brindled madtoms have at least some type of barbs on their pectoral fins. The brindled madtom's barbs are more than half the diameter of its pectoral spine (figure 44). The margined madtom's barb is less than half the diameter of the spine.

Color varies from olive to slate gray dorsally, grading to a grayish white ventrally.

Life History. The stonecat spawns in a nest located under rocks or other overhanging shelter throughout the summer from June through August. It spawns in lakes, in creek mouths, and at the edge of riffle areas in streams. Both parents guard the eggs. Stonecats feed primarily at night on aquatic insects, but molluscs, crayfish, and small fish make up a significant portion of their diet.

Distribution. The stonecat ranges from Montana and Arkansas east to the Great Lakes and St. Lawrence River and southwest of the Appalachians to Alabama. In the Northeast, it is found only in New York and Vermont, and it is endangered in Vermont. It prefers streams with rapidly flowing water and with large rocks or boulders on the bottom to provide shelter. It may also be found along the edges of large lakes with wave-swept shorelines.

Tadpole Madtom

Noturus gyrinus (Mitchill, 1817)

Identification. The tadpole madtom is a thick-bodied fish with an *attached adipose fin; well-developed procurrent rays at the anterior edge of its caudal fin, creating a fanlike shape to the fin;* no backward extension of teeth in its upper jaw; and no barbs on the posterior margin of its pectoral spine. Its color is dark gray or brown to grayish olive, darker on the back and shading to lighter hues on the belly. No distinct markings are obvious on the body.

Life History. Tadpole madtoms spawn in June or July along the shores of lakes or ponds and in slow-moving streams over a vegetated or mud bottom. They normally choose to deposit their eggs in sites under logs, rocks, or boards and, in some cases, in old tin cans. They feed primarily at night on small insects and crustaceans.

Distribution. Tadpole madtoms range from North Dakota to the St. Lawrence River to Florida and Texas. They are absent from the Appalachian Mountains. In the Northeast, they are found in the Great Lakes, Hudson, and Delaware drainages in New York; the Merrimack drainage in New Hampshire; and the Chicopee and Thames drainages in Massachusetts. They are found both in lakes and in moderate to large rivers. They are more likely to be found in lakes than are other madtoms.

Margined Madtom

Noturus insignis (Richardson, 1836)

Identification. The margined madtom has an *attached adipose fin,* relatively small barbs on its pectoral spine, and *dark margins on its dorsal, caudal, and anal fins; it lacks the well-developed procurrent rays of the caudal fin found in the tadpole madtom;* and there is no backward lateral extension to the premaxillary tooth patch in its upper jaw. The back is olive to gray, grading to yellowish white on the belly. The margins of the dorsal, caudal, and anal fins have a dark band slightly in from the outer edge, leading to the common name.

Life History. Margined madtoms spawn in midsummer, probably late June. Females produce approximately 100 eggs during spawning. Little is known of their spawning behavior. They reach sexual maturity during their second or third summer and usually live for only 4 or 5 years. They feed on insects and small fish, growing to 5–6 inches.

Distribution. Margined madtoms are found east of the Allegheny Mountains from Lake Ontario to Georgia. They are found in the Finger Lakes, Mohawk-Hudson, Delaware, and Susquehanna drainages in New York and in the Merrimack drainage in New Hampshire and Massachusetts. They prefer streams with relatively clear water and rock or coarse gravel bottoms.

Brindled Madtom

Noturus miurus Jordan, 1877

Identification. The brindled madtom is distinguished by an *adipose fin that is attached to the back and tail; large barbs on its pectoral spine,* and a distinctly *mottled coloration.* It lacks the distinct procurrent rays of the tadpole madtom, and it has no backward lateral extensions of the premaxillary tooth patch on the roof of its mouth. The back has dark blotches interspersed between lighter areas, a pattern that extends to a lesser degree down the sides. The fins often have dark blotches, and the tail has a dark band around its periphery. The belly is white.

Life History. Little is known of the life history of this species. In Michigan, it spawns relatively late in the summer when the water temperature has reached 78°F along the shore of lakes. It also spawns in quiet water in slow-moving streams. It builds nests under an overhanging object when available and tolerates a broad range of bottom types, from rock and gravel to mud and vegetation.

Distribution. The brindled madtom ranges south from the Lake Erie and Ontario drainages to the Ohio and Mississippi River drainages on to Louisiana. In the Northeast, it is known from the Mohawk, Allegheny, and Lake Ontario drainages in New York. It prefers the lower reaches of streams with vegetation and relatively soft bottoms.

Pikes

Family Esocidae

Pike are elongate physostomous fishes with the dorsal and anal fin located far back near the forked caudal fin. The head and particularly the snout are somewhat flattened. The jaws are well armed with teeth. The family comprises five species, four of which are found in the Northeast.

Species Key

1a. Prominent dark vertical bar extends downward from eye; operculum and cheeks completely scaled (figure 46a); dorsal and caudal fins without dark markings→ **2**

1b. Dark vertical bar under eye absent or faint; lower half of operculum without scales; cheeks may or may not be completely scaled (figures 46b and 46c); dorsal and caudal fins with dark markings→ **3**

2a. Dark vertical or oblique bars on sides of body; snout shorter, distance from snout tip to center of pupil less than distance from center of pupil to posterior edge of operculum; branchiostegal rays usually 11–13→ **Grass/Redfin Pickerel, *Esox americanus***

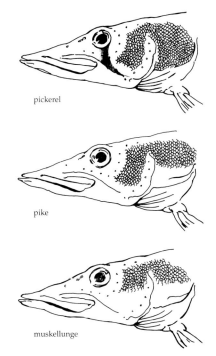

Fig. 46. Scale pattern on cheek and operculum of *(a)* pickerel, *(b)* pike, and *(c)* muskellunge.

2b. Dark chainlike pattern on sides of body; snout longer, distance from snout tip to center of pupil greater than distance from center of pupil to posterior edge of operculum; branchiostegal rays usually 14–17→ **Chain Pickerel,** *Esox niger*

3a. Cheek completely scaled; operculum scaled on upper half only (figure 46b); light spots on body and vertical fins; mandibular pores 5 or fewer (figure 47); branchiostegal rays 14–16→ **Northern Pike,** *Esox lucius*

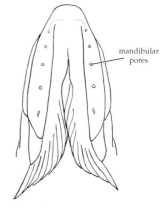

mandibular pores

3b. Cheek and operculum without scales on lower half (figure 46c); dark spots or bars on body and vertical fins; mandibular pores 6–9; branchiostegal rays 17–19→ **Muskellunge,** *Esox masquinongy*

Fig. 47. Under side of northern pike's head showing mandibular pores.

Grass Pickerel

Esox americanus vermiculatus LeSueur, 1846

Redfin Pickerel

Esox americanus americanus Gmelin, 1788

Identification. Pickerel are easily distinguished from pike and muskellunge in that *both their cheek and operculum are completely scaled;* they have a *dark vertical bar extending down from the eye,* but no markings on the dorsal and anal fins. The grass or redfin pickerel has a shorter snout than the chain pickerel and lacks the chainlike markings on the side. There are two subspecies of *Esox americanus* in the region: the grass pickerel (*E. americanus vermiculatus)* and the redfin pickerel (*E. americanus americanus).* Living specimens of the two can be distinguished by their head profiles. The *snout of the redfin pickerel, when viewed from the side, has a slightly less-concave upper profile;* the redfin also has more than 6 notched scales between the pelvic fins. The *grass pickerel has a slightly more concave upper profile* and up to 3 notched scales between the pelvic fins. The redfin pickerel is dark green dorsally, grading to white ventrally, with vertical dark bars on the sides below the lateral line. The grass pickerel is similar in coloration but a bit lighter in tone.

Life History. All members of the family spawn in the early spring shortly after the ice goes out. Ripe adult grass or redfin pickerel move into marshes, flooded meadows, or shallow bays to spawn. The eggs are broadcast in water less than 2 feet deep, each female producing between 750 and 4,600 eggs. No parental care is given to the young because the adults leave the marsh shortly after spawning. The young grow rapidly, initially feeding on zooplankton, then insects, and eventually small fish. Grass and redfin pickerel are sight feeders and thus feed only in the day. They live for approximately 7 years, achieving a length of 10–12 inches. They prefer living in a habitat with a dense stand of submerged aquatic vegetation, usually in slow-moving streams or lakes. In large lakes and rivers, they are more commonly found in stream mouths entering the lake or river than in the larger bodies of water themselves.

Grass or redfin pickerel, although not large, are scrappy fish when taken on light gear. The flesh is delicately flavored and tasty, but bony.

Distribution. The grass pickerel is primarily a subspecies of the Midwest and thus is found in the Allegheny, Lake Erie, Lake Ontario, and St. Lawrence drainages of New York. The redfin pickerel is more of a coastal subspecies and is found in all of the New England states and in the Hudson, Delaware, and Long Island drainages in eastern New York.

Chain Pickerel

Esox niger LeSueur, 1818

Identification. The chain pickerel is distinguishable from the grass or redfin pickerel by a longer snout and by the presence of *chainlike markings along the sides of its body.* In addition, if you turn either pickerel over and look at the underside of its gill covers, you will see a series of slender bones supporting the membranous portion of the edge of the gill cover. These bones are called branchiostegal rays. The chain pickerel has 14–17 branchiostegal rays, whereas the grass or redfin pickerel has 11–13. The chain pickerel's back and sides are olive green to brown, grading to white on the belly. Its sides are overlain with yellowish green blotches, which cause the darker green background color to form chainlike markings on the sides.

Life History. Chain pickerel spawn in marshy areas and shallow bays shortly after the ice goes out in the spring. Spawning lasts for approximately 7–10 days, and then the adults leave the spawning grounds. The eggs hatch in 6–12 days, and the young reach 4–5 inches by the end of September. They reach sexual maturity at age 3 or 4. In many populations, few fish live much beyond this age, although some 8- to 9-year-old individuals have been found. Larval chain pickerel initially feed on plankton, switching to insects during their first summer and finally to fish before they are 1 year old. Most adult chain pickerel are 15–18 inches long and weigh approximately $1\frac{1}{2}$ pounds.

Because chain pickerel reach a larger size, they are more important to the sport fishery than grass or redfin pickerel. If you use light spinning gear or a fly rod and a good minnow imitation as a lure, and you fish parallel to the edge of a weed bed, you are bound to get some action and a good fight from chain pickerel. They are active most of the year and can be taken through the ice.

Distribution. The chain pickerel is generally found east of the Appalachians from Nova Scotia south to Florida and west across the Gulf Coast to Texas. It is found in a variety of habitats, from heavily vegetated shallow water to deeper regions in lakes to streams or rivers in all states in the Northeast.

Northern Pike

Esox lucius Linnaeus, 1758

Identification. The northern pike *lacks scales on the lower half of its operculum,* thus separating it from the pickerels. The color pattern gives the impression of having *light spots on a dark background.* The muskellunge, in contrast, has dark spots on a lighter background and no scales on the lower half of either the cheek or operculum. The dark background color of the pike is green to brown. It is darker on the back and shades to a lighter greenish brown on the sides and eventually to a milky white on the belly. The sides are marked with oblong yellowish green spots.

Life History. Pike spawn early in the spring, shortly after the ice breaks up. They move inshore, usually at night, seeming to prefer shallow marshes or flooded meadows. The spawning run usually lasts 2–3 weeks. Spawning occurs in daylight and begins with a female leading several males slowly around the edge of the marsh in water about a foot deep. They periodically line up close to one another; she releases eggs, which the males fertilize. The males often slap the female with their tails at this time, creating an easily discernible commotion for anyone near the marsh to see. The process continues for several hours until the female has broadcast all of her eggs, which could be as many as 100,000. The eggs hatch in about 2 weeks, and the young begin feeding on microscopic crustaceans and small insects. It is not long, however, before they begin feeding on small fish, which remain the major part of their diet for the rest of their lives. Northern pike are found in clear lakes as well as in rivers and generally prefer shallow, weedy habitats. Adults are very predaceous, feeding on perches, shiners, frogs, crayfish, and even young waterfowl. Some northern pike have been shown to live up to 26 years. They reach sexual maturity at 2–5 years. They can approach 50 pounds in weight, but the average fish caught is usually less than 10 pounds.

Northern pike are caught by anglers year round but seem to be most readily taken in the spring after the spawning run, when they are exceptionally hungry. They will strike almost any lure and are readily caught on live bait.

Distribution. The northern pike's range extends in a wide band through the northern portion of North America, Europe, and Asia. In North America, its range is from Alaska to Missouri east to the Appalachian Mountains. It is found in all states in the Northeast but is native to only the Great Lakes and Allegheny drainages. It has expanded its range into the rest of the Northeast, most recently into Maine in the Belgrade Lakes and Androscoggin drainages.

Muskellunge

Esox masquinongy Mitchill, 1824

Identification. With *no scales on the lower half of either the cheek or operculum;* no dark bar below the eye; and a body that has *dark spots or bars on a lighter background,* the muskellunge is easily separated from other members of the pike family. The back and sides are green to light brown, and the belly and undersides are cream. The sides are decorated with dark brown or black markings.

Life History. Spawning of muskellunge occurs in the spring, just after the northern pike have spawned, commonly in May. Mature adults move from deeper water into shallow bays and marshy areas. The spawning behavior is similar to that of the northern pike. Each female may produce up to 200,000 eggs. The eggs hatch in 1–3 weeks, and the young begin feeding 10–14 days later. For the first few days, the young muskellunge feed on microscopic crustaceans, but after a week or two has elapsed, they switch to small fish as a food source. They persist in this habit for the rest of their lives, supplementing the fish diet with an occasional salamander, duckling, shrew, or even small muskrat. Muskellunge may live up to 20 years and approach 70 pounds in weight. The average, however, is much less.

Because the muskellunge is normally the largest predatory fish in any body of freshwater in the region, it is an important contributor to the sport fishery wherever it is abundant, such as the St. Lawrence River and Chautauqua Lake in New York. Many anglers spend a great deal of time searching for one of the great fishing thrills—the capture of a large muskellunge.

A hybrid between the northern pike and muskellunge called the tiger musky has been widely stocked in the region. It has the desirable trait of growing to a large size quickly and producing sterile males so that the population cannot reproduce.

Distribution. The muskellunge is found only in eastern North America from Ontario and Quebec south to Georgia. It is found in New York, Vermont, Maine, and Connecticut, usually preferring shallow, heavily vegetated areas, but can also be found in water up to 40 feet deep. In Maine, it has recently been found in Baker Lake in the St. John drainage. In New York, it is found in Chautauqua Lake, the St. Lawrence River, Lakes Ontario and Erie, Lake Champlain, and the Oswegatchie drainage. In Vermont, it is most abundant in Lake Champlain. Muskellunge were introduced in Connecticut in the Connecticut and Thames Rivers.

Mudminnows
Family Umbridae

Mudminnows are small, dark fish with rounded caudal fins, nonprotractile jaws, slightly flattened heads, and short snouts. Their gas bladder is connected to the esophagus, so they have some capacity to breathe air. They inhabit slow, stagnant waters frequently low in oxygen, conditions to which they are well adapted. Five species comprise the family, two of which occur in the Northeast.

Species Key

1a. Body marked with thin, dark brown, longitudinal stripes running down the sides, particularly evident on the lower half (figure 48a)→ **Eastern Mudminnow,** *Umbra pygmaea*

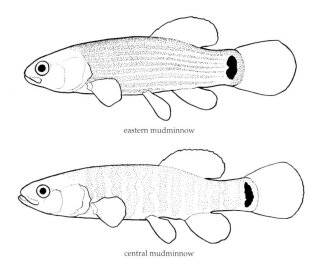

eastern mudminnow

central mudminnow

Fig. 48. Lateral view of *(a)* eastern mudminnow and *(b)* central mudminnow, showing markings.

170

1b. Body without horizontal stripes, but with faint, vertical bars (figure 48b) → **Central Mudminnow,** *Umbra limi*

Central Mudminnow

Umbra limi (Kirtland, 1840)

Identification. The Northeast has two species of mudminnows: the central mudminnow (*Umbra limi*) and the eastern mudminnow (*Umbra pygmaea*). Both are small fish, 2–3 inches long, characterized by a *rounded caudal fin, which is preceded by a distinct dark vertical bar.* The central mudminnow is more common and is distinguished from the eastern mudminnow by the absence of horizontal stripes and a *somewhat dark, mottled coloration on its sides.* Both species bear a resemblance to killifishes, but an inspection of the mouth highlights a difference. The killifishes have a deep groove that separates the snout from the upper lip. This condition is referred to as protractile, meaning that the upper lip can be projected forward when the mouth opens. Mudminnows in contrast lack the deep groove; the *upper lip is tightly attached to the snout and is not protractile.* Both the central mudminnow and the eastern mudminnow have an olive green to brown dorsal surface, with yellow brown sides and yellow to white belly. The fins are often dark.

Life History. The central mudminnow spawns in March or April, often migrating upstream to flooded areas. The female frequently attaches the adhesive eggs one at a time to the underside of overhanging rocks or vegetation. She then stands guard, gently moving her fins, creating a slight current. The young hatch in approximately 6 days. The central mudminnow feeds on ostracods when young and on insects, mollusks, and larger crustaceans as it becomes older. Central mudminnows are generalists in their feeding habits, taking prey from the surface, from midwater, and from the bottom. Some reach sexual maturity in 1 year, but most reach maturity at 2 years of age. Rarely do they live beyond 4 years. They are typically less than 5 inches long. They live in shallow water over a soft bottom, frequently in quite stagnant water. Because they can use their swim bladder as an accessory respiratory organ, they are very tolerant of low-oxygen concentrations. This capability allows them to occupy habitats unavailable to other fishes. When disturbed, they dive into the bottom mud to escape danger—hence the name mudminnow. Much of their natural habitat is being eliminated owing to the draining of wetlands and stagnant marsh areas.

Distribution. The central mudminnow is found primarily in the Midwest. It ranges from Lake Champlain and Quebec to Tennessee and Arkansas and north to the Dakotas. In the Northeast, it is found in the Connecticut River in Connecticut and Massachusetts and in Lake Champlain in Vermont, and it is fairly common in quiet water in the Allegheny, Great Lakes-St. Lawrence, and Hudson drainages in New York. It has recently been reported from Maine.

Eastern Mudminnow

Umbra pygmaea (DeKay, 1842)

Identification. The eastern mudminnow is a small, dark brown fish with a *rounded caudal fin* preceded by a dark vertical bar and with *pencil thin dark lines running horizontally along the sides. The upper lip is tightly attached to the snout.*

Life History. Adults spawn in early April. They choose a rocky or vegetated substrate to lay their eggs; some create a nest in the vegetation. Females remain with the nest, guarding it from predators until the young disperse. Eastern mudminnows feed on a variety of things, including small crustaceans and aquatic insects. They are normally less than 5 inches long. They are very hardy fish and tolerant of both low-oxygen concentrations and low pHs, which allows them to occupy small woodland pools and other difficult habitats.

Distribution. The eastern mudminnow ranges from southeastern New York, including Long Island, along the Atlantic Coastal Plain to northeastern Florida. In the Northeast, it is found only in quiet mud-bottomed and vegetated streams and ponds in southeastern New York.

Smelts

Family Osmeridae

Smelts are found in freshwater and marine environments. They are small fish with an adipose fin; cycloid scales; a lateral line; and a large mouth containing many large teeth on the jaw, tongue, and vomerine bone. They have no pelvic axillary process. The smelt family is made up of ten species. Only one occurs in the Northeast.

Rainbow Smelt

Osmerus mordax (Mitchill, 1814)

Identification. Rainbow smelts are minnowlike fishes that can be distinguished from all other fishes in the state by a *large mouth;* the presence of an *adipose fin;* and a lack of barbels, pelvic axillary process, or spines in the dorsal fin. They may superficially resemble brook silversides but can be distinguished from them in the field by the single dorsal fin and *relatively short anal fin.* They are light green on the back with silvery sides or belly. Their color tends to darken in stained waters, such as in mountain lakes.

Life History. Rainbow smelts are primarily marine fish that enter freshwater to spawn. Many have become landlocked, however, and thus move from a lake to a tributary stream when it is time to spawn. This move usually occurs around the time of ice breakup. Adults swim into the stream at night, rarely progressing more than a few hundred yards upstream. The female chooses a position over gravel or sand, and three or four smaller males position themselves downstream. She then releases up to 50,000 eggs, which the waiting males fertilize. The eggs attach to the bottom, resting on a short pedestal. The young, after hatching, return to the lake and begin feeding on plankton. Growth in females is more rapid than in males. A large female may be 10 inches long and weigh $\frac{1}{4}$ pound. A large male, in contrast, may be only $8\frac{1}{2}$ inches long and weigh $\frac{1}{6}$ pound. Rainbow smelts are lake-dwelling fish, preferring cool, deep water. They feed on plankton, often migrating inshore at night in search of food.

Rainbow smelts are an excellent food fish and are sought in both the commercial and sport fisheries. The customary procedure is for anglers to gather at night in groups, build a bonfire, and line up along the banks of a spawning stream. As the rainbow smelts swim upstream, the anglers capture them with a dip net.

Distribution. Rainbow smelts originally ranged along the Atlantic Coast from New Jersey to Labrador. Landlocked populations occurred in cool lakes throughout New England and the Maritime Provinces of Canada. The original range of the smelt has been greatly extended by introductions, however. Rainbow smelts are found in all states of the region.

Whitefishes, Trouts, and Salmons

Family Salmonidae

This large and important family of fishes possesses cycloid scales, soft rays in all fins, an adipose fin, and a pelvic axillary process. Sixty-eight species are known worldwide. The species found in the Northeast can be divided into two subfamilies: the Coregoninae and Salmoninae.

The Coregoninae, or cisco and whitefish, subfamily is characterized by having a small mouth, with the lower jaw not extending behind the eye. The scales are relatively large, with fewer than 100 scales in the lateral line. Eight species of coregonids have been reported for the region, five of which are found in deep waters of Lake Ontario or Lake Erie: the bloater (*Coregonus hoyi*), the kiyi (*C. kiyi*), the blackfin cisco (*C. nigripinnis*), the shortnose cisco (*C. reighardi*), and the shortjaw cisco (*C. zenithicus*). Most of these deep-water coregonids are quite rare, and many may in fact be extirpated from these lower Great Lakes. The remaining three coregonids are the lake whitefish (*C. clupeaformis*), the cisco (*C. artedii*), and the round whitefish (*Prosopium cylindraceum*). These three species are more common and are discussed later.

Three genera of Salmoninae occur in the Northeast: *Salvelinus* (char), *Salmo* (Atlantic salmon and brown trout), and *Oncorhynchus* (Pacific salmon and rainbow trout). All three genera of salmonids are distinguishable from the coregonids by the larger size of their mouth (it extends posteriorly to well behind the eye), the smaller size of their scales (more than 100 in the lateral line), and the presence of parr marks (dark, rectangular markings) in juveniles.

This guide provides descriptions for the three chars found in the region: the brook trout (*Salvelinus fontinalis*), the lake trout (*S. namaycush*), and the arctic char (*S. alpinus*); for the two salmonids: brown trout (*Salmo trutta*) and the Atlantic salmon (*S. salar*); and for the four Pacific salmon and rainbow trout species: the coho (*Oncorhynchus kisutch*), the Chinook (*O. tshawytscha*), the sockeye (*O. nerka*), the pink salmon (*O. gorbuscha*), and the rainbow trout (*O. mykiss*).

A key to adult salmonids is given next, followed by a separate key to young trouts and salmons less than 5 inches long is provided.

Species Key

1a. Mouth small, posterior end of upper jaw (maxilla) extends to just below eye (figure 49a); fewer than 100 scales in lateral line→ **2**

1b. Mouth large, posterior end of upper jaw extends well behind eye (figure 49b); more than 100 scales in lateral line→ **4**

2a. Only 1 single flap between the nostrils (figure 50a); gill rakers fewer than 20 (figure 51a)→ **Round White-fish,** *Prosopium cylindraceum*

2b. Two flaps between nostrils (figure 50b); gill rakers more than 23 (figures 51b and 51c)→ **3**

3a. In side view, the snout is pointed, and the mouth is terminal (figure 52a); gill rakers between 43 and 52 (figure 51b)→ **Cisco,** *Coregonus artedii*

3b. In side view, the snout is rounded, and the mouth is subterminal (figure 52b); gill rakers fewer than 32 (figure 51c)→ **Lake Whitefish,** *Coregonus clupeaformis*

4a. Anal fin with 12 or fewer developed rays; lining of mouth whitish→ **5**

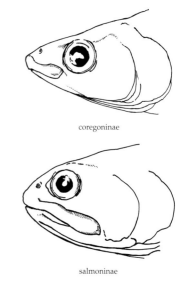

coregoninae

salmoninae

Fig. 49. Mouths of the two major subdivisions of the family Salmonidae: *(a)* Coregoninae and *(b)* Salmoninae.

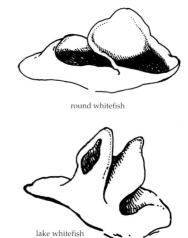

round whitefish

lake whitefish

Fig. 50. Flaps between the nostrils of *(a)* round whitefish and *(b)* lake whitefish.

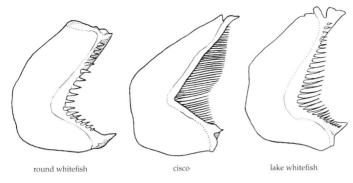

round whitefish   cisco   lake whitefish

Fig. 51. Gill rakers of *(a)* round whitefish, *(b)* cisco, and *(c)* lake whitefish.

4b. Anal fin with 13 or more developed rays; lining of mouth dark, at least in patches → **10**

5a. Color pattern composed of dark spots on lighter background; lateral line scales less than 175; teeth present on shaft of vomer (bone running down center of roof of mouth) (figure 53a) → **6**

5b. Color pattern composed of light spots on darker background; lateral line scales greater than 175; no teeth on shaft of vomer (figure 53b) → **8**

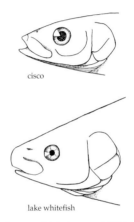

cisco

lake whitefish

Fig. 52. Snout of *(a)* cisco and *(b)* lake whitefish.

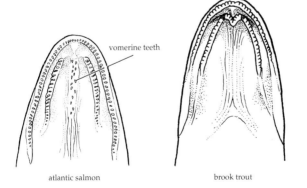

vomerine teeth

atlantic salmon   brook trout

Fig. 53. Teeth in upper part of mouth of *(a)* Atlantic salmon and *(b)* brook trout.

6a. Sides of body with numerous small black spots, particularly well developed on caudal fin→ **Rainbow Trout,** *Oncorhynchus mykiss*

6b. Sides of body with fewer large black spots (many as large or larger than pupil of eye); few spots, if any, present on caudal fin→ **7**

7a. Maxilla extends to posterior edge of eye or farther in fish longer than 6 inches; many reddish spots well developed on sides and adipose fin (may be faint or absent in populations occupying large lakes); adipose fin with a reddish orange margin; teeth on shaft of vomer well developed; 9 rays in anal fin→ **Brown Trout,** *Salmo trutta*

7b. Maxilla extends to just below posterior edge of pupil, rarely to posterior edge of eye; no reddish spots; adipose fin lacking reddish orange margin; teeth on shaft of vomer weak and deciduous; 10–13 rays in anal fin→ **Atlantic Salmon,** *Salmo salar*

8a. Caudal fin deeply forked; lower fins without black stripe, and white stripe poorly developed; body not brightly colored, generally grayish→ **Lake Trout,** *Salvelinus namaycush*

8b. Caudal fin square to only slightly forked; lower fins with the leading edge pure white; body often brightly colored with cream, pink, or red spots→ **9**

9a. Caudal fin square; lower fins with the leading edge white, followed by a black stripe; sides of body with small red spots encircled in blue halos; back and dorsal fin covered with vermiculations (wormlike markings)→ **Brook Trout,** *Salvelinus fontinalis*

9b. Caudal fin slightly forked; lower fins with the leading edge white, but not followed by a black stripe; sides with cream, pink, or red spots without blue halos; vermiculations lacking→ **Arctic Char,** *Salvelinus alpinus*

10a. Body without distinct black spots, but some very fine speckling may be present→ **Sockeye,** *Oncorhynchus nerka*

10b. Body and caudal fin with distinct black spots→ **11**

11a. Back and both lobes of caudal fin with large black spots, some as large as eye; lateral line scales 147–205; males develop a hump on the back during spawning period→ **Pink Salmon** *Oncorhynchus gorbuscha*

11b. Back and caudal fin with small black spots no larger than pupil of eye; lateral line scales 112–65→ **12**

12a. Fish can be easily picked up by the tail; both lobes of caudal fin with small black spots; when depressed, first rays of anal fin reach less than two-thirds of the way to end of anal fin→ **Chinook Salmon,** *Oncorhynchus tshawytscha*

12b. Fish cannot be picked up easily by the tail; no spots on lower lobe of caudal fin; when depressed, first rays of anal fin reach more than two-thirds of the way to end of anal fin→ **Coho Salmon,** *Oncorhynchus kisutch*

Key to Young Salmons and Trouts 2–5 Inches Long

1a. Principal anal rays 8–12→ **2**

1b. Principal anal rays 12–19→ **6**

2a. Dorsal fin with dark spots or black first dorsal ray or both→ **3**

2b. Dorsal fin lacking dark markings→ **Lake Trout,** *Salvelinus namaycush*

3a. Red or yellow spots on lateral line; width of space between parr marks generally less than or equal to width of parr marks at lateral line→ **4**

3b. Red or yellow spots missing; lighter space between dark parr marks generally greater than width of dark parr marks at lateral line→ **Rainbow Trout,** *Oncorhynchus mykiss*

4a. Caudal fin deeply forked, shortest rays approximately one-half of the length of the longest; pectoral fin as long as depressed dorsal fin; in juveniles, a single red spot between parr marks→ **Atlantic Salmon,** *Salmo salar*

4b. Caudal fin shallowly forked, shortest rays greater than one-half the length of the longest; pectoral fin shorter than depressed dorsal fin→ **5**

5a. Eight or nine parr marks; sides below lateral line without small dark spots→ **Brook Trout,** *Salvelinus fontinalis*

5b. Approximately 11 parr marks; sides below lateral line have small dark spots→ **Brown Trout,** *Salmo trutta*

6a. Parr marks missing→ **Pink Salmon,** *Oncorhynchus gorbuscha*

6b. Parr marks present→ **7**

7a. Parr marks short and stubby, none taller than diameter of eye→ **Sockeye,** *Oncorhynchus nerka*

7b. Parr marks tall, the largest greater than diameter of eye→ **8**

8a. Adipose fin evenly pigmented; anal fin with dark pigment posterior to white leading edge; first ray of anal fin elongate, producing a concave shape to outer edge of fin→ **Coho Salmon,** *Oncorhynchus kisutch*

8b. Adipose fin with pigmentation heavier on dorsal and posterior edge, lighter in center; anal fin lacking dark pigment; first ray of anal fin not elongate→ **Chinook Salmon,** *Oncorhynchus tshawytscha*

Round Whitefish

Prosopium cylindraceum (Pallas, 1784)

Identification. All members of the family Salmonidae are characterized by the presence of an *adipose fin* and a pelvic axillary process and by the absence of barbels around the mouth. Whitefishes are distinguishable from salmon and trout by their relatively *small mouth* and large scales. In whitefishes, the upper jaw extends no farther posterior than the middle of the eye, whereas in trouts and salmons it reaches well behind the eye. Lateral line scales in whitefishes are larger than in trout and salmon, with fewer than 100 in the lateral line. Round whitefish are distinguishable from other whitefishes by the *single flap of tissue between the anterior and posterior opening of each nostril.* Lake whitefish and ciscoes have a double flap of tissue. In addition, the 13–20 gill rakers of the round whitefish are short and stubby, whereas the 23 or more gill rakers in the cisco and the lake whitefish are long and slender. Round whitefish are generally dark gray dorsally, grading through silver to white ventrally. Blue, purple, green, and even a yellow sheen are apparent on the sides of adults at times. The young have several horizontal rows of black spots on their sides.

Life History. Round whitefish spawn in the fall, usually in November, over shallow shoal areas or off the mouth of streams. They pair up and broadcast their eggs preferably over a gravel bottom, although spawning over silt and vegetation has been reported. A single female may carry 2,000–10,000 eggs. Once spawning has occurred, the eggs are abandoned. The eggs are large, and they incubate over the winter and hatch in approximately 140 days, depending on temperature. The young begin feeding on plankton; as they grow, their diet switches to bottom invertebrates, with mayflies, caddis flies, midge larvae, and small molluscs appearing most commonly in their stomachs. They may reach an age of 14 years and a length of 20 inches, but adults are more commonly 4–7 years old and 9–14 inches long. Round whitefish prefer deep, clear lakes but generally venture no deeper than 150 feet. They enter shallow water only to spawn.

Distribution. Round whitefish are widely distributed throughout the upper Great Lakes, Canada, Alaska, and northeastern Asia. Although not abundant in the Northeast, they are still thought to exist in a few deep lakes in all states except Massachusetts and Rhode Island. They were reported from Lake Ontario, Lake Champlain, and many Adirondack lakes in New York in the early part of the twentieth century, but populations have declined so much that the round whitefish is now classified as endangered in New York. In Vermont, it is listed as a species of special concern. Round whitefish have not been found in many sites that reported them two or three decades ago. Threats to their survival include competition and predation from introduced fish species (yellow perch, smallmouth bass, and lake whitefish), loss of spawning sites, siltation, and lake acidification.

Lake Whitefish

Coregonus clupeaformis (Mitchill, 1818)

Identification. The lake whitefish is distinguishable from the rest of the whitefishes by its *rounded snout* (figure 52b), *subterminal mouth, and the double flap between its nostrils.* It is usually silvery gray to white, with little coloration.

Life History. Lake whitefish spawn from October to December, depending on the temperature and the locality. Males are the first to arrive on the spawning grounds, which are near shore in shallow water, less than 20 feet deep, over a gravelly or sandy bottom. Spawning occurs primarily at night. Females rise to the surface, discharging eggs as they go. Males follow, fertilizing the eggs. Because the eggs are only slightly heavier than water, they sink gently to the bottom. Females carry approximately 10,000 eggs for each pound of body weight, thus each fish produces 10,000–75,000 eggs. Spawning lasts for approximately 10 days, with many repetitions of the spawning act. The eggs hatch in 120–40 days, and the fry begin feeding within 2 weeks on microscopic crustaceans. At this time, the young lake whitefish are usually found in water less than 2 feet deep. As they grow, they move into deeper water, until finally, as adults, they are found in water at least 60 feet deep. When they reach an inch in length, their mouth turns downward, and they begin feeding off the bottom on crustaceans, mollusks, and insects. Lake whitefish up to 20 pounds have been reported, but the average is less than 4 pounds. They grow slowly, and many take up to 16 years to reach such a size.

Lake whitefish are taken in the commercial catch in the Great Lakes. They are light and delicately flavored. Angling for lake whitefish is not well developed. In Otsego Lake near Cooperstown, New York, lake whitefish are called Otsego bass. In Otsego Lake, they are taken on flies when in shallow water or by jigging, or using small pieces of fish on a small hook, when they are in deep water.

Distribution. Lake whitefish are distributed throughout Canada and Alaska and extend into many lakes in the northern United States. They are found in all the states of the Northeast except Connecticut, Massachusetts, and Rhode Island. In New York, they have been found in the following lakes: Otsego, Caroga, Canada, Champlain, Saranac, Placid, Clear, Ontario, Erie, Raquette, and the Finger Lakes. In New Hampshire, they are known from Lake Winnipesauke. They may well exist in many other deep, cool lakes because stocking programs prior to 1900 introduced them into many northern lakes.

Cisco

Coregonus artedii LeSueur, 1818

Identification. The cisco, also called the lake herring, most resembles the lake whitefish but can be distinguished from it by the shape of the snout. In the cisco, the *snout is more pointed, and the mouth is terminal* (figure 52a); in the lake whitefish, the snout is rounded, and the mouth is subterminal. The cisco has two flaps between the nasal openings, whereas the round whitefish has a single flap. The cisco's back is green to blue, its sides silvery with an iridescent sheen, and its belly and fins are generally white.

Life History. Although ciscoes move into shallow water early in the fall, spawning takes place many weeks later, usually late in November or early December. Spawning appears to be a group activity involving many individuals. The eggs are broadcast on the bottom and receive no parental care. They hatch in 110–30 days. The fry begin feeding on plankton, and most continue to feed on plankton all their lives. Ciscoes occasionally consume mayflies or small minnows. They may live up to 10 years and achieve a size approaching 20 inches; most are smaller, however. They are cold-water fish, preferring water cooler than 60°F. Consequently, during the summer they are generally found in deep water, moving into shallow areas only when the temperature has dropped.

Ciscoes, like lake whitefish, are a part of the commercial fishery in the Great

Lakes. Surprisingly, relatively few sport anglers fish for them. Ciscoes will take a fly when a large hatch is occurring in the spring, and they can be taken through the ice, fishing fairly deeply with jigs.

Distribution. The range of the cisco is from Quebec west to Alberta and north to the Northwest Territories. Its range dips into the United States in the Great Lakes and upper Mississippi drainages. In the Northeast, it has been found only in New York and Vermont in several of the Finger Lakes and in the following lakes: Erie, Ontario, Champlain, George, Oneida, Tupper, Otsego, Chautauqua, Hedges.

Brook Trout

Salvelinus fontinalis (Mitchill, 1814)

Identification. Brook trout are distinguished from whitefishes by a *large mouth* and small scales. Brook trout are included among a group of three species of trout called char (*Salvelinus*) and are separated from other trout in the genera *Salmo* and *Oncorhynchus* by *the color pattern on their bodies, which is basically a scattering of light spots over a darker background*. The brook trout has a relatively square tail, a scattering of *small red spots encircled in blue halos* over the sides of the body, and a *back and dorsal fin covered with vermiculations (wormlike markings)*. The pelvic and anal fins are orange to pink, with conspicuous white leading edges followed by a dark stripe.

Life History. Spawning occurs in the fall between September and December. In most cases, mature adults move into headwater streams, selecting a site with a gravel bottom and substantial flow of cold, clear water. Brook trout are also known to seek out and spawn in upwelling areas in streams, lakes, and ponds. The female digs a depression in the gravelly bottom while the male stands guard, chasing other fishes away. The female faces upstream and while lying on her side vibrates her body, violently kicking out gravel, which is carried a short distance downstream. She continues this process until she creates a redd, or nest, several inches deep. She frequently lies on the redd, extending her anal fin as if to measure the correct depth during the digging phase. She eventually is satisfied, and the male moves onto the redd with her. She places her vent as close as possible to the deepest part of the redd and extrudes anywhere from a few hundred to several thousand eggs. At the same time, the male produces a cloud of sperm that fertilizes the eggs. Immediately after spawning, the female moves upstream and begins to cover the redd by sweeping her tail across the bottom, dislodging gravel that falls into the redd and covers the eggs. The male stands guard for a few minutes after spawning but quickly loses interest and abandons his post. Females carry up to 7,000 eggs and thus may spawn more than once. In fact, it has been observed that after spawning a female frequently moves a short distance upstream and begins constructing a new redd.

The eggs develop slowly during the fall and winter. They may take as long as 142 days if the water is cold (35°F) or as short as 28 days if the water is warm (59°F). In the Northeast, the water temperature in streams is normally near freezing in the winter, and thus the incubation period is prolonged, lasting most of the winter. After hatching, the young fish remain in the redd, receiving nourishment from their large yolk sac. They begin feeding about a month later, at which time they leave the redd. Young trout feed initially on microcrustaceans and small insects. As they grow, they continue to feed on insects and other stream invertebrates. Large trout may switch to feeding on fish or amphibians. Most brook trout are less than 14 inches long. It is possible, however, for them to exceed 14 pounds and 31 inches in unusually productive water, as is evidenced by the capture of one fish this large in Canada. Brook trout are not long-lived, usually surviving only until their fourth or fifth year, although some strains in Canada are known to live for 10 years.

The brook trout is one of the most sensitive fishes in the region. It is very intolerant of environmental degradation. It also needs water whose temperature rarely exceeds 79°F and then for only short periods. It does better when the water remains below 65°F. In addition, oxygen levels must be above 5–6 parts per million; the bottom must not be silted over; and good sand or gravel should be present for spawning. Consequently, as land was cleared in lowland areas, farms were worked, homes built, and industries started in the Northeast, the water suitable for brook trout diminished. They survived only in headwater streams and ponds where the environmental conditions remained suitable. Unfortunately, headwater streams are small and thus give rise to small fish.

The brook trout is also one of the fishes most sought after by the angler. It readily takes flies or other artificial lures and provides a showy fight. In addition, it is one of the region's most attractive fishes and is commonly taken in beautiful surroundings.

Distribution. The brook trout's original range ran from Georgia north to Labrador and the Hudson Bay region and thence south to the Great Lakes region. It has been introduced in other parts of the world as well, but owing to its sensitivity it is not as widespread as the brown or rainbow trout. In the Northeast, it can be found in all states and every major watershed where habitat is suitable.

Arctic Char

Salvelinus alpinus (Linnaeus, 1758)

Identification. As with other chars, Arctic char are characterized by light spots overlying a darker background on their body. They have a slightly forked tail and no vermiculations (worm markings) on the dorsal part of the body. A dark band does not follow the white leading edge on the lower fins of the arctic char as it does in the brook trout. Both brook trout and lake trout have vermiculations, and the brook trout has a dark band directly behind the white band. The arctic char's body color is quite variable. Nonspawning arctic char tend to be relatively plain and silvery, with little in the way of distinctive coloration; spawning fish, in contrast, are brightly colored, with a dark green back, sides decorated with bright red or orange spots, and a brilliant orange belly.

Life History. Arctic char have two distinct life history patterns. Those in the northern part of the range are anadromous, spawning in freshwater but spending most of their adult life at sea. Others spend their entire life in freshwater and are considered to be landlocked. In the Northeast, most populations are landlocked. They spawn in streams and lakes, with the female building a redd where she deposits the fertilized eggs. In Maine, it is estimated that the spawning period runs from late November to early December after the water temperature gets below 50°F. Arctic char in Floods Pond, Maine, have shown a strong tendency to return to spawning sites when displaced. The spawning behavior of the arctic char is similar to that of the brook trout. The eggs hatch in the spring, and the young leave shallow water to move into deeper water approximately 2 weeks after hatching. In lakes, arctic char tend to remain within the deepest, coolest layer, the hypolimnion, which is usually at least 30 feet below the surface. Juveniles feed almost exclusively on zooplankton, whereas adults feed not only on zooplankton, but also on benthic organisms, aquatic insects, crustaceans, and fish. Most arctic char in the Northeast are 4 years or younger, but some may live to 5 or 6 years of age. Growth is dependent to a large extent on whether they are able to switch to fish as a major diet item. Those that can switch may achieve weights of 1½ pounds, whereas those that feed exclusively on plankton and insects are much smaller, reaching only ¼ pound. Arctic char are not abundant in the Northeast for several reasons. This region is at the very southern end of their range, and the climatic conditions are not favorable for their continued existence here. They do not compete well with lake trout, which occupy a similar habitat. Because they live in deep waters of relatively inaccessible lakes and because their populations are declining, they are not as commonly encountered as other trouts.

Distribution. Arctic char, as their name implies, are found in rivers and lakes all along the coastline of the Arctic Ocean and thus are one of the most northerly freshwater fishes in North America. They have a circumpolar distribution, being found not only in northern North America, but also in Europe and Asia. In the southern portion of their range, they prefer relatively deep oligotrophic lakes with adequate oxygen in the deeper waters. In the Northeast, they currently are found only in Maine, Vermont, and New Hampshire. Maine probably has the largest population, where they are reported from lakes in the headwaters of the St. John and Penobscot Rivers in Aroostook and Piscataquis Counties. Relatively few are found in New Hampshire and Vermont, where they are reported from Connor Pond and Averill Lake, respectively.

Lake Trout

Salvelinus namaycush (Walbaum, 1792)

Identification. The lake trout, like the brook trout, is a char and thus characterized by *light spots on a dark background.* The black stripes on the lower fins are missing, and the white stripe on the leading edge of the lower fins is not well developed. The lake trout is not a brightly colored fish, and its *caudal fin is forked.* Each of these characteristics distinguish the lake trout from the brook trout or arctic char.

Life History. Lake trout spawn in the fall between October and December. They spawn in lakes, generally in water less than 100 feet deep. They are the only trout in the region that do not move into streams to spawn. They do not build nests, but simply deposit their heavy, nonadhesive eggs over rocky bottoms with many naturally occurring cavities. Females carry 700–800 eggs per pound body weight, so a 10-pound female may carry 7,000–8,000 eggs.

Eggs hatch in approximately 110 days, and the young begin feeding on zooplankton and small insect larvae. They soon begin to feed on a wide array of insects and crustaceans, with one of the favorites being the possum shrimp (*Mysis relicta*). Larger lake trout utilize fish for forage, such as alewives, shiners, suckers, sculpins, sticklebacks, trout-perches, whitefishes, and smelts. Lake trout that weighed more than 100 pounds have been reported. This is very rare. It is quite rare even to see a fish in excess of 30 or 40 pounds. Much more common are fish that weigh 2–10 pounds.

During the warmer part of the year, lake trout are found in the deep, cool water of large lakes. They generally prefer water with adequate oxygen and with temperatures that stay between 44 and 55°F. In late fall, winter, and early spring, they may forage in shallow water as long as the temperature stays below 50°F. In much of the Northeast, lake trout are at the southern extremity of their range. As a northern species, they have not adapted well to warmer lakes. Because of the warming of the surface waters in summer, lake trout are forced to seek deeper, cooler waters. If the lake is shallow or if owing to eutrophication the deeper waters have reduced oxygen levels, they have difficulty surviving the summer. Consequently, they are found only in large, deep lakes that still maintain adequate oxygen in their deeper waters.

The lake trout was formerly a very important part of the commercial catch of fishermen in the Great Lakes. Its numbers declined owing to a variety of causes, including lamprey predation and overfishing. In recent years, with lamprey-control programs reducing predation on lake trout and with active lake trout stocking programs, it is making a strong comeback in the Great Lakes.

It is highly prized by anglers. In the spring and fall, it can be taken on light spinning gear or even on flies in shallow water. When taken in this manner, it demonstrates its fighting qualities. More commonly, however, it is taken during the summer by trolling at great depths with downriggers.

Distribution. Lake trout are generally distributed throughout Canada and Alaska. They also extend into the continental United States in Maine, New Hampshire, Vermont, Massachusetts, New York, Pennsylvania, Michigan, Wisconsin, Minnesota, Montana, and Idaho. In the Northeast, they are found in deep lakes in all states except Connecticut and Rhode Island.

Brown Trout

Salmo trutta Linnaeus, 1758

Identification. Brown trout have *dark spots on a lighter background,* as do other trout and salmon. In the case of brown trout, these spots are large (many approximately the size of the pupil of the eye) but are *rarely present on the caudal fin.* They are cast against the light brown background of the body. The belly is creamy white. In addition, numerous red or orange spots are present on the sides. The brown trout has 9–10 anal rays. Brown trout can often be confused with landlocked salmon; however, the *maxilla (upper jaw bone) in the brown trout extends at least to the posterior edge of the eye,* whereas the maxilla in the salmon reaches only to the rear edge of the pupil.

Life History. Spawning occurs in the fall, usually in October or November, in streams with clean gravel bottoms. Spawning behavior of the brown trout is similar to that of the brook trout. A female may carry anywhere from 200–2,000 eggs. The young hatch in 100–65 days, depending on temperature. They begin feeding on very small bottom organisms, such as young black fly, mayfly, and stonefly larvae. They continue to feed on bottom insects as they grow, moving to progressively larger individuals as they are capable of handling them. In addition, their menus expand to include amphipods, mollusks, terrestrial insects washed into the stream, and fishes. Brown trout may live up to 9 or 10 years, achieving a size of 20 pounds or more. Fish weighing up to 40 pounds have been reported, but the usual fish caught is less than 1 pound. Large brown trout are being taken from Lake Ontario, with a 33-pound fish the largest recorded to date.

Brown trout are found in both streams and lakes, but spawning almost always occurs in streams. For lake populations, the young may remain in the stream for several years, migrating back to the lake, where they mature, and then later returning to the stream to spawn. Stream populations, of course, spend their entire life in the stream. Brown trout are more tolerant of poor environmental conditions than are brook trout and consequently have replaced them in many marginal habitats.

Brown trout are highly regarded as a sport fish. As far back as the seventeenth century, Izaak Walton wrote many lines about the joys of fishing for them. Since that time, brown trout have continued to give millions of anglers hours of enjoyable fishing. Because they are wary, they are one of the more difficult fishes to catch. Brown trout can be taken on flies, spinners, or live bait such as worms, grasshoppers, hellagramites, or minnows.

Distribution. Brown trout were found originally only in Europe and western Asia, but they have been widely introduced throughout the world, including in most of the waters of the Northeast. No major suitable drainage in this region is without brown trout.

Atlantic Salmon

Salmo salar Linnaeus, 1758

Identification. The Atlantic salmon bears a resemblance to the brown trout, but the brown trout has two rows of strong teeth on the vomerine bone, whereas the Atlantic salmon has a single row of weak deciduous teeth. In addition, *in the Atlantic salmon the maxilla extends no farther than the back of the eye,* whereas in brown trout the maxilla extends well behind the eye. The Atlantic salmon's back and sides are grayish brown with *large dark spots,* grading to olive and eventually grayish white on the belly. Juveniles have a *red spot between parr marks.*

Life History. As with arctic char, Atlantic salmon have two distinct types of life history. They normally spend most of their adult life in the ocean, migrating into freshwater only to spawn. The young remain in freshwater for several years before migrating out to sea. In some locations, however, the species has become landlocked and does not return to the sea, spending its entire life cycle in freshwater. Atlantic salmon move into spawning streams in the fall. The female digs a redd in the gravel to receive her eggs. Several males are in attendance. After she constructs the redd and usually at night, she deposits her eggs in it, and one of the accompanying males immediately fertilizes them. This process is repeated in new mating sites until the female is spent. A female may carry up to 4,000 eggs. The eggs hatch in approximately 100 days, and the young spend several years in the stream before returning to either the sea or a lake. Growth accelerates when they leave the stream and can begin feeding on forage fish. Prior to that, their diet in the stream is predominantly insects. The oldest fish reported was a 13-year-old specimen taken in Scotland; however, most fish do not reach their tenth birthday. Average size is between 16 and 28 inches, although some that weighed 24 pounds have been taken from Lake Ontario. Sexual maturity is reached between 3 and 5 years of age. Unlike Pacific salmons, Atlantic salmon do not always die after spawning and can return to the stream to spawn again.

The Atlantic salmon is without a doubt one of the finest sport fishes in the region. It can be taken on a fly, spinner, or live bait, and the fight is spectacular, with many long runs and jumps.

Distribution. Atlantic salmon are widely distributed throughout the North Atlantic, from Portugal northward and westward to Canada and originally as far south as the Connecticut River. Landlocked Atlantic salmon are found in clear, cool lakes and rivers in all of the states in the Northeast. In many localities, they are dependent on stocking to maintain their populations. In earlier years, sea-run Atlantic salmon migrated up rivers in Maine in substantial numbers, but their numbers have now been greatly reduced because of pollution, dams, overfishing, competition with exotic species, disease, and habitat degradation—so much so that the wild sea-run Atlantic salmon has been declared endangered in Maine rivers from the Kennebec north to the Canadian border.

Rainbow Trout

Oncorhynchus mykiss Walbaum, 1792

Identification. The rainbow trout is a trout with *many small dark spots on a lighter background. The spots are particularly well developed on the caudal fin.* In contrast, brown trout and landlocked salmon have larger spots, with few on the caudal fin. *Rainbow trout have 12 or fewer anal rays.* Pacific salmons (coho, Chinook, pink, and sockeye) have 13 or more anal rays. Rainbow trout are quite variable in their coloration. Fish living in lakes are light and silvery colored and thus are often referred to as "steelheads," whereas stream-dwelling rainbows are much darker and more heavily spotted. The back is dark blue to brown, grading to silver on the belly; the sides show a characteristic pink to red band.

Life History. The rainbow, unlike most other salmonids in the Northeast, spawns in the spring in streams over good gravel. In the Finger Lakes of New York and possibly in other areas as well, some rainbows migrate into the tributary streams in the fall and wait in the lower reaches until spring to spawn, but others migrate into the stream in March or April. Redd construction and spawning itself for the rainbows are very similar to those practices for the brook trout. A female rainbow may carry 2,000–3,000 eggs. Owing to warmer water temperatures, the incubation period is shorter for rainbows than it is for fall spawners, with most young hatching within 60 days. Stream-dwelling rainbows feed on bottom invertebrates and terrestrial insects washed into the stream. Lake-dwelling rainbows also feed on insects, but cladocerans and small fish make up a substantial portion of their diet as well. Rainbows prefer water cooler than 70°F, but they can survive temperatures up to 80°F for short periods of time. The adult rainbow trout in the region are probably the most tolerant of warm water and thus, along with the brown trout, most likely to survive in marginal habitat. Rainbow trout live for 6 or 7 years. Lake-dwelling rainbows may reach 20–22 inches and 3 or 4 pounds during that time. Stream rainbows are usually smaller, 10–12 inches and less than 1 pound. In Lake Ontario, a 31-pound fish was taken.

Rainbow trout are excellent game fish and can be taken in a wide variety of ways, using flies, spinners, spoons, live bait, cheese, and even marshmallows.

Distribution. The original range of the rainbow was in lakes and streams of the Rocky Mountains and coastal areas from northern Mexico to Alaska. It has since been introduced all over the world. One of the earliest introductions was in New York in 1874. It is now found in a wide variety of habitats from small streams to large rivers to lakes in all of the major drainage basins of each state in the Northeast where suitable habitat is present.

Sockeye or Kokanee

Oncorhynchus nerka (Walbaum, 1792)

Identification. All Pacific salmons (coho, Chinook, pink, and sockeye) in the Northeast can be distinguished from other trouts and salmons by having at least 13 soft rays in their anal fin. Trouts and Atlantic salmon, in contrast, have 12 or fewer soft anal rays. Sockeyes have 13 or more anal rays and no conspicuous black spots on the body or tail, as the other species have. Their coloration ranges from dark blue on the back through silver on the sides to white on the belly.

Life History. The kokanee is the landlocked form of the sockeye salmon. It spawns from September to December in streams tributary to lakes or even in shallow areas along the lakeshore. The female digs a redd; spawning occurs; and in a few weeks or months the spawning fish die. Females normally carry approximately 450 eggs. The young hatch in 48–140 days, depending on water temperature. After leaving the redd, the young spend very little time in the stream, but instead move directly to the lake. Sockeyes feed on plankton throughout most of their lives, occasionally eating insects when they are abundant. Most mature at age 4 and range in size from 8–12 inches and usually less than 1 pound in weight. They prefer water between 50 and 59°F and thus are normally found in deep water during the summer.

Sockeyes can be taken on hook and line even though they are primarily plankton feeders. Trolling, still fishing, or fly-fishing are the most widely used techniques. When sockeyes are feeding on insects at the surface, they can be taken on flies.

Distribution. Sockeye are found in coastal lakes around the northern Pacific Ocean from California to Alaska, Russia, and Japan. In the Northeast, they have been stocked in New York, Vermont, Maine, Massachusetts, and Connecticut. In New York, they have been introduced in Lake Colby, Little Green Pond, Long Pond, Pine Pond, and Clear Pond in the Champlain drainage; in Twin Lake, Bug Lake, and Mitchell Pond in the Oswegatchie and Black drainages; and in Glass Lake in the Hudson drainage. In Connecticut and Massachusetts, they have been introduced into the Housatonic, Connecticut, and Thames River drainages. It is unclear whether any of these introductions have resulted in established populations.

Pink Salmon

Oncorhynchus gorbuscha (Walbaum, 1792)

Identification. Pink salmon have *more than 13 rays in the anal fin and very large spots (some the size of the eye) on the back, sides, and tail.* They are dark blue on the back, grading through silver on the sides to white on the belly.

Life History. Not much is known of the life history of this species in the Northeast. Elsewhere, landlocked populations of pink salmon spawn in streams tributary to the lake in which they reside. Spawning takes place in early fall, and the young hatch and leave the redds in the spring. Pink salmon feed on a variety of organisms, ranging from insects and crustaceans to fish. Under good conditions, adults may be 18 inches long and up to 4 pounds when they undertake their spawning run.

Distribution. The pink salmon ranges along the western coast from northern California to Japan. It has been introduced into the Northeast as a result of stockings in the Great Lakes and off the coast of Maine. It has been reported from Lakes Erie and Ontario as a result of these stockings. It is unknown whether they have successfully established reproducing populations in the Northeast.

Coho Salmon

Oncorhynchus kisutch (Walbaum, 1792)

Identification. Coho salmon have a *long first anal ray and more than 13 rays in their anal fin* as well as *conspicuous black spots on their back and on the upper lobe of their caudal fin.* Chinook salmon have similar black spots, but the spots extend onto the lower lobe of their caudal fin as well. Pink salmon have very large black spots, some as large as the eye. The coho is dark blue to green on its back, grading through bright silver on its side and eventually to white on its belly.

Life History. Coho salmon move into spawning streams tributary to Lakes Ontario and Erie during September and early October. The female chooses the spawning site, generally preferring a location with small- to medium-size gravel at the head of a riffle, right where the smooth water of the upstream pool begins to roughen as it flows over the riffle. The female digs the redd by lying on her side close to the bottom and violently undulating her body. Males are not known to assist in this process. Each female is frequently accompanied by more than one male, but only one male is dominant, and the others are considered accessory males. After the female constructs the redd, the dominant male joins her there, and spawning occurs. If other males are present, they usually take this opportunity to dart into the redd and release sperm. A female may move to another site and spawn more than once. She normally carries 1,400–6,000 eggs. After spawning is finished, however, the adult fish dies. In West Coast streams, the eggs hatch in 35–50 days. If spawning is successful, hatching is probably delayed in streams in the Northeast because of the cold winters. The young remain in the stream for a year, feeding heavily on aquatic insects, and then they migrate downstream to a lake. In Lakes Ontario and Erie, the populations are maintained by stocking. Some natural spawning does occur at least in the Salmon River and its tributaries, but whether it is adequate to maintain the population without stocking is doubtful. Although coho salmon remain in the lake for just two growing seasons, growth is quite rapid, and they may reach 24 inches and 8 pounds before they begin the spawning run, which leads to their eventual death. The largest fish taken from Lake Ontario was more than 33 pounds. Coho salmon are highly piscivorous, feeding in Lake Ontario primarily on alewives.

Coho salmon were introduced into New York's Great Lakes in 1968 in the hope that they would take hold and provide a fishery similar to the highly successful one developed in Michigan a few years earlier. It is now clear, based on the successful establishment of this species, that coho salmon can do extremely well in Lakes Ontario and Erie.

The best fishing for coho salmon occurs as they congregate off the mouth of spawning streams. Trolling with spinners or spoons, spin casting, or even fly-fishing with streamers are all good methods at this time. After they enter the stream to spawn, they stop feeding and are much more difficult to catch.

Distribution. Coho salmon are not native to the Northeast. They are found in streams along the west coast of North America from northern California to Alaska and over to Russia and Japan. They normally migrate to the ocean after their first year in the nursery stream. The coho salmon has been introduced in New York, New Hampshire, Maine, Massachusetts, and Connecticut. In 1968, it was introduced into Lakes Ontario and Erie and now may be found in the Niagara River. In New Hampshire, it was stocked for a few years in tributaries of the Great Bay, the Lamprey, and Exeter Rivers. In Massachusetts, it is known only from the North River drainage. In Connecticut, it has been stocked in all major drainages, but viable populations have probably not developed from those stockings.

Chinook Salmon

Oncorhynchus tshawytscha (Walbaum)

Identification. Chinook, with *large black spots on both the upper and lower lobe of their caudal fin and 14–16 relatively uniform anal rays,* are readily distinguishable from other salmonids. They are the largest of the Pacific salmons. They are blue or bluish green on their backs, grading to silver on their sides and white on their bellies.

Life History. Chinook are fall spawners, moving into streams in September or October. Spawning behavior of the Chinook is similar to that of the coho. Each female may carry 2,000–14,000 eggs depending on her size. The young hatch the following spring. The fry remain in the stream family several months before descending to the lake. They feed almost exclusively on aquatic insects at this time, in contrast to the coho, which will take fishes in the stream if available. In the lake, Chinook spend 2–3 years feeding on forage fish such as alewives, smelts, or shads and grow quite rapidly. In Alaska, a sea-run Chinook weighing 126 pounds was reported. Landlocked forms, such as those found in Lake Ontario, are smaller than sea-run fish, but the bulk of those taken by anglers are 20–30 pounds. The largest fish taken to date in New York was a 47-pound fish from the Salmon River in 1991.

Distribution. The Chinook ranges throughout the North Pacific from southern California to Alaska, west to Russia, and south to Japan. In 1969, Chinook were stocked in Lake Ontario. This was the third attempt to get a population started in Lake Ontario since the first try in 1874. They can now be found in Lake Ontario, Lake Erie, and the Niagara River and support a multi-million-dollar fishery. They have been introduced into waters of all of the states in the Northeast except Rhode Island. It is unclear whether any of these other populations can maintain themselves without stocking. In some cases, they are sea-run fish that run up coastal streams to spawn.

Trout-Perches

Family Percopsidae

The trout-perches share characteristics of the soft-rayed fishes and the spiny-rayed fishes. Their scales are ctenoid; the swim bladder is of the physoclistus type; and the dorsal, anal, and pelvic fins are preceded by 1 or 2 weak spines. They also have an adipose fin. Only two species are known in this family, one of which, the trout-perch,*Percopsis omiscomaycus,* is found in the Northeast.

Trout-Perch

Percopsis omiscomaycus (Walbaum, 1792)

Identification. The trout-perch is a small minnowlike fish, usually less than 5 inches long, with an *adipose fin, rough ctenoid scales, 2 very weak spines at the anterior edge of the dorsal fin,* and a single spine at the anterior edge of the anal and pelvic fins. The only other fishes in the state with adipose fins are: the catfishes, which are easily distinguished by their barbels; and the trouts, salmons, white-fishes, and smelts, all of which have smooth cycloid scales and no spines. The background color of the trout-perch is brownish tan to silvery and is overlain with *5 horizontal rows of dark spots on the back and sides.*

Life History. Upon reaching 1 year of age, trout-perch leave deep water and move in toward shore or into tributary streams in the spring when the water temperature approaches 68°F. They spawn over rock or gravel substrate. Each female carries approximately 350 eggs. The young are left to care for themselves. Trout-perch feed on crustaceans, zooplankton, and small insects. Most of their total growth is completed before their first winter, when they have reached approximately 3 inches. They may live up to 4 years, but most do not live beyond 2 years. Trout-perch live in lakes and slow-moving streams with sandy or gravelly bottoms. They generally are found in very deep water during the day but sometimes come into shallow water to feed at night.

Distribution. This species' range extends from Quebec to Alaska on the north and from West Virginia to Kansas on the south. It is found in Vermont; in the Housatonic River system in Connecticut; and in the Allegheny, Great Lakes-St. Lawrence, and Hudson drainages in New York.

Pirate Perches
Family Aphredoderidae

The family Aprhedoderidae has a single member, the pirate perch. It is a unique fish that shows some of the characteristics of more advanced fishes. It has spines in its dorsal fin; ctenoid scales, a type of scale with small projections (cteni) on their surface; and pelvic fins that are positioned just below the pectoral fins.

Pirate Perch

Aphredoderus sayanus (Gilliams, 1824)

Identification. The pirate perch is characterized by the *location of the adult's anus: on the throat just posterior to the gill cover.* No other species of freshwater fish in the region shares this trait. It is a stocky, dark brown fish, with slightly lighter coloration on the ventral side.

Life History. Pirate perch spawn in late spring, depositing eggs in a nest defended by the parents. The anus and urogenital pore in the young fish are initially in the normal posterior position. As development progresses, however, the anus and urogenital pore move anteriorly and reach the throat region during the second year of life. Pirate perch feed on insects, crustaceans, and oligochaetes. They typically get no larger than 4–5 inches in length and live to 3–4 years of age.

Distribution. The pirate perch is found from Ohio to Wisconsin and south to eastern Texas, along the Gulf Coast to Florida and north to eastern Long Island. It is rare or absent throughout most of the Northeast except on eastern Long Island, New York, where it is more abundant. It has also been reported from a few of the tributaries to Lakes Erie and Ontario in upstate New York. It prefers ponds, marshes, and pools in slow-flowing streams usually with mud-and-silt bottoms and abundant vegetation.

Cuskfishes
Family Lotidae

The cuskfishes are a small family of five species. Taxonomists have recently separated them from a larger family—the codfishes, family Gadidae. Members of the cuskfish family may have 1–3 dorsal fins, a rounded caudal fin, and a single median barbel on the chin that serves as a good field character. The nostrils have tubular extensions. Burbot are elongate, eel-like fish with very small cycloid scales embedded in their skin so deeply that they appear to be scaleless. They have segmented soft rays that support their fins. Of the five species in this family, the only one that truly inhabits freshwater is the burbot (*Lota lota*).

Burbot

Lota lota (Linnaeus)

Identification. The burbot is readily distinguished from other species by its somewhat elongate shape; *a single conspicuous barbel at the tip of the lower jaw;* and *2 dorsal fins, the second even longer than the single long anal fin.* Its back is dark brown in color; its sides are a yellowish tan overlain by an irregular network of dark brown markings; and its belly is yellow. The only species that the burbot might be confused with is the tomcod, *Microgadus tomcod,* which is primarily a marine species that enters brackish water and, on occasion, may be found in freshwater. The tomcod, however, has 3 dorsal fins and 2 anal fins, making it unique among any fish you might encounter in freshwater and easily distinguished from a burbot.

Life History. Burbot spawn under the ice at night in the winter. They spawn earlier in the year than any other fish in the region. Large groups frequently gather, often in shallow water, mate, and broadcast the eggs across the sandy bottom of the lake or river. Burbot are very prolific. A single female may produce more than 1 million eggs; the average fish, however, produces half that number. The eggs incubate, without benefit of a nest, for 4–5 weeks before hatching. The young drift in the open water, feeding on zooplankton. Burbot mature around 3 years of age, and some individuals are known to live for 16 years. Adult burbot average around 15–18 inches and weigh nearly 1 pound. Some grow considerably larger. Burbot up to 16 pounds have been taken in the region. Burbot are deep, cold-water fish, found primarily in large lakes and rivers, often at great depths. A few populations have surprisingly been found in relatively small streams in the upper Susquehanna River drainage. Although young burbot feed on plankton or insects, as they grow older, they feed almost exclusively on other fishes, such as perches, ciscoes, or whitefishes.

While fishing for other species, anglers often take the burbot, but it is not utilized either for food or as a sport fish to any extent in the United States.

Distribution. The burbot has a circumpolar distribution. It is found throughout Canada, the northern United States, Alaska, the Soviet Union, and Scandinavia. In the Northeast, it is reported from all states in the region except Rhode Island.

Silversides

Family Atherinidae

Silversides are small, slightly elongate, delicate physoclistus fishes with cycloid scales. Their lateral line is greatly reduced or missing.

Approximately 156 species are known, primarily from tropical waters. Only the brook silverside, *Labidesthes sicculus,* is a freshwater form. Two brackish-water species—the inland silverside, *Menidia beryllina,* and the Atlantic silverside, *Menidia menidia*—occasionally enter freshwater. The brook silverside is easily distinguished from the brackish-water forms by its rather elongate beak and relatively small scales (75–80 in lateral series). The brackish-water silversides have smaller jaws and fewer scales.

Brook Silverside

Labidesthes sicculus (Cope, 1865)

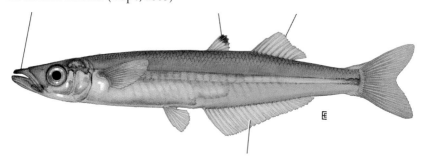

Identification. The brook silverside is a slender fish, approximately 2–4 inches long, with a *unique beaklike snout.* It has *2 dorsal fins:* the first is small, containing only 4 spines; the second is larger, containing 1 spine and 10–11 rays. The *anal fin is longer than the second dorsal fin* and extends forward to below the first dorsal fin. The unique mouth, 2 dorsal fins, and the unusually long anal fin are good field characters that will enable you to identify this fish with ease. It has relatively small scales, 75–80 of them in the lateral series. The only fish that it might be confused with is the inland silverside, which does not have the long beaklike snout and has a shorter anal fin that does not extend to below the first dorsal fin and larger scales (less than 50 in the lateral series). The brook silverside is light green dorsally with a somewhat transparent body and a light green band along its side.

Life History. The life history of the brook silverside is quite interesting. Adults gather in large groups in shallow water in the spring when the water temperature approaches 68°F. Males often outnumber females. As a female enters the spawning group, several males immediately chase her, causing her to leap out of the water. One male eventually catches up with her, approaches from the rear, and moves alongside. At this point, the other males terminate the chase. There is some evidence that the eggs are fertilized internally. The eggs possess long filaments that enable them to stick to any vegetation or rock with which they come into contact. The young hatch in a few days and move to open water away from shore. Growth is rapid, and by the end of the first summer most of the fish are nearly adult size. The following summer these young fish spawn, the majority dying before winter. The brook silverside's life span is brief, approximately 15 months, one of the shortest life spans for any species in the region. Thus, the population in any given year is totally dependent on the reproductive success of the previous year. Brook silversides have no mechanism to buffer their population as would be the case for a species that has multiple-year classes spawning each year.

Brook silversides are very active schooling fish and frequently jump out of the water, a habit that has led to the name "skipjack." They feed on insects and plankton and serve as forage for game fish. They are not a very good bait fish because they are very fragile and die quickly upon handling.

Distribution. The range of this species extends from New York to Minnesota and south to Texas and Florida. In the Northeast, it is found in the Allegheny, Great Lakes-St. Lawrence, and Mohawk-Hudson drainages of New York. It has recently been reported from Vermont in Lake Champlain. It lives just under the surface in lakes and in open portions of streams and rivers.

Topminnows
Family Fundulidae

The topminnows are soft-rayed, physoclistus fishes with cycloid scales. Their head is flattened dorsally and scaled, and their mouth is modified for surface feeding. Approximately thirty-seven species of topminnows are known, of which only one truly freshwater form is found in the region.

Banded Killifish

Fundulus diaphanus (LeSueur, 1817)

Identification. The banded killifish is a small fish with soft rays as the only support for its dorsal fin, with a rounded caudal fin, and with *pelvic fins that lie almost entirely in advance of its dorsal fin.* It has scales on its head and no lateral line. It is the only killifish species in the region that spends its entire life cycle in freshwater. It does, however, occupy brackish water occasionally and thus can be found in conjunction with three other common brackish-water species: the sheepshead minnow (*Cyprinodon variegatus*), the mummichog (*Fundulus hete-roclitus*), and the striped killifish (*Fundulus majalis*). The sheepshead minnow is a short, deep-bodied fish (its maximum depth is contained two times in its standard length) with bicuspid teeth, which distinguishes it from the other three species. The banded killifish has 35–55 scales in the lateral series, whereas the mummichog and striped killifish have 31–35 scales in their lateral series.

The banded killifish is a slender fish with a narrow caudal peduncle and a relatively *long snout that is flattened on top.* The mummichog and striped killifish, in contrast, are shorter and stockier, with a thicker caudal peduncle and a more rounded snout. The back of the banded killifish is olive green to brown; the sides are pale yellow to white, with *12–20 vertical fingers projecting down from the back.* The underside is white.

Life History. Banded killifish may spawn any time from late spring into late summer. They spawn in extremely shallow, quiet water around the shores of lakes, choosing sites with abundant aquatic vegetation. The female extrudes a cluster of eggs, which remain attached to her genital papilla by fine, transparent threads. The eggs are immediately fertilized by an attendant male and then quickly become entangled in the vegetation. Females normally carry no more than a few hundred eggs. Banded killifish have a mouth that seems to be well adapted to feeding from the water surface. Studies of the stomach contents of banded killifish in Canada, however, have shown that they feed on organisms from a wide variety of different habitats, including a large number of bottom-dwelling organisms. They generally feed on small insects, crustaceans—in particular ostracods—and plant material. Banded killifish grow to a size of 2–3 inches and may spawn at 1 year of age.

Distribution. This species is found from the Maritime Provinces of Canada south to South Carolina, with a westward salient extending through New York and the Great Lakes to Montana. It is found in all states in the Northeast.

Livebearers

Family Poecillidae

Livebearers are primarily small fish of tropical regions of South and North America as well as the Caribbean. As the name implies, they reproduce by internal fertilization and produce live young. There are approximately 140 species in the family. One species is found in the Northeast.

Western Mosquitofish

Gambusia affinis (Baird and Girard, 1853)

Identification. The livebearers are small fish with a single dorsal fin composed of segmented soft rays; a rounded caudal fin; no lateral line; scales on the head; and a mouth that points upward. They share these characteristics with the topminnows, but they differ from the topminnows in that the base of the first ray of their dorsal fin is located posterior to the base of the first ray of the anal fin, and the male's anal fin is modified into an intromittent organ adapted for internal fertilization. Western mosquitofish are olive green to brown dorsally, grading to white on the belly. Small black spots are scattered across the body and fins, forming dark lines on the caudal fin.

Life History. These fish produce live young. In tropical environments, they breed throughout the year. A female may reproduce two to four times each year. Young are retained in the mother for 3–4 weeks, at the end of which they are released at an advanced stage of development and are required to forage on their own. Reproduction in the Northeast has not been well studied, but if they reproduce at all, it would be anticipated that the breeding season would be much shorter here than it would in warmer climates. Western mosquitofishes are stocked in the Northeast primarily because they are effective in reducing mosquito populations. Mosquito larvae are one of their favorite foods. They also feed on algae, small crustaceans, and insects. They are small fish, adults usually reaching 1–1½ inches in length.

Distribution. This is a southern species, ranging from Illinois south to Mexico and Florida and northward along the coast to southern New Jersey. It has been widely introduced, but most introductions in the North fail to survive the winter. Smith (1985) reported a population on Long Island, New York, that has maintained itself through the winter and is considered established. A second population was reported (Whitworth 1996) in a pond in Connecticut but is unlikely to become established. No other self-maintaining populations have been reported in the region. Western mosquitofish occupy low-gradient streams, weedy ponds, and lakes, usually swimming very near the surface.

Sticklebacks

Family Gasterosteidae

Sticklebacks are small physoclistus fishes with a dorsal fin composed of stout, isolated spines, an extremely narrow caudal peduncle, and a rounded caudal fin. They are the only fish in the region with isolated spines unconnected by membranes along the dorsal midline. They lack scales, although some have bony plates on their sides. Approximately eight species belong to the family, four of which are found in the Northeast.

Species Keys

1a. Nine (8–11) dorsal spines (figure 54); no bony plates on sides→ **Nine-spine Stickleback,** *Pungitius pungitius*

1b. Three to six dorsal spines; bony plates on sides may or may not be present→ **2**

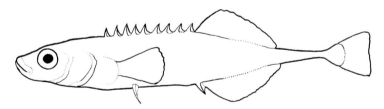

Fig. 54. Ninespine stickleback.

2a. Three dorsal spines (figure 55); bony plates on sides→ **Threespine Stickleback,** *Gasterosteus aculeatus*

2b. Four to six dorsal spines; no bony plates on sides→ **3**

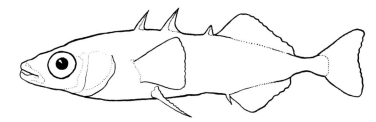

Fig. 55. Threespine stickleback.

3a. Four to six relatively short dorsal spines, approximately equal in length and evenly spaced (figure 56)→ **Brook Stickleback,** *Culaea inconstans*

3b. Four relatively long dorsal spines, varying in length and unevenly spaced (figure 57)→ **Fourspine Stickleback,** *Apeltes quadracus*

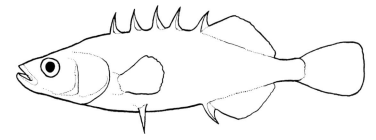

Fig. 56. Brook stickleback.

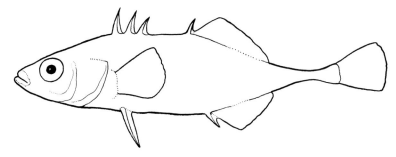

Fig. 57. Fourspine stickleback.

Fourspine Stickleback

Apeltes quadracus (Mitchill, 1815)

Identification. As its name suggests, this species has *4 spines in its dorsal fin*, although in some cases it can have 5 spines. The only other species that might be confused with the fourspine stickleback is the brook stickleback, but the brook stickleback's spines are much shorter in length, less than the diameter of the eye. The fourspine stickleback's color varies depending on the habitat, but it is generally a mottled pattern of dark brown on the back and sides, grading rather abruptly to silver or white on the belly.

Life History. Sticklebacks are an interesting group of fishes in that the male builds a rather elaborate nest and cares for the young, and the female only provides the eggs. The male locates a suitable site, usually containing some erect aquatic vegetation such as reeds or grass, and establishes a territory, which he defends very vigorously. Within the territory, the male constructs a nest out of filamentous algae and other plant material held together by a sticky secretion derived from his kidney. The nest is typically round, about the size of a baseball, and has a single opening. After the male constructs the nest, he attempts to attract a female by making extensive displays of his spawning coloration and by butting her with his head. If she is receptive, she swims into the nest and with some help from the male deposits her eggs, then swims out the opposite end of the nest. The male immediately enters, fertilizes the eggs, and leaves the nest. He then begins the process of attracting other females to spawn. After up to five females have laid eggs in the nest, the male stops and guards the nest with great aggressiveness. Throughout this process, he continually fans the nest, creating a current to help ensure that the eggs have enough oxygen. He uses a process of opercular pumping to accomplish this end, which is unique among sticklebacks.

Fourspine sticklebacks feed on plankton, reaching a little more than 2 inches in size. They are short-lived, with males living for only a year, females sometimes for 2 years.

Distribution. The fourspine stickleback is primarily a marine species found near shore along the coast. It enters rivers and streams, however, and is known to enter freshwater. In a few places, populations are restricted to freshwater. It is found near the coast in all states of the Northeast except Vermont. It is usually found in association with dense vegetation, as is true of other sticklebacks.

Brook Stickleback

Culaea inconstans (Kirtland 1841)

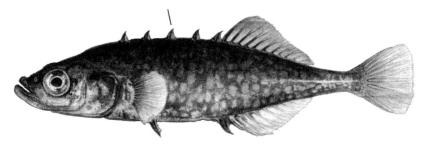

Identification. The brook stickleback is the most common stickleback in the freshwaters of the Northeast. It can be distinguished from other sticklebacks by the absence of bony plates on its side. It has 4–6 short dorsal spines (equal to or less than the diameter of the eye). The background color is olive green or brown dorsally to light green or cream ventrally, overlain by light mottling.

Life History. The spawning of the brook stickleback is similar to the spawning of the fourspine stickleback. Brook sticklebacks spawn in the spring, normally in April or May. They are short-lived, most reaching only their third birthday. They reach sexual maturity at 1 year and grow to be approximately 3 inches in length. Brook sticklebacks feed on insect larvae, in particular mosquitoes. Their behavior is quite interesting to watch, especially during the breeding season.

Distribution. Brook sticklebacks can be found from Maine to Montana and north to Canada's Northwest Territories and Nova Scotia. They are reported from Connecticut, Maine, Vermont, and New York in the Northeast. They live in weedy brooks or small ponds.

Threespine Stickleback

Gasterosteus aculeatus Linnaeus, 1758

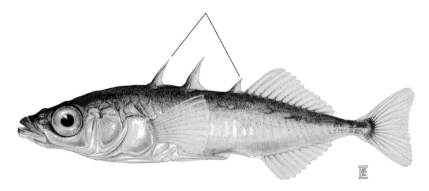

Identification. The presence of *3 spines in the dorsal fin* and bony plates along the side of the body is sufficient to distinguish the threespine stickleback from any other stickleback in the region. The back is olive green to brown, grading to silver on the belly. Breeding males develop a reddish orange breast and belly.

Life History. The reproductive behavior of the threespine stickleback is similar to that of other sticklebacks; in fact, much of the study of stickleback reproduction has been done on the threespine stickleback. It feeds on small crustaceans, insects, and occasionally larval fishes. It generally does not get larger than 2 inches in length.

Distribution. The threespine stickleback is found throughout the world in the Northern Hemisphere. In North America, it is found primarily along the Atlantic Coast from Chesapeake Bay to Hudson Bay and on the Pacific Coast from Baja California to the Seward Peninsula in Alaska. It is also known from the St. Lawrence and Ottawa Rivers as well as from Lake Ontario. In the Northeast, it has been reported from all states except Vermont. Many of the populations along the coast are marine, but some members of these populations may enter freshwater. It is typically found in shallow, vegetated water in the mouths of large rivers and in large lakes, such as Lake Ontario.

Ninespine Stickleback

Pungitius pungitius (Linnaeus, 1758)

Identification. The presence of 9–10 isolated spines in the dorsal fin of the ninespine stickleback is sufficient to distinguish it from any other fish in the region. The back is green to gray, and the lower half of the body is white.

Life History. Reproduction in ninespine sticklebacks is similar to that in other sticklebacks. They feed on small crustaceans, insects, and fish eggs and larvae. They normally do not live beyond 3 years of age.

Distribution. The ninespine stickleback is found around the world in the Northern Hemisphere. In North America, it is found in a broad band from Alaska southeastward across Canada to Nova Scotia and New Jersey. In the Northeast, it is reported from all states except Vermont. It appears in two quite different habitats: some populations are coastal, entering freshwater to spawn; others are landlocked, living in relatively deep lakes, often at great depths. It has been reported from Lake Ontario and Canandaigua Lake in New York.

Temperate Basses
Family Moronidae

The temperate basses (Moronidae) are a small family of fishes that have ctenoid scales, spines, and a swim bladder that is not connected to the gastrointestinal tract (i.e., they are physoclistus fishes). They have a complete lateral line and 2 separate dorsal fins. The anterior dorsal fin has 9 spines, and the posterior dorsal fin has 1 leading spine and 12–15 soft rays. Among freshwater fishes in the region, the distinguishing feature of the temperate basses is the presence of 2 separate dorsal fins, combined with an anal fin that has 3 spines. Members of the perch family have separate dorsal fins but only 1–2 spines in their anal fin. Some members of the sunfish family have 3 anal spines, but their dorsal fins are clearly joined. The white perch has a dorsal fin where the spinous dorsal merges slightly with the soft dorsal, but not to the extent found in sunfishes.

The family Moronidae has been revised several times, and it is uncertain exactly how many species will ultimately be allocated to it. There are four freshwater or anadromous Moronidae species in North America, three of which are found in the Northeast.

Species Key

1a. Soft anal rays 9–10; the 3 anal spines are not graduated: the second spine is almost as long as the third (figure 58a); lower and upper jaw are the same length; no patch of small teeth at base of tongue; no distinct horizontal lines on sides (figure 59)→ **White Perch,** *Morone americana*

1b. Soft anal rays 11–13; the 3 anal spines graduated in length—the first approximately one-third the length of the second, and the second approximately two-thirds the length of the third (figure 58b); lower jaw projects beyond tip of snout; 1 or more patches of small teeth at base of tongue; 5–7 dark, narrow lines running horizontally along side of body (figure 60)→ **2**

2a. Body shorter and deeper, its depth equal to or greater than head length (figure 60); 12–13 soft anal rays→ **White Bass,** *Morone chrysops*

2b. Body elongate, its depth less than head length (figure 61); 11 (7–12) soft anal rays→ **Striped Bass,** *Morone saxatilis*

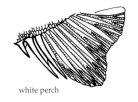

white perch

white bass

Fig. 58. Arrangement of anal spines in *(a)* white perch and *(b)* white bass.

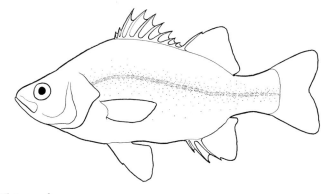

Fig. 59. White perch.

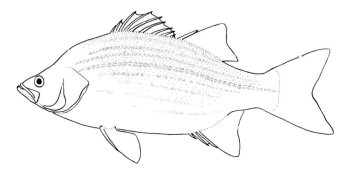

Fig. 60. White bass.

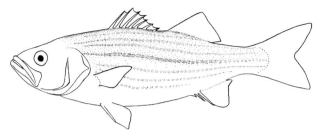

Fig. 61. Striped bass.

White Bass

Morone chrysops (Rafinesque, 1820)

Identification. The presence of 2 separate dorsal fins and 3 anal spines narrows the choices to one of the three temperate basses in the region. White bass are separated from white perch by the presence of *5–7 dark, narrow bands running horizontally along their sides*. Their *lower jaw projects beyond the tip of their snout,* and they have 12–13 anal rays, which also help to distinguish them from white perch. The only other temperate bass with dark, narrow bands is the striped bass, but it is a much more elongate fish and normally has 11 anal rays. The back of the white bass is dark green, the side silvery, and the underside white.

Life History. White bass choose shallow shoal areas or shoreline stretches with a gravel or rubble bottom in lakes for spawning in May or June. In Lake Mendota, Wisconsin, it has been shown that they are able to home to the same spawning grounds year after year, using the sun as a navigational aid. Females extrude eggs near the surface; accompanying males fertilize the eggs, which settle to the bottom, where they attach. Each female produces from 25,000 to 1 million eggs, but very few survive to maturity. Depending on the water temperature, the eggs hatch in a few days. The young absorb the yolk sac and begin feeding on zooplankton. Their growth is rapid, reaching 4–5 inches by the end of their first summer. They live for 4 or 5 years and grow to 14–15 inches and 1–2 pounds. They feed on crustaceans, insects, and small fish, including their own young.

The white bass is a schooling species and appears in great abundance in shallow water in the evening. It can be taken on flies, small spinners, and minnows.

Distribution. The range of the white bass extends from the St. Lawrence River to Lake Huron and south through the Mississippi Valley to the Gulf of Mexico. In the Northeast, it is found in New York in Lake Erie, the Niagara River, Lake Ontario, and the St. Lawrence River, as well as in Cayuga and Oneida Lakes. It is not reported from other states in the region. It prefers large bodies of water (either lakes or reservoirs normally greater than 300 acres).

White Perch

Morone americana (Gmelin, 1789)

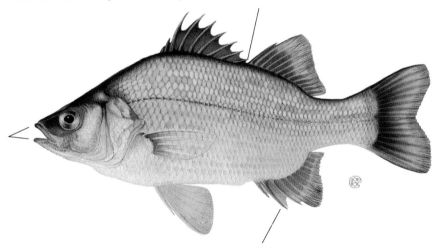

Identification. The white perch has 2 dorsal fins, *the anterior spiny dorsal and the posterior soft dorsal, slightly connected by a low membrane.* It lacks the dark horizontal lines on its sides, and *its lower and upper jaws are of approximately the same length.* In addition, the *3 anal spines are not graduated in length, but instead the first anal spine is quite short, the second and third are longer and approximately the same length* (see figure 58a). The back and base of the median fins are olive green to dark gray, with colors on the body grading to silvery gray on the sides and white on the underside.

Life History. White perch spawn in late spring in freshwater ponds, often near the ocean. They are very prolific, with each female producing hundreds of thousands of demersal (heavy and adhesive) eggs. The eggs are fertilized and broadcast across the bottom with no parental care. They hatch in a few days to a week, depending on water temperature. The species is so prolific that even with the haphazard spawning the population is not easily eliminated by over-fishing once it is established. White perch are quite tolerant of salinity changes and can be found in estuaries as well as freshwater. Young white perch feed primarily on zooplankton. Adult white perch feed on a broad range of food items, including minnows, crustaceans, and insects. They travel in schools searching for food and forage over a fairly broad area. As they get larger, their diet switches from invertebrates to fishes. Adults are usually less than 10 inches long and 1 pound in weight. They may live up to 12 years of age.

Distribution. White perch are found in coastal waters from the St. Lawrence River south to South Carolina. In the Northeast, they are found in all states, typically near the coast. There is evidence that they are extending their range farther inland into freshwater habitats as they have established populations in lakes in central New York in the past 50 years.

Striped Bass

Morone saxatilis (Walbaum, 1792)

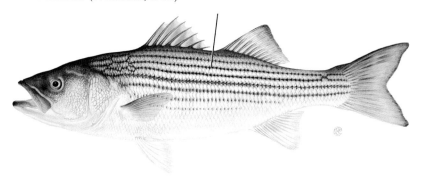

Identification. Striped bass are similar to white bass in that they have *7 or 8 dark narrow bands running horizontally along the length of the body.* They differ in that they are *more slender, with the greatest body depth less than the head length.* They also have 11 branched anal rays. These characteristics, plus their large size (1–10 pounds), aid in distinguishing striped bass from their close relative the white bass. They are gray on the back, transitioning through silver on the sides to white on the belly. Overlaying the silver sides are 7–8 narrow, dark bands running the length of the body.

Life History. Striped bass, like salmon and sea lampreys, have an anadromous spawning migration as a key element in their life history. They leave salt water and migrate into estuaries and freshwater rivers to spawn. The spawning season extends from April through June. They prefer to spawn in rivers near the mouths of tributary streams. Females normally carry 180,000–700,000 eggs, depending on their size. Several smaller males usually accompany each female. The spawning fish swim very close to the surface and on occasion turn on their side and beat the water with their tails, creating a commotion. This commotion has been referred to as a "rock fight." In reality, it is part of the spawning process. The eggs are semibuoyant and drift with the current until they hatch 2–3 days later. Young striped bass initially feed on microscopic organisms and then quickly graduate to feeding on freshwater shrimp and midge larvae. As adults, they feed heavily on small fishes. Late in the summer or early in the fall the young striped bass move downstream to overwinter in deeper water. Males reach sexual maturity in 2–3 years, females in 4–6 years. Adults normally weigh 1–10 pounds, but fish that weigh more than 30 pounds are frequently taken. Striped bass may live for 10–12 years, spawning several times during that period.

A major sport fishery for striped bass exists along the eastern coast of the United States. Some fishing for stripers occurs in the Hudson River proper. They are excellent game fish, achieving large size and exhibiting good fighting qualities.

Distribution. Striped bass are found all along the Atlantic Coast from the St. Lawrence River to the St. John's River in Florida. They are also found in the Gulf of Mexico and have been successfully introduced into the Pacific coastal waters of Oregon and California. There is evidence to suggest that there are three major spawning locations for this species on the East Coast: the Roanoke River, Chesapeake Bay, and the Hudson River. In the Northeast, they are reported from all states except Vermont. Although they are a marine fish, they move into the lower and middle reaches of most of the major rivers, and they have the capacity to become landlocked, as has been demonstrated in South Carolina. They are known to spawn in the Hudson River between West Point and Kingston, New York.

Sunfishes
Family Centrarchidae

The sunfish family includes not only sunfishes, but also the black bass and crappies. They are an important component of the warm water fishery of the Northeast. They possess spines, and most of them possess ctenoid scales. Their dorsal fins are joined and are composed of an anterior spinous portion with 6–13 spines and a posterior soft-rayed portion supported by 9–18 rays. The anal fin typically has 3 spines, but some may have up to 9 spines. The majority of the sunfishes are deep bodied, laterally compressed fishes. Thirty-two species are assigned to this family, fifteen of which are found in the Northeast.

Species Key

1a. Caudal fin rounded (figure 62)⟶ **2**

1b. Caudal fin slightly to distinctly forked (figure 63)⟶ **4**

2a. Mouth large, maxilla extends posteriorly to behind middle of eye (figure 62); cycloid scales⟶ **Mud Sunfish, *Acantharchus pomotis***

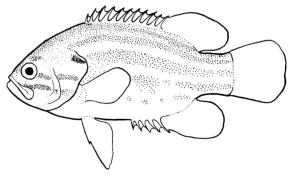

Fig. 62. Mud sunfish.

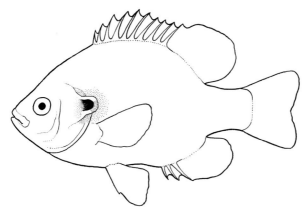

Fig. 63. Pumpkinseed.

2b. Mouth small, maxilla does not extend beyond middle of eye (figure 64); ctenoid scales→ **3**

3a. Opercular spot larger than pupil of eye; sides of body with no or indistinct crossbars (figure 64); adults with distinctive blue spots on a dark background; 16–18 scales around caudal peduncle→ **Bluespotted Sunfish,** *Enneacanthus gloriosus*

3b. Opercular spot as large as pupil of eye; sides of body with 5–8 distinct dark vertical bands (figure 65); no blue spots on sides; 19–22 scales around caudal peduncle→ **Banded Sunfish,** *Enneacanthus obesus*

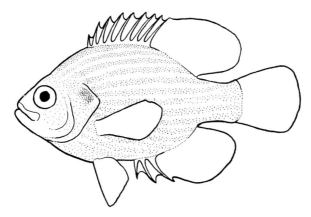

Fig. 64. Bluespotted sunfish.

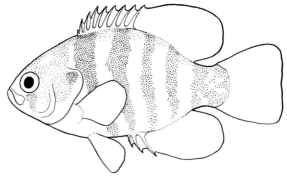

Fig. 65. Banded sunfish.

4a. Anal spines 5–7; dorsal spines 5–9 or 11–13, rarely 10 → **5**

4b. Anal spines 3; dorsal spines 10 → **7**

5a. Length of anal fin base (a) a little more than one-half the length of dorsal fin base (b) (figure 66); dorsal spines 11–13 → **Rock Bass,** *Ambloplites rupestris*

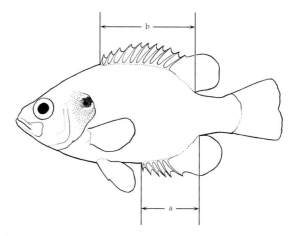

Fig. 66. Rock bass.

5b. Length of anal fin base approximately equal to length of dorsal fin base (figure 67); dorsal spines 5–9 → **6**

6a. Distance from rear of eye to base of first dorsal spine (c) equal to length of dorsal fin base (d) (figure 67); 7–8 dorsal spines; body with irregular dark markings → **Black Crappie,** *Pomoxis nigromaculatus*

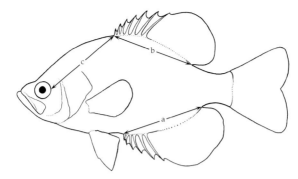

Fig. 67. Black crappie.

6b. Distance from rear of eye to base of first dorsal spine (c) greater than length of dorsal fin base (b) (figure 68); 6–7 dorsal spines; pale body→ **White Crappie,** *Pomoxis annularis*

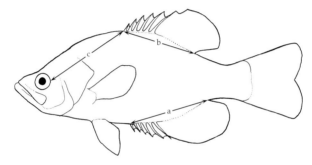

Fig. 68. White crappie.

7a. Body elongate, its standard length three times its depth in larger adults or five times its depth in younger fish (figure 69); scales small, more than 55 in lateral line→ **8**

7b. Body deep, its standard length two times its depth in large adults or three times its depth in younger fish (figure 71); scales large, less than 55 in lateral line→ **9**

8a. Distinct dark band running horizontally along sides of body; notch between 2 dorsal fins deep; shortest dorsal spine at center of the notch fits two to three times in length of longest spine (figure 69); mouth large, end of jaw extends behind posterior margin of eye→ **Largemouth Bass,** *Micropterus salmoides*

8b. Coloration variable, but normally without a distinct lateral band; notch between 2 dorsal fins not so deep; shortest dorsal spine at center of the notch fits one to two times into length of longest spine (figure 70); mouth smaller, end of jaw extends just to posterior end of eye→ **Smallmouth Bass,** *Micropterus dolomieu*

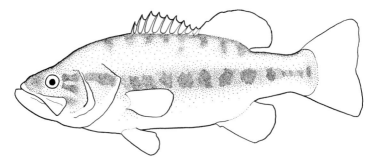

Fig. 69. Largemouth bass.

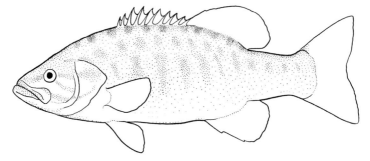

Fig. 70. Smallmouth bass.

9a. Mouth large, maxilla extends posteriorly to middle of eye (figure 71); teeth on tongue→ **Warmouth,** *Lepomis gulosus*

9b. Mouth small, maxilla does not extend beyond middle of eye; no teeth on tongue→ **10**

10a. Pectoral fin short and rounded, when laid forward only reaches posterior edge of eye (figure 72a); pectoral fin length approximately one-fourth the standard length→ **11**

10b. Pectoral fin long and pointed, when laid forward reaches anterior edge of eye or beyond (figure 72b); pectoral fin length approximately one-third the standard length→ **13**

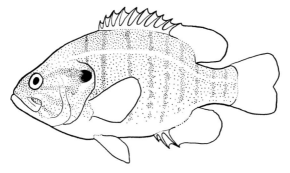

Fig. 71. Warmouth bass.

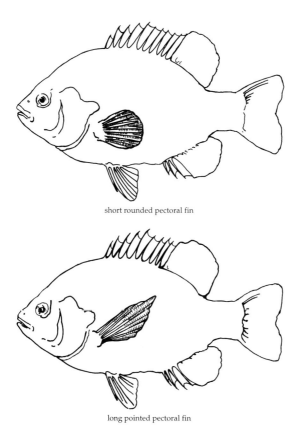

short rounded pectoral fin

long pointed pectoral fin

Fig. 72. Pectoral fins of sunfish: *(a)* the short, rounded form and *(b)* the long, pointed form.

11a. Opercular flap entirely black and not decorated with orange or red spots or bands→ **Redbreast Sunfish,** *Lepomis auritus*

11b. Opercular flap with red or orange spot or band at edge (appears white in preserved specimens)→ **12**

12a. Opercular flap as wide as long; opercle bone stiff, cannot be bent forward on itself without breaking; dusky spot on last 3 rays of dorsal and anal fins (figure 73); lateral line scales 44–51→ **Green Sunfish,** *Lepomis cyanellus*

12b. Opercular flap much longer than wide; opercle bone flexible, can be bent forward on itself; no dusky spot on dorsal or anal fin (figure 74); lateral line scales 34–38→ **Longear Sunfish,** *Lepomis megalotis*

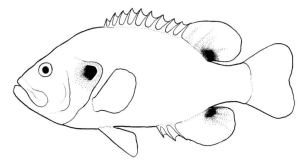

Fig. 73. Green sunfish.

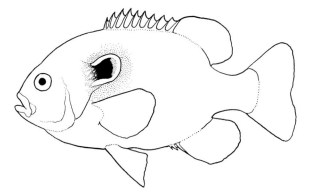

Fig. 74. Longear sunfish.

13a. Opercular flap with bright red spot at posterior end; no dark spot at base of posterior dorsal fin; gill rakers short, thick, and sometimes curved, longest gill raker less than diameter of pupil (figure 75a)→ **14**

13b. Opercular flap entirely blue to margin; dusky spot at base of posterior dorsal fin; gill rakers long and straight, longest gill raker equal to pupil diameter (figure 75b)→ **Bluegill,** *Lepomis macrochirus*

14a. Opercular flap stiff and inflexible; light green wavy bands on cheeks→ **Pumpkinseed,** *Lepomis gibbosus*

14b. Opercular flap flexible, can be bent forward upon itself; spots on cheeks→ **Redear Sunfish,** *Lepomis microlophus*

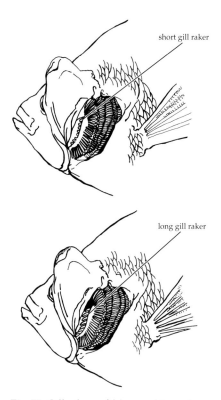

Fig. 75. Gill rakers of *(a)* pumpkinseed and *(b)* bluegill.

Mud Sunfish

Acantharchus pomotis (Baird, 1855)

Identification. All sunfishes are characterized by 2 confluent dorsal fins—an anterior spinous dorsal fin and a posterior soft dorsal—and by at least 3 spines in the anal fin. The rock bass, the black and white crappies, and the mud sunfish have 5–7 anal spines. The mud sunfish is easily identified by its *rounded caudal fin, 5 anal spines, and relatively large mouth,* the maxilla extending to under the middle of the eye. It is also the only sunfish with cycloid scales. Its back is reddish brown, grading to pale brown on the belly. Five distinct lines run along the sides down the length of its body. Its eye is brown.

Life History. Little is known of the life history of the mud sunfish in the Northeast. In North Carolina, it is reported to spawn from December through May. Males construct and defend a round nest cleared of vegetation, often over a sand bottom. Mud sunfish feed on aquatic insects and crustaceans. They may live up to 7 years and reach 6$\frac{1}{2}$ inches in length.

Distribution. The mud sunfish is found along the Atlantic Coastal Plain from New York to Florida. It is quite rare in the Northeast. It is reported from only one locality in New York, the Hackensack River. Because it has not been collected since 1935, it is listed as threatened in New York, and it may very well have been extirpated from the region. As its name suggests, it occupies weedy ponds, bogs, lakes, and lowland streams with mud or silt bottoms.

Rock Bass

Ambloplites rupestris (Rafinesque, 1817)

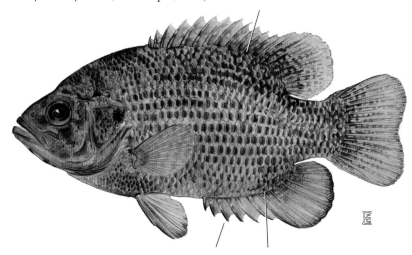

Identification. The rock bass has *5–7 anal spines,* as do both crappies and mud sunfish. In crappies, the bases of the anal and dorsal fins are approximately the same length, whereas in the rock bass the *base of the anal fin is much shorter than the base of the dorsal fin.* The mud sunfish is distinguishable from the others by its rounded tail and its cycloid scales. Rock bass have a dark olive back and light olive underside. Overlaying this background are irregular blotches and mottling above the lateral line and a series of 8–10 faint horizontal lines below the lateral line. The eye is red.

Life History. Rock bass spawn early in the summer after the water has reached 60–70°F. The male constructs a platelike depression in shallow water, guarding the nest until a female joins him. A female may carry 5,000 or more eggs, but generally she does not deposit them all in one nest. Instead, she visits several nests until she is spent. Accordingly, the male is likely to be visited by more than one female. The eggs hatch in 3–4 days, and not long after that the young leave the nest and disperse. The male aggressively guards the nest during the time that his young are using it. Later in the summer, after the young have developed scales, they are strikingly colored with large dark blotches. Rock bass feed on insects, small fish, mollusks, and crayfish. They may live for more than 10 years, reaching 1 pound and 13 inches. The usual size, however, is much smaller, approximately 8 or 9 inches and less than $\frac{1}{2}$ pound. If overcrowded, they will be stunted, not achieving even this modest size. They are frequently found in association with smallmouth bass and may compete with young smallmouth bass for food.

Anglers can easily catch rock bass, which take flies, small spinners, or live bait. They fight well when first hooked.

Distribution. Rock bass are native to the Lake Champlain drainage west to the Dakotas and then south through the Mississippi Valley to the Gulf of Mexico. They are found in all states in the Northeast except Maine. Rock bass are found in rocky areas in lakes and in larger streams, where they may be quite abundant.

Bluespotted Sunfish

Enneacanthus gloriosus (Holbrook, 1855)

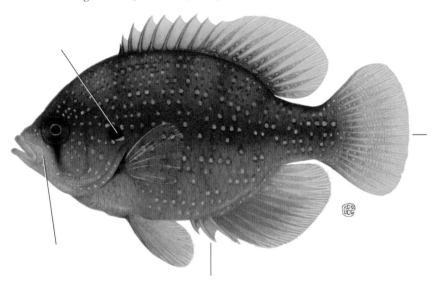

Identification. Bluespotted sunfish have a *rounded caudal fin, 3 anal spines, a maxilla that does not reach the middle of the eye, and an opercular spot that is larger than the pupil of the eye.* They are greenish brown dorsally, grading to white ventrally; the sides are highlighted by bright turquoise spots in males.

Life History. Male bluespotted sunfish build a circular nest by clearing a small depression. Females deposit their eggs in the nest, and the male defends it, the eggs, and the young until the young disperse. Bluespotted sunfish feed on small aquatic insects, crustaceans, and mollusks. They are small fish, normally reaching only 2–4 inches in length.

Distribution. The bluespotted sunfish is found along the Atlantic Coastal Plain from New York to Florida. In the Northeast, its native range is primarily in southeastern New York, but it is also found in the Delaware drainage and has been reported from Oneida Lake and Jamesville Reservoir near Syracuse, New York, in the Lake Ontario drainage. It prefers vegetated ponds, small lakes, or slow-flowing and heavily vegetated streams.

Banded Sunfish

Enneacanthus obesus (Girard, 1854)

Identification. The banded sunfish is one of three sunfishes in the region with a rounded caudal fin. In addition, it has 3 anal rays, a small mouth with the maxilla not reaching back to the middle of the eye, an opercular spot approximately as large as the pupil of the eye, and no blue spots on its sides. It is generally green to brown in color, with dark vertical bars on its sides.

Life History. The life history of the banded sunfish is not well known but is presumed to be very similar to that of the bluespotted sunfish. It builds its nest in vegetation and feeds on small aquatic insects and crustaceans. It is very tolerant of low pH. It is a small fish, normally reaching only 2–4 inches in length.

Distribution. The banded sunfish ranges along the Atlantic Coastal Plain from New Hampshire to Florida. In the Northeast, it has been reported from all of the states except Maine and Vermont. It is considered threatened in New York, where it is found only on eastern Long Island. It is often found in unproductive ponds or slow-moving streams that may be darkly stained.

Redbreast Sunfish

Lepomis auritus (Linnaeus, 1758)

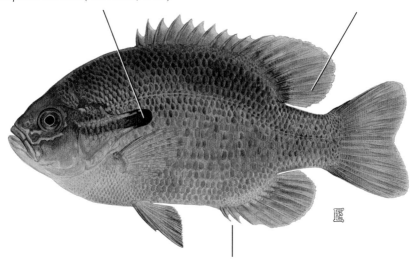

Identification. The fishes in the genus *Lepomis* are what we normally think of as "sunfishes." Three species are fairly common in the region: the redbreast, the pumpkinseed, and the bluegill. Four other species, although not as abundant, have been reported from various sites in the Northeast. All are distinguishable from other members of the sunfish family in that they have a forked tail, *3 anal spines,* and a body depth that fits only two to three times into the standard length. The redbreast is distinguished from the bluegill and pumpkinseed by its short pectoral fin, which, if laid forward, would reach no farther than the eye. The bluegill and pumpkinseed have longer pectoral fins, which almost reach the tip of the snout when laid forward. *The earflap on the redbreast is entirely blue.* The pumpkinseed has a red spot on its earflap. Although the bluegill has a dark blue earflap like the redbreast, it has one distinguishing field character that makes it easy to identify: a large dusky spot at the posterior base of the dorsal fin. *The redbreast sunfish lacks this spot.* The back of the redbreast sunfish is olive to dark brown, the lower sides gray to green, the belly gray white, and the breast a bright orange. The opercular flap is dark blue. Turquoise bands radiate backward across the head. The other similar species (warmouth, green, longear, and redear sunfishes) are relatively rare in the Northeast.

Life History. The redbreast spawns in early summer, constructing a nest in shallow water near shore or in a protected portion of a stream. Females carry 1,000–8,000 eggs. The male guards the nest until the young hatch. Little is known of the early life history of this species. It feeds primarily on insects but is known to consume small fish occasionally. Adults grow to 6–8 inches. During the winter, they move into deeper water and form a fairly inactive wintering aggregation.

The redbreast is too small to be a major sport fish. It does, however, take bait or a lure readily and commonly appears in the catch of children fishing near shore.

Distribution. The range of this species extends from New Brunswick to Florida east of the Appalachians. It is found in all states in the region.

Green Sunfish

Lepomis cyanellus Rafinesque, 1819

Identification. The green sunfish, unlike all of the other sunfishes except the warmouth, has a large mouth, with the maxilla extending almost to the middle of the eye. It has a relatively short and rounded pectoral fin, which when bent forward does not reach beyond the eye. The opercular flap has an orange margin and is quite rigid and stiff. Fairly heavy pigmentation can be seen at the base of the last few rays in the dorsal and anal fins, giving the impression of a dusky spot in those locations (see figure 73). Green sunfish are basically green in color, darker on the back and grading to lighter tones on the belly.

Life History. Green sunfish spawn in the summer when water temperatures range from 68 to 82°F. Males construct nests in very shallow water, often less than 1 foot deep. They guard the nest until the young have dispersed. Green sunfish feed on aquatic insects, mollusks, and fishes. They may reach 10 inches in length, but that is quite unusual; more typical are fish 4–6 inches long.

Distribution. The original range of this species was from New York west to North Dakota and south to Mexico and Georgia. Because it is very tolerant of a wide variety of ecological conditions, however, it has been introduced well outside of its original range. In the Northeast, it is reported from New York, Connecticut, and Massachusetts.

Pumpkinseed

Lepomis gibbosus (Linnaeus, 1758)

Identification. The pumpkinseed is readily distinguished from most other sunfish by the *long and pointed pectoral fins,* a stiff opercular bone, and the *red spot on its opercular flap.* It is quite common and, along with the yellow perch and brown bullhead, is probably the most familiar fish in the region. The back is olive to yellowish brown, shading to yellow or orange ventrally. The sides of the *head and cheek have several wavy turquoise bands.*

Life History. Spawning occurs in early summer; the pattern is essentially the same as for other sunfish. The male creates a circular depression in shallow water by fanning his tail and using his mouth to carry away larger objects. The nest usually has a diameter approximately twice the length of the fish constructing it. After the male builds the nest, the female is attracted to enter it to spawn. They swim together in a slow circle over the nest, emitting eggs and sperm, which settle to the bottom of the nest. The eggs are sticky and attach to the first thing they contact. The male guards the nest and the young until they disperse. A female may carry 1,500–3,000 eggs, and more than one female may spawn in a single nest. The males are very brightly colored at this time and defend the nest with great vigor. They are not easily frightened, and, in fact, a hand placed near the nest might get nipped. Pumpkinseeds live for 8 or 9 years and rarely exceed 10 inches and $1/2$ pound. They feed on insects, small invertebrates, mollusks, and occasionally a small fish.

If for no other reason than that the pumpkinseed has introduced thousands of young people to the joys of angling, it would have to be considered an important species. The pumpkinseed, however, has also proved to be a scrappy fighter when taken on light gear. It strikes flies, spinners, or live bait readily and puts up a good fight, considering its size.

Distribution. The pumpkinseed was originally found from New Brunswick to Georgia and west to the Dakotas. It has been widely introduced into many of the western states, however. It is widespread throughout the Northeast and has been reported from all states. It is a resident primarily of lakes and ponds, but also of quiet water in streams and rivers. It normally chooses to live in or near vegetation or brush cover.

Warmouth

Lepomis gulosus (Cuvier, 1829)

Identification. The warmouth is distinguishable from any other sunfish in the region by a forked tail, a large mouth (the maxilla extends beyond the middle of the eye), and the presence of a significant patch of teeth on its tongue. It is brown on the back, grading to whitish on the belly. It has dark vertical bars on its sides.

Life History. The warmouth has an extended spawning season. In Illinois, where it has been studied, spawning begins in mid-May, peaks in early June, and is normally over by early July. Males build and defend the nests, choosing sites with a rubble bottom covered by a thin layer of sand or silt. They are very aggressive, attacking any intruder that may approach. When a female is ready to spawn, the pair swim in a tight circle over the nest, depositing eggs onto the bottom. The male guards the nest until the young have left. Eggs hatch in 1–2 days, and the young begin to feed about a week after hatching. The young begin to disperse into the vegetation after feeding is initiated. Warmouths initially feed on plankton, but as they grow, they switch to a variety of organisms, including crayfish, mollusks, aquatic insects, crustaceans, worms, and small fishes. They live for 6–8 years and reach 4–7 inches in length. A large specimen may approach 1 pound in weight.

Distribution. The warmouth ranges from Kansas and Iowa east to Virginia and south to Florida and Texas. It is known from only two locations in southeastern New York, Woodbury Creek in Orange County and Saw Kill in Dutchess County. It apparently was introduced but is not spreading from these areas. It typically occupies slow-moving, heavily vegetated areas with muck or soft bottoms.

Bluegill

Lepomis macrochirus (Rafinesque, 1819)

Identification. The name *bluegill* is a good key to the identification of this species because it has a *blue opercular flap,* but this character is not sufficient for certain identification because the opercular flap on the redbreast sunfish is entirely blue as well. *Long, pointed pectoral fins* that reach beyond the eye when pulled forward and the *dusky thumb print at the posterior edge of the soft dorsal fin* are the other clues for positive identification of the bluegill. Although the dusky thumb print does not show up well on the illustration here, it is a good and reliable field character. The back is dark green to brown, shading to white on the belly and yellow to orange on the breast.

Life History. Bluegills spawn in early summer, as do the other sunfishes. Their reproductive behavior is very similar to that of the pumpkinseed and need not be repeated here. The young leave the nest when they are $\frac{1}{4}$ to $\frac{1}{3}$ inch in length. There is evidence that at this very young age they leave the weedy shore of the lake and move into the open water, where their transparent bodies make them essentially invisible. At approximately 1 inch, they have developed scales, which can protect them from insect predators, and at that size they return to the vegetated portion of the lake. When young, bluegills feed on zooplankton. Larger fish feed on insects, invertebrates, and on occasion small fish. They may live for 10 years, reaching 10 inches in length. Most individuals are between 6 and 9 inches long.

When you are fishing for bluegill, the use of light gear can produce a great deal of enjoyment. Like the pumpkinseed, they readily take flies, spinners, or bait and put up a solid fight when hooked. If you reduce your gear to match their capabilities, you will find that they will repay you with a strong fight. They are commonly stocked in farm ponds, but they have a tendency to become stunted if they are not fished regularly.

Distribution. The bluegill was originally found in an area that extended from the St. Lawrence River south to Georgia and then west to Texas and Minnesota. It has been introduced in areas well beyond this range. It is reported from all states of the Northeast except Maine. Bluegills tend to live in lakes and occupy more open habitat than the pumpkinseed, even though both may be found in the same lake.

Longear Sunfish

Lepomis megalotis (Rafinesque, 1820)

Identification. A *forked tail*, a small mouth, a *short, rounded pectoral fin, a red spot on its dark opercular flap, and a relatively long and flexible opercular bone* are characteristics that identify the longear sunfish. It is dark brown to gray dorsally, grading to a bright orange or yellow ventrally. Males during breeding season are particularly colorful, as shown in the illustration.

Life History. The longear sunfish builds a nest and spawns in summer, as do most of the other sunfishes. It normally spawns when the water temperature warms to 74–77°F. Nests are constructed in shallow water, preferably on gravel, or on a sand-and-silt bottom. Nests are often aggregated into a colony, with many males on nests in a limited area. Males aggressively defend the nest site, both from neighboring longear sunfish and from other intruders. Longear sunfish feed on small aquatic insects and crustaceans. They may reach 10 years old, but they tend to be relatively small sunfish, ranging from 2 to 4 inches in length.

Distribution. The longear sunfish ranges from Wisconsin, Michigan, and Ohio south to the Gulf of Mexico in Texas to Florida. It is an inhabitant of slow-moving streams. In the Northeast, it is found in western New York, where it is rare and considered a threatened species.

Redear Sunfish

Lepomis microlophus (Günther, 1859)

Identification. The redear sunfish has a long, pointed pectoral fin that when bent forward almost reaches the tip of its snout and a flexible opercular flap with a bright red spot on its posterior end—thus the name *redear*. It is greenish gray on its back, grading through mottled sides to a white belly.

Life History. Redear sunfish spawn throughout the summer in the South, where they are native. The spawning period in the North may be shorter. The male builds a nest near aquatic vegetation, defends it, and cares for the young, as do other male sunfishes. Redear sunfish feed on a variety of bottom organisms, including mollusks and crustaceans. They are relatively large for sunfishes, reaching 2–4 pounds in the southern part of their range. Sizes are much smaller in the North.

Distribution. The original distribution of this species was from southern Illinois and Indiana south to Texas and peninsular Florida. It has been introduced outside of this range and has been reported from Vermont, the only location within the Northeast where it is found. It is found in slow-moving water—ponds, lakes, and slow-moving streams—usually near submerged aquatic vegetation.

Smallmouth Bass

Micropterus dolomieu Lacépède, 1802

Identification. Many people do not realize that the smallmouth bass and the largemouth black bass are members of the sunfish family and thus share the characteristics that distinguish this family from other freshwater fishes. Both the largemouth and smallmouth have 3 anal spines and a relatively elongate body whose standard length is three to four and one-half times its greatest depth. The largemouth has a dark band running horizontally along its side; *the smallmouth lacks this dark band.* In addition, the notch between the first and second dorsal fin is deeper in the largemouth than in the smallmouth, and the *posterior end of the upper jaw extends behind the orbit of the eye in the adult largemouth, but no farther than the posterior edge of the orbit in the adult smallmouth.* The back and sides of the smallmouth are olive to gray, shading into a light yellow green on the lower flank. The undersides are grayish white. Juveniles have a distinct color pattern on the caudal fin, beginning with yellow at the base of the fin, followed by a dark band and then a white outer edge.

Life History. Smallmouth bass spawn in May or early June, typically over a gravel or rocky bottom. The male constructs a round nest and is then joined by the female, who releases several thousand eggs, which the male quickly fertilizes. She carries 5,000–7,000 eggs and thus may visit other nests until she is spent. The male guards the nest, chasing any intruders away. The young hatch in 4–8 days, and they leave the nest 2–3 weeks later as very dark black fry. Smallmouths initially feed on microscopic crustaceans, switching to insects, crayfish, and fishes as they grow. They may live for up to 14 or 15 years and reach 18–20 inches. Record fish in the region exceed 8 pounds. In the spring, they are in shallow water, but as the water warms, they move deeper to escape the heat. During winter, under the ice, they remain rather listlessly near the bottom. They do not feed in winter and thus contribute little to the ice fishery.

The smallmouth is one of the species that makes angling in the Northeast such a pleasure. It can be taken with wet or dry flies, spinners, spoons, plugs, or live bait such as crayfish, minnows, night crawlers, or hellgrammites. When caught, it puts up a magnificent fight with lots of leaping and aerial acrobatics.

Distribution. The original range of the smallmouth bass was the Great Lakes, St. Lawrence, and Mississippi drainages. It has been widely introduced and is now found throughout the United States, in southern Canada, and in localities in Europe and Africa. It is found in all of the states in the Northeast. Smallmouth bass prefer cool water, with rock or gravel bottoms. They are found in both lakes and streams.

Largemouth Bass

Micropterus salmoides (Lacépède, 1802)

Identification. The largemouth bass resembles the smallmouth bass in many ways. It, however, has a fairly distinct *dark, wide band that extends horizontally along its side;* a deep notch between the two dorsal fins; and *a jaw that extends beyond the posterior margin of the eye,* except in young individuals. The back and sides are olive to gray to black, grading to grayish white on the undersides.

Life History. Largemouth bass spawn in late spring or early summer. They tend to choose shallower, weedier sites than the smallmouth, but otherwise their spawning behavior is quite similar. A female may carry up to 60,000 eggs, although the average is probably fewer than 10,000. The eggs hatch in 3–5 days, and it is another week before the fry are able to swim well enough to feed. They tend to remain together for another month, with the male parent guarding them. At this early stage, they are a light green color instead of the striking black color of smallmouth fry. Largemouths begin life feeding on microscopic crustaceans, switch soon to insects, and eventually graduate to fish, frogs, worms, and crayfish. Individuals may live up to 15 years, some exceeding 20 inches and a weight of 8 pounds. Record fish exceed 11 pounds. More common, however, are fish that weigh 2–3 pounds.

The largemouth is an important game fish. It is very common in small farm ponds as well as in lakes. It can be taken on live bait or on anything that resembles live bait; one of the more popular lures is the plastic night crawler. It can also be taken on spinners, plugs, or spoons as well as on flies or streamers.

Distribution. The original distribution of this species was the Great Lakes and Mississippi drainages and up the East Coast from Florida to Virginia. Because of many introductions, it is now found throughout the United States and also in the British Isles, France, Germany, South Africa, Brazil, the Philippines, and Hong Kong. It is found in all states in the Northeast. Largemouth bass are fish of quiet weedy water. They are common in shallow bays, small lakes, and ponds. They are rarely found in streams and rivers. They also seem to prefer siltier, softer bottoms than the smallmouth. Consequently, even though both the largemouth and smallmouth may live in the same lake, they are seldom found in the same habitat. The largemouth inhabits weedy bays, whereas the smallmouth prefers deeper water with less vegetation.

White Crappie

Pomoxis annularis Rafinesque, 1818

Identification. The crappies are the only other members of the sunfish family besides the rock bass and mud sunfish that have 5–7 anal spines. Their shape and the fact that the base of their anal fin is approximately the same length as the base of their dorsal fin easily distinguish them from other members of the family. Two species are known, the white crappie (*Pomoxis annularis)* and the black crappie (*Pomoxis nigromaculatus).* In the white crappie, the length of the base of the dorsal fin is less than the distance from the base of its first dorsal spine to its eye. In the black crappie, in contrast, these two distances are approximately equal. In addition, the white crappie has 6–7 dorsal spines, whereas the black crappie has 7–8 dorsal spines. The white crappie's body is gray to brown dorsally, grading to a gray white ventrally. This background is overlain with a mottled dark gray to brown pattern.

Life History. White crappies spawn after the water has warmed to 57°F and may continue to spawn until water temperatures reach 73°F, thus placing their spawning period in May and June for much of the region. Their spawning behavior is similar to that of other sunfishes, with the male constructing and defending the nest until the young leave. They tend to be colonial nesters, with many males guarding nests in a limited area. They feed initially on zooplankton, switching to aquatic insects and small fish as they get older. They normally reach 12–14 inches and may weigh around 1 pound.

Distribution. The original distribution of the white crappie was from South Dakota to southern Ontario and western New York, south to the Gulf coast in Alabama, and west to Texas. It has been introduced to many localities outside of this range. It is found in four states in the Northeast: New York, Connecticut, Massachusetts, and Vermont. It prefers lakes, large ponds, and impoundments and is quite tolerant of silt and turbidity. It may also be found in smaller numbers in slow-moving, low-gradient streams and rivers.

Black Crappie

Pomoxis nigromaculatus (LeSueur, 1829)

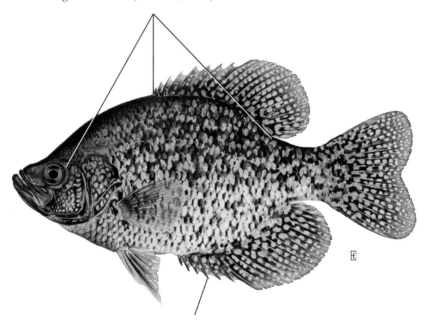

Identification. The black crappie has *5–7 anal spines;* its dorsal and anal fin bases are approximately the same length, as you would find in a white crappie. The *distance from the eye to the base of the first dorsal spine in the black crappie, however, is equal to the length of the base of the dorsal fin* instead of being greater than the length of the dorsal fin base, as it is in the white crappie. The black crappie has 7–8 dorsal spines in contrast to the 6–7 spines in the white crappie. It has a very narrow or thin body when viewed from the front. In both crappies, the snout tends to curve upward, giving these fish a distinctive profile. The black crappie's back is green, olive, or gray, grading quickly to cream on the sides and belly. Overlaying the base coloration on the sides and median fins are a large number of irregular brown to black spots.

Life History. The black crappie spawns in early summer. Its habits are quite similar to other nest-building sunfishes. Females may carry up to 150,000 eggs, but most have 20,000–50,000 eggs. Little is known about the early life history of this species. They apparently feed on plankton for the first few years, supplementing this diet with insect larvae. In later years, they switch to fish, usually selecting individuals less than 2 inches long. Crappies may live for 8 or 9 years and reach 1 foot in length and 1 pound or more in weight. Record fish are up to 3–4 pounds in weight. They tend to school and provide excellent fishing in the spring when they gather in prespawning congregations.

They can be taken on live bait, preferably small minnows, spinners, or flies. One good method is to hook a minnow to a line, place a large bobber several feet up from the bait, and cast this toward a likely spot, allowing it to drift until a school is contacted. Although crappies are not large, they put up a respectable, albeit short, fight, and they are delicious eating. In areas where crappies are abundant, ice fishing is a productive method of taking them.

Distribution. The black crappie originally was found from Florida and Texas north to the upper Mississippi Valley and Quebec. It, too, has been introduced beyond its normal range and is now commonly found throughout the United States. In the Northeast, it is found in all of the states in the region. Black crappies are rarely if ever found in running water. They are lake or pond dwellers, preferring clear water with abundant vegetation.

Darters and Perches
Family Percidae

Members of the perch family are small to moderately large physoclistus fishes with ctenoid scales, 2 separate dorsal fins, pelvic fins located under their pectoral fins, and 1 or 2 spines in the anal fin. They can be separated from other families that have 2 separate dorsal fins by several unique characteristics. Members of this family have only 1 or 2 spines at the forward edge of their anal fin. They have scales, and the pelvic fins are not joined to form a suckerlike disc. They lack barbels and isolated dorsal spines. The base of the anal fin is shorter than the length of the base of both dorsal fins. The family is divided into two groups: the relatively small darters and a group of three game fishes—the yellow perch, the walleye, and the sauger. All darters have 2 separate dorsal fins; the anterior fin is composed entirely of spines, the posterior fin entirely of soft rays. Darters have either 1 or 2 spines in their anal fin. The spines are quite soft and flexible and easily confused with rays unless one looks carefully for the lack of segmentation or the lack of flaring at the end of the ray. Of course, darters are considerably smaller than perches, walleyes, or saugers, but they can also be distinguished from their larger relatives by the rounded tail and the smooth edge on their preoperculum.

The family is composed of 165 species, 21 of which are found in the Northeast; 18 of the 21 are darters.

Species Key

1a. Preoperculum with a serrated edge (figure 76); mouth large, maxilla extends to at least the middle of the eye; adults usually longer than 6 inches → **2**

1b. Preoperculum smooth; mouth small, maxilla extends only to anterior edge of eye; adults usually less than 5 inches → **4**

2a. No canine teeth present on lower jaw—that is, all teeth are approximately the same length; anal soft rays 6–8; dorsal soft rays 12–13; dark vertical bars along sides→ **Yellow Perch,** *Perca flavescens*

2b. Canine teeth present on lower jaw; anal soft rays 11–14; dorsal soft rays 17–23; no dark vertical bars→ **3**

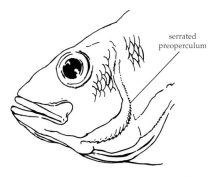

Fig. 76. Serrated preoperculum on yellow perch.

3a. Distinct round, black markings on spiny dorsal fin; no black blotch at posterior base of spiny dorsal fin (figure 77a); dorsal soft rays 17–21→ **Sauger,** *Sander canadense*

3b. Diffuse black markings on spiny dorsal fin; large black blotch at posterior base of spiny dorsal fin (figure 77b); lower lobe of caudal fin has white tip; dorsal soft rays 19–23→ **Walleye,** *Sander vitreum*

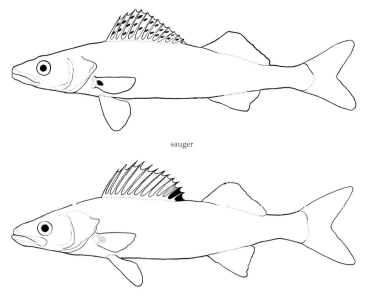

sauger

Fig. 77. Markings on dorsal fin of *(a)* sauger and *(b)* walleye.

4a. Body translucent and partially naked; scales found on midline of sides, but not on rest of body; slender shape, body depth fits seven or more times into standard length; 1 spine in anal fin→ **Eastern Sand Darter,** *Ammocrypta pellucida*

4b. Body opaque and completely scaled; has a more robust shape, body depth fits less than seven times into standard length; usually 2 spines in anal fin (exceptions: johnny and tessellated darter)→ **5**

5a. Ventral midline of body contains a distinct row of specialized scales separated from scales on either side by small groove (figure 78); area of anal fin approximately equal to area of second dorsal→ **6**

5b. Ventral midline without specialized scale row; area of anal fin less than area of second dorsal fin→ **11**

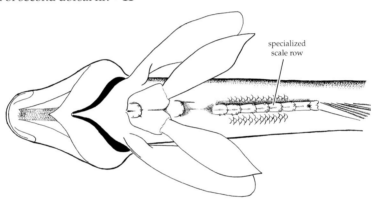

specialized
scale row

Fig. 78. Specialized scale row on ventral midline of *Percina* sp.

6a. Premaxillary bones protractile, groove separates upper lip from snout→ **Channel Darter,** *Percina copelandi*

6b. Premaxillary bones not protractile, thin fleshy connection (frenum) between upper lip and tip of snout→ **7**

7a. Snout conical and extending beyond upper lip (figure 79a); sides of body with 14–16 vertical bars, every other one expanded at lower end→ **Logperch,** *Percina caprodes*

7b. Snout does not extend beyond upper lip (figure 79b); sides of body with dark blotches that tend to run together along lateral line → **8**

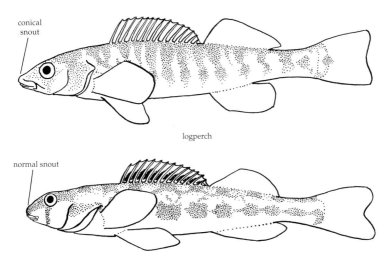

Fig. 79. Snout and pattern of markings on side of *(a)* logperch and *(b)* shield darter.

8a. Cheeks completely scaleless→ **9**

8b. Cheeks more or less scaled→ **Blackside Darter,** *Percina maculata*

9a. Head and snout elongated (figure 80a); more than 70 scales in lateral line→ **Longhead Darter,** *Percina macrocephala*

9b. Head and snout not elongated (figure 80b); fewer than 65 scales in lateral line→ **10**

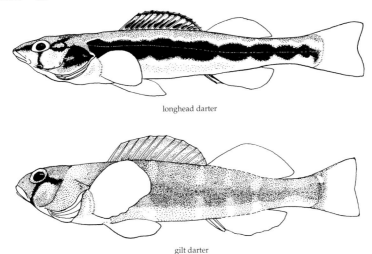

Fig. 80. Head and snout of *(a)* longhead darter and *(b)* gilt darter.

10a. Color olive and bronze; 7 dark blotches more or less confluent along lateral line→ **Gilt Darter,** *Percina evides*

10b. Color pale yellow; 6 dark blotches usually not confluent along lateral line→ **Shield Darter,** *Percina peltata*

11a. Premaxillary bones protractile→ **12**

11b. Premaxillary bones not protractile→ **14**

12a. Two anal spines; snout blunt; no groove separating maxilla from preorbital region except at posterior end (figure 81)→ **Greenside Darter,** *Etheostoma blennioides*

12b. One anal spine (first soft ray is unbranched and thus resembles a spine, but it is segmented); snout pointed; a groove separates maxilla from preorbital region over most of its length→ **13**

groove missing

Fig. 81. Head of greenside darter showing attachment to preorbital region of head.

13a. Six to eight markings on sides resembling X, V, or W; 10–12 rays in second dorsal fin; mouth horizontal, with snout steeply sloping, giving a blunt-nosed appearance (lower jaw not visible when head viewed from above)→ **Johnny Darter,** *Etheostoma nigrum*

13b. Nine to eleven X-, V-, or W-shaped markings on sides; 12–14 rays in second dorsal fin; mouth more oblique, with pointed snout and more gradual slope (tip of lower jaw can be seen when head viewed from above)→ **Tessellated Darter,** *Etheostoma olmstedi*

14a. Lateral line incomplete, normally not extending beyond posterior end of soft dorsal fin→ **15**

14b. Lateral line complete or nearly so, lacking only last 5 or 6 scales→ **18**

15a. No more than 3 scale rows between lateral line and base of spiny dorsal fin→ **Swamp Darter,** *Etheostoma fusiforme*

15b. At least 4 scale rows between lateral line and base of spiny dorsal→ **16**

16a. Spiny dorsal low, approximately one-half the height of the soft dorsal; knobs on tips of spines in males (figure 82); shoulder region has a markedly enlarged black humeral scale→ **Fantail Darter,** *Etheostoma flabellare*

l6b. Spiny dorsal nearly as high as soft dorsal; shoulder region without a black humeral scale→ **17**

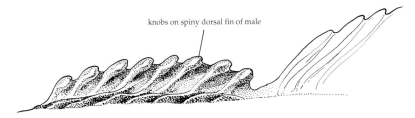

knobs on spiny dorsal fin of male

Fig. 82. Detail of spiny dorsal fin of male fantail darter.

17a. Cheeks almost naked, opercula with scales; body deep, greatest depth beneath first dorsal fin, fitting four to four and one-half times into standard length; scales in lateral series less than 50→ **Rainbow Darter,** *Etheostoma caeruleum*

17b. Both cheeks and opercula more or less scaled; body slender, greatest depth fits five and one-half to six and one-half times into standard length; scales in lateral series more than 50→ **Iowa Darter,** *Etheostoma exile*

18a. Gill covers not united by a membrane extending across the isthmus→ **19**

18b. Gill covers broadly connected by a membrane extending across the isthmus→ **20**

19a. Relatively small scales, usually 60 scale rows in body length; no black band around margin of soft dorsal, anal, and caudal fins; head length fits approximately three and one-fifth to three and three-fifths times into standard length; round tail→ **Spotted Darter,** *Etheostoma maculatum*

19b. Relatively large scales, 55 or fewer scale rows in body length; a black band around margin of soft dorsal, anal, and caudal fins; head length fits approximately three and one-half to three and four-fifths times into standard length; square tail→ **Bluebreast Darter,** *Etheostoma camurum*

20a. Twelve or more dorsal spines; no scales on cheeks; membrane connecting gill covers forms a nearly U-shaped arc; dark band extends from in front of dorsal fin down either side to just above pectoral fin; rear of body has 5–7 bluish green bands separated by orangish red spots→ **Variegate Darter,** *Etheostoma variatum*

20b. Fewer than 12 dorsal spines; embedded scales on cheeks, sometimes difficult to see; membrane connecting gill covers forms a nearly straight line (may form a shallow angle, but not a U-shaped angle); no dark band in front of dorsal fin; body color greenish except in breeding male, where 9 or more dark green vertical bars encircle body→ **Banded Darter,** *Etheostoma zonale*

Eastern Sand Darter

Ammocrypta pellucida (Putnam, 1863)

Identification. The eastern sand darter is distinct from any other darter in the region because its body is translucent in life and nearly naked, being covered by scales only down the middle of its sides and on the caudal peduncle. The rest of the body lacks scales. It is a slender fish; its body depth fits seven or more times in its standard length. It is one of only three species of darters in the region to have a single anal spine. The other two (johnny and tessellated darters) are scaled.

Life History. As its name implies, the sand darter prefers streams with a sand bottom, usually in slow-moving, shallow water. Its preference for sand bottoms is quite strong, and it is unlikely to be found if adequate sand is not available. It tends to bury itself in the sand to avoid predators, to capture prey, or simply to conserve energy. It is known to spawn in early to mid-June in Vermont when water temperatures are between 69 and 78°F. Adults are typically 2 inches in length. This species appears to be declining throughout its range, owing possibly to increased siltation of streams, which reduces the amount of sand-bottom habitat available.

Distribution. The eastern sand darter is found in Illinois and Kentucky, ranging east in the Mississippi, Ohio, and Great Lakes drainages to western New

York, the St. Lawrence River, and tributaries of Lake Erie and Lake Champlain. In the Northeast, it is found only in New York and Vermont. In New York, it is found in Lake Erie as well as in the Grasse, St. Regis/Deer, and Mettawee Rivers. In Vermont, it is found in the Poultney, Winooski, Lamoille, and Missisquoi Rivers. It is considered threatened in both states.

Greenside Darter

Etheostoma blennioides Rafinesque, 1819

Identification. The greenside darter has a *blunt, rounded snout that extends beyond the mouth and a groove that separates the upper lip from the snout; the maxilla, which lies above and behind the upper lip, is attached to the preorbital region throughout most of its length* (see figure 81). The area of the anal fin is less than the area of the second dorsal fin when the fish is viewed from the side. The greenside darter also has 2 anal spines; a complete lateral line; and 6–7 dark markings across the back, one directly in front of the dorsal fin and the others along the base of the dorsal fin all the way to the base of the tail. Prior to and during the breeding season, males exhibit dark green vertical bars on their sides.

Life History. Greenside darters are most commonly found in deep riffle areas in streams with gravel to rock bottoms and rapidly flowing water. Smaller individuals can also be found searching for food in quieter water. They feed on small insects, primarily midge and mayfly larvae. When not searching for food, they rest on the bottom, using their pectoral fins for support. They spawn in the spring when water temperatures reach 50–55°F, with males occupying and defending a territory on the bottom of the stream. Eggs are attached to bottom vegetation or algae and fertilized. They hatch in approximately $2\frac{1}{2}$ weeks at temperatures of 55–60°F. Greenside darters live for 3–4 years, achieving a size of $2\frac{1}{2}$–$4\frac{1}{2}$ inches in length. They first spawn 1 year after hatching.

Distribution. The greenside darter has several isolated populations: one in the Ozark Mountains in Missouri and Arkansas; one in the Great Lakes drainages of southern Michigan and northern Ohio; and one along the Atlantic Coast in the Potomac River system. Its main center of abundance, however, is the Ohio River drainage, including the Allegheny River. In the Northeast, the greenside darter is known only from New York, where it is found in the Allegheny, Genesee, Great Lakes, Susquehanna, and Mohawk drainages.

Rainbow Darter

Etheostoma caeruleum Storer, 1845

Identification. The rainbow darter is a relatively stocky darter with its *greatest body depth one-fourth to one-fifth the standard length.* The body is deepest under the first dorsal fin. It has an *incomplete lateral line,* which ends under the second dorsal fin; large scales, with less than 50 in the lateral series; and 2 anal spines. Its *cheeks are almost naked, but the opercula have scales;* 9–14 vertical dark bars cross the sides; and 6–10 dark saddles cross the back from in front of the spiny dorsal fin to near the caudal fin. In breeding season, males develop unusually bright color patterns. The fins take on a reddish tinge; the belly becomes orangish red; the dark saddles and vertical bars become very distinct; and a red band near the base of the first dorsal fin parallels a blue band on the outer edge of the fin.

Life History. Rainbow darters live in streams and rivers, usually occupying riffle areas where the current is the fastest. They are very adept at locating small spaces behind rocks or other shelter where the current is reduced. They spawn in the early spring in riffles over gravel. Females leave an adjoining pool to join a male, who defends a territory around her until they spawn. She buries the lower half of her body into the substrate and releases her eggs; the male fertilizes them, and they fall into the gravel, where they develop. She normally deposits 8 or so eggs at each spawning and repeats this process over the spawning season up to thirty-nine times. The young darters initially feed on small crustaceans, but they switch to small insect larvae by the time they reach an inch or so in length. Maximum size for rainbow darters is approximately $2^3/_4$ inches.

Distribution. The rainbow darter ranges from Minnesota, Wisconsin, and the Ozarks in Missouri eastward to New York. In the Northeast, it is found only in New York in the Allegheny, Lake Erie, and western Lake Ontario watersheds.

Bluebreast Darter

Etheostoma camurum (Cope, 1870)

Identification. The bluebreast darter is a stocky darter with a square to slightly rounded caudal fin. A bridge of tissue (frenum) connects the upper lip to the snout; the lateral line is complete; the gill covers are not united by a membrane extending across the isthmus. The bluebreast has relatively large scales, with 55 or fewer scale rows along the length of the body. It is distinguished from the spotted darter by a slender, clear band just in from the margin of the soft dorsal, anal, and caudal fins. Its head length fits approximately three and one-half to three and four-fifths times into the standard length. Its body is dark brown to olive, grading to clear on the belly. In breeding males, distinct reddish orange spots cover the sides.

Life History. Bluebreast darters spawn in late spring or early summer in riffles over gravel in large clear streams. They tend to move upstream from their winter habitat to spawn. A female locates an area attended by a male and burrows into the gravel until her back is level with the bottom. The male rests over her, and eggs are released and fertilized. This process is repeated several times, producing approximately 100 fertilized eggs. The eggs hatch in about 10 days. Bluebreast darters feed on small aquatic insects such as dipteran larvae. They often reach 3 inches in length.

Distribution. The bluebreast darter has a relatively limited range. It is found in eastern Illinois, Indiana, Kentucky, and Tennessee, eastward through Ohio, West Virginia, and northwestern Pennsylvania, and up to southwestern New York. It occupies the lower Allegheny in Pennsylvania and has recently been discovered upstream in two locations in the New York portion of the Allegheny drainage. It is considered endangered in New York. It has not been reported from elsewhere in the Northeast.

Iowa Darter

Etheostoma exile (Girard, 1859)

Identification. The Iowa darter is a slender fish; its greatest depth goes five and one-half to six and one-half times into its standard length; it has *2 anal spines* and *an incomplete lateral line,* with more than 50 scales in the lateral series; a bridge of tissue (frenum) connects the upper lip to the snout; and both cheeks and opercula are more or less scaled. The back has *7–10 dark brown saddles;* the anterior dorsal fin has a blue outer margin underlain by a red band. Vertical blotches decorate the sides.

Life History. Iowa darters are commonly found in downstream stretches of streams and lakes, where flow is reduced or nonexistent. They seem to prefer still water with vegetation and a mud bottom. Iowa darters are often found in recently flooded areas adjacent to streams or small rivers. They feed primarily on aquatic insects but also consume small crustaceans, snails, rotifers, and fish eggs. Adults are usually between 2 and $2\frac{1}{2}$ inches long. They spawn in early spring on gravel, algae, or other vegetation. A female mates with several males and lays a small number of eggs each time she mates.

Distribution. The Iowa darter is one of the most northerly darters. Its range stretches eastward from Saskatchewan to Quebec in Canada and then south into Wyoming and Montana and east to New York and Vermont. It is found in two states in the Northeast, New York and Vermont, and it has been placed on the special concern list in Vermont.

Fantail Darter

Etheostoma flabellare Rafinesque, 1819

Identification. The fantail darter is readily distinguished from other darters in the region by a *spiny dorsal fin that is approximately one-half the height of the soft dorsal fin behind it* and by *fleshy knobs at the tips of the dorsal spines (in breeding males)* (see figure 82). Most other darters have a taller spiny dorsal fin without fleshy knobs. Fantail darters have an incomplete lateral line, which ends under the soft dorsal fin a terminal mouth and a frenum. The back has approximately 8 saddles, and the sides have a similar number of vertical bars. The males become darker during breeding season but do not develop the bright coloration of some other darters.

Life History. Fantail darters prefer a rock or cobble substrate and tend to hide themselves between and under rocks on the bottom of streams. They spawn in late spring or early summer when the water temperature reaches 60°F. Males choose a nest site under an overhanging rock at the head of a riffle. Females lay eggs on the underside of the rock, and males guard and groom the eggs with the fleshy knobs on their dorsal fin. A male spawns with several females and accumulates as many as 500 eggs in a nest. Fantail daters feed primarily on mayfly and midge larvae but also feed on other insects, crustaceans, and snails as the opportunity permits. They live for approximately 4 years, at which age they may be 2¾ inches long.

Distribution. The fantail darter ranges along the southern Great Lakes from Wisconsin to New York and Vermont. It is also found in the Ozarks, in the Tennessee River, and along the Atlantic Coast from South Carolina to New York State. It is found in two states in the Northeast, New York and Vermont. In New York, it is found in the western and northern parts of the state as well as in the Mohawk River.

Swamp Darter

Etheostoma fusiforme (Girard, 1854)

Identification. The swamp darter is a relatively plain brown to tan darter that lacks the bright breeding colors of other darters. A frenum connects the upper lip to the snout; an incomplete lateral line ends below the soft dorsal fin; and there are no more than 3 scale rows between the lateral line and the base of the spiny dorsal fin. The swamp darter's tan background color is decorated with dark brown markings along the sides, back, and fins.

Life History. Swamp darters are typically found in still, quiet water with abundant vegetation, preferring small lakes, ponds, or swamps where the water is darkly stained. They are rarely found in streams or rivers, but if so, only in quiet water. They depend on vegetation for shelter and as a source of food. The markings and color of their bodies provides cryptic coloration for these kinds of habitats. They are relatively tolerant of low-oxygen concentrations. Spawning occurs in April or May, with the females laying their eggs on vegetation. Adults feed on very small aquatic insects and crustaceans found in the vegetation. Swamp darters are small, reaching only $1\frac{1}{4}$ inches as adults, and they are short-lived, dying not long after spawning at the end of their first year.

Distribution. The swamp darter ranges along the Atlantic Coastal Plain from southern Maine to Florida and then west to Kentucky, Tennessee, and Oklahoma. The range of this darter extends farther south than the range of other darters. It is recorded in lowland areas for all of the states in the region except Vermont. It is considered endangered in Maine and threatened in New York, where it is known only from eastern Long Island.

Spotted Darter

Etheostoma maculatum Kirtland, 1841

Identification. The spotted darter is distinguished in the field by a *very long and sharp snout* and a relatively stocky body with a *deep caudal peduncle.* In addition, the lip is joined to the snout by a fleshy bridge; the lateral line is complete (57–62 scales); and the sides have *thin, dark lines extending down the length of the body.* The body is generally light to dark brown, with a scattering of small red spots; the back is relatively darker, and the undersides are relatively lighter; the outer margins of both the dorsal and caudal fins are clear.

Life History. Spotted darters are found in relatively deep streams and prefer the fastest current where large rocks and algae are present. They breed in May or June in Pennsylvania, usually at the head of a riffle. As with the fantail darter, they place eggs on the underside of rocks, and the males guard them. Adults feed primarily on aquatic insects. They can live up to 5 years and typically achieve a size of approximately 2 inches. In recent years, they have suffered from a reduction in habitat owing to siltation and increasing nutrient and pesticide loads in streams.

Distribution. The spotted darter is not very common anywhere within its range, which extends from northwestern Pennsylvania through southern Ohio and Kentucky. It is found in only one location in the Northeast: French Creek in the Allegheny drainage of New York. It is considered threatened in New York.

Johnny Darter

Etheostoma nigrum Rafinesque, 1820

Identification. The johnny darter is a slender, straw-colored darter with a single anal spine and W-, V-, or X-shaped markings along its sides. Its upper lip is separated from the snout by a deep groove. It most resembles the tessellated darter but can be distinguished from it by only 6–8 markings on its side and 10–12 rays in the second dorsal fin; the tessellated darter has 9–11 markings and 12–14 rays in the second dorsal fin. The johnny darter has a blunt snout with a horizontal mouth. These two species are difficult to separate and were once considered the same species.

Life History. Johnny darters are quite tolerant of a variety of habitats and thus can be found in both streams and lakes. In streams, they prefer slower water than do most other darters; they are found more often in pools and deep runs than in riffle areas. Adults spawn in the spring. The female deposits her adhesive eggs on the underside of a rock, and the male guards the nest until the eggs hatch. Johnny darters feed on small crustaceans and aquatic insects. They live for approximately 3 years and achieve a length of $2\frac{1}{2}$ inches.

Distribution. The johnny darter is primarily a midwestern species, ranging from Saskatchewan, Manitoba, Ontario, and Quebec south through the Mississippi Valley to the Tennessee River. Its range stretches eastward into western New York and Pennsylvania and southward into Virginia and North Carolina. In the Northeast, it is found only in the Allegheny and the Great Lakes-St. Lawrence drainages in New York.

Tessellated Darter

Etheostoma olmstedi Storer, 1842

Identification. The tessellated darter is a common, fairly plain fish recognizable by the presence of a series of *9–11 X-, W-, M-, or V-shaped dark marks running horizontally along its sides and 12–14 rays in the second dorsal fin.* It has a *single spine in its anal fin,* which distinguishes it from most other darters except the eastern sand darter and the johnny darter. The eastern sand darter is largely colorless and scaleless, and the johnny darter has a blunter snout and fewer soft rays (10–12) in the dorsal fin. The tessellated darter's background color is a light brown or straw color, occasionally with a green tinge.

Life History. Spawning takes place in late April or May in shallow streams with rocky bottoms. Males enter the spawning area first and establish territories, which they defend vigorously. When the females are ready to spawn, they approach the spawning site and are met by a territorial male. The female lays her eggs on the underside of a rock. Accompanied by the male, she moves upside down along the rock. As she extrudes eggs, the male fertilizes them. Each female normally lays 30–200 eggs. After spawning, the male stands guard over the nest and fans it to keep water circulating over the eggs. The eggs hatch in 5–8 days. Tessellated darters feed on microscopic crustaceans and small insects as well as on organic debris from the bottom. They live for 3 or 4 years and reach approximately $2\frac{1}{2}$ inches when full grown. They are widespread throughout the region, generally preferring running water with a sandy bottom. They may also be found near shore or stream mouths in lakes and ponds and over silty or gravelly bottoms.

The darters are not significant to the sport fishery, but they may serve as forage for a number of game species. They are interesting fishes to observe in an aquarium and are relatively hardy.

Distribution. The tessellated darter is found east of the Appalachians from the St. Lawrence River to North Carolina. In the Northeast, it is found in all states except Maine.

Variegate Darter

Etheostoma variatum Kirtland, 1838

Identification. The variegate darter is a fairly large darter, with older adults reaching 4 inches. Field characters include the unique color pattern, which includes a *dark band that extends from in front of the spiny dorsal fin down either side to just above the pectoral fin.* The forward half of the body is relatively unmarked, but the *rear of the body has 5–7 bluish green bands separated by orangish red spots or bands.* The upper lip is connected to the snout by a fleshy bridge; the lateral line is complete or nearly so, lacking only the last 5 or 6 scales; *it has 12 or more dorsal spines;* there are no scales on its cheeks; and the membrane connecting the gill covers forms a nearly U-shaped arc.

Life History. The variegate darter prefers streams that are intermediate between small creeks and small rivers. They spawn in these streams at the head of riffles after the water temperature has reached 50°F. Adults feed on aquatic insect larvae.

Distribution. The variegate darter ranges along the Ohio River valley from Indiana to New York. In the Northeast, it is found only in the Allegheny River system in western New York.

Banded Darter

Etheostoma zonale (Cope, 1868)

Identification. The banded darter is a relatively small darter, adults averaging 2 inches or less in length. The *upper lip is connected to the snout by a fleshy bridge;* the *membrane connecting the gill covers forms a nearly straight line (may form a shallow angle, but not a U shape);* the lateral line is complete or nearly so, lacking only the last 5 or 6 scales; there are fewer than 12 spines in the first dorsal fin; *it has 2 anal spines;* embedded scales are found on its cheeks, although they are sometimes difficult to see; *a dark bar extends from the front of the eye to the tip of the snout;* 6–7 inconspicuous dark saddles are present on the back; body color is greenish except in breeding males, where 9 or more dark green vertical bars encircle the body.

Life History. Very little is known of the life history of the banded darter. Adults are known to reach 2½ inches in length.

Distribution. The banded darter is found widely through the Mississippi and Ohio River drainages from southern Minnesota to northern Mississippi and from Kentucky and Tennessee to western New York. In the Northeast, it is found only in the Allegheny and Susquehanna River systems in New York.

Yellow Perch

Perca flavescens (Mitchill, 1814)

Identification. Yellow perch are quickly recognized in the field by the *broad, vertical, olive green bands overlaying the yellow background color.* Even more dependable distinguishing characters are *2 separate dorsal fins: an anterior spiny dorsal fin and a posterior soft dorsal fin.* The *anal fin has only 2 spines* and 6–8 soft rays. The preoperculum has a serrated edge, and the teeth are uniform in size—that is, there are no canine teeth.

Life History. Spawning occurs in early spring when the water has warmed up to at least 44°F and before it reaches 54°F. Adults move into shallow water, sometimes entering tributary streams. Spawning occurs at night over brush or vegetation. A single female leads a long double line of males around a circuitous course and eventually extrudes a long gelatinous string of eggs, which the attendant males then fertilize. No nest is built, but the eggs are retained and protected in a unique and very interesting way. They rest in a long gelatinous tube, which is folded like a partially extended accordion and may reach up to 7 feet in length. The egg mass is semibuoyant and tends to oscillate with the movements of the water. Such movement creates a pumping action that draws water into the hollow center of the tube and expels stale water through small, inconspicuous holes along its length. This system is an adaptation for providing the eggs protection from mechanical shock and desiccation while still allowing for aeration. The yellow perch egg mass is somewhat reminiscent of the bullhead egg mass, except that the bullhead has to work very hard to keep enough water flowing over the eggs to ensure proper aeration. Each female yellow perch may carry from 3,000 to 100,000 eggs, depending on her size, the average being approximately 20,000–30,000. The young hatch in 7–10 days and remain close to the bottom and relatively inactive until they absorb their yolk sacs. They begin feeding on zooplankton, switching to small insects or crustaceans before the end of their first year. As adults, they continue to eat insects but feed on crayfish and small fishes as well. Yellow perch live for approximately 8 or 9 years and grow to 10–11 inches; they become sexually mature at 3 or 4 years. They are shallow-water fish and move in large, loosely organized groups. They are inactive at night, and on a summer evening you can see them resting on the bottom if you shine a powerful light into the water. They do not become inactive in the winter but continue to move and feed under the ice.

Of all the different kinds of fishes in the region, the yellow perch has to rate very near the top in numbers caught by anglers. It is not a particularly good fighting fish, but it is easily caught and very good eating. It is most often taken on live bait fished just off the bottom; it can be taken winter or summer. Yellow perch have a tendency to become stunted if their populations get too large for the food supply. They also compete successfully with salmonids for food and thus create difficulties in the management of trout fisheries. In addition to providing food and sport for humans, young perch are an important forage fish for many large game fishes.

Distribution. Yellow perch range from Nova Scotia to Florida, then westward in a broad band to Montana and Great Slave Lake. In the Northeast, they are found in all major drainages.

Logperch

Percina caprodes (Rafinesque, 1818)

Identification. The logperch is a darter in the genus *Percina* and has all of the distinctive darter characteristics: small size, smooth preoperculum, and rounded or at least nonforked tail. The genus *Percina* is distinguishable from the genera *Ammocrypta* and *Etheostoma* by the presence of modified scales between the pelvic fins and by either the absence of scales on the midline of the belly or a row of enlarged scales on the midline (see figure 78). In the genus *Etheostoma*, there are no modified scales between the pelvic fins, and the belly is scaled over. *Ammocrypta* has no scales on the belly. When *Percina* is viewed from the side, the *anal fin of is normally as large or larger than the posterior dorsal fin*. In many but not all *Etheostoma*, in contrast, the anal fin is smaller than the posterior dorsal fin. Darters in the genus *Percina* are pigmented and thus are readily distinguished from the clear and transparent eastern sand darter, *Ammocrypta*. In addition, the sand darter has only 1 anal spine, whereas *Percina* has 2 anal spines. The logperch is separated from the other members of the genus *Percina* by its *long snout, which protrudes beyond its upper lip* and by the *narrow, dark vertical bars* instead of large blotches on its sides. The background color is yellowish green.

Life History. Logperch are primarily a lake-dwelling species, but they are also known from large streams and rivers. They spawn late in June, moving in from deep water to water less than 6 feet deep. Males congregate in a large group of several hundred individuals over a sandy bottom. A female periodically enters this group and swims circuitously through it. Many males follow her, and one eventually catches up with her. The two then settle to the bottom, the male resting on the back of the female. They both make violent movements with their bodies, creating a small pit in the sand and throwing up a large sand cloud in the process; 10–20 eggs are laid and fertilized at this time, which fall back into the pit and are covered by the settling sand. Waiting males eat any eggs that are not covered. This process continues until the female has spawned several times. She carries from 1,000 to 3,000 eggs, but whether she deposits all of them during spawning is unknown. No parental care of the eggs after spawning has been observed. The young feed on microscopic crustaceans, switching to insects as they grow. Adults feed primarily on insects and are reported to use their long snout to poke under leaves and turn rocks over in a search for food. Adults may reach 4–5 inches when fully grown.

Distribution. The logperch can be found from the St. Lawrence River south on the western side of the Appalachians to the Gulf of Mexico and northwest to Saskatchewan. In the Northeast, it is found in Vermont and New York in all major drainages except the Delaware, Susquehanna, and Long Island systems.

Channel Darter

Percina copelandi (Jordan, 1877)

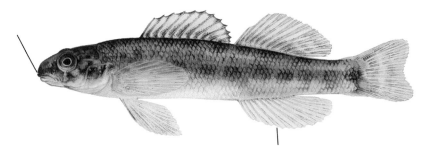

Identification. The distinguishing feature of the channel darter is the lack of a frenum—that is, a *groove completely separates the upper lip from the snout.* All other members of the genus *Percina* in the region have a frenum. The channel darter superficially looks similar to a tessellated or johnny darter except that it has a number of star-shaped scales between the bases of the pelvic fins; the breast and the ventral midline are either naked or with a few of these specialized scales, characteristic of all *Percina.* The *anal fin is roughly as large as the second dorsal fin* in the channel darter, but much smaller in the tesselated and johnny darters. The snout of the channel darter is blunt and rounded in contrast to the pointed snout of the logperch. The sides of the channel darter are decorated with 10–15 dark blotches over a yellow to olive background color.

Life History. Channel darters spawn in the summer when the water temperature is around 70°F. They move into tributary streams, and males establish territories behind large rocks. Eggs are deposited in the gravel. Adults feed on small insect larvae, primarily chironomids, midges, mayflies, and caddisfly larvae. They are also known to consume algae and detritus. They are normally found in lakes or larger streams where the current is relatively weak.

Distribution. The channel darter is found in the Ohio River drainage, including the Tennessee River, and in the Great Lakes drainage eastward from Lake Huron to the St. Lawrence River and Lake Champlain. In the Northeast, it is found in New York and Vermont. In Vermont, it has been placed on the endangered species list.

Gilt Darter

Percina evides (Jordan and Copeland, 1877)

Identification. The gilt darter's snout does not extend beyond the upper lip as it does in the logperch, and there is a well-developed frenum, unlike in the channel darter; its cheeks are scaleless, and it has less than 65 scales in its lateral line, which is complete. The base color of the gilt darter's body is olive and bronze, with 7 dark blotches more or less confluent along the lateral line. In breeding males, the lateral markings develop bluish green bands, unique among *Percina* darters in the region.

Life History. Very little work has been done on the life history of this species. In Minnesota, it spawns over a rock-and-cobble bottom in early summer at water temperatures that range from 63 to 73°F. Males reach sexual maturity at 1 year and females at 2 years of age. Females may carry from 100 to 400 eggs. They are known to live for 3–4 years and achieve a size of approximately 3 inches.

Distribution. In the Northeast, the gilt darter is reported only from a collection made by the New York State Biological Survey in 1937 in the Allegheny River in New York, where it is considered endangered and possibly extirpated.

Longhead Darter

Percina macrocephala (Cope, 1869)

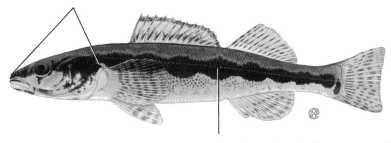

Identification. The longhead darter is very similar to the gilt darter except that it has 74–80 scales in the lateral line, as opposed to 65 in the gilt darter. Its *head is quite long,* approximately 31 percent of the standard length, longer than the head of any other *Percina* darter in the region. It has a frenum, and its cheeks are without scales. Its color pattern is variable, but often a *dark band, irregular in width, extends along its sides.* The sides are lighter brown above the lateral band, and the belly and lower sides are white.

Life History. Unlike other darters, the longhead darter appears to spend considerable time in pools and midwater portions of moderate to large streams. It feeds on crayfish and mayflies and may exceed 4 inches in length.

Distribution. In the Northeast, the longhead darter is found only in the Allegheny drainage of New York, where it is listed as threatened.

Blackside Darter

Percina maculata (Girard, 1859)

Identification. The blackside darter is characterized by *scales on its cheeks;* a *snout that does not extend beyond its upper lip;* and an upper lip that is joined to the snout by a frenum. The sides of its body have approximately *8 dark blotches that tend to run together along the lateral line,* overlying an olive to bronze coloration.

Life History. The blackside darter seeks shelter among vegetation or brush in relatively quiet water in streams. It spawns over sand or gravel bottoms when the water temperature rises to approximately 62°F. Adults feed on aquatic insects, crustaceans, and even small fish. They range widely in search of food, feeding not only on the bottom, but also in midwater and at the surface. Blackside darters have retained a functional swim bladder, which allows them to move up and down the water column with relative ease. Adults may reach 4 inches in length.

Distribution. The blackside darter's range extends from central Canada, south in the Mississippi drainage to Oklahoma and Louisiana, and then east along the southern Great Lakes to western New York. In the Northeast, the blackside darter is found only in western New York in the Allegheny, Lake Erie, and Lake Ontario drainages.

Shield Darter

Percina peltata (Stauffer, 1864)

Identification. The shield darter looks much like the blackside darter in the field except that *it does not have scales on its cheeks.* It has fewer than 65 scales in its lateral line. Its base color is pale yellow, with *6 large, dark blotches usually not confluent along the lateral line.* These two species are rarely found in the same area. The blackside darter is found in western New York; the shield darter is found primarily in southern New York.

Life History. Shield darters breed in New York between mid-April until the end of May in medium-size streams with gravel bottoms. The males defend territories. Eggs are deposited in the gravel at the bottom of the stream or in sand pockets behind boulders. Little is known of their diet, but it is likely to be similar to that of other darters: aquatic insect larvae. Shield darters grow to 3 inches in length.

Distribution. The shield darter is found in streams along the Atlantic Coast from New York to North Carolina. In the Northeast, it is found only in New York in the Hudson, Delaware, and Susquehanna drainages.

Sauger

Sander canadense (Smith, 1834)

Identification. The sauger resembles a walleye except that *it does not have the prominent dusky spot on the posterior base of its first dorsal fin or the white spot on the lower lobe of its caudal fin.* It does have several rows of fairly distinct black spots on the membranes of the first dorsal fin. These spots, however, are considerably smaller than the large, dark blotches on the walleye. The sauger's body is basically a light brown overlain with darker brown blotches.

Life History. Saugers are spring spawners, normally beginning slightly later than walleyes but in roughly the same type of habitat. Females, with attending males, broadcast their eggs over the spawning gravel and then leave the spawning site. The eggs hatch, and the young begin life feeding on zooplankton. As adults, they reach a foot or so in length. Saugers prefer even larger bodies of water than walleyes and are quite tolerant of turbidity.

Distribution. Saugers are found in a region that extends from the St. Lawrence River to Alabama and north to Alberta. They are found only in New York and Vermont in the Northeast. A significant population can be found in Lake Champlain.

Walleye

Sander vitreum (Mitchill, 1818)

Identification. Walleyes are large perchlike fish with serrations on the posterior edge of their preoperculum, a forked tail, and canine teeth in the lower jaw. Adults do not have the regular dark vertical bars like the perches, but instead have a pattern of irregular dark blotches on a brown to yellow background. The *first dorsal fin of the walleye has a characteristic large black spot at its posterior base,* and the tip of the lower lobe of the caudal fin tends to be whitish. These characters distinguish walleyes from saugers, which are missing the large spot on the dorsal fin and the white spot on the caudal fin, but have many smaller black spots scattered over the entire first dorsal fin, usually arranged in horizontal rows. *Sander vitreum* is composed of two subspecies: the walleye (*S. vitreum vitreum*) and the blue pike (*S. vitreum glaucum*). The blue pike was formerly found in Lake Erie but is now thought to be extinct.

Life History. Walleyes are early spring spawners, often initiating spawning not long after ice-out. They migrate up into tributary streams, choosing sites with good flow and gravel bottoms. Some may remain in lakes, spawning over gravel shoals. They do not build nests but are broadcast spawners, simply depositing their eggs over the bottom. The eggs sink, becoming entangled in vegetation or falling into spaces between the gravel. A large female may lay more than half a million eggs. Survival to hatching is not good, however, if 20 percent of the eggs hatch, the survival rate is considered excellent. More commonly, less than 5 percent of the eggs hatch under natural conditions. This percentage still leaves 25,000 fry from a female that produced 500,000 eggs. In a stable population, you can expect 24,998 of these fish to die before they reach sexual maturity. Because of the high egg mortality rate, it has become common management practice to take eggs from walleyes, fertilize them, and incubate them in a hatchery until they hatch. Then they are either stocked as fry or held for a longer period and stocked as fingerlings. When this practice is followed, the survival rate is greatly increased. Under natural conditions, the eggs hatch in 2–2½ weeks, and the young fish, encumbered by their yolk sac, drift into deeper water.

Young walleyes feed initially on zooplankton but switch to small fishes in a short while. In Oneida Lake, New York, where Cornell University has studied walleyes for many years, it has been shown that they depend heavily on young perch for food. Perch spawn a few weeks after the walleye, and perch fry appear in the lake just about the time young walleye are switching from zooplankton to fish. They continue this beneficial relationship (from the walleye's point of view) throughout their lives. Walleyes feed on other forage fish as well and even occasionally on insects. Walleyes feed primarily during periods of darkness or low light. The insides of their eyes are lined with a reflective surface called the tapetum lucidum, which allows them to see quite well in the dark. It is the tapetum lucidum that causes the eye shine observed when a walleye is brought into a lighted boat at night. Walleyes may live up to 15 years and achieve a weight of 17 pounds. The walleye caught by anglers is more commonly less than 3 pounds, however, and only 3 or 4 years old.

Large lakes and rivers are walleyes' preferred habitat. They are rarely found in lakes less than 100 acres in size. In addition, they seem to prefer water that is somewhat turbid, thus reducing the light exposure on their eyes. The tapetum lucidum, which is very useful when light intensities are low, causes these fish to be very sensitive to bright light. Thus, clear lakes with good light penetration are poor habitats for walleyes. To anglers, the walleye is one of the most highly prized fish. Its flesh is light and tasty. Although not a spectacular fighting fish, the walleye achieves a large enough size that catching it is always a challenge.

Distribution. Walleyes range from Quebec south, west of the Appalachians, to the Gulf Coast and then northwestward to the Mackenzie River. In the Northeast, they are found in all of the states except Maine and Rhode Island.

Drums

Family Sciaenidae

The drums are primarily coastal tropical marine fishes. They have a physoclistus swim bladder, which can be used to make drumming sounds—hence the name. They have ctenoid scales and a lateral line that extends onto the caudal fin. Approximately 160 species belong to the family, 1 of which is known from the freshwaters of the Northeast.

Freshwater Drum

Aplodinotus grunniens (Rafinesque, 1819)

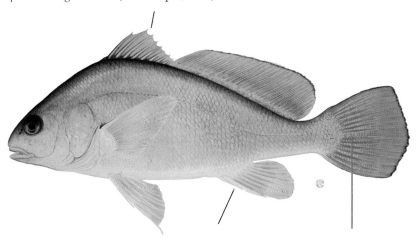

Identification. The freshwater drum, a heavy-bodied fish, superficially resembles the carp. The drum, however, has *8–9 spines in the anterior dorsal fin; 2 spines in the anal fin, one small and the second quite large;* and a *lateral line that extends well onto the rounded caudal fin.* It is a yellow to silvery fish with a green to brown back and yellowish white undersides.

Life History. It is thought that freshwater drums spawn in open water and produce planktonic eggs. Large numbers of freshwater drum have been seen swimming together near the surface far from shore. The supposition is that they are spawning aggregations. Plankton tows often take drum eggs when sampling in the summer, thus strengthening the case for planktonic eggs. Although producing planktonic eggs is the rule with marine fishes, it is unique among freshwater fishes in the Northeast.

After spawning occurs, the eggs hatch in a day or two, and the young begin feeding on minute crustaceans. As they get older and larger, they switch to feeding on a variety of invertebrates, including insect larvae and leeches. They are well adapted for feeding on mollusks. They have large, powerful sets of teeth in their pharynx, which they use to crush snail or clam shells; they then spit out the shell and swallow the soft body. This ability has made them a major consumer of the zebra mussel, a recent invader in the Great Lakes and in many smaller lakes throughout the Northeast. Drums commonly range in size from 1 to 5 pounds. Individuals that exceeded 35 pounds are known, however. Some freshwater drums live to be 14 years of age.

The male freshwater drum has the capacity to make a grunting noise that is quite audible to the human ear. This noise is made not with vocal cords as in humans, but by vibrations of the swim bladder, which create sound waves that pass through the water. The function of this sound is unknown, but because it occurs most noticeably during the spawning season, some people believe that it may play a role in courtship behavior. The freshwater drum's ear stones (otoliths) are also interesting. They are large and marked with an L-shaped groove that resembles a boomerang. Many people have discovered these stones on a beach and consider them lucky charms.

Distribution. The freshwater drum is found in the Great Lakes and Mississippi River drainages. In the Northeast, it is found in New York and Vermont in Lakes Erie, Ontario, Champlain, and Oneida. It inhabits deep water in large lakes and deep pools in large rivers where the water is clean and the bottom well supplied with food.

Gobies
Family Gobiidae

The gobies are a large family of small marine fishes. Limited numbers, however, are also found in brackish water and even in freshwater. There are approximately 1,875 species in the family worldwide, with 2 freshwater species in (or potentially in) the Northeast. Both were introduced as a result of ballast-water discharges in the St. Clair River, near Detroit, Michigan, in 1990. Since that time, they have spread rapidly. One species, the round goby, has been reported from Lake Erie, Lake Ontario, and connecting waters. The other species, the tubenose goby, is known for western Lake Erie and may soon spread into the New York waters of Lake Erie, if it has not already done so. These 2 species are characterized by 2 dorsal fins and no lateral line; most important, their 2 pelvic fins are joined to form a suckerlike disc. These characteristics distinguish gobies from any other fishes in the region.

Species Key

1a. A prominent black blotch on rear of first dorsal fin; no tubelike extension of anterior nostrils over lips; 49–55 scales in the lateral series, no lateral line; larger fish, adults usually longer than 5 inches→ **Round Goby,** *Neogobius melanostomus*

1b. No prominent black blotch on rear of first dorsal fin; a tubelike extension of anterior nostrils reaches over the upper lip; 45–48 scales in lateral series, no lateral line; smaller fish, adults usually less than 5 inches long→ **Tubenose Goby,** *Proterorhinus marmoratus*

Round Goby

Neogobius melanostomus (Pallas, 1811)

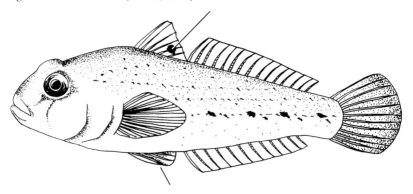

Identification. Gobies are the only fish in the region with 2 dorsal fins, no lateral line, and a *suckerlike disc on their ventral side.* They are bottom-dwelling fishes, as are the only two groups with which they might be confused: the sculpins and darters. Both the sculpins and darters, however, have separate pelvic fins and thus lack the suckerlike disc. The round goby is easily distinguished from the tubenose goby by *the dark spot on the rear of its first dorsal fin* and by the lack of the tubelike extensions of the anterior nostrils. Round gobies often get to be quite large for a goby, with adults reaching 10 inches in length. Young fish tend to be a relatively uniform slate gray in color. They develop black and brown blotches over their body as they get older. The dorsal fin has a greenish border.

Life History. Round gobies are benthic fishes that rest on the bottom, often under cover of stones, occasionally burying themselves in sand or small gravel. In the summer, they tend to be found in the nearshore region, in rocky or weedy habitat, but in the winter they move into deeper water. They have been taken in water 70 feet deep in the Great Lakes. Round gobies are very tolerant of low-oxygen concentrations, which may have facilitated their transport in the ballast water of ships. They have a protracted spawning period, from early spring to late summer. They deposit eggs in sheltered areas, using rocks or logs for protection. Males spread a gluelike material on the underside of a rock or log, and the female attaches the eggs to it. Males guard the nest and are thought to die after spawning. Females are known to spawn several times over the course of the spawning season, and each nest may receive the eggs of several females, ultimately resulting in up to 10,000 eggs in a nest. Adults feed on mollusks, crustaceans, worms, insects, fish eggs, and young fishes. In the laboratory, round gobies have been shown to feed on darters, lake trout eggs, and fry. It is probable that their diet includes the young stages of fishes that co-occur with them, such as sculpins, darters, logperch, and other bottom-dwelling fishes. There is evidence that mottled sculpin populations in the Detroit River have been strongly depressed by the presence of round gobies. Round gobies have well-developed molariform teeth, which allow them to feed heavily on zebra mussels. Laboratory studies have demonstrated that they may consume from thirty to fifty zebra mussels per day. Males reach 4–5 inches in length by the end of their first year. Females are a little smaller at that age, reaching 3–4 inches. Maximum size is reported to be approximately 10 inches. They live up to 4 years of age.

Distribution. The native range of this species is in Eurasia, where it is found in the Black and Caspian Seas, in the Sea of Azov, and in tributaries to these waters. It was apparently transported to the Great Lakes in the ballast water of freighters traveling between ports within the species' native range and the Great Lakes. It was first reported for the United States in Lake St. Clair in 1990. It has become well established in the United States and is spreading rapidly. It is currently known for Minnesota, Wisconsin, Illinois, Indiana, Michigan, Ohio, Pennsylvania, and New York. It is also known from many locations on the Canadian side of the Great Lakes. It has been reported from the New York waters of Lake Erie, the Niagara River, and Lake Ontario. At this time, it has not reached any other state in the Northeast.

Tubenose Goby

Proterorhinus marmoratus (Pallas, 1814)

Identification. The tubenose goby is easily identified by the suckerlike disc formed from its pelvic fins; the long tubelike extensions from its anterior nostrils that reach over its upper lips; and the lack of a dark spot on the posterior portion of its spiny dorsal fin. Tubenose gobies are relatively small fish, with adults normally 3 inches in length.

Life History. Tubenose gobies occupy nearshore weedy habitats. They are not as aggressive as round gobies or as some of the Northeast's native benthic fishes. They build nests in sheltered areas under rocks or logs. The male defends the nest. After spawning, the male dies. Tubenose gobies' diet consists of aquatic insects and an occasional larval fish. They may live up to 5 years of age. To date, it appears that they are not having as severe an impact on native fish communities as the round goby. Tubenose gobies are not as aggressive; their populations are not as dense; and they are not spreading as rapidly.

Distribution. The tubenose goby is also from the same general region as the round goby—that is, the Black and Caspian Seas, the Sea of Azov, and their tributaries. In these regions, it is considered endangered. It was first discovered in the United States in Lake St. Clair, Michigan, in 1990. It has not been as successful as the round goby in establishing populations here and does not appear to be spreading as quickly, although there have been reports of it in Lake Erie. It is possible that it will expand its range and enter the New York waters of Lake Erie in the future. Further expansion might take it into Lake Ontario and the St. Lawrence River.

Sculpins

Family Cottidae

Sculpins are small, bottom-dwelling fishes with large, flattened heads and spines on their preoperculum. They are normally scaleless but may have limited patches of reduced ctenoid scales on their body. The only groups with which they might be confused are the darters and gobies. Gobies' pelvic fins are joined to form a unique suckerlike disc on the underside of their bodies, whereas both sculpins and darters have separate pelvic fins. Darters have scales over their entire body; sculpins do not. The family Cottidae is composed of three hundred species, two of which are found in freshwater in the Northeast. Two additional species were originally found in Lakes Ontario and Erie but are now thought to be extinct: the spoonhead sculpin (*Cottus ricei*) and the deepwater sculpin (*Myoxocephalus thompsoni*). Both were deepwater forms, typically found in depths of at least 200 feet or more in Lakes Ontario and Erie. The deepwater sculpin is the only member of the family whose gill membranes are free from the flesh of the throat (isthmus). The spoonhead sculpin has as distinguishing characteristics an unusually flattened head, a complete lateral line, and a spine on the preoperculum that curves upward and forward.

Species Key

1a. Pelvic fin with 1 spine closely attached to the first of 3 rays, giving the impression that only 3 rays support the pelvic fin (figure 83); anal rays 11–13; membrane between rays of anal fin is deeply notched, giving a scalloped outline to anal fin→ **Slimy Sculpin, *Cottus cognatus***

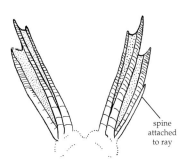

Fig. 83. Pelvic fin of slimy sculpin showing attachment of spine to ray.

1b. Pelvic fin with 1 spine closely attached to the first of 4 rays, giving the impression that only 4 rays support the pelvic fin; anal rays 13–15; membrane between rays of anal fin is not as deeply notched, giving a smoother outline to anal fin→ **Mottled Sculpin,** *Cottus bairdi*

Mottled Sculpin

Cottus bairdi Girard, 1850

Identification. Sculpins are small fish, usually 3–4 inches long, with large pectoral fins, 2 dorsal fins, and a large, flat head. They are scaleless, with weak, slender spines in the anterior dorsal fin. The mottled sculpin can be distinguished from the slimy sculpin in that it has 4 soft rays and 1 spine in its pelvic fin. The pelvic spine is so small and so closely attached to the large anterior soft ray, however, that it is essentially invisible without dissection. Thus, the field characters to look for in the mottled sculpin are the 4 soft rays supporting the pelvic fin. The slimy sculpin has only 3 rays. The mottled sculpin's anal fin has a relative smooth outline and 13–15 rays. The mottled sculpin is light to dark brown with darker brown mottling across its back and sides. The belly is light cream.

Life History. The mottled sculpin spawns in the spring in rapidly flowing water of streams. The male constructs a small nest under stones or vegetation. He then undertakes a reproductive display, which may include the production of sound by striking his head against the substrate in an effort to entice a female into his nest. If he is successful, she will deposit several hundred eggs, often on the underside of the sheltering stones or vegetation. The male then fertilizes the eggs and guards the nest until the young begin to feed, which may take more than a month.

Mottled sculpins are known to feed on algae and insects. They have been blamed for feeding on trout eggs. The extent to which they inflict any real damage to trout populations by this practice is unclear. It may be that they feed only on those eggs that are scattered and would have died anyway. There is no evidence that they have any negative effect on trout populations; on the contrary, they may be beneficial to trout as prey.

Distribution. The range of the mottled sculpin extends from Labrador south to Georgia, west to the Ozarks, and northwest to Manitoba. It is also found in the Missouri and Columbia River drainages. In the Northeast, it is found in New York and Vermont in the Great Lakes-St. Lawrence, Allegheny, and Susquehanna drainages. The mottled sculpin normally occupies headwater streams and the margins of large lakes. It prefers rocky or gravelly bottoms and also frequents moderately deep water in lakes.

Slimy Sculpin

Cottus cognatus Richardson, 1836

Identification. The slimy sculpin is a small scaleless fish with a *flattened head and large pectoral fins,* thus resembling the mottled sculpin except that it has *3 rather than 4 pelvic rays,* 11–13 anal rays, and a distinctly scalloped shape to the anal fin. Its color is similar to that of the mottled sculpin.

Life History. Spawning occurs in the spring when the water temperature reaches 40–50°F. Males choose the spawning site. Females are attracted to the site, where they leave some of their eggs on the underside of an overhanging rock or stick. A 4-inch female will carry approximately 1,400 eggs. The male guards the nest for a month or so until the young leave. Adults feed on small invertebrates and insects off the bottom of a stream or lake. They rarely grow beyond 4 inches.

Distribution. The slimy sculpin's distribution is more northerly than the mottled sculpin's, extending throughout most of Canada, Alaska, and even Siberia. In the United States, it is found in the northern tier of states from the Great Lakes drainage eastward. In the Northeast, it is found in all of the states except Rhode Island. It is found in lakes and cold streams, often in small springs and headwater reaches of swiftly flowing streams.

Glossary

References

Index

Glossary

Abbreviate heterocercal: The condition in the caudal fin of primitive fishes such as gars and bowfin where the vertebral column turns upward, but only partially extends into the caudal fin; intermediate between homocercal and heterocercal.

Adipose eyelid: A pair of transparent membranes, one covering the anterior third of the eye, the other covering the posterior third of the eye; commonly found in the herring family.

Adipose fin: A small flap of fleshy tissue on the dorsal midline posterior to the dorsal fin. It is found in the catfish, trout, smelt, and trout-perch families, among others.

Ammocoete: The larval, nonparasitic stage of all lampreys.

Anadromous: Describes the migration from the sea to freshwater for spawning, characteristic of salmon, lampreys, and herring, among others; the term is sometimes used when a landlocked species migrates from a large lake into a stream to spawn.

Anal fin: The fin located on the ventral midline of the body, usually just posterior to the vent.

Anterior: A relative position on the fish's body; anterior is more forward, toward the head.

Anus: See *vent.*

Barbel: An elongate fleshy flap of skin with a sensory function, commonly found around mouth of fish.

Bicuspid: A tooth with two cusps or points.

Branchiostegal rays: A series of elongate bones extending fanlike from under the gill covers.

Buccal funnel: The oral chamber in lampreys; it lies anterior to the esophageal opening and is commonly lined with teeth.

Bulla: An extension of the swim bladder into the inner ear.

Canine teeth: Sharp conical teeth typically longer than other teeth in the mouth and found on the forward part of jaw.

Catadromous: Describes the migration from freshwater to the sea to spawn, characteristic of the eel family.

Caudal fin: The tail fin of fishes.

Caudal peduncle: The part of the fish's body between the caudal fin base and the posterior portion of the anal fin.

Cheek: The portion of the side of the head between the eye and the anterior edge of the gill cover.

Circumoral teeth: Teeth in the buccal funnel of lampreys that encircle the esophageal opening.

Complete lateral line: A condition that exists when the lateral line extends from the head to the base of the tail in a regularly spaced series of pores.

Ctenoid scales: Bony ridge scales that possess small spines or ctenii on their exposed (posterior) margins. Ctenoid scales are characteristic of spiny-rayed fishes.

Cycloid scales: Smooth, largely circular bony ridge scales lacking small spines or ctenii. Cycloid scales are characteristic of soft-rayed fishes.

Deciduous: A condition where a structure such as scales or teeth have a tendency to fall off at some stage of development.

Demersal eggs: Eggs heavier than water, with a sticky coating, that sink and remain on the bottom.

Dentary bone: The major bone in the lower jaw; it normally contains the lower jaw teeth.

Dorsal: A relative position on the fish's body; dorsal is more toward the back or upper part of the body.

Dorsal fin: The fin located on the midline of the back between the head and the tail; in some species, more than one dorsal fin may be present.

Drumlin: An elongate hill formed by glacial movement composed of glacial till with relatively blunt and rounded ends.

Elvers: Young eels intermediate in development between the transparent, leaflike larvae and the adult eels.

Esker: An elongate ridge from 10 to 100 feet high with very steep sides.

Family: A group of related fishes that form a taxonomic category above a genus and below an order.

Frenum: A membrane located on the midline that connects the skin on the snout to the upper jaw.

Ganoid scales: Strong diamond-shaped scales with a hard enamel covering; found on gars.

Genus: A taxonomic category between family and species levels comprising a group of structurally or phylogenetically related species.

Genital papilla: A small fleshy projection just posterior to the anal opening.

Gill arch: The skeletal element of the gill that contains the gill rakers and gill filaments. Located under the gill cover.

Gill cover: See *operculum.*

Gill filaments: Feathery tissue arising from the bony gill arch under the gill cover. Used in respiration.

Gill rakers: Bony projections arising from the anterior edge of the gill arch. Most prominent on the first gill arch, where they are often used in fish identification.

Gular plate: A large flat bone lying between the bones of the lower jaw in the bowfin.

Head length: The greatest straight-line distance from the most anterior portion of the snout to the most posterior portion of the opercular membrane.

Heterocercal: A condition of the caudal fin in which the vertebral column turns dorsally and enters the upper lobe of the caudal fin; found in sturgeons and paddlefishes.

Homocercal: A condition of the caudal fin in which the vertebral column ends in a flat bony plate and does not enter either lobe of the caudal fin; found in the vast majority of the fishes in the Northeast.

Humeral scale: A large scalelike structure located behind the head and directly above the base of the pectoral fins in darters. It is often darkly pigmented.

Incomplete lateral line: A lateral line that either is interrupted or does not extend all the way to the base of the caudal fin.

Inferior mouth: A mouth located on the underside of the head and often overhung by the snout, as in many suckers.

Isthmus: A narrow band of flesh (actually part of the breast) that lies between the gill covers on the ventral side and separates them; in some fishes, the gill membranes are broadly connected to the isthmus; in others, they are not.

Kettle lake: A lake formed as the result of a large block of glacial ice melting in glacial till or outwash.

Lateral line: A line running from the head region posteriorly to the base of the caudal fin; composed of canals and small pores that pass through the lateral line scales opening to the outside.

Lateral line scales: Scales lying over the lateral line, each with a lateral line pore passing through it.

Laterally compressed: Refers to a body shape that appears to have been compressed from both sides, as in sunfishes.

Leptocephalus: The transparent, leaflike larval stage of eels, a strictly marine stage in the life history of the eel.

Mandible: The lower jaw, which is composed primarily of the dentary bones.

Mandibular pores: Small openings on the ventral side of the mandible.

Maxilla: One of the bones in the upper jaw, the maxilla lies posterior and dorsal to the premaxilla; the maxilla and the premaxilla together form the upper jaw.

Median fins: Fins that lie on the midline, such as the dorsal, anal, and caudal fins.

Moraine: A landform composed of glacial till deposited during glacial retreat.

Myomeres: Along the flanks of fishes, blocks of muscle that are divided by connective tissue; in adult fishes, they are most readily visible after the skin has been removed.

Nunatak: An area of high ground such as a hill or mountain that is surrounded by glacial ice.

Nuptial tubercles: Small horny projections that appear on the head, body, and fins of some fishes during the breeding season; they are generally sloughed off after the breeding season is over; commonly appear in minnows and suckers.

Operculum: The thin flat bone that forms the posterior portion of the gill cover.

Oral disc: The round circular disc surrounding the mouth of lampreys.

Orbit: The bony socket that surrounds the eyeball.

Order: A group of related fishes forming a taxonomic category above a family and below a class.

Orogeny: The geological process by which mountains are formed.

Ovipositor: A specialized organ that allows the female bitterling to deposit eggs in a position suitable for their development in the mantle cavity of clams.

Paired fins: Fins found on either side of the midline—the pelvic and pectoral fins.

Palatine teeth: Teeth rooted in the pair of palatine bones located in the roof of the mouth behind the median vomer.

Papillae: Small fleshy protrusions.

Parr: The stage in the early life of a trout or salmon characterized by the presence of parr marks.

Parr marks: Dark rectangular markings on the sides of young trout and salmon.

Pectoral fin: The paired fins located along the sides of the body, behind the head and anterior or dorsal or both to the pelvic fins.

Pelagic: Pertaining to the open-water habitat.

Pelvic axillary process: A small triangular flap of tissue located at the base of the pelvic fin.

Pelvic fins: The paired fins located near the ventral midline posterior or ventral or both to the pectoral fins.

Peritoneum: The thin membranous lining of the abdominal cavity.

Pharyngeal teeth: Small teeth found on the pharyngeal bone in some fishes.

Physoclistus: Refers to a fish possessing a gas bladder without a direct tubular connection to the alimentary canal.

Physostomous: Refers to a fish possessing a gas bladder with a direct connection to the alimentary canal; this connection is called the pneumatic duct.

Piscivorous: An adjective describing a predator that feeds primarily on fishes.

Plicae: Ridges or folds of skin on the lips of suckers.

Posterior: A relative position on the fish's body; posterior is more toward the rear or tail region.

Predorsal region: Area of the back directly anterior to the dorsal fin.

Premaxilla: The bone that forms the most anterior and medial portion of the upper jaw; it normally bears teeth.

Preoperculum: One of the thin flat bones forming the gill cover; it lies anterior to the operculum and below and behind the eye. It is the forward portion of the gill cover.

Preorbital region: Area just in front of the eye.

Principal unbranched ray: A ray that is not branched, but is fully developed and reaches to the outer edge of the fin.

Procurrent rays: Small rays at the anterior edge of the upper and lower portion of the caudal fin. Well developed in the tadpole madtom.

Protractile: A condition of the upper jaw in which a deep groove separates the upper jaw from the snout, allowing the upper jaw to protrude forward when the mouth is opened. The presence of a frenum prevents this from happening.

Radii: Markings on a fish scale that radiate outward from the central focus of the scale.

Ray or soft ray: A segmented, paired, and generally branched supporting element in fins.

Redd: The gravelly nest of a trout or salmon formed by the female's digging and covering movements prior to and just after spawning.

Refugium: An area of relatively moderate climate in which plants and animals can survive during an ice age. Serves as a center for dispersal of species after glaciers retreat.

Rudimentary ray: A small, relatively undeveloped and unbranched ray.

Scutes: Pointed scales that protrude from the body in a row along the ventral midline of herrings; they give a sawlike edge to the herring's belly.

Snout: The region of the head anterior to the forward edge of the eye.

Species: Populations of actual or potentially interbreeding individuals reproductively isolated from other such groups.

Spine: An unsegmented, unpaired, and generally stiff supporting element in the fins of many fishes, pointed at its distal end.

Spinous ray: A soft ray that has become hardened and is not branched; segmentation may be retained in the form of serrations on its posterior edge; found in carp, goldfish, and catfishes.

Spiracle: An opening from the outside into the mouth cavity, located dorsally and posterior to the eye.

Standard length: Distance from tip of the snout to the base of the rays of the caudal fin; determined by gently bending the caudal fin and noting the crease at the base.

Subterminal mouth: A mouth whose position is intermediate between terminal (at the most anterior end) and inferior (ventrally located); it is normally just slightly more ventral than a terminal mouth.

Terminal mouth: A mouth whose position is at the most anterior end of the fish.

Terrane: A rock formation created as a result of pieces of exotic crustal material attaching themselves to a continent; the terrane has unique characteristics that distinguish it from the adjacent continental material.

Unicuspid: A tooth with a single cusp or point.

Vent: The opening of the intestine to the outside; anus.

Ventral: A relative position on the fish's body; ventral is more toward the underneath portion or belly region of the fish.

Viscera: Internal organs.

Vomerine teeth: Teeth located on the vomerine bone; found in the roof of the mouth on the midline, just posterior to the upper jaw bone.

References

General

Becker, G. C. 1983. *Fishes of Wisconsin*. Madison: Univ. of Wisconsin Press. 1,052 pp.

Carlander, K. D. 1969. *Handbook of Freshwater Fishery Biology*. Vol. 1. Ames: Iowa State Univ. Press. 752 pp.

———. 1977. *Handbook of Freshwater Fishery Biology*. Vol. 2. Ames: Iowa State Univ. Press. 431 pp.

Carlson, D. M., R. A. Daniels, and S. W. Eaton. 1999. "Status of Fishes of the Allegheny River Watershed of New York State." *Northeastern Naturalist* 4: 305–26.

Everhart, W. H. 1976. *Fishes of Maine*. 4th ed. Augusta: Maine Department of Inland Fish and Game. 96 pp.

George, C. J. 1981. *The Fishes of the Adirondack Park*. Albany: New York State Department of Environmental Conservation, Lake Monograph Program. 94 pp.

Greeley, J. R. 1927. "Fishes of the Region with Annotated List." In *A Biological Survey of the Genesee River System*. Supplement. 16th Annual Report of the New York Conservation Department, 47–66.

———. 1928. "Fishes of the Oswego Watershed with Annotated List." In *A Biological Survey of the Oswego River System*. Supplement. 17th Annual Report of the New York Conservation Department, 84–107.

———. 1929. "Fishes of the Erie-Niagara Watershed with Annotated List." In *A Biological Survey of the Erie-Niagara System*. Supplement. 18th Annual Report of the New York Conservation Department, 150–79.

———. 1930. "Fishes of the Lake Champlain Watershed." In *A Biological Survey of the Champlain Watershed*. Supplement. 19th Annual Report of the New York Conservation Department, 44–87.

———. 1934. "Fishes of the Raquette Watershed with Annotated List." In *A Biological Survey of the Raquette Watershed*. Supplement. 23rd Annual Report of the New York Conservation Department, 53–108.

———. 1935. "Fishes of the Watershed with Annotated List." In *A Biological Survey at the Mohawk-Hudson Watershed*. Supplement. 24th Annual Report of the New York Conservation Department, 63–101.

———. 1936. "Fishes of the Area with Annotated List." In *A Biological Survey of the*

Delaware and Susquehanna Watersheds. Supplement. 25th Annual Report of the New York Conservation Department, 45–88.

———. 1937. "Fishes of the Area with Annotated List." In *A Biological Survey of the Lower Hudson Watershed.* Supplement. 26th Annual Report of the New York Conservation Department, 45–103.

———. 1938. "Fishes of the Area with Annotated List." In *A Biological Survey of the Allegheny and Chemung Watersheds.* Supplement. 27th Annual Report of the New York Conservation Department, 48–73.

———. 1939. "The Freshwater Fishes of Long Island and Staten Island with Annotated List." In *A Biological Survey of the Fresh Waters of Long Island.* Supplement. 28th Annual Report New York Conservation Department, 29–44.

———. 1940. "Fishes of the Watershed with Annotated List." In *A Biological Survey of the Lake Ontario Watershed.* Supplement. 29th Annual Report of the New York Conservation Department, 42–81.

Greeley, J. R., and S. C. Bishop. 1932. "Fishes of the Area with Annotated List." In *A Biological Survey of the Oswegatchie and Black River Systems.* Supplement. 21st Annual Report of the New York Conservation Department, 54–93.

———. 1933. "Fishes of the Upper Hudson Watershed with Annotated List." In *A Biological Survey of the Upper Hudson Watershed.* Supplement. 22nd Annual Report of the New York Conservation Department, 64–101.

Greeley, J. R., and C. W. Greene. 1931. "Fishes of the Area with Annotated List." In *A Biological Survey of the St. Lawrence Watershed.* Supplement. 20th Annual Report of the New York Conservation Department, 44–94.

Halliwell, D. B., T. R. Whittier, and N. H. Ringler. 2001. "Distributions of Lake Fishes in the Northeast. III. Salmonids and Associated Coldwater Species." *Northeastern Naturalist* 8, no. 1: 189–206.

Hartel, K. E., D. B. Halliwell, and Alan E. Launer. 2002. *Inland Fishes of Massachusetts.* Lincoln, Mass.: Massachusetts Audubon Society. 328 pp.

Hocutt, C. H., and E. O. Wiley, eds. 1986. *The Zoogeography of North American Freshwater Fishes.* New York: John Wiley and Sons. 866 pp.

Hubbs, C. L., and K. F. Lagler. 1964. *Fishes of the Great Lakes Region.* Ann Arbor: Univ. of Michigan Press. 213 pp.

Jenkins, R. E., and N. M. Burkhead. 1994. *Freshwater Fishes of Virginia.* Bethesda, Md.: American Fisheries Society. 1,079 pp.

Kendall, W. C. 1914. "The Fishes of Maine." *Proceedings of the Portland Society of Natural History* (Maine) 3, no. 1: 1–198.

Kendall, W. C., and W. A. Dence. 1929. "The Fishes of the Cranberry Lake Region." *Roosevelt Wildlife Bulletin* 5, no. 2: 219–309.

Kircheis, F. W. 1994. "Update on Freshwater Fish Species Reproducing in Maine." *Maine Naturalist* 2, no. 1: 25–28.

Lee, D. S., C. R. Gilbert, C. H. Hocutt, R. E. Jenkins, D. E. McAllister, and J. R. Stauffer Jr. 1980. *Atlas of North American Fishes.* Raleigh: North Carolina Biological Survey. 854 pp.

McClane, A. J., ed. 1998. *McClane's New Standard Fishing Encyclopedia and International Angling Guide.* New York: Gramercy. 1,156 pp.

Nelson, J. S. 1994. *Fishes of the World.* New York: John Wiley. 600 pp.

Page, L. M., and B. M. Burr. 1991. *A Field Guide to Freshwater Fishes.* Boston: Houghton Mifflin. 432 pp.

Robins, C. R., R. M. Bailey, C. E. Bond, J. R. Brooker, E. A. Lachner, R. M. Lea, and W. B. Scott. 1991. *Common and Scientific Names of Fishes from the United States and Canada.* 5th ed. American Fisheries Society Special Publication no. 20. Bethesda, Md.: American Fisheries Society. 183 pp.

Scarola, J. F. 1973. *Freshwater Fishes of New Hampshire.* Concord: New Hampshire Fish and Game Department, Division of Inland and Marine Fisheries. 131 pp.

Schmidt, R. E. 1986. "Zoogeography of the Northern Appalachians." In *The Zoogeography of North American Freshwater Fishes,* edited by C. H. Hocutt and E. O. Wiley. New York: John Wiley and Sons.

Scott, W. B., and E. J. Crossman. 1973. *Freshwater Fishes of Canada.* Fisheries Research Board of Canada Bulletin no. 184. Ottawa: Fisheries Research Board of Canada. 966 pp.

Scott, W. G. 1967. *Freshwater Fishes of Eastern Canada.* 2d ed. Toronto: Univ. of Toronto Press. 137 pp.

Smith, C. L. 1985. *The Inland Fishes of New York State.* Albany: New York State Department of Environmental Conservation. 522 pp.

———. 1994. *Fish Watching: An Outdoor Guide to Freshwater Fishes.* Ithaca, N.Y.: Cornell Univ. Press. 216 pp.

Strange, R. M., and B. Burr. 1997. "Intraspecific Phylogeography of North American Highland Fishes: A Test of the Pleistocene Vicariance Hypothesis." *Evolution* 51, no. 3: 885–97.

Trautman, M. 1981. *The Fishes of Ohio.* Columbus: Ohio State Univ. Press. 782 pp.

Werner, R. G. 1980. *Freshwater Fishes of New York State: A Field Guide.* Syracuse, N.Y.: Syracuse Univ. Press. 186 pp.

Whittier, T. R., D. B. Halliwell, and R. A. Daniels. 1999. "Distributions of Lake Fishes in the Northeast. I. Centrarchidae, Percidae, Esocidae, and Moronidae." *Northeastern Naturalist* 6: 283–304.

———. 2000. "Distributions of Lake Fishes in the Northeast. II. The Minnows (Cyprinidae)." *Northeastern Naturalist* 7: 131–56.

Whittier, T. R., D. B. Halliwell, and S. G. Paulsen. 1997. "Cyprinid Distributions in Northeast USA Lakes: Evidence of Regional-Scale Minnow Biodiversity Losses." *Canadian Journal of Fisheries and Aquatic Sciences* 54: 1593–607.

Whitworth, W. R. 1996. *Freshwater Fishes of Connecticut.* State Geological and Natural History Survey of Connecticut Bulletin no. 114. Hartford: Connecticut Department of Environmental Protection. 243 pp.

Whitworth, W. R., P. L. Berrien, and W. T. Keller. 1968. *Freshwater Fishes of Connecticut.* State Geological and Natural History Survey of Connecticut Bulletin no. 101. Hartford: Connecticut Department of Environmental Protection. 134 pp.

Selected References by Family

Lampreys, Family Petromyzontidae

Anderson, A. A., and A. M. White. 1988. "Habitat Selection of *Ichthyomyzon fossor* and *Lampetra appendix* in a Northeastern Ohio Stream." *Ohio Journal of Science* 88, no. 2: 7.

Barnes, M. D., D. L. Rice, and G. J. Phinney. 1993. "Ohio Lamprey, *Ichthyomyzon bdellium* (Petromyzontidae), in Ohio." *Ohio Journal of Science* 93, no. 3: 42–43.

Beamish, F. W. H. 1980. "Biology of the North American Anadromous Sea Lamprey, *Petromyzon marinus.*" *Canadian Journal of Fisheries and Aquatic Sciences* 37, no. 11: 1924–43.

Beamish, F. W. H., and L. S. Austin. 1985. "Growth of the Mountain Brook Lamprey *Ichthyomyzon greeleyi* Hubbs and Trautman." *Copeia* no. 4: 881–90.

Carpenter, S. R., C. D. Baker, and B. J. Forsyth. 1987. "Nesting Silver Lampreys, *Ichthyomyzon unicuspis,* in the Little Blue River (Southern Indiana, Crawford County, Ohio River Drainage)." *Proceedings of the Indiana Academy of Sciences* 97: 525–26.

Cochran, P. A., and J. E. Marks. 1995. "Biology of the Silver Lamprey, *Ichthyomyzon unicuspis,* in Green Bay and the Lower Fox River, with a Comparison to the Sea Lamprey, *Petromyzon marinus.*" *Copeia* no. 2: 409–21.

Christie, W. J., and D. P. Kolenosky. 1980. "Parasitic Phase of the Sea Lamprey (*Petromyzon marinus*) in Lake Ontario." *Canadian Journal of Fisheries and Aquatic Sciences* 37, no. 11: 2021–38.

Farmer, G. J., and F. W. H. Beamish. 1973. "Sea Lamprey (*Petromyzon marinus*) Predation on Freshwater Teleosts." *Journal of the Fisheries Research Board of Canada* 30, no. 5: 601–5.

Gage, S. H. 1928. "The Lampreys of New York State—Life History and Economics." In *A Biological Survey of the Oswego River System.* Supplement. 17th Annual Report of the New York Conservation Department, 158–91.

Hardisty, M. W., and I. C. Potter, eds. 1971. *The Biology of the Lampreys.* New York: Academic.

Hoff, J. G. 1988. "Some Aspects of the Ecology of the American Brook Lamprey, *Lampetra appendix,* in the Mashpee River, Cape Cod, Massachusetts." *Canadian Field-Naturalist* 102: 735–37.

Holmes, J. A., and P. Lin. 1994. "Thermal Niche of Larval Sea Lamprey, *Petromyzon marinus.*" *Canadian Journal of Fisheries and Aquatic Sciences* 51, no. 2: 253–62.

Jensen, A. L. 1994. "Larkin's Predation Model of Lake Trout (*Salvelinus namaycush*) Extinction with Harvesting and Sea Lamprey (*Petromyzon marinus*) Predation: A Qualitative Analysis." *Canadian Journal of Fisheries and Aquatic Sciences* 51, no. 4: 942–45.

Lawrie, A. H. 1970. "The Sea Lamprey in the Great Lakes." *Transactions of the American Fisheries Society* 99, no. 4: 766–75.

Lennon, R. E. 1954. "Feeding Mechanism of the Sea Lamprey and Its Effect on Host Fishes." *U.S. Fish and Wildlife Service Fishery Bulletin* 98, no. 56: 247–93.

Pearce, W. A., R. A. Braem, S. M. Dustin, and J. J. Tibbles. 1980. "Sea Lamprey (*Petromyzon marinus*) in the Lower Great Lakes." *Canadian Journal of Fisheries and Aquatic Sciences* 37, no. 11: 1802–10.

Raney, E. C. 1939. "The Breeding Habits of *Ichthyomyzon greeleyi* Hubbs and Trautman." *Copeia* no. 2: 111–12.

Schneider, C. P., R. W. Owens, R. A. Bergstedt, and R. O'Gorman. 1996. "Predation by Sea Lamprey (*Petromyzon marinus*) on Lake Trout (*Salvelinus namaycush*) in Southern Lake Ontario, 1982–1992." *Canadian Journal of Fisheries and Aquatic Sciences* 53, no. 9: 1921–32.

Seagle, H. H., Jr., and J. W. Nagel. 1982. "Life Cycle and Fecundity of the American Brook Lamprey, *Lampetra appendix,* in Tennessee." *Copeia* no. 2: 362–66.

Stier, K., and B. Kynard. 1986a. "Abundance, Size, and Sex Ratio of Adult Sea-Run Sea Lampreys, *Petromyzon marinus,* in the Connecticut River." *Fishery Bulletin* 84, no. 2: 476–80.

———. 1986b. "Movement of Sea-Run Sea Lampreys, *Petromyzon marinus,* During the Spawning Migration in the Connecticut River." *Fishery Bulletin* 84, no. 3: 749–53.

Surface, A. H. 1898. "The Lampreys of Central New York." *U.S. Fishery Commission Bulletin 1897* 17: 209–15.

Wigley, R. L. 1959. "Life History of the Sea Lamprey of Cayuga Lake, New York." *U.S. Fish and Wildlife Service Fishery Bulletin* 154, no. 59: 561–617.

Wilson, F. W. 1955. "Lampreys in the Lake Champlain Basin." *American Midland Naturalist* 54, no. 1: 168–72.

Young, R. J., J. R. M. Kelso, and J. G. Weise. 1990. "Occurrence, Relative Abundance, and Size of Landlocked Sea Lamprey (*Petromyzon marinus*) Ammocoetes in Relation to Stream Characteristics in the Great Lakes." *Canadian Journal of Fisheries and Aquatic Sciences* 47, no. 9: 1773–78.

Sturgeons, Family Acipenseridae

Bain, M. B. 1997. "Atlantic and Shortnose Sturgeons of the Hudson River: Common and Divergent Life History Attributes." *Environmental Biology of Fishes* 48: 347–58.

Beamish, F. W. H., D. L. G. Noakes, and A. Rossiter. 1998. "Feeding Ecology of Juvenile Lake Sturgeon, *Acipenser fulvescens,* in Northern Ontario." *Canadian Field-Naturalist* 112, no. 3: 459–68.

Binkowski, F. P., and S. I. Doroshov, eds. 1985. *North American Sturgeons: Biology and Aquaculture Potential.* Dordrecht, Netherlands: W. Junk. 163 pp.

Buckley, J., and B. Kynard. 1985. "Habitat Use and Behavior of Pre-spawning and Spawning Shortnose Sturgeon, *Acipenser brevirostrum,* in the Connecticut River." In *North American Sturgeons: Biology And Aquaculture Potential,* 111–18. Dordrecht, Netherlands: W. Junk.

Carlson, D. M. 1995. "Lake Sturgeon Waters and Fisheries in New York State." *Journal of Great Lakes Research* 21: 35–41.

Chiasson, W. B., D. L. G. Noakes, amd W. H. Beamish. 1997. "Habitat, Benthic Prey, and Distribution of Juvenile Lake Sturgeon (*Acipenser fulvescens*) in Northern Ontario Rivers." *Canadian Journal of Fisheries and Aquatic Sciences* 54, no. 12: 2866–71.

Dadswell, M. J. 1979. "Biology and Population Characteristics of the Shortnose Sturgeon, *Acipenser brevirostrum* LeSueur 1818 (Osteichthyes: Acipenseridae), in the Saint

John River Estuary, New Brunswick, Canada." *Canadian Journal of Zoology* 57, no. 11: 2186–210.

Dovel, W. L. 1978. *Biology and Management of Atlantic Sturgeons* (Acipenser oxyrhynchus) *Mitchill, and Shortnose Sturgeons* (Acipenser brevirostrum) *LeSueur, of the Hudson Estuary.* Cincinnati: Wapora. 181 pp.

Fortin, R., J. R. Mongeau, G. Desjardins, and P. Dumont. 1993. "Movements and Biological Statistics of Lake Sturgeon *(Acipenser fulvescens)* Populations from the St. Lawrence and Ottawa River Systems, Quebec." *Canadian Journal of Zoology* 71: 638–50.

Fried, S. M., and J. D. McCleave. 1973. "Occurrence of the Shortnose Sturgeon *(Acipenser brevirostrum),* an Endangered Species, in Montsweag Bay, Maine." *Journal of the Fisheries Research Board of Canada* 30, no. 4: 563–64.

Kynard, B. 1997. "Life History, Latitudinal Patterns, and Status of the Shortnose Sturgeon, *Acipenser brevirostrum.*" *Environmental Biology of Fishes* 48, nos. 1–4: 319–34.

McCleave, J. D., S. M. Fried, and A. K. Towt. 1977. "Daily Movements of Shortnose Sturgeon, *Acipenser brevirostrum,* in a Maine Estuary." *Copeia* no. 1: 149–57.

Richmond, A. M., and B. Kynard. 1995. "Ontogenetic Behavior of Shortnose Sturgeon, *Acipenser brevirostrum.*" *Copeia* no. 1: 172–82.

Smith, T. I. J. 1985. "The Fishery, Biology, and Management of Atlantic Sturgeon, *Acipenser oxyrhynchus,* in North America. North American Sturgeons: Biology and Aquaculture Potential." *Environmental Biology of Fishes* 14, no. 1: 61–72.

Smith, T. I. J., and E. K. Dingley. 1984. "Review of Biology and Culture of Atlantic *(Acipenser oxyrhynchus)* and Shortnose Sturgeon *(A. brevirostrum).*" *Journal of the World Mariculture Society* 14: 210–18.

Stevenson, J. T., and D. H. Secor. 2000. "Age Determination and Growth of Hudson River Atlantic Sturgeon, *Acipenser oxyrhynchus.*" *Fishery Bulletin* 98, no. 1: 153–66.

Taubert, B. D. 1980. "Reproduction of Shortnose Sturgeon *(Acipenser brevirostrum)* in Holyoke Pool, Connecticut River, Massachusetts." *Copeia* no. 1: 114–17.

Taubert, B. D., and M. J. Dadswell. 1980. "Description of Some Larval Shortnose Sturgeon *(Acipenser brevirostrum)* from the Holyoke Pool, Connecticut River, Massachusetts, U.S.A., and the Saint John River, New Brunswick, Canada." *Canadian Journal of Zoology* 58, no. 6: 1125–28.

Vladykov, V. D., and J. R. Greeley. 1963. "Order Acipenseroidei. Fishes of the Western North Atlantic." *Memoir, Sears Foundation for Marine Research* 1, no. 3: 24–60.

Walsh, M. G., M. B. Bain, T. Squiers Jr., J. R. Waldman, and I. Wirgin. 2001. "Morphological and Genetic Variation among Shortnose Sturgeon *(Acipenser brevirostrum)* from Adjacent and Distant Rivers." *Estuaries* 24, no. 1: 41–48.

Webb, P. W. 1986. "Kinematics of Lake Sturgeon, *Acipenser fulvescens,* at Cruising Speeds." *Canadian Journal of Zoology* 64, no. 10: 2137–41.

Paddlefishes, Family Polyodontidae

Boone, E. A., Jr., and T. J. Timmons. 1995. "Density and Natural Mortality of Paddlefish, *Polyodon spathula,* in an Unfished Cumberland River Subimpoundment, South Cross Creek Reservoir, Tennessee." *Journal of Freshwater Ecology* 10, no. 4: 421–31.

Devitsina, G. V., and A. A. Kazhlaev. 1993. "Chemoreceptor Organs in Early Juvenile Paddlefish, *Polyodon spathula.*" *Journal of Ichthyology* 33, no. 1: 142–46; 33, no. 5: 143–49.

Graham, L. K. 1997. "Contemporary Status of the North American Paddlefish, *Polyodon spathula.*" *Environmental Biology of Fishes* 48: 279–89.

Paukert, C. P., and W. L. Fisher. 2000. "Abiotic Factors Affecting Summer Distribution and Movement of Male Paddlefish, *Polyodon spathula,* in a Prairie Reservoir." *Southwestern Naturalist* 45, no. 2: 133–40.

Pitman, V. M., and J. O. Parks. 1994. "Habitat Use and Movement of Young Paddlefish (*Polyodon spathula*)." *Journal of Freshwater Ecology* 9, no. 3: 181–89.

Purkett, C. A., Jr. 1961. "Reproduction and Early Development of the Paddlefish." *Transactions of the American Fisheries Society* 90, no. 2: 125–29.

Robinson, J. W. 1967. "Observations on the Life History, Movement, and Harvest of the Paddlefish, *Polyodon spathula,* in Montana." *Proceedings of the Montana Academy of Science* 26: 33–44.

Gars, Family Lepisosteidae

Crumpton, J. 1970. "Food Habits of Longnose Gar (*Lepisosteus osseus*) and Florida Gar (*Lepisosteus platyrhincus*) Collected from Five Central Florida Lakes." In *Proceedings of the Twenty-fourth Annual Conference, Southeastern Association of Game and Fish Commissioners,* 419–24. Columbia, S.C.: Southeastern Association of Game and Fish Commissioners.

Echelle, A. A., and C. D. Riggs. 1972. "Aspects of the Early Life History of Gars (*Lepisosteus*)." *Transactions of the American Fisheries Society* 101, no. 1: 106–12.

Netsch, Lt. Norval F., and A. Witt Jr. 1962. "Contributions to the Life History of the Longnose Gar (*Lepisosteus osseus*) in Missouri." *Transactions of the American Fisheries Society* 91, no. 3: 251–62.

Suttkus, R. D. 1963. "Order Lepisostei. Fishes of the Western North Atlantic." *Memoir, Sears Foundation for Marine Research* 1, no. 3: 61–88.

Trembley, F. J. 1930. "The Gar-Pike of Lake Champlain." In *A Biological Survey of the Champlain Watershed.* Supplement. *19th Annual Report of the New York State Conservation Department (1929),* 139–45.

Webb, P. W., D. H. Hardy, and V. L. Mehl. 1992. "The Effect of Armored Skin on the Swimming of Longnose Gar, *Lepisosteus osseus.*" *Canadian Journal of Zoology* 70, no. 6: 1173–79.

Bowfins, Family Amiidae

Dugas, C. N., M. Konikoff, and M. F. Trahan. 1976. "Stomach Contents of Bowfin (*Amia calva*) and Spotted Gar (*Lepisosteus oculatus*) Taken in Henderson Lake, Louisiana." *Proceedings of the Louisiana Academy of Sciences* 39: 28–34.

Katula, R. S., and L. M. Page. 1998. "Nest Association Between a Large Predator, the Bowfin (*Amia calva*), and Its Prey, the Golden Shiner (*Notemigonus crysoleucas*)." *Copeia* no. 1: 220–21.

Lagler, K. F., and C. L. Hubbs. 1940. "Food of the Long-nosed Gar (*Lepisosteus osseus oxyurus*) and the Bowfin (*Amia calva*) in Southern Michigan." *Copeia* no. 4: 239–41.

Mooneyes, Family Hiodontidae

D'Amours, J. S. Thibodeau, and R. Fortin. 2001. "Comparison of Lake Sturgeon (*Acipenser fulvescens*), *Stizostedion* spp., *Catostomus* spp., *Moxostoma* spp., Quillback (*Carpiodes cyprinus*), and Mooneye (*Hiodon tergisus*) Larval Drift in Des Prairies River, Quebec." *Canadian Journal of Zoology* 79, no. 8: 1472–89.

Glenn, C. L. 1975. "Seasonal Diets of Mooneye, *Hiodon tergisus*, in the Assiniboine River." *Canadian Journal of Zoology* 53, no. 3: 232–37.

———. 1976. "Seasonal Growth Rates of Mooneye (*Hiodon tergisus*) from the Assiniboine River." *Journal of the Fisheries Research Board of Canada* 33, no. 9: 2078–82.

Glenn, C. L., and R. R. G. Williams. 1976. "Fecundity of Mooneye, *Hiodon tergisus*, in the Assiniboine River." *Canadian Journal of Zoology* 54, no. 2: 156–61.

Van Oosten, J. 1961. "Records, Ages, and Growth of the Mooneye, *Hiodon tergisus*, of the Great Lakes." *Transactions of the American Fisheries Society* 90, no. 2: 170–74.

Wallus, R., and J. P. Buchanan. 1989. "Contributions to the Reproductive Biology and Early Life Ecology of Mooneye in the Tennessee and Cumberland Rivers." *American Midland Naturalist* 122: 204–7.

Freshwater Eels, Family Anguillidae

Barbin, G. P., and J. D. McCleave. 1997. "Fecundity of the American Eel *Anguilla rostrata* at 45 Degrees N in Maine, U.S.A." *Journal of Fish Biology* 51, no. 4: 840–47.

Denoncourt, C. E., and J. R. Stauffer Jr. 1993. "Feeding Selectivity of the American Eel *Anguilla rostrata* (LeSueur) in the Upper Delaware River." *American Midland Naturalist* 129, no. 2: 301–8.

Facey, D. E., and G. W. Labar. 1981. "Biology of American Eels in Lake Champlain, Vermont." *Transactions of the American Fisheries Society* 110, no. 3: 396–402.

Haro, A., T. Castro-Santos, and J. Boubee. 2000. "Behavior and Passage of Silver-Phase American Eels, *Anguilla rostrata* (LeSueur), at a Small Hydroelectric Facility." *Dana. Charlottenlund* (Dana) 12: 33–42.

Haro, A. J., and W. H. Krueger. 1988. "Pigmentation, Size, and Migration of Elvers (*Anguilla rostrata*, LeSueur) in a Coastal Rhode Island Stream." *Canadian Journal of Zoology* 66, no. 11: 2528–33.

Kleckner, R. C., J. D. McCleave, and G. S. Wippelhauser. 1983. "Spawning of American Eel, *Anguilla rostrata*, Relative to Thermal Fronts in the Sargasso Sea." *Environmental Biology of Fishes* 9, nos. 3–4: 289–93.

Labar, G. W. 1982. "Local Movements and Home-Range Size of Radio-Equipped American Eels (*Anguilla rostrata*) from Lake Champlain, with Notes on Population Estimation." In *Proceedings of the 1980 North American Eel Conference*, 72. Ontario Fisheries Technical Report Series no. 4. Toronto: Ontario Ministry of Natural Resources.

Labar, G. W., and D. E. Facey. 1983. "Local Movements and Inshore Population Sizes of American Eels in Lake Champlain, Vermont." *Transactions of the American Fisheries Society* 112, no. 1: 111–16.

Levesque, J. R., and W. R. Whitworth. 1987. "Age Class Distribution and Size of American Eel (*Anguilla rostrata*) in the Shetucket/Thames River, Connecticut." *Journal of Freshwater Ecology* 4, no. 1: 17–22.

Oliveira, K. 1999. "Life History Characteristics and Strategies of the American Eel, *Anguilla rostrata*." *Canadian Journal of Fisheries and Aquatic Sciences* 56, no. 5: 795–802.

Oliveira, K., and J. D. McCleave. 2000 . "Variation in Population and Life History Traits of the American Eel, *Anguilla rostrata*, in Four Rivers in Maine." *Environmental Biology of Fishes* 59, no. 2: 141–51.

Sorensen, P. W., M. L. Bianchini, and H. E. Winn. 1986. "Diel Foraging Activity of American Eels, *Anguilla rostrata* (LeSueur), in a Rhode Island Estuary." *Fishery Bulletin* 84, no. 3: 746–47.

Wippelhauser, G. S., and J. D. McCleave. 1987. "Precision of Behavior of Migrating Juvenile American Eels (*Anguilla rostrata*) Utilizing Selective Tidal Stream Transport." *Journal Conseil International pour l'Exporation de la Mer* 44, no. 1: 80–89.

Herrings, Family Clupeidae

Bodola, A. 1966. "Life History of the Gizzard Shad, *Dorosoma cepedianum* (LeSueur), in Western Lake Erie." *U.S. Fish and Wildlife Service Fishery Bulletin* 65, no. 2: 391–425.

Cheek, R. P. 1968. *The American Shad.* U.S. Fish and Wildlife Service Fishery Leaflet no. 614. Washington, D.C.: U.S. Fish and Wildlife Service. 13 pp.

Crecco, V. A., and T. F. Savoy. 1985. "Effects of Biotic and Abiotic Factors on Growth and Relative Survival of Young American Shad, *Alosa sapidissima*, in the Connecticut River." *Canadian Journal of Fisheries and Aquatic Sciences* 42, no. 10: 1640–48.

Crowder, L. B., and F. P. Binkowki. 1983. "Foraging Behaviors and the Interaction of Alewife, *Alosa pseudoharengus,* and Bloater, *Coregonus hoyi*." *Environmental Biology of Fishes* 8, no. 2: 105–13.

Dodson, J. J., and W. C. Leggett. 1973. "Behavior of Adult American Shad (*Alosa sapidissima)* Homing to the Connecticut River from Long Island Sound." *Journal of the Fisheries Research Board of Canada* 30, no. 12, pt. 1: 1847–60.

Domermuth, R. B., and R. J. Reed. 1980. "Food of Juvenile American Shad, *Alosa sapidissima,* Juvenile Blueback Herring, *Alosa aestivalis,* and Pumpkinseed, *Lepomis gibbosus,* in the Connecticut River below Holyoke Dam, Massachusetts." *Estuaries* 3, no. 1: 65–68.

Durbin, A. G., S. W. Nixon, and C. A. Oviatt. 1979. "Effects of the Spawning Migration of the Alewife, *Alosa pseudoharengus,* on Freshwater Ecosystems." *Ecology* 60, no. 1: 8–17.

Havey, K. 1973. "Production of Juvenile *Alosa pseudoharengus* at Love Lake, Washington County, Maine." *Transactions of the American Fisheries Society* 102, no. 2: 434–37.

Hildebrand, S. F. 1963. "Family Clupeidae. Fishes of the Western North Atlantic." *Memoir, Sears Foundation for Marine Research* 1, no. 3: 257–454.

Jessop, B. M. 1994. *Homing of Alewives* (Alosa pseudoharengus) *and blueback herring* (A. aestivalis) *to and Within the Saint John River, New Brunswick, as Indicated by Tagging Data.* Canadian Technical Report of Fisheries and Aquatic Sciences no. 2015. Ottawa: Department of Fisheries and Oceans. 27 pp.

Kissil, G. W. 1974. "Spawning of the Anadromous Alewife, *Alosa pseudoharengus,* in Bride Lake, Connecticut." *Transactions of the American Fisheries Society* 103, no. 2: 312–17.

Leggett, W. C., and J. E. Carscadden. 1978. "Latitudinal Variation in Reproductive Characteristics of American Shad (*Alosa sapidissima):* Evidence for Population Specific Life History Strategies in Fish." *Journal of the Fisheries Research Board of Canada* 35, no. 11: 1469–78.

Levesque, R. C., and R. J. Reed. 1972. "Food Availability and Consumption by Young Connecticut River Shad *Alosa sapidissima."* *Journal of the Fisheries Research Board of Canada* 29, no. 10: 1495–99.

Limburg, K. E. 1996. "Modeling the Ecological Constraints on Growth and Movement of Juvenile American Shad (*Alosa sapidissima*) in the Hudson River Estuary." *Estuaries* 19, no. 4: 794–813.

Loesch, J. G. 1987. "Overview of Life History Aspects of Anadromous Alewife and Blueback Herring in Freshwater Habitats." *American Fishery Society Symposium* 1: 89–103.

Miller, R. R. 1957. "Origin and Dispersal of the Alewife, *Alosa pseudoharengus,* and the Gizzard Shad, *Dorosoma cepedianum,* in the Great Lakes." *Transactions of the American Fisheries Society* 86, no. 1: 97–111.

———. 1960. "Systematics and Biology of the Gizzard Shad (*Dorosoma cepedianum)* and Related Fishes." *U.S. Fish and Wildlife Service Fishery Bulletin* 173, no. 60: 371–92.

Mills, E. L., R. O'Gorman, E. F. Roseman, C. Adams, and R. W. Owens. 1995. "Planktivory by Alewife (*Alosa pseudoharengus)* and Rainbow Smelt (*Osmerus mordax)* on Microcrustacean Zooplankton and Dreissenid (Bivalvia: Dreissenidae) Veligers in Southern Lake Ontario." *Canadian Journal of Fisheries and Aquatic Sciences* 52, no. 5: 925–35.

Neves, R. J., and L. Depres. 1979. "The Oceanic Migration of American Shad, *Alosa sapidissima,* along the Atlantic Coast." *Fishery Bulletin* 77, no. 1: 199–212.

Odell, T. T. 1934. "The Life History and Ecological Relationships of the Alewife (*Pomolobus pseudoharengus* [Wilson]), in Seneca Lake, New York." *Transactions of the American Fisheries Society* 64, no. 1: 118–24.

O'Leary, J., and D. G. Smith. 1987. "Occurrence of the First Freshwater Migration of the Gizzard Shad, *Dorosoma cepedianum,* in the Connecticut River, Massachusetts." *Fishery Bulletin* 85: 380–83.

Owens, R. W., R. O'Gorman, E. L. Mills, L. G. Rudstam, J. J. Hasse, B. H. Kulik, and D. B. MacNeill. 1998. "Blueback Herring (*Alosa aestivalis)* in Lake Ontario: First Record, Entry Route, and Colonization Potential." *Journal of Great Lakes Research* 24, no. 3: 723–30.

Rideout, S. G., J. E. Johnson, and C. F. Cole. 1979. "Periodic Counts for Estimating the Size of the Spawning Population of Alewives, *Alosa pseudoharengus* (Wilson)." *Estuaries* 2, no. 2: 119–23.

Talbot, G. B. 1954. "Factors Associated with Fluctuations in Abundance of Hudson River Shad." *U.S. Fish and Wildlife Service Fishery Bulletin* 101, no. 56: 373–413.

Walton, C. J., D. Libby, and S. Collins. 1979. *Population Biology and Management of the*

Alewife (Alosa pseudoharengus) *in Maine.* Augusta: Maine Department of Marine Resources. 29 pp.

Warshaw, S. J. 1972. "Effects of Alewives (*Alosa pseudoharengus*) on the Zooplankton of Lake Wononskopomuc, Connecticut." *Limnology and Oceanography* 17, no. 6: 816–25.

Carp and Minnows, Family Cyprinidae

Aadland, L. P. 1993. "Stream Habitat Types: Their Fish Assemblages and Relationship to Flow." *North American Journal of Fisheries Management* 13, no. 4: 790–806.

Aldridge, D. C. 1999. "Development of European Bitterling in the Gills of Freshwater Mussels." *Journal of Fish Biology* 54, no. 1: 138–51.

Beers, C. E., and J. M. Culp. 1990. "Plasticity in Foraging Behaviour of a Lotic Minnow (*Rhinichthys cataractae*) in Response to Different Light Intensities." *Canadian Journal of Zoology* 68, no. 1: 101–5.

Brazo, D. C., C. R. Liston, and R. C. Anderson. 1978. "Life History of the Longnose Dace, *Rhinichthys cataractae,* in the Surge Zone of Eastern Lake Michigan near Ludington, Michigan." *Transactions of the American Fisheries Society* 107, no. 4: 550–56.

Carlson, D. M. 1997. "Status of the Pugnose and Blackchin Shiners in the St. Lawrence River in New York, 1993–95." *Journal of Freshwater Ecology* 12, no. 1: 131–39.

Cochran, P. A., D. M. Lodge, J. R. Hodgson, and P. G. Knapik. 1988. "Diets of Syntopic Finescale Dace, *Phoxinus neogaeus,* and Northern Redbelly Dace, *Phoxinus Eos:* A Reflection of Trophic Morphology." *Environmental Biology of Fishes* 22, no. 3: 235–40.

Culp, J. M. 1989. "Nocturnally Constrained Foraging of a Lotic Minnow (*Rhinichthys cataractae*)." *Canadian Journal of Zoology* 67, no. 8: 2008–12.

Danehy, R. J., N. H. Ringler, S. V. Stehman, and J. M. Hassett. 1998. "Variability of Fish Densities in a Small Catchment." *Ecology of Freshwater Fish* 7, no. 1: 36–48.

Daniels, R. A., and S. J. Wisniewski. 1994. "Feeding Ecology of Redside Dace, *Clinostomus elongatus.*" *Ecology of Freshwater Fish* 3, no. 4: 176–83.

Findlay, C. S., D. G. Bert, and L. Zheng. 2000. "Effect of Introduced Piscivores on Native Minnow Communities in Adirondack Lakes." *Canadian Journal of Fisheries and Aquatic Sciences* 57, no. 3: 570–80.

Garman, G. C., and J. R. Moring. 1993. "Diet and Annual Production of Two Boreal River Fishes Following Clearcut Logging." *Environmental Biology of Fishes* 36, no. 3: 301–11.

Gascon, D., and W. C. Leggett. 1977. "Distribution, Abundance, and Resource Utilization of Littoral Zone Fishes in Response to a Nutrient/Production Gradient in Lake Memphremagog." *Journal of the Fisheries Research Board of Canada* 34, no. 8: 1105–17.

Gauthier, S., and D. Boisclair. 1997. "The Energetic Implications of Diel Onshore-Offshore Migration by Dace (*Phoxinus eos X P. neogaeus*) in a Small Oligotrophic Lake." *Canadian Journal of Fisheries and Aquatic Sciences* 54, no. 9: 1996–2006.

Gillen, A. L., and T. Hart. 1980. "Feeding Interrelationships Between the Sand Shiner and the Striped Shiner." *Ohio Journal of Science* 80, no. 2: 71–76.

Gorski, P. R., R. C. Lathrop, S. D. Hill, and R. T. Herrin. 1999. "Temporal Mercury Dynamics and Diet Composition in the Mimic Shiner." *Transactions of the American Fisheries Society* 128, no. 4: 701–12.

Harrington, R. W., Jr. 1948a. "The Food of the Bridled Shiner, *Notropis bifrenatus* (Cope)." *American Midland Naturalist* 40, no. 2: 353–61.

———. 1948b. "The Life Cycle and Fertility of the Bridled Shiner, *Notropis bifrenatus* (Cope)." *American Midland Naturalist* 39: 83–92.

Hubbs, C. L., and G. P. Cooper. 1936. *Minnows of Michigan.* Cranbrook Institute of Science Bulletin no. 8. Bloomfield Hills, Mich.: Cranbrook Institute of Science. 95 pp.

Johnson, J. H. 1982. "Summer Feeding Ecology of the Blacknose Dace, *Rhinichthys atratulus,* in a Tributary of Lake Ontario." *Canadian Field-Naturalist* 96, no. 3: 282–86.

Johnson, J. H., D. S. Dropkin, and P. G. Shaffer. 1992. "Habitat Use by a Headwater Stream Fish Community in North-Central Pennsylvania." *Rivers* 3, no. 2: 69–79.

Johnson, J. H., and E. Z. Johnson. 1982. "Observations on the Eye-Picking Behavior of the Cutlips Minnow, *Exoglossum maxillingua.*" *Copeia* no. 3: 711–12.

Magnan, P., and G. J. Fitzgerald. 1984. "Mechanisms Responsible for the Niche Shift of Brook Charr, *Salvelinus fontinalis* Mitchill, When Living Sympatrically with Creek Chub, *Semotilus atromaculatus* Mitchill." *Canadian Journal of Zoology* 62, no. 8: 1548–55.

Magnan, P., and G. J. Fitzgerald. 1984. "Ontogenetic Changes in Diel Activity, Food Habits, and Spacial Distribution of Juvenile and Adult Creek Chub, *Semotilus atromaculatus.*" *Environmental Biology of Fishes* 11, no. 4: 301–7.

Matthews, M. M., and D. C. Heins. 1984. "Life History of the Redfin Shiner, *Notropis umbratilis* (Pisces: Cyprinidae), in Mississippi." *Copeia* no. 2: 385–90.

Matthews, W. J., A. J. Stewart, and M. E. Power. 1987. "Grazing Fishes as Components of North American Stream Ecosystems: Effects of *Campostoma anomalum.*" In *Community and Evolutionary Ecology of North America Stream Fishes,* edited by W. J. Matthews and D. C. Heins, 128–35. Norman: Univ. of Oklahoma Press.

McCann, J. A. 1959. "Life History Studies of the Spottail Shiner of Clear Lake, Iowa, with Particular Reference to Some Sampling Problems." *Transactions of the American Fisheries Society* 88, no. 4: 336–43.

McCoy, C. M., III, C. P. Madenjian, J. V. Adams, and W. N. Harman. 2001. "The Fish Community of a Small Impoundment in Upstate New York." *Journal of Freshwater Ecology* 16, no. 3: 389–94.

Mendelson, J. 1975. "Feeding Relationships among Species of Notropis (Pisces: Cyprinidae) in a Wisconsin Stream." *Ecological Monographs* 45, no. 3: 199–230.

Miller, R. J. 1964. "Behavior and Ecology of Some North American Cyprinid Fishes." *American Midland Naturalist* 72, no. 2: 313–57.

Ming, F. W., and D. L. Q. Noakes. 1984. "Spawning Site Selection and Competition in Minnows (*Pimephales notatus* and *P. promelas)* (Pisces, Cyprinidae)." *Behavioral Biology* 9, no. 3: 227–34.

Moring, J. R., and P. H. Nicholson. 1994. "Evaluation of Three Types of Artificial Habitats for Fishes in a Freshwater Pond in Maine, USA." From the Fifth International Conference on Aquatic Habitat Enhancement, 1994 *Bulletin of Marine Science* 55, nos. 2–3: 1149–59.

Mullen, D. M., and T. M. Burton. 1995. "Size-Related Habitat Use by Longnose Dace (*Rhinichthys cataractae).*" *American Midland Naturalist* 133, no. 1: 177–83.

Pappantoniou, A., and G. Dale. 1983. "Comparative Food Habits of Two Minnow Species: Blacknose Dace, *Rhinichthys atratulus*, and Longnose Dace, *Rhinichthys cataractae.*" *Journal of Freshwater Ecology* 1, no. 4: 361–64.

Pappantoniou, A., G. Dale, and R. E. Schmidt. 1984. "Aspects of the Life History of the Cutlips Minnow, *Exoglossum maxillingua*, from Two Eastern Pennsylvania Streams." *Journal of Freshwater Ecology* 2, no. 5: 449–58.

Parker, B., and P. Mckee. 1984. "Status of the Silver Shiner, *Notropis photogenis*, in Canada." *Canadian Field-Naturalist* 98, no. 1: 91–97.

Powles, P. M., S. Finucan, M. Van Haaften, and R. A. Curry. 1992. "Preliminary Evidence for Fractional Spawning by the Northern Redbelly Dace, *Phoxinus eos.*" *Canadian Field-Naturalist* 106, no. 2: 237–40.

Raney, E. C. 1940a. "The Breeding Behavior of the Common Shiner, *Notropis cornutus* (Mitchill)." *Zoologica* 25, no. 1: 1–14.

———. 1940b. "Comparison of the Breeding Habits of Two Subspecies of Blacknose Dace, *Rhinichthys atratulus* (Hermann)." *American Midland Naturalist* 23, no. 2: 399–403.

Reed, R. J. 1959. "Age, Growth, and Food of the Longnose Dace, *Rhinichthys cataractae*, in Northwestern Pennsylvania." *Copeia* no. 2: 160–62.

Ross, M. R., and R. J. Reed. 1978. "The Reproductive Behavior of the Fallfish *Semotilus corporalis.*" *Copeia* no. 2: 215–21.

Sabaj, M. H., E. G. Maurakis, and W. S. Woolcott. 2000. "Spawning Behaviors in the Bluehead Chub, *Nocomis leptocephalus*, River Chub, *N. micropogon*, and Central Stoneroller, *Campostoma anomalum.*" *American Midland Naturalist* 144, no. 1: 187–201.

Schlosser, I. J., M. R. Doeringsfeld, J. F. Elder, and L. F. Arzayus. 1998. "Niche Relationships of Clonal and Sexual Fish in a Heterogeneous Landscape." *Ecology* 79, no. 3: 953–68.

Schmidt, R. E., and J. McGurk. 1982. "Biology of the European Bitterling *Rhodeus sericeus* (Pisces: Cyprinidae) in the Bronx River, New York, USA: An Apparently Benign Exotic Species." *Biological Conservation* 24, no. 2: 157–62.

Shao, B. 1997. "Nest Association of Pumpkinseed, *Lepomis gibbosus*, and Golden Shiner, *Notemigonus crysoleucas.*" *Environmental Biology of Fishes* 50, no. 1: 41–48.

Van Duzer, E. M. 1939. "Observations on the Breeding Habits of the Cutlips Minnow, *Exoglossum maxillingua.*" *Copeia* no. 2: 65–75.

Victor, B. C., and E. B. Brothers. 1982. "Age and Growth of the Fallfish *Semotilus corporalis* with Daily Otolith Increments as a Method of Annulus Verification." *Canadian Journal of Zoology* 60, no. 11: 2543–50.

Vives, S. P. 1990. "Nesting Ecology and Behavior of Hornyhead Chub *Nocomis biguttatus*, a Keystone Species in Allequash Creek, Wisconsin." *American Midland Naturalist* 124, no. 1: 46–56.

Wallace, D. C. 1973. "The Distribution and Dispersal of the Silverjaw Minnow, *Ericymba buccata* Cope." *American Midland Naturalist* 89, no. 1: 145–55.

———. 1976. "Feeding Behaviour and Developmental, Seasonal, and Diel Changes in the Food of the Silverjaw Minnow, *Ericymba buccata* Cope." *American Midland Naturalist* 95, no. 2: 361–76.

Westman, J. R. 1938. "Studies on Reproduction and Growth of the Bluntnosed Minnow, *Hyborhynchus notatus* (Rafinesque)." *Copeia* no. 2: 57–60.

Whittier, T. R., D. B. Halliwell, and R. A. Daniels. 2000. "Distributions of Lake Fishes in the Northeast. II. The Minnows (Cyprinidae)." *Northeastern Naturalist* 7, no. 2: 131–56.

Yager, R. O., and T. S. McComish. 1976. "Food Habits of the Spottail Shiner in Indiana Waters of Lake Michigan in 1973." *Proceedings of the Indiana Academy of Science* 86: 203–8.

Zambrano, L., M. Scheffer, and M. Martinez-Ramos. 2001. "Catastrophic Response of Lakes to Benthivorous Fish Introduction." *Oikos* 94, no. 2: 344–50.

Suckers, Family Catostomidae

Aadland, L. P. 1993. "Stream Habitat Types: Their Fish Assemblages and Relationship to Flow." *North American Journal of Fisheries Management* 13, no. 4: 790–806.

Ahlgren, M. O. 1996. "Selective Ingestion of Detritus by a North Temperate Omnivorous Fish, the Juvenile White Sucker, *Catostomus commersoni.*" *Environmental Biology of Fishes* 46, no. 4: 375–81.

Bailey, M. M. 1969. "Age, Growth, and Maturity of the Longnose Sucker, *Catostomus catostomus*, of Western Lake Superior." *Journal of the Fisheries Research Board of Canada* 26: 1289–99.

Brodeur, P., P. Magnan, and M. Legault. 2001. "Response of Fish Communities to Different Levels of White Sucker (*Catostomus commersoni*) Biomanipulation in Five Temperate Lakes." *Canadian Journal of Fisheries and Aquatic Sciences* 58, no. 10: 1998–2010.

Bunt, C. M., and S. J. Cooke. 2001. "Post-spawn Movements and Habitat Use by Greater Redhorse, *Moxostoma valenciennesi.*" *Ecology of Freshwater Fish* 10, no. 1: 57–60.

Burr, B. M., and M. A. Morris. 1977. "Spawning Behavior of the Shorthead Redhorse, *Moxostoma macrolepidotum*, in Big Rock Creek, Illinois." *Transactions of the American Fisheries Society* 10, no. 1: 80–82.

Cooke, S. J., and C. M. Bunt. 1999. "Spawning and Reproductive Biology of the Greater Redhorse, *Moxostoma valenciennesi*, in the Grand River, Ontario." *Canadian Field-Naturalist* 113, no. 3: 497–502.

Curry, K. D., and A. Spacie. 1984. "Differential Use of Stream Habitat by Spawning Catostomids." *American Midland Naturalist* 111, no. 2: 267–79.

Dence, W. A. 1948. "Life History, Ecology, and Habits of the Dwarf Sucker, *Catostomus commersoni utawana* (Mather), at the Huntington Wildlife Station." *Roosevelt Wildlife Bulletin* 8, no. 4: 81–150.

Hart, T. F., Jr., and R. G. Werner. 1987. Effects of Prey Density on Growth and Survival of White Sucker, *Catostomus commersoni*, and Pumpkinseed, *Lepomis gibbosus*, Larvae. *Environmental Biology of Fishes* 18, no. 1: 41–50.

Jenkins, R. E., and D. J. Jenkins. 1980. "Reproductive Behavior of the Greater Redhorse, *Moxostoma valenciennesi*, in the Thousand Islands Region." *Canadian Field-Naturalist* 94, no. 4: 426–30.

Kwak, T. J., and T. M. Skelly. 1992. "Spawning Habitat, Behavior, and Morphology as

Isolating Mechanisms of the Golden Redhorse, *Moxostoma erythrurum*, and the Black Redhorse, *M. duquesnei*, Two Syntopic Fishes." *Environmental Biology of Fishes* 34, no. 2: 127–37.

Kwak, T. J., M. J. Wiley, L. L. Osborne, and R. W. Larimore. 1992. "Application of Diel Feeding Chronology to Habitat Suitability Analysis of Warmwater Stream Fishes." *Canadian Journal of Fisheries and Aquatic Sciences* 49, no. 7: 1417–30.

Mandrak, N. E., and E. J. Crossman. 1996. "The Status of the Lake Chubsucker, *Erimyzon sucetta*, in Canada." *Canadian Field-Naturalist* 110: 478–82.

Matheney, M. P., IV, and C. F. Rabeni. 1995. "Patterns of Movement and Habitat Use by Northern Hog Suckers in an Ozark Stream." *Transactions of the American Fisheries Society* 124, no. 6: 886–97.

Page, L. M., and C. E. Johnston. 1990. "Spawning in the Creek Chubsucker, *Erimyzon oblongus*, with a Review of Spawning Behavior in Suckers (Catostomidae)." *Environmental Biology of Fishes* 27, no. 4: 265–72.

Parker, B. R., and W. G. Franzin. 1991. "Reproductive Biology of the Quillback, *Carpiodes cyprinus*, in a Small Prairie River." *Canadian Journal of Zoology* 69, no. 8: 2133–39.

Peterson, J. T., and C. F. Rabeni. 1996. "Natural Thermal Refugia for Temperate Warmwater Stream Fishes." *North American Journal of Fisheries Management* 16, no. 4: 738–46.

Quinn, S. P., and M. R. Ross. 1985. "Non-annual Spawning in the White Sucker, *Catostomus commersoni*." *Copeia* no. 3: 613–18.

Raney, E. C., and E. A. Lachner. 1946. "Age, Growth, and Habits of the Hog Sucker, *Hypentelium nigricans* (LeSueur), in New York." *American Midland Naturalist* 36, no. 1: 76–86.

Raney, E. C., and D. A. Webster. 1942. "The Spring Migration of the Common White Sucker, *Catostomus commersoni* (Lacepede) in Skaneateles Lake and Inlet, New York." *Copeia* no. 3: 139–48.

Saint-Jacques, N., H. H. Harvey, and D. A. Jackson. 2000. "Selective Foraging in the White Sucker *(Catostomus commersoni)*." *Canadian Journal of Zoology* 78, no. 8: 1320–31.

Sayigh, L., and R. Morin. 1986. "Summer Diet and Daily Consumption of Periphyton of the Longnose Sucker, *Catostomus catostomus* in the Lower Matamek River, Quebec." *Naturaliste Canadien* 113, no. 4: 361–68.

Tremblay, S., and P. Magnan. 1991. "Interactions Between Two Distantly Related Species, Brook Trout *(Salvelinus fontinalis)* and White Sucker *(Catostomus commersoni)*." *Canadian Journal of Fisheries and Aquatic Sciences* 48, no. 5: 857–67.

Trippel, E. A., and H. H. Harvey. 1987. "Abundance, Growth, and Food Supply of White Suckers *(Catostomus commersoni)* in Relation to Lake Morphometry and pH." *Canadian Journal of Zoology* 65, no. 3: 558–64.

Werner, R. G. 1979. "Homing Mechanism of Spawning White Suckers in Wolf Lake, New York." *New York Fish and Game Journal* 26, no. 1: 48–58.

Werner, R. G., and M. J. Lannoo. 1994. "Development of the Olfactory System of the White Sucker *Catostomus commersoni*, in Relation to Imprinting and Homing: A Comparison to the Salmonid Model." *Environmental Biology of Fishes* 40: 125–40.

Woodward, R. L., and T. E. Wissing. 1976. "Age, Growth, and Fecundity of the Quillback

(*Carpiodes cyprinus*) and Highfin (*C. velifer*) Carpsuckers in an Ohio Stream." *Transactions of the American Fisheries Society* 105, no. 3: 411–15.

Yoder, C. O., and R. A. Beaumier. 1986. "The Occurrence and Distribution of River Redhorse, *Moxostoma carinatum*, and Greater Redhorse, *Moxostoma valenciennesi* in the Sandusky River, Ohio." *Ohio Journal of Science* 86, no. 1: 18–21.

Bullhead Catfishes, Family Ictaluridae

Blumer, L. S. 1985. "Reproductive Natural History of the Brown Bullhead *Ictalurus nebulosus* in Michigan." *American Midland Naturalist* 114, no. 2: 318–30.

———. 1986. "The Function of Parental Care in the Brown Bullhead, *Ictalurus nebulosus.*" *American Midland Naturalist* 115, no. 2: 234–38.

Campbell, R. D., and B. A. Branson. 1978. "Ecology and Population Dynamics of the Black Bullhead, *Ictalurus melas* (Rafinesque), in Central Kentucky." *Tulane Studies in Zoology and Botany* 20, nos. 3–4: 99–136.

Clugston, J. P., and E. L. Cooper. 1960. "Growth of the Common Eastern Madtom in Central Pennsylvania." *Copeia* no. 1: 9–16.

Devaraj, K. V. 1974. "Food of White Catfish, *Ictalurus catus* (Linn.) (Ictaluridae) Stocked in Farm Ponds." *Internationale Revue der Gesamten Hydrobiologie* 59, no. 1: 147–51.

Gutowski, M. J., and J. R. Stauffer Jr. 1993. "Selective Predation by *Noturus insignis* (Richardson) (Teleostei: Ictaluridae) in the Delaware River." *American Midland Naturalist* 129, no. 2: 309–18.

Keast, A. 1985. "Implications of Chemosensory Feeding in Catfishes: An Analysis of the Diets of *Ictalurus nebulosus* and *I. natalis.*" *Canadian Journal of Zoology* 63, no. 3: 590–602.

Raney, E. C., and D. A. Webster. 1940. "The Food and Growth of the Young of the Common Bullhead, *Ameiurus nebulosus nebulosus* (LeSueur), in Cayuga Lake, New York." *Transactions of the American Fisheries Society* 69: 205–9.

Repsys, A. J., R. L. Applegate, and D. C. Hales. 1976. "Food and Food Selectivity of the Black Bullhead, *Ictalurus melas,* in Lake Poinsett, South Dakota." *Journal of the Fisheries Research Board of Canada* 33, no. 4, pt. 1: 768–75.

Sinnott, T. J., and N. H. Ringler. 1987. "Population Biology of the Brown Bullhead (*Ictalurus nebulosus* LeSueur)." *Journal of Freshwater Ecology* 4, no. 2: 225–34.

Wallace, C. R. 1972. "Spawning Behavior of *Ictalurus natalis* (LeSueur)." *Texas Journal of Science* 24, no. 3: 307–10.

Walsh, S. J., and B. M. Burr. 1985. "Biology of the Stonecat, *Noturus flavus* (Siluriformes: Ictaluridae), in Central Illinois and Missouri Streams, and Comparisons with Great Lakes Populations and Congeners." *Ohio Journal of Science* 85, no. 3: 85–96.

Whiteside, L. A., and B. M. Burr. 1986. "Aspects of the Life History of the Tadpole Madtom, *Noturus gyrinus* (Siluriformes: Ictaluridae), in Southern Illinois." *Ohio Journal of Science* 86, no. 4: 153–60.

Pikes, Family Esocidae

Bozek, M. A., T. M. Burri, and R. V. Frie. 1999. "Diets of Muskellunge in Northern Wisconsin Lakes." *North American Journal of Fisheries Management* 19, no. 1: 258–70.

Casselman, J. M., C. J. Robinson, and E. J. Crossman. 1999. "Growth and Ultimate Length of Muskellunge from Ontario Water Bodies." *North American Journal of Fisheries Management* 19, no. 1: 271–90.

Chapman, L. J., and W. C. Mackay. 1990. "Ecological Correlates of Feeding Flexibility in Northern Pike (*Esox lucius*)." *Journal of Freshwater Ecology* 5, no. 3: 313–22.

Crossman, E. J. 1966. "A Taxonomic Study of *Esox americanus* and Its Subspecies in Eastern North America." *Copeia* no. 1: 1–20.

———. 1990. "Reproductive Homing in Muskellunge, *Esox masquinongy.*" *Canadian Journal of Fisheries and Aquatic Sciences* 47, no. 9: 1803–12.

Crossman, E. J., and J. M. Casselman. 1987. *An Annotated Bibliography of the Pike,* Esox lucius (*Osteichthyes: Salmoniformes.* Toronto: Royal Ontario Museum Life Science Miscellaneous Publications. 585 pp.

Dombeck, M. P., B. W. Menzel, and P. N. Hinz. 1984. "Muskellunge Spawning Habitat and Reproductive Success." *Transactions of the American Fisheries Society* 113, no. 2: 205–16.

Farrell, J. M. 2001. "Reproductive Success of Sympatric Northern Pike and Muskellunge in an Upper St. Lawrence River Bay." *Transactions of the American Fisheries Society* 130, no. 5: 796–808.

Farrell, J. M., and R. G. Werner. 1999. "Distribution, Abundance, and Survival of Age-0 Muskellunge in Upper St. Lawrence River Nursery Bays." *North American Journal of Fisheries Management* 19: 309–20.

Farrell, J. M., R. G. Werner, S. R. Lapan, and K. A. Claypoole. 1996. "Egg Distribution and Spawning Habitat of Northern Pike and Muskellunge in a St. Lawrence River Marsh." *Transactions of the American Fisheries Society* 125: 127–31.

Frith, H. R., and R. W. Blake. 1995. "The Mechanical Power Output and Hydromechanical Efficiency of Northern Pike (*Esox lucius*) Fast-Starts." *Journal of Experimental Biology* 198, no. 9: 1863–73.

Hoyle, J. A., and A. Keast. 1988. "Prey Handling Time in Two Piscivores, *Esox americanus vermiculatus* and *Micropterus salmoides,* with Contrasting Mouth Morphologies." *Canadian Journal of Zoology* 66, no. 2: 540–42.

Kleinert, S. J., and D. Mraz. 1966. *Life History of the Grass Pickerel* (Esox americanus vermiculatus) *in Southeastern Wisconsin.* Wisconsin Conservation Department Technical Bulletin no. 37. Madison: Wisconsin Conservation Department. 40 pp.

Margenau, T. L. 1994. "Evidence of Homing of a Displaced Muskellunge, *Esox masquinongy.*" *Journal of Freshwater Ecology* 9, no. 3: 253–56.

Raat, A. J. P. 1988. *Synopsis of Biological Data on the Northern Pike* Esox lucius Linnaeus, *1758.* Fao Fisheries Synopsis no. 30. Rome: Food and Agricultural Organization. 178 pp.

Rand, D. M., and G. V. Lauder. 1981. "Prey Capture in the Chain Pickerel, *Esox niger:* Correlations Between Feeding and Locomotor Behavior." *Canadian Journal of Zoology* 59, no. 6: 1072–78.

Raney, E. C. 1942. "The Summer Food and Habits of the Chain Pickerel (*Esox niger*) of a Small New York Pond." *Journal of Wildlife Management* 6, no. 1: 58–66.

Werner, R. G., R. Klindt, and B. Jonckheere. 1996. "Vegetative Characteristics of Muskellunge (*Esox masquinongy*) Spawning and Nursery Habitat in the 1000 Islands Section of the St. Lawrence River." *Great Lakes Research Review* 2, no. 2: 29–35.

Zorn, S. A., T. L. Margenau, J. S. Diana, and C. J. Edwards. 1998. "The Influence of Spawning Habitat on Natural Reproduction of Muskellunge in Wisconsin." *Transactions of the American Fisheries Society* 127, no. 6: 995–1005.

Mudminnows, Family Umbridae

Gee, J. H. 1981. "Coordination of Respiratory and Hydrostatic Functions of the Swimbladder in the Central Mudminnow, *Umbra limi*." *Journal of Experimental Biology* 92, no. 6: 37–52.

Klinger, S. A., J. J. Magnuson, and G. W. Gallepp. 1982. "Survival Mechanisms of the Central Mudminnow (*Umbra limi*), Fathead Minnow (*Pimephales promelas*), and Brook Stickleback (*Culaea inconstans*) for Low Oxygen in Winter." *Environmental Biology of Fishes* 7, no. 2: 113–20.

Martin-Bergmann, K. A., and J. H. Gee. 1985. "Central Mudminnow, *Umbra limi* (Kirtland), a Habitat Specialist and Resource Generalist." *Canadian Journal of Zoology* 63, no. 8: 1753–64.

Panek, F. M. 1981. "The Life History and Ecology of the Eastern Mudminnow (*Umbra pygmaea*) with Notes on Ecological and Zoogographic Relationships with the Central Mudminnow (*Umbra limi*)." *Dissertation Abstracts International, Part B* 42, no. 4: 1351–52.

Paszkowski, C. A. 1984. "The Foraging Behavior of a Generalist Feeder, the Central Mudminnow (*Umbra limi*)." *Canadian Journal of Zoology* 62, no. 3: 457–62.

Peckham, R. S., and C. F. Dineen. 1957. "Ecology of the Central Mudminnow, *Umbra limi* (Kirtland)." *American Midland Naturalist* 58, no. 1: 222–31.

Slavin, P. T., E. Bradford, R. Halpin, and D. McCormick. 1977. "The Eastern Mud Minnow, *Umbra pygmaea* (Dekay): A Potential Control Agent of Woodland Pool *Aedes* sp." *Mosquito News* 37, no. 2: 301.

Tonn, W. M., and C. A. Paszkowski. 1987. "Habitat Use of the Central Mudminnow (*Umbra limi*) and Yellow Perch (*Perca flavescens*) in Umbra-Perca Assemblages: The Roles of Competition, Predation, and the Abiotic Environment." *Canadian Journal of Zoology* 65, no. 4: 862–70.

Smelts, Family Osmeridae

Appenzeller, A. R., and W. C. Leggett. 1995. "An Evaluation of Light-Mediated Vertical Migration of Fish Based on Hydroacoustic Analysis of the Diel Vertical Movements of Rainbow Smelt (*Osmerus mordax*)." *Canadian Journal of Fisheries and Aquatic Sciences* 52, no. 3: 504–11.

Bigelow, H. B., and W. C. Schroeder. 1963. "Family Osmeridae. Fishes of the Western North Atlantic." *Memoir, Sears Foundation for Marine Research* 1, no. 3: 533–97.

Brandt, S. B., and S. P. Madon. 1986. "Rainbow Smelt (*Osmerus mordax*) Predation on Slimy Sculpin (*Cottus cognatus*) in Lake Ontario." *Journal of Great Lakes Research* 12, no. 4: 322–25.

Copeman, D. G., and D. E. McAllister. 1978. "Analysis of the Effect of Transplantation on

Morphometric and Meristic Characters in Lake Populations of the Rainbow Smelt, *Osmerus mordax* (Mitchill)." *Environmental Biology of Fishes* 3, no. 3: 253–59.

Evans, D. O., and D. H. Loftus. 1987. "Colonization of Inland Lakes in the Great Lakes Region by Rainbow Smelt, *Osmerus mordax:* Their Freshwater Niche and Effects on Indigenous Fishes." From the International Symposium on Stocks Assessment and Yield Prediction, 1987. *Canadian Journal of Fisheries and Aquatic Sciences* (supplement) 44, no. 2: 249–66.

Hrabik, T. R., and J. Magnuson. 1999. "Simulated Dispersal of Exotic Rainbow Smelt *(Osmerus mordax)* in a Northern Wisconsin Lake District and Implications for Management." Selected Proceedings of the Symposium Entitled "Space, Time, and Scale: New Perspectives in Fish Ecology and Management." *Canadian Journal of Fisheries and Aquatic Sciences* 56, no. 1: 35–42.

Lantry, B. F., and D. J. Stewart. 2000. "Population Dynamics of Rainbow Smelt *(Osmerus mordax)* in Lakes Ontario and Erie: A Modeling Analysis of Cannibalism Effects." *Canadian Journal of Fisheries and Aquatic Sciences* 57, no. 8: 1594–1606.

Murawski, S. A., G. R. Clayton, R. J. Reed, and C. F. Cole. 1980. "Movements of Spawning Rainbow Smelt, *Osmerus mordax,* in a Massachusetts Estuary." *Estuaries* 3, no. 4: 308–14.

Murawski, S. A., and C. F. Cole. 1978. "Population Dynamics of Anadromous Rainbow Smelt, *Osmerus mordax,* in a Massachusetts River System." *Transactions of the American Fisheries Society* 107, no. 4: 535–42.

Mills, E. L., R. O'Gorman, E. F. Roseman, C. Adams, and R. W. Owens. 1995. "Planktivory by Alewife *(Alosa pseudoharengus)* and Rainbow Smelt *(Osmerus mordax)* on Microcrustacean Zooplankton and Dreissenid (Bivalvia: Dreissenidae) Veligers in Southern Lake Ontario." *Canadian Journal of Fisheries and Aquatic Sciences* 52, no. 5: 925–35.

Zilliox, R. G., and W. D. Youngs. 1958. "Further Studies on the Smelt of Lake Champlain." *New York Fish and Game Journal* 5, no. 2: 164–74.

Trouts, Salmons, and Whitefishes, Family Salmonidae

Aku, P. M. K., L. G. Rudstam, and W. M. Tonn. 1997. "Impact of Hypolimnetic Oxygenation on the Vertical Distribution of Cisco *(Coregonus artedii)* in Amisk Lake, Alberta." *Canadian Journal of Fisheries and Aquatic Sciences* 54, no. 9: 2182–95.

Armstrong, J. W., C. R. Liston, P. I. Tack, and R. C. Anderson. 1977. "Age, Growth, Maturity, and Seasonal Food Habits of Round Whitefish, *Prosopium cylindraceum,* in Lake Michigan near Ludington, Michigan." *Transactions of the American Fisheries Society* 106, no. 2: 151–55.

Baldigo, B. P., and P. S. Murdoch. 1997. "Effect of Stream Acidification and Inorganic Aluminum on Mortality of Brook Trout *(Salvelinus fontinalis)* in the Catskill Mountains, New York." *Canadian Journal of Fisheries and Aquatic Sciences* 54, no. 3: 603–15.

Balon, E. K., ed. 1980. *Charrs. Salmonid Fishes of the Genus* Salvelinus. Dordrecht, Netherlands: W. Junk. 928 pp.

Bardonnet, A., and J-L. Bagliniere. 2000. "Freshwater Habitat of Atlantic Salmon *(Salmo salar)*." *Canadian Journal of Fisheries and Aquatic Sciences* 57, no. 2: 497–506.

Beauchamp, J. J., S. W. Christensen, and E. P. Smith. 1992. "Selection of Factors Affecting the Presence of Brook Trout (*Salvelinus fontinalis*) in Adirondack Lakes: A Case Study." *Canadian Journal of Fisheries and Aquatic Sciences* 49, no. 3: 597–608.

Behnke, R. J. 1972. "The Systematics of Salmonid Fishes of Recently Glaciated Lakes." *Journal of the Fisheries Research Board of Canada* 29: 639–71.

———. 1992. *Native Trout of Western North America.* American Fisheries Society Monograph no. 6. Bethesda, Md.: American Fisheries Society.

Bernatchez, L., J. G. Rhydderch, and F. W. Kircheis. 2002. "Microsatellite Gene Diversity Analysis in Landlocked Arctic Char from Maine." *Transactions of the American Fisheries Society* 131, no. 6: 1106–18.

Berube, P., and F. Levesque. 1998. "Effects of Forestry Clear-Cutting on Numbers and Sizes of Brook Trout, *Salvelinus fontinalis* (Mitchill), in Lakes of the Mastigouche Wildlife Reserve, Quebec, Canada." *Fisheries Management and Ecology* 5, no. 2: 123–37.

Blanchfield, P. J., and M. S. Ridgway. 1997. "Reproductive Timing and Use of Redd Sites by Lake-Spawning Brook Trout (*Salvelinus fontinalis*)." *Canadian Journal of Fisheries and Aquatic Sciences* 54, no. 4: 747–56.

Bodaly, R. A., J. W. Clayton, C. C. Lindsey, and J. Vuorinen. 1992. "Evolution of Lake Whitefish (*Coregonus clupeaformis*) in North America During the Pleistocene: Genetic Differentiation Between Sympatric Populations." *Canadian Journal of Fisheries and Aquatic Sciences* 49, no. 4: 769–79.

Bradford, M. J., and P. S. Higgins. 2001. "Habitat-, Season-, and Size-Specific Variation in Diel Activity Patterns of Juvenile Chinook Salmon (*Oncorhynchus tshawytscha*) and Steelhead Trout (*Oncorhynchus mykiss*)." *Canadian Journal of Fisheries and Aquatic Sciences* 58, no. 2: 365–74.

Bridges, C. H., and J. W. Mullan. 1958. *A Compendium of the Life History and Ecology of the Eastern Brook Trout,* Salvelinus fontinalis (*Mitchill*). Massachusetts Fishery Bulletin no. 23. Boston: Massachusetts Division of Fish and Game. 38 pp.

Casselman, J. M., D. M. Brown, and J. A. Hoyle. 1996. "Resurgence of Lake Whitefish, *Coregonus clupeaformis*, in Lake Ontario in the 1980s." *Great Lakes Research Review* 2, no. 2: 20–28.

Chipps, S. R., and D. H. Bennett. 2000. "Zooplanktivory and Nutrient Regeneration by Invertebrate (*Mysis relicta*) and Vertebrate (*Oncorhynchus nerka*) Planktivores: Implications for Trophic Interactions in Oligotrophic Lakes." *Transactions of the American Fisheries Society* 129, no. 2: 569–83.

Curry, R. A., and D. L. G. Noakes. 1995. "Groundwater and the Selection of Spawning Sites by Brook Trout (*Salvelinus fontinalis*)." *Canadian Journal of Fisheries and Aquatic Sciences* 52, no. 8: 1733–40.

Davis, B. M., and T. N. Todd. 1998. "Competition Between Larval Lake Herring (*Coregonus artedi*) and Lake Whitefish (*Coregonus clupeaformis*) for Zooplankton." *Canadian Journal of Fisheries and Aquatic Sciences* 55, no. 5: 1140–48.

Dittman, A. H., T. P. Quinn, and G. A. Nevitt. 1996. "Timing of Imprinting to Natural and Artificial Odors by Coho Salmon (*Oncorhynchus kisutch*)." *Canadian Journal of Fisheries and Aquatic Sciences* 53, no. 2: 434–42.

Dymond, J. R. 1963. "Family Salmonidae. Fishes of the Western North Atlantic." *Memoir, Sears Foundation for Marine Research* 1, no. 3: 457–502.

Elliott, J. M., and M. A. Hurley 1999. "A New Energetics Model for Brown Trout, *Salmo trutta*." *Freshwater Biology* 42, no. 2: 235–46.

Engel, S., and J. J. Magnuson. 1976. "Vertical and Horizontal Distribution of Coho Salmon (*Oncorhynchus kisutch*), Yellow Perch (*Perca flavescens*), and Cisco (*Coregonus artedii*) in Pallette Lake, Wisconsin." *Journal of the Fisheries Research Board of Canada* 33, no. 12: 2710–15.

Essington, T. E., P. W. Sorensen, and D. G. Paron. 1998. "High Rate of Redd Superimposition by Brook Trout (*Salvelinus fontinalis*) and Brown Trout (*Salmo trutta*) in a Minnesota Stream Cannot Be Explained by Habitat Availability Alone." *Canadian Journal of Fisheries and Aquatic Sciences* 55, no. 10: 2310–16.

Everhart, W. H., and C. A. Waters. 1965. "Life History of the Blueback Trout (Arctic Char, *Salvelinus alpinus* [Linnaeus]) in Maine." *Transactions of the American Fisheries Society* 94, no. 4: 393–97.

Fausch, K. D. 1993. "Experimental Analysis of Microhabitat Selection by Juvenile Steelhead (*Oncorhynchus mykiss*) and Coho Salmon (*O. kisutch*) in a British Columbia Stream." *Canadian Journal of Fisheries and Aquatic Sciences* 50, no. 6: 1198–207.

Ford, J. E., and D. G. Lonzarich. 2000. "Over-winter Survival and Habitat Use by Juvenile Coho Salmon (*Oncorhynchus kisutch*) in Two Lake Superior Tributaries." *Journal of Great Lakes Research* 26, no. 1: 94–101.

Ford, M. J. 1998. "Testing Models of Migration and Isolation among Populations of Chinook Salmon (*Oncorhynchus tshawytscha*). *Evolution* 52, no. 2: 539–57.

Hartman, W. L. 1959. "Biology and Vital Statistics of Rainbow Trout in the Finger Lakes Region, New York." *New York Fish and Game Journal* 6, no. 2: 121–78.

Harwood, A. J., N. B. Metcalfe, J. D. Armstrong, and S. W. Griffiths. 2001. "Spatial and Temporal Effects of Interspecific Competition Between Atlantic Salmon (*Salmo salar*) and Brown Trout (*Salmo trutta*) in Winter." *Canadian Journal of Fisheries and Aquatic Sciences* 58, no. 6: 1133–40.

Hatch, R. W. 1957. "Success of Natural Spawning of Rainbow Trout in the Finger Lakes Region of New York." *New York Fish and Game Journal* 4, no. 1: 69–87.

Havey, K. A., and K. Warner. 1970. *The Landlocked Salmon* (Salmo salar): *Its Life History and Management in Maine.* Washington, D.C.: Sport Fishery Institute and Maine Department of Inland Fish and Game. 129 pp.

Heggenes, J., J. L. Bagliniere, and R. A. Cunjak. 1999. "Spatial Niche Variability for Young Atlantic Salmon (*Salmo salar*) and Brown Trout (*S. trutta*) in Heterogeneous Streams." *Ecology of Freshwater Fish* 8, no. 1: 1–21.

Ihssen, P. E., D. O. Evans, W. J. Christie, J. A. Reckahn, and R. L. DesJardine. 1981. "Life History, Morphology, and Electrophoretic Characteristics of Five Allopatric Stocks of Lake Whitefish (*Coregonus clupeaformis*) in the Great Lakes Region." *Canadian Journal of Fisheries and Aquatic Sciences* 38, no. 12: 1790–807.

Irvine, J. R., and N. T. Johnston. 1992. "Coho Salmon (*Oncorhynchus kisutch*) Use of Lakes and Streams in the Keogh River Drainage, British Columbia." *Northwest Science* 66, no. 1: 15–25.

Jansen, P. A., H. Slettvold, A. G. Finstad, and A. Langeland. 2002. "A Niche Segregation Between Arctic Char (*Salvelinus alpinus*) and Brown Trout (*Salmo trutta*): An Experimental Study of Mechanisms." *Canadian Journal of Fisheries and Aquatic Sciences* 59, no. 1: 6–11.

Jensen, A. L. 1997. "Limiting Similarity for Coexistence of Lake Herring (*Coregonus artedii*) and Chubs (*Coregonus hoyi*)." *Ecological Modeling* 95, no. 1: 11–15.

Joergensen, L., M. Halvorsen, and P-A. Amundsen. 2000. "Resource Partitioning Between Lake-Dwelling Atlantic Salmon (*Salmo salar* L.) Parr, Brown Trout (*Salmo trutta* L.), and Arctic Charr (*Salvelinus alpinus* [L.])." *Ecology of Freshwater Fish* 9, no. 4: 202–9.

Johnson, J. H., and D. S. Dropkin. 1996. "Seasonal Habitat Use by Brook Trout, *Salvelinus fontinalis* (Mitchill), in a Second-Order Stream." *Fisheries Management and Ecology* 3, no. 1: 1–11.

Jones, M. L., G. W. Eck, D. O. Evans, M. C. Fabrizio, M. H. Hoff, P. L. Hudson, J. Janssen, D. Jude, R. O'Gorman, and J. F. Savino. 1995. "Limitations to Lake Trout (*Salvelinus namaycush*) Rehabilitation in the Great Lakes Imposed by Biotic Interactions Occurring at Early Life Stages." From the Proceedings of the International Conference on Restoration of Lake Trout in the Laurentian Great Lakes. *Journal of Great Lakes Research* 21, no. 1 (supplement): 5050–17.

Josephson, D. C., and W. D. Youngs. 1996. "Association Between Emigration and Age Structure in Populations of Brook Trout (*Salvelinus fontinalis*) in Adirondack Lakes." *Canadian Journal of Fisheries and Aquatic Sciences* 53, no. 3: 534–41.

Jutila, E., A. Ahvonen, and M. Julkunen. 2001. "Instream and Catchment Characteristics Affecting the Occurrence and Population Density of Brown Trout, *Salmo trutta* L., in Forest Brooks of a Boreal River Basin." *Fisheries Management and Ecology* 8, no. 6: 501–11.

Kemp, S. J., and J. R. Spotila. 1997. "Effects of Urbanization on Brown Trout *Salmo trutta*, Other Fishes, and Macroinvertebrates in Valley Creek, Valley Forge, Pennsylvania." *American Midland Naturalist* 138, no. 1: 55–68.

Kocik, J. F., W. W. Taylor, and W. C. Wagner. 1991. "Abundance, Size, and Recruitment of Pink Salmon (*Oncorhynchus gorbuscha*) in Selected Michigan Tributaries of the Upper Great Lakes, 1984–1988." *Journal of Great Lakes Research* 17, no. 2: 203–13.

Kwain, W. 1982. "Spawning Behavior and Early Life History of Pink Salmon (*Oncorhynchus gorbuscha*) in the Great Lakes." *Canadian Journal of Fisheries and Aquatic Sciences* 39, no. 10: 1353–60.

Kwain, W., and G. A. Rose. 1986. "Spawning Migration of Great Lakes Pink Salmon (*Oncorhynchus gorbuscha*): Size and Sex Distributions, River Entrance and Exit." *Journal of Great Lakes Research* 12, no. 2: 101–8.

Morin, R., J. J. Dodson, and G. Power. 1982. "Life History Variations of Anadromous Cisco (*Coregonus artedii*), Lake Whitefish (*C. clupeaformis*), and Round Whitefish (*Prosopium cylindraceum*) Populations of Eastern James-Hudson Bay." *Canadian Journal of Fisheries and Aquatic Sciences* 39, no. 7: 958–67.

Normandeau, D. A. 1969. "Life History and Ecology of the Round Whitefish *Prosopium cylindraceum* (Pallas), of Newfound Lake, Bristol, New Hampshire." *Transactions of the American Fisheries Society* 98, no. 1: 7–13.

Proceedings of the Third International Charr Symposium, June 13–18, 1994, Trondheim, Norway. 1995. Special issue of *Nordic Journal of Freshwater Research* 71.

Quinn, N. W. S. 1995. "General Features of Brook Trout, *Salvelinus fontinalis,* Spawning Sites in Lakes in Algonquin Provincial Park, Ontario." *Canadian Field-Naturalist* 109, no. 2: 205–9.

Rosenfield, J. A., T. Todd, and R. Greil. 2000. "Asymmetric Hybridization and Introgression Between Pink Salmon and Chinook Salmon in the Laurentian Great Lakes." *Transactions of the American Fisheries Society* 129, no. 3: 670–79.

Rudstam, L. G., and J. J. Magnuson. 1985. "Predicting the Vertical Distribution of Fish Populations: Analysis of Cisco, *Coregonus artedii,* and Yellow Perch, *Perca flavescens.*" *Canadian Journal of Fisheries and Aquatic Sciences* 42, no. 6: 1178–88.

Ryan, P. A., and T. R. Marshall. 1994. "A Niche Definition for Lake Trout (*Salvelinus namaycush)* and Its Use to Identify Populations at Risk." *Canadian Journal of Fisheries and Aquatic Sciences* 51, no. 11: 2513–19.

Sauter, S. T., L. I. Crawshaw, and A. G. Maule. 2001. "Behavioural Thermoregulation by Juvenile Spring and Fall Chinook Salmon, *Oncorhynchus tshawytscha,* During Smoltification." *Environmental Biology of Fishes* 61, no. 3: 295–304.

Savitz, J., and L. Bardygula-Nonn. 1997. "Behavioral Interactions Between Coho (*Oncorhynchus kisutch)* and Chinook Salmon (*Oncorhynchus tshawytscha)* and Prey Fish Species." *Ecology of Freshwater Fish* 6, no. 4: 190–95.

Sellers, T. J., B. R. Parker, D. W. Schindler, and W. M. Tonn. 1998. "Pelagic Distribution of Lake Trout (*Salvelinus namaycush)* in Small Canadian Shield Lakes with Respect to Temperature, Dissolved Oxygen, and Light." *Canadian Journal of Fisheries and Aquatic Sciences* 55, no. 1: 170–79.

Shirvell, C. S. 1990. "Role of Instream Rootwads as Juvenile Coho Salmon (*Oncorhynchus kisutch)* and Steelhead Trout (*O. mykiss)* Cover Habitat under Varying Streamflows." *Canadian Journal of Fisheries and Aquatic Sciences* 47, no. 5: 852–61.

———. 1994. "Effect of Changes in Streamflow on the Microhabitat Use and Movements of Sympatric Juvenile Coho Salmon (*Oncorhynchus kisutch)* and Chinook Salmon (*O. tshawytscha)* in a Natural Stream." *Canadian Journal of Fisheries and Aquatic Sciences* 51, no. 7: 1644–52.

Shuter, B. J., M. L. Jones, R. M. Korver, and N. P. Lester. 1998. "A General, Life History Based Model for Regional Management of Fish Stocks: The Inland Lake Trout (*Salvelinus namaycush)* Fisheries of Ontario." *Canadian Journal of Fisheries and Aquatic Sciences* 55, no. 9: 2161–77.

Simmons, K. R., P. G. Cieslewicz, and K. Zajicek. 1996. "Limestone Treatment of Whetstone Brook, Massachusetts. 2. Changes in the Brown Trout (*Salmo trutta)* and Brook Trout (*Salvelinus fontinalis)* Fishery." *Restoration Ecology* 4, no. 3: 273–83.

Steedman, R. J., and R. S. Kushneriuk. 2000. "Effects of Experimental Clearcut Logging on Thermal Stratification, Dissolved Oxygen, and Lake Trout (*Salvelinus namaycush)* Habitat Volume in Three Small Boreal Forest Lakes. Impacts of Major Watershed Perturbations on Aquatic Ecosystems." *Canadian Journal of Fisheries and Aquatic Sciences* 57 (supplement 2): 82–91.

Trudel, M., A. Tremblay, R. Schetagne, and J. B. Rasmussen. 2001. "Why Are Dwarf Fish So Small? An Energetic Analysis of Polymorphism in Lake Whitefish (*Coregonus clupeaformis).*" *Canadian Journal of Fisheries and Aquatic Sciences* 58, no. 2: 394–405.

Van Oosten, J., and H. J. Deason. 1939. "The Age, Growth, and Feeding Habits of the Whitefish, *Coregonus clupeaformis* (Mitchill), of Lake Champlain." *Transactions of the American Fisheries Society* 68: 152–62.

Voellestad, L. A., and J. H. L'Abee-Lund. 1994. "Evolution of the Life History of Arctic Charr, *Salvelinus alpinus.*" *Evolutionary Ecology* 8, no. 3: 315–27.

Weiss, S., and S. Schmutz. 1999. "Response of Resident Brown Trout, *Salmo trutta* L., and Rainbow Trout, *Oncorhynchus mykiss* (Walbaum), to the Stocking of Hatchery-Reared Brown Trout." *Fisheries Management and Ecology* 6, no. 5: 365–75.

Wilson, C. C., and P. D. N. Hebert. 1998. "Phylogeography and Postglacial Dispersal of Lake Trout (*Salvelinus namaycush)* in North America." *Canadian Journal of Fisheries and Aquatic Sciences* 55, no. 4: 1010–24.

Wilson, C. C., P. D. N. Hebert, J. D. Reist, and J. B. Dempson. 1996. "Phylogeography and Postglacial Dispersal of Arctic Charr *Salvelinus alpinus* in North America." *Molecular Ecology* 5, no. 2: 187–97.

Wooster, G. A., P. R. Bowser, S. B. Brown, and J. P. Fisher. 2000. "Remediation of Cayuga Syndrome in Landlocked Atlantic Salmon *Salmo salar* Using Egg and Sac-Fry Bath Treatments of Thiamine-Hydrochloride." *Journal of the World Aquaculture Society* 31, no. 2: 149–57.

Trout-Perches, Family Percopsidae

House, R., and L. Wells. 1973. "Age, Growth, Spawning Season, and Fecundity of the Trout-Perch (*Percopsis omiscomaycus)* in Southeastern Lake Michigan." *Journal of the Fisheries Research Board of Canada* 30, no. 8: 1221–25.

Magnuson, J. L., and L. L. Smith. 1963. "Some Phases of the Life History of the Trout-Perch." *Ecology* 44, no. 1: 83–95.

Muth, S. E., and D. C. Tarter. 1975. "Reproductive Biology of the Trout Perch, *Percopsis omiscomaycus* (Walbaum), in Beech Fork of Twelvepole Creek, Wayne County, West Virginia." *American Midland Naturalist* 93, no. 2: 434–39.

Pereira, D. L., and G. W. Labar. 1983. "Age and Growth of Trout-Perch in Lake Champlain." *New York Fish and Game Journal* 30, no. 2: 201–9.

Pirate Perches, Family Aphredoderidae

Boltz, J. M., and J. R. Stauffer Jr. 1993. "Systematics of *Aphredoderus sayanus* (Teleostei: Aphredoderidae)." *Copeia* no. 1: 81–98.

Fontenot, Q. C., and D. A. Rutherford. 1999. "Observations on the Reproductive Ecology of Pirate Perch, *Aphredoderus sayanus.*" *Journal of Freshwater Ecology* 14, no. 4: 545–49.

Martin, F. D., and C. Hubbs. 1973. "Observations on the Development of Pirate Perch, *Aphredoderus sayanus* (Pisces: Aphredoderidae), with Comments on Yolk Circulation Patterns as a Possible Taxonomic Tool." *Copeia* no. 2: 377–79.

Parker, N. C., and B. A. Simco. 1975. "Activity Patterns, Feeding, and Behavior of the Pirate Perch, *Aphredoderus sayanus.*" *Copeia* no. 3: 572–74.

Cuskfishes, Family Lotidae

Bailey, M. M. 1972. "Age Growth, Reproduction, and Food of the Burbot, *Lota lota* (Linnaeus), in Southwestern Lake Superior." *Transactions of the American Fisheries Society* 101, no. 4: 667–74.

Clemens, H. P. 1951a. "The Food of the Burbot, *Lota lota maculosa* (LeSueur), in Lake Erie." *Transactions of the American Fisheries Society* 80, no. 1: 56–66.

———. 1951b. "The Growth of the Burbot, *Lota lota maculosa* (LeSueur), in Lake Erie." *Transactions of the American Fisheries Society* 80, no. 1: 163–73.

Ghan, D., and W. G. Sprules. 1993. "Diet, Prey Selection, and Growth of Larval and Juvenile Burbot *Lota lota* (L.)." *Journal of Fish Biology* 42, no. 1: 47–64.

McPhail, J. D. 1997. *A Review of Burbot* (Lota lota) *Life-History and Habitat Use in Relation to Compensation and Improvement Opportunities.* Canadian Manuscript Report of Fisheries and Aquatic Sciences. Vancouver: Department of Fisheries and Oceans. 45 pp.

Robins, C. R., and E. E. Deubler Jr. 1955. *The Life History and Systematic Status of the Burbot,* Lota lota lacustris (Walbaum), *in the Susquehanna River System.* New York State Museum Science Service Circular no. 39:. Albany: New York State Museum. 49 pp.

Silversides, Family Atherinidae

Grier, H. J., D. P. Moody, and B. C. Cowell. 1990. "Internal Fertilization and Sperm Morphology in the Brook Silverside, *Labidesthes sicculus* (Cope)." *Copeia* no. 1: 221–26.

Marsden, J. E., R. W. Langdon, and S. P. Good. 2000. "First Occurrence of the Brook Silverside (*Labidesthes sicculus)* in Lake Champlain, Vermont." *Northeastern Naturalist* 7, no. 3: 248–54.

Nelson, J. S. 1968. "Life History of the Brook Silverside, *Labidesthes sicculus,* in Crooked Lake, Indiana." *Transactions of the American Fisheries Society* 97, no. 3: 293–96.

Topminnows, Family Fundulidae

Fournier, P., and E. Magnin. 1975. "Reproduction of the Banded Killifish *Fundulus diaphanus diaphanus* (LeSueur)." *Naturaliste Canadien* 102, no. 2: 181–88.

Fritz, E. S., and E. T. Garside. 1975. "Comparison of Age Composition, Growth, and Fecundity Between Two Populations Each of *Fundulus heteroclitus* and *F. diaphanus* (Pisces: Cyprinodontidae)." *Canadian Journal of Zoology* 53, no. 4: 361–69.

Godin, J-G. J. 1986. "Risk of Predation and Foraging Behaviour in Shoaling Banded Killifish (*Fundulus diaphanus).*" *Canadian Journal of Zoology* 64, no. 8: 1675–78.

Krause, J., and J-G. J. Godin. 1994. "Shoal Choice in the Banded Killifish (*Fundulus diaphanus,* Teleostei, Cyprinodontidae): Effects of Predation Risk, Fish Size, Species Composition, and Size of Shoals." *Ethology* 98, no. 2: 128–36.

Livebearers, Family Poecillidae

Clem, P. D., and J. O. Whitaker Jr. 1995. "Distribution of the Mosquitofish, *Gambusia affinis* (Baird and Girard), in Indiana, with Comments on Resource Competition." *Proceedings of the Indiana Academy of Sciences* 104, nos. 3–4: 249–58.

Harrington, R. W., Jr., and E. S. Harrington. 1961. "Food Selection among Fishes Invading a High Subtropical Salt Marsh: From Onset of Flooding Through the Progress of a Mosquito Brood." *Ecology* 42: 646–66.

Rosen, D. E., and R. M. Bailey. 1963. "The Poeciliid Fishes (Cyprinodontiformes): Their Structure, Zoogeography, and Systematics." *Bulletin of the American Museum of Natural History* 126: 1–176.

Vondracek, B., W. A. Wurtsbaugh, and J. J. Cech Jr. 1988. "Growth and Reproduction of the Mosquitofish, *Gambusia affinis*, in Relation to Temperature and Ration Level: Consequences for Life History." *Environmental Biology of Fishes* 21, no. 1: 45–57.

Sticklebacks, Family Gasterosteidae

Andraso, G. M. 1997. "A Comparison of Startle Response in Two Morphs of the Brook Stickleback (*Culaea inconstans*): Further Evidence for a Trade-off Between Defensive Morphology and Swimming Ability." *Evolutionary Ecology* 11, no. 1: 83–90.

Chivers, D. P., G. E. Brown, and R. J. F. Smith. 1995. "Acquired Recognition of Chemical Stimuli from Pike, *Esox lucius*, by Brook Sticklebacks, *Culaea inconstans* (Osteichthyes, Gasterosteidae)." *Ethology* 99, no. 3: 234–42.

Cleveland, A. 1994. "Nest Site Habitat Preference and Competition in *Gasterosteus aculeatus* and *G. wheatlandi*." *Copeia* no. 3: 698–704.

Courtenay, S. C. 1985. "Simultaneous Multinesting by the Fourspine Stickleback, *Apeltes quadracus*." *Canadian Field-Naturalist* 99, no. 3: 360–63.

Courtenay, S. C., and M. H. A. Keenleyside. 1983. "Nest Site Selection by the Fourspine Stickleback, *Apeltes quadracus* (Mitchell)." *Canadian Journal of Zoology* 61, no. 7: 1443–47.

Fitzgerald, G. J., F. G. Whoriskey, J. Morrissette, and M. Harding. 1992. "Habitat Scale, Female Cannibalism, and Male Reproductive Success in Three-spined Sticklebacks (*Gasterosteus aculeatus*)." *Behavioral Ecology* 3, no. 2: 141–47.

Foster, S. A., and J. A. Baker. 1995. "Evolutionary Interplay Between Ecology, Morphology, and Reproductive Behaviour in Threespine Stickleback, *Gasterosteus aculeatus*." *Environmental Biology of Fishes* 44, nos. 1–3: 213–23.

Gaudreault, A., T. Miller, W. L. Montgomery, and G. J. Fitzgerald. 1986. "Interspecific Interactions and Diet of Sympatric Juvenile Brook Charr, *Salvelinus fontinalis*, and Adult Ninespine Sticklebacks, *Pungitius pungitius*." *Journal of Fish Biology* 28, no. 2: 133–40.

Keivany, Y., and J. S. Nelson 2000. "Taxonomic Review of the Genus *Pungitius*, Ninespine Sticklebacks (Gasterosteidae)." *Cybium (Paris)* 24, no. 2: 107–22.

Klinger, S. A., J. J. Magnuson, and G. W. Gallepp. 1982. "Survival Mechanisms of the Central Mudminnow *(Umbra limi)*, Fathead Minnow *(Pimephales promelas)*, and

Brook Stickleback *(Culaea inconstans)* for Low Oxygen in Winter." *Environmental Biology of Fishes 7,* no. 2: 113–20.

Reisman, H. M., and T. J. Cade. 1967. "Physiological and Behavioral Aspects of Reproduction in the Brook Stickleback, *Culaea inconstans." American Midland Naturalist 77,* no. 2: 257–95.

Rowland, W. J. 1974. "Reproductive Behavior of the Fourspine Stickleback, *Apeltes quadracus." Copeia* no. 1: 183–94.

Tompkins, A. M., and J. H. Gee. 1983. "Foraging Behavior of Brook Stickleback, *Culaea inconstans* (Kirtland): Optimization of Time, Space, and Diet." *Canadian Journal of Zoology 61,* no. 11: 2482–90.

Winn, H. E. 1960. "Biology of the Brook Stickleback *Eucalia inconstans* (Kirtland)." *American Midland Naturalist 63,* no. 2: 424–38.

Temperate Basses, Family Moronidae

Alsop, R. G., and J. L. Forney. 1962. "Growth and Food of White Perch in Oneida Lake." *New York Fish and Game Journal 9,* no. 2: 133–36.

Bath, D. W., and J. M. O'Connor. 1982. "The Biology of the White Perch, *Morone americana,* in the Hudson River Estuary." *Fishery Bulletin 80,* no. 3: 599–610.

Boileau, M. G. 1985. "The Expansion of White Perch, *Morone americana,* in the Lower Great Lakes." *Fisheries 10,* no. 1: 6–10.

Buckel, J. A., D. O. Conover, N. D. Steinberg, and K. A. McKown. 1999. "Impact of Age-0 Bluefish *(Pomatomus saltatrix)* Predation on Age-0 Fishes in the Hudson River Estuary: Evidence for Density-Dependent Loss of Juvenile Striped Bass *(Morone saxatilis)." Canadian Journal of Fisheries and Aquatic Sciences 56,* no. 2: 275–87.

Busch, W-D. N., D. H. Davies, and S. J. Nepszy. 1977. "Establishment of White Perch, *Morone americana,* in Lake Erie. *Journal of the Fisheries Research Board of Canada 34,* no. 7: 1039–41.

Danehy, R. J., N. H. Ringler, and J. E. Gannon. 1991. "Influence of Nearshore Structure on Growth and Diets of Yellow Perch *(Perca flavescens)* and White Perch *(Morone americana)* in Mexico Bay, Lake Ontario." *Journal of Great Lakes Research 17,* no. 2: 183–93.

Dence, W. A. 1952. "Establishment of White Perch, *Morone americana,* in Central New York." *Copeia* no. 3: 200–201.

Dew, C. B. 1988. "Stomach Contents of Commercially Caught Hudson River Striped Bass, *Morone saxatilis,* 1973–75." *Fishery Bulletin 86,* no. 2: 397–401.

Forney, J. L., and C. B. Taylor. 1963. "Age and Growth of White Bass in Oneida Lake, New York." *New York Fish and Game Journal 10,* no. 2: 194–200.

Hocutt, C. H., S. E. Seibold, R. M. Harrell, K. V. Jeslen, and W. II. Bason. 1990. "Behavioral Observations of Striped Bass *(Morone saxatilis)* on the Spawning Grounds of the Choptank and Nanticoke Rivers, Maryland, USA." *Journal of Applied Ichthyology 6,* no. 4: 211–22.

Hurley, D. A. 1992. "Feeding and Trophic Interactions of White Perch *(Morone americana)* in the Bay of Quinte, Lake Ontario." *Canadian Journal of Fisheries and Aquatic Sciences 49,* no. 11: 2249–59.

Hurst, T. P., and D. O. Conover. 1998. "Winter Mortality of Young-of-the-Year Hudson River Bass (*Morone saxatilis*): Size-Dependent Patterns and Effects on Recruitment." *Canadian Journal of Fisheries and Aquatic Sciences* 55, no. 5: 1122–30.

Marcy, B. C., Jr., and P. P. Richards. 1974. "Age and Growth of the White Perch *Morone americana* in the Lower Connecticut River." *Transactions of the American Fisheries Society* 103, no. 1: 117–20.

Monteleone, D. M., and E. D. Houde. 1992. "Vulnerability of Striped Bass *Morone saxatilis* Waldbaum Eggs and Larvae to Predation by Juvenile White Perch *Morone americana* Gmelin." *Journal of Experimental Marine Biology and Ecology* 158, no. 1: 93–104.

Pace, M. L., S. B. Baines, H. Cyr, and J. A. Downing. 1993. "Relationships among Early Life Stages of *Morone americana* and *Morone saxatilis* from Long-Term Monitoring of the Hudson River Estuary." *Canadian Journal of Fisheries and Aquatic Sciences* 50, no. 9: 1976–85.

Parrish, D. L., and F. J. Margraf. 1990. "Interactions Between White Perch (*Morone americana*) and Yellow Perch (*Perca flavescens*) in Lake Erie as Determined from Feeding and Growth." *Canadian Journal of Fisheries and Aquatic Sciences* 47, no. 9: 1779–87.

Raney, E. C. 1952. "The Life History of the Striped Bass, *Roccus saxatilis* (Walbaum)." *Bulletin of the Bingham Oceanographic Collection* 14, no. 1: 5–97.

Schaeffer, J. S., and F. J. Margraf. 1987. "Predation on Fish Eggs by White Perch, *Morone americana*, in Western Lake Erie." *Environmental Biology of Fishes* 18, no. 1: 77–80.

Tupper, M., and K. W. Able. 2000. "Movements and Food Habits of Striped Bass (*Morone saxatilis*) in Delaware Bay (USA) Salt Marshes: Comparison of a Restored and a Reference Marsh." *Marine Biology* 137, nos. 5–6: 1049–59.

Van Winkle, W., D. S. Vaughan, L. W. Barnthouse, and B. L. Kirk. 1981. "An Analysis of the Ability to Detect Reductions in Year-Class Strength of the Hudson River White Perch (*Morone americana*) Population." *Canadian Journal of Fisheries and Aquatic Sciences* 38, no. 6: 627–32.

Voigtlander, C. W., and T. E. Wissing. 1974. "Food Habits of Young and Yearling White Bass, *Morone chrysops* (Rafinesque), in Lake Mendota, Wisconsin." *Transactions of the American Fisheries Society* 103, no. 1: 25–31.

Sunfishes, Family Centrarchidae

Arendt, J. D., and D. S. Wilson. 1997. "Optimistic Growth: Competition and an Ontogenetic Niche-Shift Select for Rapid Growth in Pumpkinseed Sunfish (*Lepomis gibbosus*)." *Evolution* 51, no. 6: 1946–54.

Breder, C. M., Jr. 1936. "I. The Reproductive Habits of the North American Sunfishes (Family Centrarchidae)." *Zoologica* 21, no. 1: 1–48.

Brown, G. E., and S. Brennan. 2000. "Chemical Alarm Signals in Juvenile Green Sunfish (*Lepomis cyanellus*, Centrarchidae)." *Copeia* no. 4: 1079–82.

Coleman, K., and D. S. Wilson. 1996. "Behavioral and Ecological Determinants of Home Range Size in Juvenile Pumpkinseed Sunfish (*Lepomis gibbosus*)." *Ethology* 102, no. 11: 900–914.

Dewoody, J. A., D. E. Fletcher, S. D. Wilkins, W. S. Nelson, and J. C. Avise. 1998. "Molecular Genetic Dissection of Spawning, Parentage, and Reproductive Tactics in a Population of Redbreast Sunfish, *Lepomis auritus.*" *Evolution* 52, no. 6: 1802–10.

Domermuth, R. B., and R. J. Reed. 1980. "Food of Juvenile American Shad, *Alosa sapidissima,* Juvenile Blueback Herring, *Alosa aestivalis,* and Pumpkinseed, *Lepomis gibbosus,* in the Connecticut River below Holyoke Dam, Massachusetts." *Estuaries* 3, no. 1: 65–68.

Dupuis, H. M. C., and M. H. A. Keenleyside. 1988. "Reproductive Success of Nesting Male Longear Sunfish (*Lepomis megalotis peltastes*). I. Factors Influencing Spawning Success." *Behavioral Ecology and Sociobiology* 23, no. 2: 109–16.

Eisner, T., and D. J. Aneshansley. 2000. "Chemical Defense: Aquatic Beetle (*Dineutes hornii*) vs. Fish (*Micropterus salmoides*)." *Proceedings of the National Academy of Sciences* 97, no. 21: 11313–318.

Elliott, J. K., J. M. Elliott, and W. C. Leggett. 1997. "Predation by Hydra on Larval Fish: Field and Laboratory Experiments with Bluegill (*Lepomis macrochirus*)." *Limnology and Oceanography* 42, no. 6: 1416–23.

Fletcher, D. E. 1993. "Nest Association of Dusky Shiners (*Notropis cummingsae*) and Redbreast Sunfish (*Lepomis auritus*), a Potentially Parasitic Relationship." *Copeia* no. 1: 159–67.

George, E. L., and W. F. Hadley. 1979. "Food and Habitat Partitioning Between Rock Bass (*Ambloplites rupestris*) and Smallmouth Bass (*Micropterus dolomieui*) Young of the Year." *Transactions of the American Fisheries Society* 108, no. 3: 253–61.

Gerber, G. P., and J. M. Haynes. 1988. "Movements and Behaviour of Smallmouth Bass, *Micropterus dolomieui,* and Rock Bass, *Ambloplites rupestris,* in South-Central Lake Ontario and Two Tributaries." *Journal of Freshwater Ecology* 4, no. 4: 425–40.

Gonzalez, R. J., and W. A. Dunson. 1991. "Does Water pH Control Habitat Segregation of Sibling Species of Sunfish (*Enneacanthus*)? *Wetlands* 11, no. 2: 313–23.

Guy, C. S., R. M. Neumann, and D. W. Willis. 1992. "Movement Patterns of Adult Back Crappie, *Pomoxis nigromaculatus,* in Brant Lake, South Dakota." *Journal of Freshwater Ecology* 7, no. 2: 137–47.

Hart, T. F., Jr., and R. G. Werner. 1987. "Effects of Prey Density on Growth and Survival of White Sucker, *Catostomus commersoni,* and Pumpkinseed, *Lepomis gibbosus,* Larvae." *Environmental Biology of Fishes* 18, no. 1: 41–50.

Hatzenbeler, G. R., M. A. Bozek, M. J. Jennings, and E. E. Emmons. 2000. "Seasonal Variation in Fish Assemblage Structure and Habitat Structure in the Nearshore Littoral Zone of Wisconsin Lakes." *North American Journal of Fisheries Management* 20, no. 2: 360–68.

Kieffer, J. D., and P. W. Colgan. 1993. "Foraging Flexibility in Pumpkinseed (*Lepomis gibbosus*): Influence of Habitat Structure and Prey Type." *Canadian Journal of Fisheries and Aquatic Sciences* 50, no. 8: 1699–705.

Laughlin, D. R., and E. E. Werner. 1980. "Resource Partitioning in Two Coexisting Sunfish: Pumpkinseed (*Lepomis gibbosus*) and Northern Longear Sunfish (*Lepomis megalotis peltastes*)." *Canadian Journal of Fisheries and Aquatic Sciences* 37, no. 9: 1411–20.

Lukas, J. A., and D. J. Orth. 1993. "Reproductive Ecology of Redbreast Sunfish *Lepomis auritus* in a Virginia Stream." *Journal of Freshwater Ecology* 8, no. 3: 235–44.

MacRae, P. S. D., and D. A. Jackson. 2001. "The Influence of Smallmouth Bass (*Micropterus dolomieu*) Predation and Habitat Complexity on the Structure of Littoral Zone Fish Assemblages." *Canadian Journal of Fisheries and Aquatic Sciences* 58, no. 2: 342–51.

McKinley, R. S., J. S. Griffiths, H. E. Kowalyk, G. R. McKenna, and S. J. Cooke. 2000. "Reproductive Activity and Summer Residency Patterns of Smallmouth Bass, *Micropterus dolomieu*, in a Thermal Discharge Canal on Lake Erie." *Journal of Freshwater Ecology* 15, no. 3: 307–16.

Newcomb, T. J., S. A. Perry, and W. B. Perry. 1995. "Comparison of Habitat Suitability Criteria for Smallmouth Bass (*Micropterus dolomieu*) from Three West Virginia Rivers." *Rivers* 5, no. 3: 170–83.

Nibbelink, N. P., and S. R. Carpenter. 1998. "Interlake Variation in Growth and Size Structure of Bluegill (*Lepomis macrochirus*): Inverse Analysis of an Individual-Based Model." *Canadian Journal of Fisheries and Aquatic Sciences* 55, no. 2: 387–96.

Noltie, D. B., and M. H. A. Keenleyside. 1987. "Breeding Ecology, Nest Characteristics, and Nest-Site Selection of Stream- and Lake-Dwelling Rock Bass, *Ambloplites rupestris* (Rafinesque)." *Canadian Journal of Zoology* 65, no. 2: 379–90.

Pardue, G. B. 1993. "Life History and Ecology of the Mud Sunfish (*Acantharchus pomotis*)." *Copeia* no. 2: 533–40.

Popiel, S. A., A. Perez-Fuentetaja, D. J. McQueen, and N. C. Collins. 1996. "Determinants of Nesting Success in the Pumpkinseed (*Lepomis gibbosus*): A Comparison of Two Populations under Different Risks from Predation." *Copeia* no. 3: 649–56.

Ridgway, M. S., and T. G. Friesen. 1992. "Annual Variation in Parental Care in Smallmouth Bass, *Micropterus dolomieu*." *Environmental Biology of Fishes* 35, no. 3: 243–55.

Robinson, B. W., D. S. Wilson, and A. S. Margosian. 2000. "A Pluralistic Analysis of Character Release in Pumpkinseed Sunfish (*Lepomis gibbosus*)." *Ecology* 81, no. 10: 2799–812.

Sabat, A. M. 1994. "Costs and Benefits of Parental Effort in a Brood-Guarding Fish (*Ambloplites rupestris*, Centrarchidae)." *Behavioral Ecology* 5, no. 2: 195–201.

Schaefer, J. F., W. I. Lutterschmidt, and L. G. Hill. 1999. "Physiological Performance and Stream Microhabitat Use by the Centrarchids *Lepomis megalotis* and *Lepomis macrochirus*." *Environmental Biology of Fishes* 54, no. 3: 303–12.

Scott, R. J., M. S. Ridgway, and D. L. G. Noakes. 1997. "The Nest Range of Smallmouth Bass (*Micropterus dolomieu*): Parental Care after Swim-up." *Canadian Journal of Zoology* 75, no. 12: 2058–62.

Shao, B. 1997. "Nest Association of Pumpkinseed, *Lepomis gibbosus*, and Golden Shiner, *Notemigonus crysoleucas*." *Environmental Biology of Fishes* 50, no. 1: 41–48.

Shoup, D. E., and L. G. Hill. 1997. "Ecomorphological Diet Predictions: An Assessment Using Inland Silverside (*Menidia beryllina*) and Longear Sunfish (*Lepomis megalotis*) from Lake Texoma." *Hydrobiologia* 350, nos. 1–3: 87–98.

Snyder, D. J., and M. S. Peterson. 1999a. "Foraging and Prey Selection by Bluespotted Sunfish *Enneacanthus gloriosus* (Holbrook) in Backwater, Vegetated Ponds in Coastal Mississippi." *Journal of Freshwater Ecology* 14, no. 2: 187–96.

———. 1999b. "Life History of a Peripheral Population of Bluespotted Sunfish *Ennea-*

canthus gloriosus (Holbrook), with Comments on Geographic Variation." *American Midland Naturalist* 141, no. 2: 345–57.

Thorp, J. H., L. D. Goldsmith, J. A. Polgreen, and L. M. Mayer. 1989. "Foraging Patterns of Nesting and Non-nesting Sunfish (Centrarchidae: *Lepomis auritus* and *L. gibbosus*)." *Canadian Journal of Fisheries and Aquatic Sciences* 46, no. 8: 1342–46.

Weaver, M. J., J. J. Magnuson, and M. K. Clayton. 1997. "Distribution of Littoral Fishes in Structurally Complex Macrophytes." *Canadian Journal of Fisheries and Aquatic Sciences* 54, no. 10: 2277–89.

Webb, P. W. 1986. "Effect of Body Form and Response Threshold on the Vulnerability of Four Species of Teleost Prey Attacked by Largemouth Bass (*Micropterus salmoides*)." *Canadian Journal of Fisheries and Aquatic Sciences* 43, no. 4: 763–71.

Webster, D. W. 1954. *Smallmouth Bass, Micropterus dolomieui, in Cayuga Lake.* Part 1, *Life History and Environment.* Agricultural Experiment Station Cornell Univ. Memoir no. 327. Ithaca: Cornell Univ. 39 pp.

Werner, R. G. 1969. "Ecology of Limnetic Bluegill Fry in Crane Lake, Indiana." *American Midland Naturalist* 81: 164–81.

———. 1972. "Bluespotted Sunfish, *Enneacanthus gloriosus,* in Lake Ontario Drainage." *Copeia* no. 4: 878–79.

Whittier, T. R., and K. E. Hartel. 1997. "First Records of Redear Sunfish (*Lepomis microlophus*) in New England." *Northeastern Naturalist* 4, no. 4: 237–40.

Wildhaber, M. L., and L. B. Crowder. 1991. "Mechanisms of Patch Choice by Bluegills (*Lepomis macrochirus*) Foraging in a Variable Environment." *Copeia* no. 2: 445–60.

Williamson, M., and A. Keast. 1988. "Retinal Structure Relative to Feeding in the Rock Bass (*Ambloplites rupestris*) and Bluegill (*Lepomis macrochirus*)." *Canadian Journal of Zoology* 66, no. 12: 2840–46.

Wright, D. I., and W. J. O'Brien. 1984. "The Development and Field Test of a Tactical Model of the Planktivorous Feeding of White Crappie (*Pomoxis annularis*)." *Ecological Monographs* 54, no. 1: 65–98.

Perches and Darters, Family Percidae

Bunt, C. M., S. J. Cooke, and R. S. McKinley. 1998. "Creation and Maintenance of Habitat Downstream from a Weir for the Greenside Darter, *Etheostoma blennioides*—a Rare Fish in Canada." *Environmental Biology of Fishes* 51, no. 3: 297–308.

Chapleau, F., and G. Pageau. 1985. "Morphological Differentiation of *Etheostoma olmstedi* and *E. nigrum* (Pisces: Percidae) in Canada." *Copeia* no. 4: 855–65.

Chivers, D. P., B. D. Wisenden, and R. J. F. Smith. 1995. "Predation Risk Influences Reproductive Behaviour of Iowa Darters, *Etheostoma exile* (Osteichthyes, Percidae)." *Ethology* 99, no. 4: 278–85.

Constantz, G. D. 1985. "Allopaternal Care in the Tessellated Darter, *Etheostoma olmstedi* (Pisces: Percidae)." *Environmental Biology of Fishes* 14, nos. 2–3: 175–83.

Cooper, J. E. 1979. "Description of Eggs and Larvae of Fantail (*Etheostoma flabellare*) and Rainbow (*E. caeruleum*) Darters from Lake Erie Tributaries." *Transactions of the American Fisheries Society* 108, no. 1: 46–56.

Czesny, S., K. Dabrowski, and P. Frankiewicz. 2001. "Foraging Patterns of Juvenile

Walleye (*Stizostedion vitreum*) in a System Consisting of a Single Predator and Two Prey Species: Testing Model Predictions." *Canadian Journal of Zoology* 79, no. 8: 1394–400.

Daniels, R. A. 1989. "Significance of Burying in *Ammocrypta pellucida*." *Copeia* no. 1: 29–34.

———. 1993. "Habitat of the Eastern Sand Darter, *Ammocrypta pellucida*." *Journal of Freshwater Ecology* 8, no. 4: 287–95.

Eisenhour, D. J. 1995. "Systematics of *Etheostoma camurum* and *E. chlorobranchium* (Osteichthyes: Percidae) in the Tennessee and Cumberland River Drainages with Analysis of Hybridization in the Nolichucky River System." *Copeia* no. 2: 368–79.

Facey, D. E. 1998. "The Status of the Eastern Sand Darter, *Ammocrypta pellucida*, in Vermont." *Canadian Field-Naturalist* 112: 596–601.

Fuller, R. C. 1998. "Fecundity Estimates for Rainbow Darters, *Etheostoma caeruleum*, in Southwestern Michigan." *Ohio Journal of Science* 98, no. 2: 2–5.

———. 1999. "Costs of Group Spawning to Guarding Males in the Rainbow Darter, *Etheostoma caeruleum*." *Copeia* no. 4: 1084–88.

Guill, J. M., and D. C. Heins. 2000. "Interannual Variation in Clutch and Egg Size of the Banded Darter, *Etheostoma zonale*." *Copeia* no. 1: 230–33.

Harding, J. M., A. J. Burky, and C. M. Way. 1998. "Habitat Preferences of the Rainbow Darter, *Etheostoma caeruleum*, with Regard to Microhabitat Velocity Shelters." *Copeia* no. 4: 988–97.

Hatch, J. T. 1983. "Life History of the Gilt Darter, *Percina evides* (Jordan and Copeland), in the Sunrise River, Minnesota." *Dissertation Abstracts International, Part B: Science and Engineering* 43, no. 11: 3502.

Heath, D. D., and D. A. Roff. 1996. "The Role of Trophic Bottlenecks in Stunting: A Field Test of an Allocation Model of Growth and Reproduction in Yellow Perch, *Perca flavescens*." *Environmental Biology of Fishes* 45, no. 1: 53–63.

Heins, D. C., J. A. Baker, and D. J. Tylicki. 1996. "Reproductive Season, Clutch Size, and Egg Size of the Rainbow Darter, *Etheostoma caeruleum*, from the Homochitto River, Mississippi, with an Evaluation of Data from the Literature." *Copeia* no. 4: 1005–10.

Hlohowskyj, I., and T. E. Wissing. 1986. "Substrate Selection by Fantail (*Etheostoma flabellare*), Greenside (*E. blennioides*), and Rainbow (*E. caeruleum*) Darters." *Ohio Journal of Science* 86, no. 3: 126–29.

Kessler, R. K., and J. H. Thorp. 1993. "Microhabitat Segregation of the Threatened Spotted Darter (*Etheostoma maculatum*) and Closely Related Orangefin Darter (*E. bellum*)." *Canadian Journal of Fisheries and Aquatic Sciences* 50, no. 5: 1084–91.

Knight, R. L., and B. Vondracek. 1993. "Changes in Prey Fish Populations in Western Lake Erie, 1969–88, as Related to Walleye, *Stizostedion vitreum*, Predation." *Canadian Journal of Fisheries and Aquatic Sciences* 50, no. 6: 1289–98.

Kuehne, R. A., and R. W. Barbour. 1983. *The American Darters*. Lexington: Univ. Press of Kentucky. 177 pp.

Lake, C. T. 1936. "The Life History of the Fantailed Darter." *American Midland Naturalist* 17: 816–30.

Leidy, R. A. 1992. "Microhabitat Selection by the Johnny Darter, *Etheostoma nigrum* Rafinesque, in a Wyoming Stream." *Great Basin Naturalist* 52, no. 1: 68–74.

Matthews, W. J. 1985. "Critical Current Speeds and Microhabitats of the Benthic Fishes *Percina roanoka* and *Etheostoma flabellare.*" *Environmental Biology of Fishes* 12, no. 4: 303–8.

McKeown, P. E., C. H. Hocutt, R. P. Morgan II, and J. H. Howard. 1984. "An Electrophoretic Analysis of the *Etheostoma variatum* Complex (Percidae: Etheostomatini), with Associated Zoogeographic Considerations." *Environmental Biology of Fishes* 11, no. 2: 85–95.

Murray, A., and D. Tarter. 1979. "Food Habits of the Logperch, *Percina caprodes* (Rafinesque), from East Lynn Lake, Wayne County, West Virginia." *Proceedings of the West Virginia Academy of Science* 51, no. 2: 73–78.

Page, L. M. 1978. "Redescription, Distribution, Variation, and Life History Notes on *Percina macrocephala* (Percidae)." *Copeia* no. 4: 655–64.

———. 1983. *Handbook of Darters.* Neptune City, N.J.: Tropical Fish Hobbyist. 271 pp.

Paine, M. D., and E. K. Balon. 1984. "Early Development of the Rainbow Darter, *Etheostoma caeruleum,* According to the Theory of Saltatory Ontogeny." *Environmental Biology of Fishes* 11, no. 4: 277–99.

Phillips, E. C., and R. V. Kilambi. 1996. "Food Habits of Four Benthic Fish Species (*Etheostoma spectabile, Percina caprodes, Noturus exilis, Cottus carolinae*) from Northwest Arkansas Streams." *Southwestern Naturalist* 41, no. 1: 69–73.

Rahel, F. J. 1989. "Nest Defense and Aggressive Interactions Between a Small Benthic Fish (the Johnny Darter, *Etheostoma nigrum*) and Crayfish." *Environmental Biology of Fishes* 24, no. 4: 301–6.

Raney, E. C., and E. A. Lachner. 1943. "Age and Growth of Johnny Darters, *Boleosoma nigrum olmstedi* (Storer) and *Boleosoma longimanum* (Jordan)." *American Midland Naturalist* 29: 229–38.

Roseman, E. F., E. L. Mills, J. L. Forney, and L. G. Rudstam. 1996. "Evaluation of Competition Between Age-0 Yellow Perch (*Perca flavescens*) and Gizzard Shad (*Dorosoma cepedianum*) in Oneida Lake, New York." *Canadian Journal of Fisheries and Aquatic Sciences* 53, no. 4: 865–74.

Schlosser, I. J., and L. A. Toth. 1984. "Niche Relationships and Population Ecology of Rainbow (*Etheostoma caeruleum*) and Fantail (*E. flabellare*) Darters in a Temporally Variable Environment." *Oikos* 42, no. 2: 229–38.

Schmidt, R. E., and W. R. Whitworth. 1979. "Distribution and Habitat of the Swamp Darter (*Etheostoma fusiforme*) in Southern New England." *American Midland Naturalist* 102: 408–13.

Simon, T. P. 1991. "Startle Response and Causes of Burying Behavior in Captive Eastern Sand Darters, *Ammocrypta pellucida* (Putnam)." *Proceedings of the Indiana Academy of Sciences* 100, nos. 3–4: 155–60.

Simon, T. P., and D. J. Faber. 1987. "Descriptions of Eggs, Larvae, and Early Juveniles of the Iowa Darter, *Etheostoma exile* (Girard), from Lac Heney, Quebec." *Canadian Journal of Zoology* 65, no. 5: 1264–69.

Smart, H. J., and J. H. Gee. 1979. "Coexistence and Resource Partitioning in Two Species of Darters (Percidae), *Etheostoma nigrum* and *Percina maculata*." *Canadian Journal of Zoology* 57, no. 10: 2061–71.

Strange, R. M. 1993. "Seasonal Feeding Ecology of the Fantail Darter, *Etheostoma flabellare*, from Stinking Fork, Indiana." *Journal of Freshwater Ecology* 8, no. 1: 13–18.

———. 1997. "Food Items of Channel Darters (*Percina copelandi*) Collected from the Ohio River." *Journal of Freshwater Ecology* 12, no. 2: 339–40.

Todd, T. N., and C. O. Hatcher. 1993. "Genetic Variability and Glacial Origins of Yellow Perch (*Perca flavescens*) in North America." *Canadian Journal of Fisheries and Aquatic Sciences* 50, no. 9: 1828–34.

Tsai, C-F., and E. C. Raney. 1974. "Systematics of the Banded Darter, *Etheostoma zonale* (Pisces: Percidae)." *Copeia* no. 1: 1–23.

Wahl, C. M., E. L. Mills, W. N. McFarland, and J. S. DeGisi. 1993. "Ontogenetic Changes in Prey Selection and Visual Acuity of the Yellow Perch, *Perca flavescens*." *Canadian Journal of Fisheries and Aquatic Sciences* 50, no. 4: 743–49.

Wahl, D. H., and L. A. Nielsen. 1985. "Feeding Ecology of the Sauger (*Stizostedion canadense*) in a Large River." *Canadian Journal of Fisheries and Aquatic Sciences* 42, no. 1: 120–28.

Walters, J. P. 1994. "Spawning Behavior of *Etheostoma zonale* (Pisces: Percidae)." *Copeia* no. 3: 818–21.

Winn, H. E. 1958. "Comparative Reproductive Behavior and Ecology of Fourteen Species of Darters (Pisces—Percidae)." *Ecological Monographs* 28: 155–91.

Drums, Family Sciaenidae

Dreves, D. P., T. J. Timmons, and J. Henson. 1996. "Age, Growth, and Food of Freshwater Drum, *Aplodinotus grunniens* (Sciaenidae), in Kentucky Lake, Kentucky/Tennessee." *Transactions of the Kentucky Academy of Science* 57, no. 1: 22–26.

Edsal, T. A. 1967. "Biology of the Freshwater Drum in Western Lake Erie. *Ohio Journal of Science* 67, no. 6: 31–40.

French, J. R. P., III. 1997. "Pharyngeal Teeth of the Freshwater Drum (*Aplodinotus grunniens*), a Predator of the Zebra Mussel (*Dreissena polymorpha*)." *Journal of Freshwater Ecology* 12, no. 3: 495–98.

Gobies, Family Gobiidae

Crossman, E. J., E. Holm, R. Cholmondeley, and K. Tuininga. 1992. "First Record for Canada of the Rudd, *Scardinius erythrophthalmus*, and Notes on the Introduced Round Goby, *Neogobius melanostomus*." *Canadian Field-Naturalist* 106, no. 2: 206–9.

Charlebois, P. M., R. G. Goettel, D. J. Jude, J. E. Marsden, R. K. Wolfe, and S. Rudnika. 1997. *The Round Goby*, Neogobius melanostomus (*Pallas*), *a Review of European and North American Literature*. Illinois Natural History Survey (INHS) Special Publication no. 20. Champaign: INHS. 76 pp.

Dubs, D. O. L., and L. D. Corkum. 1996. "Behavioral Interactions Between Round Gobies (*Neogobius melanostomus*) and Mottled Sculpins (*Cottus bairdi*)." *Journal of Great Lakes Research* 22, no. 4: 838–44.

Jude, D. J., R. H. Reider, and G. R. Smith. 1992. "Establishment of Gobiidae in the Great Lakes Basin." *Canadian Journal of Fisheries and Aquatic Sciences* 49, no. 2: 416–21.

MacInnis, A. J., and L. D. Corkum. 2000a. "Age and Growth of Round Goby *Neogobius melanostomus* in the Upper Detroit River." *Transactions of the American Fisheries Society* 129, no. 3: 852–58.

———. 2000b. "Fecundity and Reproductive Season of the Round Goby *Neogobius melanostomus* in the Upper Detroit River." *Transactions of the American Fisheries Society* 129, no. 1: 136–44.

Miller, P. J. 1986. "Gobiidae." In *Fishes of the Northeast Atlantic and the Mediterranean,* vol. 3, edited by P. J. P. Whitehead, M-L. Bauchot, J-C. Hureau, J. Nielsen, and E. Tortonese, 1019–95. Paris: UNESCO.

Sculpins, Family Cottidae

Brandt, S. B. 1986. "Disappearance of the Deepwater Sculpin (*Myoxocephalus thompsoni*) from Lake Ontario: The Keystone Predator Hypothesis." *Journal of Great Lakes Research* 12, no. 1: 18–24.

Foltz, J. W. 1976. "Fecundity of the Slimy Sculpin, *Cottus cognatus,* in Lake Michigan." *Copeia* no. 4: 802–4.

Godkin, C. M., W. J. Christie, and D. E. McAllister. 1982. "Problems of Species Identity in the Lake Ontario Sculpins *Cottus bairdi* and *C. cognatus.*" *Canadian Journal of Fisheries and Aquatic Sciences* 39, no. 10: 1373–82.

Janssen, J., S. Coombs, and S. Pride. 1990. "Feeding and Orientation of Mottled Sculpin, *Cottus bairdi,* to Water Jets." *Environmental Biology of Fishes* 29, no. 1: 43–50.

Janssen, J., and D. J. Jude. 2001. "Recruitment Failure of Mottled Sculpin *Cottus bairdi* in Calumet Harbor, Southern Lake Michigan, Induced by the Newly Introduced Round Goby *Neogobius melanostomus.*" *Journal of Great Lakes Research* 27, no. 3: 319–28.

Koster, W. J. 1937. "The Food of Sculpins (Cottidae) in Central New York." *Transactions of the American Fisheries Society* 66: 374–82.

Miller, J. E., J. F. Savino, and R. K. Neely. 1992. "Competition for Food Between Crayfish (*Orconectes virilis*) and the Slimy Sculpin (*Cottus cognatus*)." *Journal of Freshwater Ecology* 7, no. 2: 127–36.

Mohr, L. C. 1984. *The General Ecology of the Slimy Sculpin* (Cottus cognatus) *in Lake 302 of the Experimental Lakes Area, Northwestern Ontario.* Canadian Fisheries and Aquatic Sciences Technical Report no. 1227. Winnipeg: Department of Fisheries and Oceans. 20 pp.

Morgan, C., and N. Ringler. 1994. "Influence of a Benthic Predatory Fish (*Cottus cognatus*) on Invertebrate Community Structure and Secondary Production in a Tributary of the Susquehanna River." *Journal of Freshwater Ecology* 9, no. 1: 63–78.

Mousseau, T. A., N. C. Collins, and G. A. Cabana. 1988. "A Comparative Study of Sexual Selection and Reproductive Investment in the Slimy Sculpin, *Cottus cognatus. Oikos* 51, no. 2: 156–62.

Owens, R. W., and G. E. Noguchi. 1998. "Intra-lake Variation in Maturity, Fecundity, and Spawning of Slimy Sculpins (*Cottus cognatus*) in Southern Lake Ontario." *Journal of Great Lakes Research* 24, no. 2: 383–91.

Owens, R. W., and P. G. Weber. 1995. "Predation on *Mysis relicta* by Slimy Sculpins (*Cottus cognatus*) in Southern Lake Ontario." *Journal of Great Lakes Research* 21, no. 2: 275–83.

Roseman, E. F., D. J. Jude, M. K. Raths, T. G. Coon, and W. W. Taylor. 1998. "Occurrence of the Deepwater Sculpin (*Myoxocephalus thompsoni*) in Western Lake Erie." *Journal of Great Lakes Research* 24, no. 2: 479–83.

Savage, T. 1963. "Reproductive Behavior of the Mottled Sculpin, *Cottus bairdi* Girard." *Copeia* no. 2: 317–25.

Whang, A., and J. Janssen. 1994. "Sound Production Through the Substrate During Reproduction in the Mottled Sculpin, *Cottus bairdi* (Cottidae)." *Environmental Biology of Fishes* 40, no. 2: 141–48.

Index

Fundulus heteroclitus, 206
Fundulus majalis, 206

Gambusia affinis, 15, 208
Gander Terrane, 5
Gars, 33, 58–59
Gasterosteidae, 35, 210
Gasterosteus aculeatus, 15, 210, 214
Genesee River, N.Y., 99, 254
Genus, 25
Geological history, 3–7
Georgia, 91, 102, 109, 115, 119, 129, 132, 140,
   143, 146, 161, 169, 186, 235, 237, 239, 280
Gilt darter, 16, 250, 267
Gizzard shad, 11, 66, 72
Glacial rebound, 7
Glaciers, 6–7
Glass Lake, N.Y., 194
Gobies, 39, 275
Gobiidae, 39, 275
Golden redhorse, 13, 138, 148
Golden shiner, 12, 74, 88, 109
Goldfish, 11, 74–75, 91
Gondwana, 5
Grasse River, N.Y., 253
Grass/redfin pickerel, 14, 163–64
Gravel chub, 11, 80, 97
Great Bay, 196
Greater redhorse, 13, 137, 150
Great Lakes, 19, 45, 48–50, 54, 59, 63, 69–70,
   73, 92, 95, 101, 103, 108, 112–13, 117,
   123–25, 127, 140, 145–46, 148–50, 155, 158,
   160–61, 168, 172, 181–82, 184, 186, 188,
   194, 199, 205, 242–43, 252–54, 257, 260,
   266, 268, 274, 277, 280, 281
Great Slave Lake, 264
Greenland, 50
Green Mountains, 5–6
Greenside darter, 16, 250, 253
Green sunfish, 16, 228, 235
Grenville Orogeny, 4, 6
Gular plate, 60
Gulf of Mexico, 9, 65, 113

Habitat, 18
Hackensack River, N.Y., 230
Hedges Lake, N.Y., 184
Herrings, 66, 73

Heterocercal caudal fin, 51, 56, 58, 60
Hiodon tergisus, 11, 62
Hiodontidae, 36, 62
Holyoke Dam, 53
Hornyhead chub, 12, 80, 107
Housatonic River, 8, 9–10, 100, 155, 194, 199
Hudson Bay, 48, 54, 130, 186, 214
Hudson River, 1, 8, 9, 10, 17, 48, 53, 55, 72, 94,
   97, 100, 111, 113, 116, 145, 161, 165, 172,
   199, 221, 269
Hudson River Valley, 6
Human impact, 19–21
Hybognathus hankinsoni, 12, 84, 100
Hybognathus regius, 12, 84, 101
Hypentelium nigricans, 13, 136, 145

Ice Age, 19
Ichthyomyzon bdellium, 10, 44–45
Ichthyomyzon fossor, 10, 44–45
Ichthyomyzon greeleyi, 10, 44, 46
Ichthyomyzon unicuspis, 10, 44, 47
Ictaluridae, 34, 151
Ictalurus punctatus, 14, 153, 158
Idaho, 188
Ide, 12, 74, 89, 102
Illinois, 111, 116, 143, 144, 209, 240, 252, 255,
   277
Indiana, 111, 143–44, 150, 240, 255, 262, 277
Inland silverside, 204
Iowa, 116, 237
Iowa darter, 16, 251, 256
Ironcolor shiner, 12, 75, 87, 115

James River, 109
Jamesville Reservoir, N.Y., 233
Johnny darter, 16, 250, 259

Kansas, 105, 199, 237
Kennebec River, Me., 9–10, 53, 102, 191
Kentucky, 45, 92, 252, 255, 258–59, 262
Key, using, 31–32
Kingston, N.Y., 221
Kiyi, 175

Labidesthes sicculus, 15, 204
Labrador, 55, 65, 143, 174, 186, 280
Lake Champlain, N.Y./Vt., 1, 7, 9, 17, 43, 45,
   48, 50, 54, 59, 63, 69, 101, 113, 119, 122, 127,

Mississippi River (*cont.*)
140, 143, 146–47, 149, 162,184, 242–43, 245,
252, 262, 268, 274
Mississippi Valley Refugium, 19
Missouri, 45, 97, 101, 115–16, 118–19, 124,
148–49, 168, 253, 255
Missouri River, 280
Mitchell Ponds, N.Y., 194
Mohawk/Hudson drainage, 8, 19, 94, 113,
161, 205
Mohawk River, N.Y., 5, 69, 91–92, 94, 108, 162,
254, 257
Montana, 107, 132, 155, 159, 160, 188, 205, 213,
256, 264
Montpelier, Vt., 5
Mooneye, 11, *62*
Moosehead Lake, Me., 1, 5, 10
Mopus Brook, Conn., 111
Moraines, 7
Morone americana, 15, 216, *219*
Morone chrysops, 15, 217, *218*
Morone saxatilis, 15, 217, *220*
Moronidae, 40, 216
Morphology, 26–30
Mottled sculpin, 17, 280
Mountain brook lamprey, 10, 44, *46*
Mount Monadnock, N.H., 6
Moxostoma anisurum, 13, 138, *146*
Moxostoma carinatum, 13, 138, 146
Moxostoma duquesnei, 13, 138, 147
Moxostoma erythrurum, 13, 138, *148*
Moxostoma macrolepidotum, 13, 138, *149*
Moxostoma valenciennesi, 13, 137, *150*
Mudminnows, 38, 170
Mud sunfish, 15, 222, *230*
Mummichog, 206
Muskellunge, 14, 164, *168*
Myoxocephalus thompsoni, 279
Mysis relicta, 188
Myxini, 2

Naming fishes, 25–26
Nebraska, 102
Neogobius melanostomus, 17, 275, *276*
Neuse River, 114
New Brunswick, 53, 235
Newburgh, N.Y., 97
Newfoundland, 71–72

New Hampshire, 1, 2, 3, 5, 6, 8, 10, 23, 49, 107,
118, 161, 183, 187, 188, 196, 233
New Jersey, 174, 209, 215
New River, 99
New York, 1–6, 9–10, 17, 23, 43, 45, 47–50,
53–54, 57, 59, 63, 70, 73, 91–92, 94–95,
97–98, 100–1, 105–6, 108–9, 111–13, 115–18,
120–23, 131–32, 134, 140, 144–50, 155,
160–62, 165, 169, 172, 181, 183–84, 188,
193–94, 199, 201, 205, 209, 213, 215, 220,
230, 233, 235, 240, 244, 252–60, 262,
265–66, 268–70, 274, 277, 280
New York City, 9–10, 130
New York State Biological Survey, 267
New York State Department of
Environmental Conservation, 54, 57
Niagara River, N.Y., 9, 59, 118, 150, 194, 197,
219, 277
Ninespine stickleback, 15, 210, 214
Nocomis biguttatus, 12, 80, *107*
Nocomis micropogon, 12, 80, *108*
North American Native Fishes Association,
23
North Carolina, 19, 71, 94, 99, 100, 109, 111,
114, 260–61, 269
North Dakota, 110, 112, 118, 156, 161, 235
Northern brook lamprey, 10, 44–5
Northern hogsucker, 13, 136, *145*
Northern pike, 14, 18, 164, *167*
Northern redbelly dace, 12, 74, 83, *124*
North River, Mass., 196
Northwest Territories, 119, 130, 143, 184, 213
Notemigonus crysoleucas, 12, 88, *109*
Notropis amblops, 12, 80, *110*
Notropis amoenus, 12, 88, *111*
Notropis anogenus, 12, 86, *112*
Notropis atherinoides, 12, 88, *113*
Notropis bifrenatus, 12, 85, *114*
Notropis buccatus, 12, 81, *114*
Notropis chalybaeus, 12, 87, *115*
Notropis dorsalis, 12, 87, *116*
Notropis heterodon, 12, 87, *117*
Notropis heterolepis, 12, 86, *118*
Notropis hudsonius, 12, 86, *119*
Notropis photogenis, 12, 88, *120*
Notropis procne, 12, 85, *120*
Notropis rubellus, 12, 88, *121*
Notropis stramineus, 12, 85, *122*